MEDIEVAL
AND
RENAISSANCE
DRAMA
IN ENGLAND

Editorial Board

MEDIEVAL AND RENAISSANCE DRAMA IN ENGLAND

Volume 20

Edited by
S. P. Cerasano

Book Review Editor
Heather Anne Hirschfeld

Madison • Teaneck
Fairleigh Dickinson University Press

Associated University Presses
2010 Eastpark Boulevard
Cranbury, NJ 08512

The paper used in this publication meets the requirements
of the American National Standard for Permanence of Paper
for Printed Library Materials Z39.48-1984.

International Standard Book Number 978-0-8386-4127-9 (vol. 20)
International Standard Serial Number 0731-3403

All editorial correspondence concerning *Medieval and Renaissance Drama in England* should be addressed to Prof. S. P. Cerasano, Department of English, Colgate University, Hamilton, N.Y., 13346. Orders and subscriptions should be directed to Associated University Presses, 2010 Eastpark Boulevard, Cranbury, New Jersey 08512.

Medieval and Renaissance Drama in England disclaims responsibility for statements, either of face or opinion, made by contributors.

Contents

Foreword   7

Contributors   9

Forum: Race, Racism, and Performance on the Early Modern Stage

Racial Impersonation on the Elizabethan Stage: The Case of
Shakespeare Playing Aaron   17
  IMTIAZ HABIB

The Folly of Racism: Enslaving Blackface and the "Natural" Fool
Tradition   46
  ROBERT HORNBACK

Moorish Dancing in *The Two Noble Kinsmen*   85
  SUJATA IYENGAR

Articles

Ophelia's "Old Lauds": Madness and Hagiography in *Hamlet*   111
  ALISON A. CHAPMAN

"Now wole I a newe game begynne": Staging Suffering in *King
Lear,* the Mystery Plays, and Grotius's *Christus Patiens*   136
  BEATRICE GROVES

Curtains on the Shakespearean Stage   151
  FREDERICK KIEFER

Imagining the Actor's Body on the Early Modern English Stage   187
  JEREMY LOPEZ

"Ick verstaw you niet": Performing Foreign Tongues on the Early
Modern Stage   204
  ANDREW FLECK

Notes and Documents

The Succession of Sots, or Fools and Their Fathers   225
  JOHN H. ASTINGTON

An Early Seventeenth-Century Playhouse in Tonbridge, Kent   236
  JAMES M. GIBSON

Review Essays

This Strange, Eventful History . . .   259
ANDREW JAMES HARTLEY

Drugs, Medicine, and the Early Modern Stage   273
STANTON B. GARNER JR.

Reviews

Celia R. Daileader, *Racism, Misogyny, and the "Othello" Myth: Inter-racial Couples from Shakespeare to Spike Lee*   281
CHRISTY DESMET

Gail Kern Paster, *Humoring the Body: Emotions and the Shakespearean Stage*   284
ERIC JOHNSON-DEBAUFRE

Pascale Aebischer, *Shakespeare's Violated Bodies: Stage and Screen Performance*   286
DENEEN SENASI

Susan Zimmerman, *The Early Modern Corpse and Shakespeare's Theatre*   289
HEATHER HIRSCHFELD

Virginia Mason Vaughan, *Performing Blackness on English Stages, 1500–1800*   292
FRANCESCA T. ROYSTER

Matthew Biberman, *Masculinity, Anti-Semitism and Early Modern English Literature: From the Satanic to the Effeminate Jew*   297
PETER BEREK

Index   300

Foreword

The publication of volume 20 of *Medieval and Renaissance Drama in England* features a forum concerning issues of race, racism, and performance on the early modern stage. Following this are articles addressing madness and hagiography in *Hamlet* and staging suffering in *King Lear* and the mystery plays, along with three pieces that take up historical and theoretical issues relating to the actor's body, foreign tongues, and stage curtains. Additionally, we are pleased to print extended notes concerning a seventeenth-century playhouse in Tonbridge, Kent, and the professional lineage of Robert Armin. *MaRDiE* continues its custom of publishing review essays in Andrew James Hartley's overview of two books relating to the English history play and Stanton B. Garner's commentary on drugs, medicine, and the early modern stage. Reviews—long and short—complete the volume.

S. P. CERASANO
Editor

Contributors

JOHN H. ASTINGTON is Professor of English and Drama, and director of the Graduate Centre for Study of Drama, University of Toronto. He is the author of *English Court Theatre, 1558–1642* (1999), and of numerous essays on the drama and theater history of the English Renaissance.

PETER BEREK, Professor of English at Mount Holyoke College, has published recently on Renaissance Jews, cross-dressing in the Beaumont and Fletcher plays, and generic terms on early modern titled pages and the authority of print.

ALISON A. CHAPMAN is Associate Professor of English Renaissance literature at the university of Alabama at Birmingham. She is currently working on a book manuscript tentatively titled *Patron Saints: Authors, Patrons and Medieval Hagiography in Early Modern England.* Her research for the past few years has concerned the persistence of the saints, and her essay in this volume of *MaRDiE* emerges from that interest.

CHRISTY DESMET, Associate Professor of English at the University of Georgia, is the author of *Reading Shakespeare's Characters: Rhetoric, Ethics, and Identity* (1992). With Robert Sawyer, she has edited *Shakespeare and Appropriation* (1999) and *Harold Bloom's Shakespeare* (2001). With Sujata Iyengar, she is cofounder and general editor of *Borrowers and Lenders: The Journal of Shakespeare and Appropriation* (http://www.borrowers.uga.edu), whose inaugural issue (2005) was concerned with "Shakespeare in the American South."

ANDREW FLECK is Associate Professor of English at San Jose State University. He has published articles in *Modern Philology, Studies in English Literature, Shakespeare Yearbook,* and *Studies in Philology.* He is working on a book, *The Dutch Device: English National Identity and the Image of the Dutch.*

STANTON B. GARNER JR. is Professor of English at the University of Tennessee. In addition to *The Absent Voice: Narrative Comprehension in the Theater* (1989), *Bodied Spaces: Phenomenology and Performance in Contemporary Drama* (1994), and *Trevor Griffiths: Politics, Drama, History* (1999), he has

9

published articles on medieval, Renaissance, and modern drama. He is currently working on the intersections of theater and medicine.

JAMES M. GIBSON is an independent scholar currently editing the Kent records for the Records of Early English Drama series. *Kent: Diocese of Canterbury* was published in three volumes in 2002, and *Kent: Diocese of Rochester* is now nearing completion.

BEATRICE GROVES is a Junior Research Fellow at Wolfson College, Oxford University. Her most recent publication is a book entitled *Texts and Traditions: Religion in Shakespeare's Plays, 1592–1604* (2006).

IMTIAZ HABIB is Associate Professor of English at Old Dominion University in Virginia. He is the author of *Shakespeare and Race: Postcolonial Praxis in the Early Modern Period* (2000), *Black Lives in the English Archives, 1500–1676,* and essays on early modern English literature and culture.

ANDREW JAMES HARTLEY is Distinguished Professor of Shakespeare in the Department of Dance and Theatre at the University of North Carolina, Charlotte. He is the author of *The Shakespearean Dramaturg: A Theoretical and Practical Guide* (2006) and the editor of the performance journal *Shakespeare Bulletin.*

HEATHER ANNE HIRSCHFELD is Associate Professor of English at the University of Tennessee, Knoxville. Her latest book is entitled *Joint Enterprises: Collaborative Drama and the Institutionalization of the English Renaissance Theater.* For several years she has served as book review editor of *Medieval and Renaissance Drama in England.*

ROBERT HORNBACK is Associate Professor of English at Oglethorpe University. With articles published or forthcoming in *SEL, ELR, Comparative Drama, Renaissance and Reformation,* and the Blackwell *Companion to Tudor Literature and Culture,* he is currently writing a book that brings to light long-overlooked comic traditions, ranging from blackface fools and early evangelical comedy to stupid puritan clown-types.

SUJATA IYENGAR teaches at the University of Georgia. Her books include *Shades of Difference: Mythologies of Skin Color in Early Modern England* (2005) and *Shakespeare's Medical Language* (forthcoming).

ERIC JOHNSON-DEBAUFRE is a doctoral candidate in English at Boston University. He is currently working on a dissertation that explores the growth and influence of cartographic consciousness in early modern England.

FREDERICK KIEFER is Professor of English at the University of Arizona. His most recent book is *Shakespeare's Visual Theatre: Staging the Personified Characters* (2003).

JEREMY LOPEZ is Assistant Professor of English at the University of Toronto. He is the theater review editor of *Shakespeare Bulletin* and the author of *Theatrical Convention and Audience Response in Early Modern Drama* (2003).

FRANCESCA T. ROYSTER is Associate Professor of English and Associate Dean of Undergraduate Studies at DePaul University, she is the author of *Becoming Cleopatra: the Shifting Image of an Icon* (2003) and has published essays in *Shakespeare Quarterly, Shakespeare Studies, Approaches to Teaching Shakespeare's "Othello"* (2005), and other volumes.

DENEEN SENASI is a lecturer at the University of Tennessee, Knoxville. Her work has appeared recently in the *Journal for Early Modern Cultural Studies* and *Religion and Literature*. She has an essay forthcoming in the collection entitled *Desire and the Analysts* from SUNY Press.

MEDIEVAL
AND
RENAISSANCE
DRAMA
IN ENGLAND

Forum: Race, Racism, and Performance on the Early Modern Stage

Racial Impersonation on the Elizabethan Stage: The Case of Shakespeare Playing Aaron

IMTIAZ HABIB

I

IF racial construction is a clairvoyant performance, the creation of a virtual human reality from another psychic realm, its greatest provenance will be in the theater. Acting, as the production of virtual persons, is predicated on another that will be fabricated, so that different sexual or ethnic lives are the staple of the industry of the stage. This symbiotic relationship between drama and the other, that is to say between mimesis and alterity, is what drives the postcolonial philosopher Michael Taussig, following Walter Benjamin, to assert that "the ability to mime, and mime well," which is to say act and act well, "is the capacity to Other."[1] Insofar as early modern racial discourse is a heavily colonial product,[2] from a postcolonial standpoint it follows, then, and is a neglected truism for post-structularist cultural studies in general, that the rise of racial discourse in early modern England is intimately connected to the rise of popular drama in the early colonial reign of Elizabeth I.[3] The multiplicity of racialized representations in the popular English drama between 1587 and 1640 testify to the onset of this otherwise unnoticed and only recently studied discourse that traditional historical acknowledgments have been wont to see as operating clearly only from the middle of the seventeenth century onward, most notoriously in the transatlantic slave trade. But while over the last decade and a half important analyses of late sixteenth- and early seventeenth-century English racial constructions have focused on the *figurative* representations of race in elements of material texts and in discrete cultural formations, including language,[4] there has been little opportunity to examine the political dynamics of the *literal* impersonation of race onstage.[5] If, however, that has been due in part to the paucity of documentary details of racial acting in Elizabethan drama, a significant breakthrough for race studies as a whole in the period is afforded by the plausible albeit speculative data of Donald Foster's stylometric SHAXICON tests regarding specific roles Shakespeare may have played, specifically that he may have played Aaron in *Titus Andronicus,* as well as Morocco and Antonio in *The Merchant*

17

of Venice and Brabantio in *Othello.* Unraveling the complex psychosocial transactions involved in such possibilities provide valuable new insights into the compulsions and difficulties of racial discourse in Shakespeare and his world.

The usefulness of the data produced by SHAXICON stems from its reasonably cautious methodology, and from its generally corroborative compatibility with the existing information of traditional scholarship on Elizabethan playhouse documents and theater history, and on the beginnings of Shakespeare's professional career. "Electronically map[ping] Shakespeare's language so that we can now tell usually which texts influence which other texts, and when," SHAXICON'S "lexical database indexes all words that appear in the canonical plays 12 times or less. (These are called 'rare words')." What this demonstrates, in Foster's own words, is that:

> The rare words in Shakespearean texts are not randomly distributed either diachronically or synchronically, but are mnemonically "structured." Shakespeare's active lexicon as a writer was systematically influenced by his reading, and by his apparent activities as a stage player. When writing, Shakespeare was measurably influenced by plays then in production, and by particular stage-roles most of all. Most significant is that, while writing, he disproportionately "remembers" the rare–word lexicon of plays concurrently "in repertoire"; and from these plays he always registers disproportionate lexical recall (as a writer) of just one role (or two or three smaller roles); and these remembered roles, it can now be shown, are most probably those roles that Shakespeare himself drilled in stage performance.
>
> (SHAXICON '95, 1)

Applying this test Foster finds that in *Titus Andronicus* Shakespeare played "probably Aaron or old Lucius, or possibly alternating between these roles" (SHAXICON '95, 4). Additionally, SHAXICON indicates that in *The Merchant Venice* "Shakespeare seems to have played Antonio in all productions; but Morocco is a second 'remembered' role," and that in *Othello* he played "Brabantio" (SHAXICON '95, 3).

The cautiousness of SHAXICON's methodology is indicated, first by the fact that it has no knowledge of traditionally ascribed play dates and of Shakespearean authorship, and second, despite the test's confirmation of three roles traditionally attributed to Shakespeare, that of Adam in *As You Like It,* the Ghost in *Hamlet,* and Old Kno'well in Jonson's *Every Man in His Humour,* by Foster's emphatic (and subsequently repeated) warning that "this catalogue cannot be *proven* to represent historical reality" (emphasis added).[6] Although in the intervening decade since its release SHAXICON has been successfully challenged, that has focused mainly on its claim of Shakespearean authorship for the nondramatic text *Funeral Elegy,* which Foster himself has subsequently withdrawn.[7] But despite its controversial reputation, and despite being now regarded by some as a "moribund" study, and akin to "counterfeiting Shakespeare" (fueled, one suspects, by an understandable but unnecessary traditional humanities apprehension about the mechanization of things literary by the emergence of statistical and electronic studies), its method of statistically derived internal stylistic analyses of Shakespeare texts, particularly of "rare words," for deriving a variety of insights about Shakespeare's writing and performing life, has proven useful and drawn cautious adherents.[8] Overall, and without implying a position for or against the validity of SHAXICON's methodology and findings as such, it is possible to suggest that the list of probable acting roles for Shakespeare that it indicates is not incredible, because it is congruent with traditional scholarly knowledge of Shakespeare's early career.

To take as a case in point SHAXICON's indications about *Titus,* the uncertain history of the play's origins, between 1592 and 1594, associated as references to the play are with Pembroke's-Strange's-Sussex's-Chamberlain's Men singly and in combination (ignoring here the "early start" argument of E. A. J. Honigmann ascribing a late 1580s date, and the even more dubious but ingeniously constructed Oxfordian argument ascribing a 1570s date), does not affect the possibility and the significance of Shakespeare playing Aaron.[9] The conflicts and issues within that history all point to Shakespeare beginning his theater career as an actor and writer (as the Robert Greene, Henry Chettle references to him suggest),[10] for whom it is perfectly consistent to write crowd-winning lines/roles/texts that he could himself help to make successful in performance while seeking employment in times that were uncertain for both, the industry as a whole (plague years, playing companies' breakups and reformations) and the playwright in terms of his struggling beginnings in the London/Southwark performance scene. Traditional scholarship has already noted that *Titus* is one of the two early tragedies that seems to have been written to impress, in terms of the unusual demands it makes on its producers.[11] In the racial discourse of an early colonial environment, a key crowd winner is the impersonation of a racialized life on the stage, as is witnessed by the fact that according to the payment records in Henslowe's *Diary Titus Andronicus* was performed five times between 1593 and 1594, with the fattest takings on his lists for each of those occasions, including sometimes three times per week.[12] In what follows, this paper will not try to analyze how Shakespeare played Aaron and the other related racial roles or to prove that he did in fact play them. Rather, it will explore the psychosocial dynamics of what it meant for him to have probably done so. SHAXICON's findings provide not the proof but the cue for such a speculative exploration.

II

The impersonation of a racialized life is a preference on the part of the actor-playwright, and in that racial impersonation is primarily projective, striving to cast a perceived similitude of difference for the enjoyment of a kind of virtual solidarity. Irrespective of whether *Titus Andronicus* is a revision of the older *Titus and Vespasian* held by Strange's Men and given for reworking to a young Shakespeare seeking to show his mettle or is a fresh script composed by him with the same compulsions, and irrespective of whether the scripting of a black role in the play is the first instance of the representation of color on the popular Elizabethan stage or whether that scripting merely follows the seminal lead of George Peele's *Battle of Alcazar* racially played with such success by Edward Alleyn in 1587,[13] the writing and playing of race in *Titus* is a Shakespearean choice. The developed independent role of the doubly demonized Moor with the Jewish name, identifiable in no source but directly evocative of the additional racialization potential of anti-Semitic dramatization popularized by the endless success of Marlowe's *Jew of Malta,* is "peculiarly Shakespearian."[14] It is a choice with a particular psychic signature. It is indicative not so much of a knowledge of the black life or of a desire to know it as of a need to project it exploitatively to make it known, to render it usably into a larger social imaginary. At this fundamental level, racial playing is unavoidably implicated in an identificatory impetus, the gesture of oneness with the object of representation that is the quintessence of the mimetic act.

The cosmetic details of race's physical depiction on the Shakespearean stage, first catalogued by Eldred Jones, and cited recently by Dympna Callaghan,[15] aim at external phenotypical conflation, facing white with black, which is consistent with the "externalized" quality of late Elizabethan acting as opposed to the "subtler" effect of the later acting of Burbage as differentiated by Andrew Gurr.[16] The physical staging of the black life in Aaron, inscribing and reinforcing conventional traits of that life gathered from the morphology of popular Elizabethan cultural constructions such as the travel writings of Richard Hakluyt, Richard Eden, and others,[17] as well as from novel experiential encounters with the small but growing numbers of captured African populations in London, constitutes for playwright-actor and his protocolonial audience an enjoyment of the black other who with his "cloudy melancholy . . . [and] . . . fleece of woolly hair" fights to save his species against the imperial order that has enslaved him and in revenge busily plots its destruction. Carried by a logic of representative inclusion, the demonizing performance of Aaron functions obscurely as a kind of virtual solidarity with the marked-down black subject who is by that very representation added to the protocolonial English socius's circuit of visibility. For the denigratory impersonator and his audience, the "wretch-ing" of the marginal black wretch is acceptably enjoyable, in other words, because it offers to culturally showcase him in return.

At the same time, the obscurity and the virtual (rather than real) nature of the instinct of solidarity within the projective performance of racial impersonation makes the latter also racial critique. Critique is implicit in the act of impersonation itself, in that the act substitutes the real with its mimesis, which can become a denial and cancellation of the real and hence a critique of it. To ask, as Dympna Callaghan does in her seminal essay, why if there were blacks were they not used on the Elizabethan stage,[18] is to confront the expurgatory regime of Shakespearean racial acting in which the black subject can be *re-presented* but not allowed to present itself. A homologous instance of this is the performance, six years after the first staging of Aaron in *Titus Andronicus,* of the historical Mary Frith or Moll Cutpurse in *The Roaring Girl* at the Fortune theater, in which she can watch the performance but not participate in it.[19] This is the similitude of difference that serves as a reminder of separation from the enacted product (beyond the instinct of solidarity and empathy with it), and thereby works as a critique of it. The contrarious mimetic reflex between critiquing re-presentation and projective presentation has been described by Alexander Leggatt as the distance between the early modern English actor standing "as it were, beside the character, commenting on it," and "showing it off,"[20] which is to say, performing it. This is the self-pointing gesture of the Aaron actor's onstage likening of his "fleec[y]" hair to the uncoiling of "an adder" about to do "some fatal execution," and of his explication of his "deadly-standing eye . . . [and] . . . silence," as signs of "vengeance," "blood," and "revenge" (2.3.32–39) that makes his projective enactment of the black life a simultaneous denunciation of it.

If to Robert Weimann, discussing the psychic mechanics of performative disfigurement in *Richard III,* the phenomenon marks "the difference between the closure of representation and the aperture of its transaction," and the "gap inhabited by the player presenting himself in the act of disfiguring the object of representation,"[21] that same performative disfigurement underwrites Shakespeare-as-Aaron's coloring of his "soul black like his face" (3.1.205), in the precise syntax of popular Anglo-European iconographic tradition. The negative projectivity of the role and its personal enactment by Shakespeare becomes, then, a censorious collective ritual between personator and audience of a reduction of the black life, and because of the known collaborative nature of Elizabethan popular drama, an enacted communal critique of its existence. According to the experienced theatergoer Edmund Gayton, writing in 1654 but describing what could plausibly be held to apply five decades earlier, Elizabethan spectators come to a performance "not to study . . . but [to] love such expressions and passages which with ease insinuate themselves into their capacities."[22] Since for the typically substantial and already excitable audience at the Rose the power of performance is accelerated by its closely packed atmosphere, the effect on that audience of the fantasy of performance cannot have been only to direct their energies instantly on to "the nearest available women" as Leggat observes,[23] but also to inculcate long-term attitudes toward minority ethnic prey in the neighborhood at large. In this popular theater would perform what Leggatt, citing a modern sociologist of popular drama, says such demotic performances do, which is to "inform members of a community about social structure."[24] The nullifying review of the black life in the Shakespearean performance of Aaron assumes a still clearer point in SHAXICON's additional indication that he also alternated as "old Lucius,"[25] the character that is Aaron's formal judge and sentencer at performance's end, the latter role formally emphasizing and ensuring the critiquing depiction of the former. Shakespeare's acting of both roles is nothing more than the literalization of his direction of the racial roles written by him, in keeping with his habit of directing the acting as noted by his colleagues such as John Lowin and Joseph Taylor, and suggested by Andrew Gurr, and a part of the general practice of Elizabethan playwrights as remembered by the seventeenth-century English antiquarian and biographer John Aubrey in 1681, and by foreign visitors such as Johannes Rhenanus, a German physician impressed with the English public theaters in 1613.[26]

Furthermore, solidarity exists uncertainly with, and is punctuated by, the drive of the writer-player's nascent colonial culture to govern and control the differential threat of the black other who exists for it paradigmatically on a sliding scale between attraction and repulsion, fascination and fear. This simultaneous anxious containment is what in different ways Ania Loomba and Dympna Callaghan have both described. For Loomba this is early modern English drama's subliminal obligation to manage popular fears about, and reverse the historical reality of, the subsumption of English cultural ideology by Turkish and Eastern nonwhite cultures by rehearsing its obverse, and for Callaghan this is Elizabethan cultural discourse's reduction of the potency of the black life by the othered mimesis of it onstage.[27] Not merely are victorious Ottoman Turkish military assaults on Europe relentless throughout Elizabeth's and James's reigns, so are their cultural triumphs, as the succession of considerable and continuous Christian conversions to Islam in both reigns attest. Whereas this alarming development inspires a popular English play (Robert Daborne's *A Christian Turned Turke*) and coins the word "renegado" in James's reign as Nabil Matar and C. A. Patrides before him have both shown, this popular trepidation of the non-English/non-European/non-Christian/nonwhite Other gathers force earlier and is a part of the popular imagination of London in the 1590s.[28] Within the conflationary habit of early modern racial othering described, for instance, by the Jacobean figure who inherits the pioneering colonial ethnography of Richard Hakluyt, Samuel Purchas, in which peoples of different regions and cultures are indistinguishably lumped together,[29] Turks, East and West Indians, and Muslims also become black, which then stands in, not just for Africans, but for all those others as well. More specifically, in the 1590s in London itself, the numbers of "veritable negro[es]" themselves, to use the infamous words of one modern Shakespeare editor,[30] are considerable and growing, as parish registry records across central, east, and south London, in and near neighborhoods and areas of Shakespeare's known residences and workplaces such as Bishopsgate, Clerkenwell, Aldgate, and particularly, Shoreditch and Southwark, indicate. In the last three decades of the sixteenth century, captured black people, individually and in families, in a variety of bondages and relationships, including cross-racial ones, are living in parish neighborhoods such as St. Bottolph, Aldgate; St. Mary Bothaw; St. Olave, Hart Street; St. Olave, Tooley Street, Southwark; Christchurch, Newgate; All Hallaws, Honey Lane; St. Pancras, Soper Lane; St. Benet Fink; St. Mary, Mounthaw; St. James, Clerkenwell.[31] Elizabethan black existence is also documented in tax returns as Eldred Jones showed long ago, in court papers, as in the case against the Marrano Jewish physician Hector Nunes in 1588, in which his blackamoor maids are made to testify against him but not in their own person, and in medical records, as in Simon Foreman's casebooks describing his treatment of a black maid named Polonia in 1597.[32] Hostile popular English responses to the assimilatory struggle of the sixteenth-century Tudor black subject, while being documented as far back as the beginning of the century by Robert Fabyan's amazed recollection of two Westminister Africans perfectly turned out in English manners and clothing, are best typified by George Best's well-known troubled ruminations in 1576 about a black man fathering a black child with a white woman in London.[33] Several entries about cross-racial unions in the parish registers record more tersely the same animus.[34] The growing number of blacks eventually prompts, of course, Elizabeth's three deportation orders for them in 1596 and 1601.[35] Irrespective of the exact numbers of black people resident in Elizabethan London in the closing decades of the sixteenth century, that population must have been numerous enough to be instantly noticeable to a young Shakespeare first arriving in London at the end of the 1580s and living amid, and in proximity to, such neighborhoods for him to have immediately recognized their spectacular theatrical potential and for him to have decided to represent them onstage in one of his earliest dramatic enterprises and his very first tragedy.

Seen against this specific history and material context, and particularly within the now-compelling possibility that Shakespeare may have encountered black people firsthand, more than his conception of the negatively marked black man in Aaron, his performance of the role himself (in the Rose in Southwark, in the early 1590s) acquires a particular charge. It parallels, and responds to, the repressed historical black subject's struggle for acceptance, which is to say pass for white, in late Tudor London. If assimilation is the successful assumption of a particular kind of social being, the becoming of someone else and the entering into a new life, the colonized black Elizabethan subject's struggle to assimilate is the symptom and cue for his derisive racialized impersonation onstage. In this symbiotic exchange, black passing for white is profiled and reversed in the performative recasting of black by

white as unsuitable for assimilation.[36] As the engine of Titus's "tragic" failure to reconstruct both, the feuding body politic of imperial Rome and the
body of his ravaged family, Aaron (who is an unofficial slave just as the majority of blacks in the Elizabethan parish records are unofficially bonded, i.e.,
personally possessed "servants") is also the undesirable racial outsider in the
white metropolis who in the words of Shakespeare's own monarch has
"crepte" in.[37] More crucially, not only is he attempted to be, but cannot be,
expelled, he has now written himself into the civic life of the city. In a vague
multiculturalist critical practice, Aaron's black child may make an estheti-
cally pleasing composite twin with the fairer but equally racially mixed one
of his countryman Muletius that is substituted for it as the emperor's heir and
Rome's future potentate, but both together reactively highlight the dangerous
miscegenic inroads into the Elizabethan human landscape being made by
real-life blacks outside the playhouse. Shakespeare's designing and enactment of the role of Aaron in the public theater is thus plausibly proximate if
not exactly coterminus with popular Elizabethan culture's xenophobic resistance to the entry of the colonized black subject into its living mainstream,
even as it enjoys and showcases the exoticism of that presence.[38]

III

To the extent that racial impersonation involves racial embodiment, the assumption of a racial life and the entering into it and possessing it, racial acting is also a form of surveillance. The enactment of the racial subject is an
acquisitive knowing of that otherwise unavailable life and a sketching of its
exigencies. For compulsively inquisitorial Elizabethan officials such as William Cecil and Francis Walsingham, the government's multiple and minute
cartographic surveys of the realm are accompanied by its detailed watchful-
ness over the population in repeated enforcements of parish record keeping
orders inherited from Elizabeth's father's reign, particularly in and around
London.[39] But whereas the deadly distrustfulness of a post-Reformation England throughout Elizabeth's reign is focused chiefly on Spanish Catholic
conspiracy, its ancillary effect is to establish a relentless spying, on everyone
and everything, as the normative procedure of the government, and massively
prosecuted by the court's intricate network of intelligencers.[40] As such, performance and the public playhouse are under constant scrutiny, not just from
Puritan polemicists and the city alderman, but also from the privy councillors
who in allowing the theaters to exist repeatedly inquire into and strictly regulate their operation.[41] The stage's personation of the black life, like the rest
of its business, must therefore bear the impress of the government's variable
but endless vigilance and a relationship of conformity to it. In this case, the
design and the enactment of the politically and sexually subversive role of

Aaron is for the public an instructive illumination and exposure of the incurable perfidy of the black subject hidden in its midst, a symbolic confirmatory examination of the civic treachery and sexual riot that popular travel literature has already paradigmatically suspected him to possess.[42] Shakespeare's necessary connections to powerful Elizabethan personalities and government officials, possibly to Lord Strange, as well as to Lord Hunsdon, and the earls of Pembroke and Southampton, visible a few years later in the public mention of him in the city's theater documents,[43] thus give his performance of Aaron and its ethnic investigation the proportions of a believable deliberateness.

The public inquisition of the black life in the playing of Aaron is most explicit in Lucius's interrogation of him in the play's closing scenes, Shakespeare's agenda of ethnic inquiry becoming more palpable, as mentioned earlier, by SHAXICON's revelation that occasionally he also himself played Lucius. As the total effect of Aaron's black life in the play's white Roman community is evident only at the end of the play, the full review of that life is available only to Lucius as the final redeemer of Roman political order after the bloody carnage of the Saturninuns-Tamora-Titus internecine feud. As Aaron is the primary architect of the destruction of the play's civic body (even if Tamora is the secondary one), he is the cancer that is Lucius's immediate responsibility to probe and reveal. That examination of the hidden danger of the black life begins with Lucius's first interrogative encounter with the "the incarnate devil" and "wall'ey'd slave," even before Lucius has entered Rome, and turning as that catechism does on the promise that Aaron holds for Lucius, described by the former himself as the "wonderous things / That highly may advantage thee to hear" (5.1.40–55), it is what presages and initiates his victorious journey to Rome as its new leader.[44] The secret discoveries that the hearing reveals are extensions of the desolate location of the "ruinous monastery" that is the black subject's abode, shown elsewhere in the performance to be either in streets and alleys or in solitary if idyllic gardens (as with Tamora), that is, unfixed and unkowable habitations just like Aaron's historical Elizabethan counterparts. If the design of the forced interview of the captive black subject is basically that of a life for a life, that exchange involves not just the offer of Aaron's life for that of his colored child but more importantly the life of the latter in return for information necessary for the recovery of Rome. That is, it is the surreptitious black life's revelations that will restore the white community to health, accentuated in the urgency of Lucius's opening words: "Say . . . / Why dost not speak? What, deaf? not a word?" (5.1.44–47). Notable in the knowledge thus acquired is not so much the catalog of perfidious deeds ranging from the harmless to the serious, but the discernible, casually rehearsed undertone of its language in which what is learned is already surmised and only in need of confirmation:

> For I must talk of murthers, rapes, and massacres
> Acts of black nights, abominable deeds
> Complots of mischiefs, treason, villainies . . .

(5.1.62–65)

The invisible compulsion of this performed confession is a bit more detectable in Aaron's words in the next scene:

> Some devil whisper curses in my ear,
> And prompt me that my tongue may utter forth
> The venomous malice of my swelling heart!

(5.3.11–13)

The traceable internal pressures of such lines identify the self-vindicating nature of the investigation of the black life in Shakespeare's textual and theatrical portrayal of Aaron and Lucius, in which the marked body of the racial other is mimicked, possessed, and voiced over to iterate a life suspected and predesigned for it.

It follows, then, that to a degree racial impersonation is also racial programming, as the inscription of dominant culture the psychoanalytic scripting of the repressed black life. If colonialism is a drama of power between colonizer and colonized, or, to use a supplementary scenario, if race relations are an enacted script of control between the power perpetuation of the white and the disempowerment of the black, then the early modern English playwright and his agent, the actor, are surrogate colonizers as Terence Hawkes has suggested[45]—with racializing intent. To this paradigm may be added the third element of psychoanalyses, since, assuming in the fashion of Fredric Jameson that all cultural production is a socially symbolic act, symbiotic homologies can be established between drama and psychoanalysis.[46] Popular drama in particular could be seen as the liminal symbiosis of a collective social surveillance, the assembling, through the examination, of the elements of an imagined social life. In Stephen Greenblatt's words about the Elizabethan stage, these are "the public uses of spectacle to impose normative ethical patterns on the urban masses."[47] If the analyst-patient relationship is thought of as a drama, with role, dialogue, and a linear plot (diagnosis-treatment-cure), the popular English drama can be understood as the psychoanalysis of a national being, the natural programming, that is, the prognosis, intervention in, and production of a desired socius with its particular codes of privilege and prohibition. Given what Jacqueline Rose has insisted is the inherent ethnocentrism of psychoanalysis,[48] this heuristic could be applied to race to describe popular Elizabethan drama's performative fashioning of deviant colonized ethnicity into assimilative compliance in the script of nationhood.

Seen in this fashion, the performative agenda of the scene of Lucius's questioning of Aaron is not only to obtain information from him but also through that very cooperation to manipulatively attempt to render the recalcitrant black subject suitable for a conformable metropolitan citizenship. The real object of this doubly recessed enactment (Lucius as manipulative inquisitor and Aaron as the canny confessor, within the other actor and Shakespeare playing Lucius and Aaron reversibly), however, is not the success of the interrogation but in fact *its failure*. The scripting of an acceptable civic personality in the black subject is not the successful achievement of true repentance and probity in Aaron, but its opposite: the self-demonstration of his essential inability to acquire civility, which will then be his psychic passport to a justifiably disempowered white colonial national life. In other words, the real collective psychoanalysis of the scenes of Aaron's questioning by Lucius is the public modeling of the unredeemability of the black life as the norm for it, otherwise a demotic theatricalization of the proverbial Elizabethan wisdom of not trying to "wash an Ethiope white."[49] The prosecution of this complex stage agenda is the burden of not just Aaron's gleeful confession of malevolence but also of his emphatic denial of any transformational penitence in himself, the closing scenes of his role being merely the climactic summary of the overall lesson of his portraiture. That, unlike the case of Mary Frith, it is still unknown whether any Elizabethan blacks see their negative framing by Shakespeare in Aaron is irrelevant, for that demonizing black stage iconography, while meant for the black subject, is not dependant on him. Rather, it is dependant on the two thousand white spectators of the Rose who will stamp it into progressively wider cultural currency from each performance of the play.[50] In the circuit of transmission between author-actor and spectator, as the popularity of the negative model of the black life is the popularity of its propagator and vice versa so Shakespeare's exemplary racial profiling of the black life in the role of Aaron is the molding of his public career.

To review the ground covered so far, Shakespeare's racial impersonation in his playing of Aaron may issue from an obscure instinct of racial solidarity but may also involve an instinct of racial critique deployed across the triple agendas of ethnic control, surveillance, and programming. The obverse relationship between racial impersonation as solidarity and as critique is not chronologic but synchronous, and not linear but dialectical, so that the white enactment of the black life is at once projecting and suppressing race, showcasing and defacing it at the same time. These complex crossovers in the regimes of racial impersonation's progress describe the uncertainties of its operation and suggest its variable relationship to the authority of the impersonator. Together, the heterogenous features of Shakespeare's racial impersonation might be said to constitute its instability of *intention*.

IV

It remains to be considered briefly how racial impersonation involves a col-
lateral cost for the impersonator. Even if in early modern English usage there
is a distinction between playing and acting in today's sense, as for instance
in Thomas Hobbes's definition in *Leviathan* in 1651 of acting as personation,
that distinction, involving a later, more formalized performance with scripted
and naturally plausible role depiction for acting as distinct from the earlier,
diversely free-form entertainment of playing,[51] is fuzzy and at best merely
emergent in the early 1590s. Shakespeare's playing of a black character, no
matter how projective and external, involves a substitution of one identity
with another, a wearing of black over white. Even if transient, the miming of
a person of another race requires the leaving of one's home self for another
and the transference of one kind of self-knowing of one kind of phenotypical
external to another kind imagined to be flowing from a different skin color.
For the white actor staging a black, the reversibility of this transaction is en-
tropic on two levels, that of the social and the psychic: a descent to the reduced material allowances of the mimicked black life for the former, and in
consequence, a vulnerability to the constructed opprobrious living practices
of that life for the latter. For Shakespeare to impersonate the black subject is
to be unavoidably even if incrementally tainted by him, particularly to the
white community of his impersonation. This is the reflexive self-marking of
racial impersonation, the infection of whiteness by blackness.

As the deepest of all colors, black resists its absorption and has the potential to appropriate all others. Contrary to Callaghan's observation that "black
. . . can neither be written on, nor returned . . . to white,"[52] the strength of
black's hue does not preclude its whitening but cumulatively threatens the
latter's obliteration in the event of white's impersonation of it. This is to say
that black can more easily take on and mimic white and retain its integrity
than can the latter, which is a function of the converse direction of the resultant pigmentary accretion in the two interactions: black going on white will
eventually discolor white more than white going on black will gradually
streak black. Transferred symbolically to its human effects, this lesser reversibility of the blacking up of white compared to the greater one of the blanch-
ing out of black, puts the white theatrical Elizabethan racial impersonator in
a threshold zone that is not quite black and yet no longer just white either.
His physical assumption of blackness may be temporary, but in terms of an
experience of the black life that cannot be mnemonically disowned even as
the accoutrements of its theatrical illusion can at performance's end be shed,
his loss of a simple and exclusive whiteness must be permanent. The communal and individual signs of this residual loss in Shakespeare's playing of
Aaron operate discretely in the text of the social performance to which it

is contributing and in the psychic performance of the theatrical script itself, although the former perhaps in ways that can be theoretically generalized rather than historically demonstrated with precision. In the interests of fore-grounding the importance of such theoretical generalizations, it is worth in-voking here Loomba's question "Why is it, for example, that while men dressing as women can be regarded as potentially 'unsettling' gender catego-ries, no such radical meaning attaches to 'blacking up'?"[53]

Early modern English social response to the assumption of blackness, for cosmetic fashion or for performative entertainment, runs a complex range from the silently tolerant to the pointedly critical, and it is complicated fur-ther by the busy dialogue against face painting and by the animosity toward the theatrical industry as a whole, within which it is overwritten. Callaghan's earlier cited insistence that beneath the racial dressing up onstage in *Titus* it is white actors appropriating black lives is suggestive not only of the indeli-bility of whiteness (and of the early capitalist politics of mimesis, which fe-tishizes and commodifies both the ethnic and the sexual real for commercial gain, so that the blackfaced but white Shakespearean Aaron's claim that "black is better . . . in that it scorns to bear another hue" is actually an inside joke between impersonator and audience), but also of the incarceration of white in black even if momentarily so, and hence of its potential for drowning in it. As Loomba sharply observes, in the early colonialist English age of Anglo-European domination and suppression of people of color Elizabethan racial impersonation onstage stands for the ironic, counterpointing depen-dence and submission of the white man to the black.[54] Some anxiety about this meaning is visible about a decade later in Dudley Carleton's noticeable unease at the blacked-up spectacle of Queen Anne and her troupe in Jonson's *Masque of Blackness* when he comments that "it became them nothing so well as their red and white," for, as Callaghan explains, it was "a defilement of their pure aristocratic body" (198–99).[55] Whether William Bourne (Bird, Byrd), who plays black roles in the *Battle of Alcazar, 1 Tamar Cham,* and *Frederick and Basilea* (all plays with racial roles) at the Rose a few years earlier in 1597, is the focus in part at least of this same discomfort, in the tavern fight for which he receives an official sentence,[56] and whether that ex-perience is typical of the boisterous lives of his close colleagues such as Charles Massey, Samuel Rowley, Anthony Jeffes, George Somerset, William Cartwright, and Wilbraham, all of whom had also repeatedly played such roles, is uncertain. Irrespective of these and other uncertainties, including how blackface was achieved at the Rose, since there is no evidence of face painting being used, it is the ramifications of assuming a black face onstage that bear significance.

Functioning in the dubious space between a discreet and fluctuating Privy Council support on the one hand, and the relentless hostility of the city alder-men on the other, the Elizabethan player is, in the words of one social historian of Shakespeare, "always disliked by some."[57] Pressured perpetually to conform to the limits of his profession set by the Privy Council, maneuvering constantly to avoid becoming the target of puritanical civic attacks on the stage, and scrambling continually to please unpredictable and volatile spectators, dangerous missteps and faux pas with violent consequences must have been the norm rather than the exception in the lives of the performers. While even within their brevity and frequent opacity, records of described or implied violence involving early modern Tudor and Stuart actors, playwrights, and stages describe a spectrum of originary scenarios, several among them leave open the possibility of that violence issuing from animosities toward players for what they are performing onstage. Between 1580 and 1626 there are multiple documented instances of acts of deliberate hostility shown toward players by the public, including open fights between them.[58] Among them is the warrant issued for Shakespeare's arrest in 1596.[59] This is to say that even if players were a boisterous and violent lot, some of their violence may have been their response to the social pressures *on them* for what they were performing onstage.

But the stage's own admission of the lingering effects of the white impersonation of black is underlined by Callaghan in her above-cited discussion, when she says that "Dense black face painting (which because of the practical difficulty of washing it off meant that the transformation of black to white promised at the end [of *The Masque of Blackness*] had to wait until *The Masque of Beauty*."[60] Such a metatheatrical acknowledgment is more directly evident in Richard Brome's *The English Moor,* when Quicksand while painting Millicent up as a black moor and describing to her how to put on black face, apologizes to her that "Heavan's workmansip [*sic*]" in her face will have to be lost for a while: "For a small time; farewell."[61] Shakespeare's own silent signal of the reflexive price of racial impersonation may be the fact that at least according to the evidence of SHAXICON, he does not himself play another racial character again, even when he continues to compose racial roles with greater complexity, and even as he plays some of the roles that support the racialization of minorities onstage (Antonio in *Merchant* and Brabantio in *Othello*). To Elizabethans critical of theater such as Geoffrey Fenton, Stephen Gosson, Philip Stubbes, Anthony Munday, and John Northbrooke, playing someone is to take on his vices—that's what becoming someone means.[62] As Callaghan has pointed out, even as successful an actor as Nathan Field was denied communion at his parish church.[63] The commonly repeated strictures of Fenton, Gosson, and the others against stage role-playing must have had a pronounced effect in the social experience of Elizabethan racial impersonators.

The psychic reflux of Shakespeare's racial impersonation in Aaron does, however, register in the slight but significant reversals that Lucius encounters in his interrogation of Aaron. Drawing on the assumption afforded by SHAX-

ICON that Shakespeare played both Aaron and Lucius in different performances, and designating for the purpose of this analysis the Aaron of 5.1 and
5.3 *only* as the psyche of the impersonated black subject and Lucius as that
of the Shakespeare actor impersonating him, the quick points that Aaron
scores off Lucius amount to the self-pricking of the Shakespeare impersonator by his very impersonation. This is to use the Aaron of the role's final
appearances as the performative doppelgänger of the Shakespearen author-
actor who plays him in the overall script as a whole. For one thing, the trans-
actional exchange between Aaron and Lucius (the offer to talk and incrimi-
nate himself in return for his black baby's life, which will be the gain of the
survival of his kind) is itself proposed by Aaron, so that he is more in charge
than Lucius. This is akin to the role taking over the actor. For another thing,
Aaron extracts more conditions from Lucius than he from him—Lucius has
to agree to saving the baby before the confessional therapy can begin:

> *Aar.* Swear that he shall, and then I will begin . . .
> *Luc.* Even by my god, I swear to thee I will.
>
> (5.1.70–86)

Furthermore even though he invokes a Christian ethic in making Lucius
swear by his Christian God that he will keep his word to save Aaron's baby,
which is to say that he is willing to rely on Christian belief, his invocation of
such an ethic is only to test and probe Lucius's moral integrity, to in fact
"adjust" *Lucius's* psychic life (the semantic codes of his belief systems) to
include Aaron. This is almost a case of the analyst analyzed, and if psychoanalysis is a hermeneutics of suspicion,[64] then that is here applied by the "patient" on the analyst. Finally, Aaron's confessions do not lead to repentance,
despite the urging of Lucius:

> *Luc.* Art thou not sorry for these heinous deeds?
> *Aar.* Ay, that I had not done a thousand more . . .
>
> (5.1.123–24)

That Lucius's attempted psychological ministrations fall back upon him is
implicit in the ironic fact that the session ends with the analyst silencing the
patient: "Sirs, stop his mouth, and let him speak no more" (5.1.119–51).
This, one might say, is the breaking down of the analyst by the patient, instead of the other way around. In 5.3 what resonate more, possibly because
of their terminal location, are Aaron's curses on Lucius and the Romans
rather than their invectives on him:

> Ah, why should wrath be mute and fury dumb?
> I am no baby, I, that with base prayers
> I should repent the evils I have done.
>
> (5.3.184–87)

Even if it is the cultural politics of the play's race performance to make the black subject's "wrath" and "fury" have the show's final say, in order to propagate his congenital reprobation as detailed earlier, the unspoken indictment that design silently allows of the ideology of the impersonator's culture, and therefore of his psychic comfort, is the price such impersonation has to pay.

In sum, that in two immediately successive essays in the same critical volume, and in a kind of responsive relationship with each other, Dympna Callaghan and Ania Loomba have posited two generally opposite but equally compelling results in the endgame of early modern racial stage replication, namely that it is white remaining white in playing black cosmetically for the former and it is white losing itself in black for the latter, indicates that the product of such replication has a variable valency. This might spell another kind of discrepancy between the performance and the outcome of Elizabethan racial impersonation and symptomize another kind of instability in Elizabethan racial impersonation than what was described earlier in this essay. This could be termed the instability of *effect.* If so, both reflexive phenomena— racial impersonation as solidarity and as critique passing into each other, and racial programming passing into racial self inflection—have an operative simultaneity and equivalence, despite their mutually retrograde movements. A contrary *intention* and *effect* inversely collude with each other typically in the Shakespearean playing of the black subject in Aaron. In this sense, *Titus* may constitute as complex, if not a more complex, case of racial impersonation than *Othello* and even *Antony and Cleopatra.*[65]

V

Whether Shakespeare actually played the role of Aaron must of course remain unknowable. That is a fundamental difficulty that even SHAXICON's tempting analysis cannot alleviate. But even if it is uncertain exactly who played that role at the Rose, this much is certain: someone did, and it was a white male actor. Furthermore, even if Shakespeare did not play that role himself, as far as existing scholarly knowledge is concerned it is highly probable that he wrote it and the play of which it is a vital part. It is equally plausible, as this essay has tried to show, that he was involved in the crafting of the performance of both role and play. In the ultimate analysis, this essay's observations apply to the white Elizabethan acting of the role of black Aaron, irrespective of the particular identity of the actor. Although "rare words" analyses such as that of SHAXICON and other stylometric studies cannot indicate the incidence of unusual word usage, because they deal with word frequency and not word meaning, physiologically self-descriptive phrases such as "woolly hair," "thick lipp'd," "deadly standing eye," and "cloudy melancholy" that are part of Aaron's lexical repertoire occur nowhere else in Shakespeare. These reflect deliberate aspects of the physical staging of the black man that necessarily become affective elements of the writer recreating him and of the actor playing him. Shakespeare's undeniable historical proximity to this fact merely makes him a useful discursive stand-in for reconstructing its complex psychosocial ramifications.

If, in the one representation of Shakespeare's face with the longest reputation of authenticity, including in the recent evaluation of extant competing portraits by the National Portrait Gallery in London, namely the early seventeenth-century Chandos portrait, the playwright-actor has seemed to his nineteenth-century viewers as "a dark, heavy man, with a foreign expression, . . . thin curly hair, a somewhat lubricious mouth, red-edged eyes, wanton lips, with a coarse expression," and to his contemporary modern ones as being "swarthy" and "foreign" looking, are these perceived attributes the effects of his racial personification of a black man in his early career?[66] Even if some of these elements may either be the products of the portrait's aging, or of later retouchings, those phenomena would not account for the fundamental alienness of the face in the painting common to the perceptions of its historical and contemporary viewers. If the portrait has always seemed not recognizably English, could that misrecognition be the spectral aftereffect of racial impersonation's self-inflection in the moment of its performance?[67]

Any serious consideration of the root developments of Elizabethan theatrical history has a number of competing dates to consider. If the traditional choice for the beginning moment of early modern English popular drama is Burbage's construction of the Theatre playhouse in Shoreditch in 1576, that choice is challenged by the event that preceded and drove that, namely the Privy Council's ordinance of two years earlier allowing the Earl of Leicester's players the permanent authority to perform at times and places of their choosing, and even more significantly by the relatively recently understood construction plans of the Red Lion in 1567. However, if the paucity of actual performances and texts to accompany these early events render them intriguing but not central moments in the true efflorescence of Elizabethan theater,[68] the great volume of documented productions, texts, and professional playwrights in the late 1580s and nineties inevitably claims for this later period the status of a more dependable turning point in the growth of the late Tudor public stage. But whether the emphasis then is on the fortunes of the Admiral's Men, on the founding of the Lord Chamberlain's Men, on the construction of the Globe in 1599, or on the birth and evolution of personated acting within the older tradition of playing in the last decade of the sixteenth century, the time frame of importance becomes the ten years between 1585 and 1595. As it so happens, this window includes the arrival of Shakespeare in the London playing scene and the beginning of his career. It also encompasses the critical moment of the racial impersonation of the black man in Aaron.

Irrespective of the precise circumstances that lie behind the first practice of Elizabethan theatrical racial impersonation, and irrespective of whether Shakespeare truly starts that practice or whether he merely renders more professionally powerful and successful an innovation originated by Edward Alleyn (and George Peele),[69] it is the black subject that is located precisely at and within the apotheosis of what will be early modern England's proudest national achievement. To say this is to further suggest that this location is causative, and that the figure of the black man must be seen as crucially contributive to the true success of the theatrical arts of Shakespeare and his colleagues. That is consistent with a postcolonial critical practice's overall view of the still insufficiently recognized debt of an etiolatory Anglo-European cultural and political history to the colonized black peoples of the world. To iterate that debt has been the purpose of this essay.

Notes

1. *Mimesis and Alterity,* 19.

2. Ann Laura Stoler, *Carnal Knowledge and Imperial Power,* 24. For a summary discussion of the derivation of early modern and modern notions of race from early modern colonialism, as well as other arguments about the origins of racism, see my book, *Shakespeare and Race,* 3–4.

3. A responsible postcolonial critical practice seeks to trace both the consequences as well as the origins of the early modern Anglo-European colonial project, that is, examines colonialism's phenomenology in the temporal modes of both its post- and prehistories, within period- and region-specific narratives. Such a critical practice sees sixteenth-century England as early colonial in the sense that the English territorial colonialism that is fully visible later has its ideological inception and impetus in the transoceanic commercial explorations in the reign of the Tudors. Early English colonialism, which I have elsewhere termed the "protocolonial" ("Shakespeare's Spectral Turks," 2), is neither a formally organized project nor a fully formed ideology, but a discernible, rapidly growing national instinct of assertion, domination, and possession, that in its eventual production of colonialism proper bears a viably metonymic relation to it in critical analysis.

4. Some typical examples of this burgeoning field of scholarship are the works of Michael Neill, Martin Orkin, Emily Bartels, Peter Erickson, Kim Hall, Ania Loomba, Margo Hendricks, Dympna Callaghan, my own work, and that of Stanley Wells and Catherine Alexander.

5. This lacuna has been pointed out by Ania Loomba, "Shakespeare and Cultural Difference," 189–90.

6. That it has no knowledge of traditionally ascribed play dates and Shakespearean authorship is emphasized by David Kathman in "Critically Examining Oxfordian Claims," part 7. Foster's disavowal of historical conclusions is in SHAXICON '95,

1. Foster repeats the warning in his response to the pointed questions asked by Steve Sohmer in the electronic discussion list called SHAKSPER in November 1995.

7. Two of the strongest challenges to SHAXICON were those of Diana Price, "Shaxicon and Shakespeare's Acting Career," and Ward E. Y. Elliott and Robert J. Valenza, "Glass Slippers and Seven-League Boots: C-Prompted Doubts About Ascribing *A Funeral Elegy* and *A Lover's Complaint* to Shakespeare." For Foster's recantation, see William S. Niederkorn, "A Scholar Recants on His 'Shakespeare' Discovery."

8. Brian Vickers calls it counterfeiting (*"Counterfeiting" Shakespeare: Evidence, Authorship and John Ford's Funerall Elegye*, 450–52), and Gabriel Egan calls it "moribund" (personal Web page at http://www.gabrielegan.com/index.htm last accessed September 4, 2006). Others who have used the rare words approach include Bradley Efron and Ronald Thisted, "Estimating the Number of Unseen Species: How Many Words did Shakespeare Know?" (for a comment on Efron and Thisted's study, see Stanley Wells, "The Year's Contribution to Shakespearian Study," p. 228); Gabriel Egan, who has taken it up in his program called SHAXICAN (http://www.gabrielegan.com/index.htm); and Gary Taylor (Stanley Wells et al., eds., in *William Shakespeare: A Textual Companion*, 451).

9. E. K. Chambers, *Elizabethan Stage*, 2:122–23; David George, "Shakespeare and Pembroke's Men," 305–21; Sidney Thomas, "On the Dating of Shakespeare's Early Plays," 186–93; Carol Chillington Rutter, *Documents of the Rose Playhouse*, 78; and "Shakespeare's Life," 5; David L. Roper, "Henry Peacham's Chronogram: The Dating Of Shakespeare's Titus Andronicus."

10. Chambers, vol. 4, appendix C.

11. Andrew Gurr, *Staging in Shakespeare's Theatres*, 46.

12. Rutter, 78. Equally popular were other plays with racialized characters in them, such as Peele's *Mully Mahomet* and Marlowe's *The Jew of Malta.*

13. Anthony Gerard Barthelemy, *Black Face, Maligned Race*, 43.

14. J. C. Maxwell, ed., *Titus Andronicus*, xxx; Naomi Liebler, *Shakespeare's Festive Tragedy*, 133, 145.

15. Eldred Jones, "The Physical Representations of African Characters," 18–19; Dympna Callaghan, "'Othello Was a White Man,'" 195, 198.

16. *Shakespearean Stage*, 69–81; also see Peter Thomson, *Shakespeare's Professional Career*, 103–6.

17. The extensive body of travel writing known to the Elizabethans would typically include John Mandeville's *Travels;* Leo Africanus's *A Geographical Historie of Africa;* William Towerson's "Voyage to Guinea in 1555"; Richard Eden's *The Decades of the New World and West Indies* and *The History of Travel;* Richard Hakluyt's *The Principall Navigations, Voiages, and Discoveries of the English Nation;* and Samuel Purchas's *Hakluytus Posthumus.*

18. "'Othello Was a White Man,'" 193.

19. Alexander Legatt, *Jacobean Public Theatre*, 80.

20. Ibid., 80–81.

21. *Author's Pen and Actor's Voice*, 90 and 82, respectively.

22. *Pleasant Notes from Don Quixote*, cited by Leggatt, 33.

23. *Jacobean Public Theatre*, 37.

24. Ibid., 34.

25. SHAXICON '95, 5.

26. Chambers 2:329, 346. Chambers, in the same page in which he records the reference, does point out, however, that the dates involved cast some doubt over Joseph Taylor's acting direction by Shakespeare; Gurr, *Staging,* 45; A. M. Nagler, *Shakespeare's Stage,* 76.

27. "Shakespeare and Cultural Difference," 189, and "'Othello Was a White Man,'" 194, respectively.

28. See the essays by Nabil Matar, "The Renegade in English Seventeenth Century Imagination," and C. A. Patrides, "'The Bloody and Cruell Turke': The Background of a Renaissance Commonplace." The *Oxford English Dictionary* (*OED*) (2:2490) lists two instances of this use of the word in the late 1590s, one in 1598 and one in 1599, the latter by Hakluyt himself in the second volume of his *Principall Navigations.* John Florio's Italian-English dictionary lists this use of the word once in 1598: "Rinegato, a renegado, a foresworne man, one that hath renounced his religion"; see the Early Modern English Dictionaries Database (EMEDD) compiled by Ian Lancashire at the University of Toronto, accessible at http://www.chass.utoronto.ca/english/emed/emedd.html.

29. See 539 of his *Purchas His Pilgrimage,* for his frank confession of the English "confus[ion] of nations . . . [and] names."

30. M. R. Ridley, ed., *Othello,* l–li. The expression is originally Samuel Taylor Coleridge's in his *Shakespearean Criticism* 1:42, but Ridley's discussion of what *he* tries to imply is absurdly racist Victorian criticism is of course itself deeply inflected with racist assumptions; for a discussion of the unfortunate racism of Ridley's remarks, see Karen Newman's "'And Wash an Ethiop White,'" 143–45.

31. Following the tentative initial citations of a few of these records by W. E. Miller ("Negroes in Elizabethan London"), Eldred Jones (*The Elizabethan Image of Africa*), Thomas Forbes (*Chronicle from Aldgate*), and Roslyn Knutson ("A Caliban in St. Mildred Poultry"), I present my comprehensive study of these records in my forthcoming book, *Imprints of the Invisible: Black Lives in the Engliish Archives, 1500–1676,* in which there are 137 documentations of black people in London as well as elsewhere in England in Shakespeare's lifetime alone. The total number of documented references to black people in early sixteenth- and seventeenth-century England that I have found are several times that number.

32. See "The Elizabethan Image of Africa," 20; Meyers, "Lawsuits," 157, 163, and "Elizabethan Marranos Unmasked"; and entry for May 5, 1597, vol. 234 in Simon Foreman's unpublished medical casebooks.

33. Best, in *Principall Navigations,* 2:155 and 7:262–64.

34. For instance, in St. Martin in the Fields, Westminster, in 1573; in St. Mary Magdalene, Bermondsey, also in 1573; in St. Botolph, Bishopsgate, in 1575; in St. Pancras, Soper Lane, in 1578; in St. Mary Magdalene, Milk Street, in 1593; in St. Olave, Hart Street, in 1598; in St. Margaret, Westminster, in 1601; in All Hallows, London Wall, in 1606; in St. Nicholas, Deptford, in 1613; and in St. Botolph, Aldgate, in 1618. Even if the opacity of Elizabethan naming practices, the inconsistencies of improvisatory documentation procedures, the vagaries of sixteenth-century English orthography, and errors in the antiquarian Victorian transcriptions of these records

prevent certainty of racial identification in some cases, the majority of the records quite clearly specify black people through a consistent use of descriptors such as "Negro"/"negra," "neger," "blackamore/blackamoor(e)," "moor," "Blackman"/ "blacky," "Ethiop," singly and in combination with all variations thereof.

35. *Acts of the Privy Council,* 26:16–17, 20–21.

36. For an extended discussion of this point, see my essay "Shakespeare's Spectral Turks."

37. In the deportation order of 1601. The original manuscript has the expression "crepte," whereas John Roche Dasent in his *Acts of the Privy Council* (which is the first publication of these orders) incorrectly transcribed this as "carried." See the facsimile of the original manuscript of the order in the Marquess of Salisbury Collections in Hatfield House, which Eldred Jones provides on p. 19 of his *Elizabethan Image of Africa.*

38. On Elizabethan xenophobia, even against other Europeans, see Linda Yungblutt's revealing study, *Strangers Settled Here among Us: Policies, Perceptions, and the Presence of Aliens in Elizabethan England.*

39. Mark Koch, "Ruling the World," 118–21; J. Charles Cox *The Parish Registers of England,* 1–7; W. E. Tate, *The Parish Chest,* 43–45. Also see generally, G. R. Elton's *Policy and Police: The Enforcement of the Reformation in the Age of Thomas Cromwell.*

40. See Alastair Plowden, *The Elizabethan Secret Service,* 16–17, 44; A. Haynes, *Invisible Power: The Elizabethan Secret Service,* 6–8.

41. Rutter, 9–12.

42. On the contribution of Elizabethan travel literature to popular racial morphologies, see Emily Bartels's two essays, "Richard Hakluyt and the Elizabethan Construction of Africa," and "Making More of the Moor."

43. Entry of March 15, 1595, in the Declared Accounts of the Treasurer of the Queen's Chamber, in which Shakespeare is listed as a payee, along with Richard Burbage and William Kempe, for a Christmas performance before the queen (Public Record Office, Exchequer, Pipe Office, Declared Accounts, E351/542 f107v; cited Schoenbaum, 136).

44. My text of the play here, and throughout this essay, is G. Blakemore Evans, ed., *The Riverside Sghakespeare.*

45. *Shakespeare's Talking Animals,* 212.

46. I am implying the basic thesis of his book, *The Political Unconscious: Narrative as a Socially Symbolic Act.*

47. "The Improvisation of Power," 50. Leggatt also says something close to this when in discussing the atmosphere of the Jacobean public playhouse he refers to the "sustained flow of excitement" it generated as "the sense of community popular culture seeks to create" (43). His discussion of the effect of Jacobean public performances (39–45) is helpful overall, and supportive of what I am saying here.

48. In Wolf Sachs, "Introductions: Part Two," in *Black Hamlet,* 52.

49. For a cultural history of the phrase, and its pervasive Elizabethan usage, see Karen Newman's essay, "'And Wash the Ethiop White,'" 140–41ff.

50. The number of spectators at the Rose is based on the calculations of Carol Chillington Rutter from the dimensions of the theater foundations excavated in 1989.

Her estimates are 1,600 spectators before the Rose was enlarged in 1592, and 400 more after that date (*Documents of the Rose Playhouse,* xi, xiv). This figure is compatible with the greater one of the Globe reported by the Spanish ambassador in 1624 (Gurr, *Playgoing,* 20).

51. *Leviathan,* 1.16, cited by Stephen Orgel, *Impersonations,* front matter ff. xi; for discussions of the distinctions between "playing," "acting," and "personation," and the progressive development over the course of the sixteenth century of "playing" into "acting" into "personation," see William Ingram, *The Business of Playing,* 67–91 for the first, Weimann, 131–36, for the first and the second; and both Gurr, *Shakespearean Stage,* 73–81 and Thomson, 104–8 for the second and third. The distinction between "playing" and both "acting" and "personation," is greater than that between "acting" and "personation," and my point here is that the later distinction is discernible only in the late 1590s onward. The natural plausibility we attribute to or expect of acting corresponds to the evolving, late Elizabethan notion of "personation."

52. " 'Othello was a White Man,' " 198.

53. "Shakespeare and Cultural Difference," 189–90.

54. Ibid.

55. " 'Othello was a White Man,' " 198–99.

56. *Casting Shakespeare's Plays,* 28; Gurr, *Shakespearean Stage,* 58.

57. Ivor Brown, *Shakespeare and the Actors,* 139.

58. In addition to the incident of William Bird cited above, and of Nathan Field cited below, there are the following: In April 13, 1580, Robert Leveson and Lawrence Dutton, two of the Earl of Oxford's players, were involved in a scuffle with gentlemen of the Inns of Court, for which they were jailed at Marshalsea prison (Dasent's *Acts of the Privy Council,* 11:445, 11:37, 112; Chambers, 14:280; Gurr, *Playgoing,* 118). Gurr believes, however, that the incident is not a part of the "hostility of pulpit or Guildhall" (*Playgoing,* 119). On May 26, 1580 there "was a certayne fraye betwene the sevauntes of th'earle of Oxforde and the gentlemen of the Innes of Courtes" (*Acts of the Privy Council,* 11:445, 12: 37, 112; Chambers, 4:280). In July 1580 Thomas Chesson, an Oxford player, is released from Gatehouse jail on a one-year bond of good behavior (Dasent, *Acts of the Privy Council,* 11:445, 12:37, 112; Gurr, *Playgoing,* 118–19). On July 11, 1581, certain gentlemen of the Inns of Court (Parr Stafferton and his group) assaulted Arthyr Kynge, Thomas Goodale, and others (Lord Berkeley's Men), because of which all parties were detained by the Lord Mayor's City of London order, as was reported to Burghley by William Fleetwood (Gurr, *Playgoing,* 67–68, 119–20). According to Gurr, the incident is also not a part of the "hostility of pulpit or Guildhall" (*Playgoing,* 119), and "must have had a social origin, the common players facing the arrogant and idle young gentlemen in a hot summer" (Gurr, *Playgoing,* 68). In 1583, at the Red Lion, there was a scuffle over one of the payment boxes when a local man tried to see the play being performed without paying, "A scuffle ensued, two sharers left the stage to assist the gatherers; the culprit was eventually chased and stabbed. . . . the cheated box-holder was John Singer, a sharer and one of the founding-players of Queen Elizabeth's company" (G. M. Pinciss, "The Queen's Men, 1583–1592," *Theatre Survey* 11 (1970): 51–52; cited in Bentley, *Profession,* 95). In 1596 a warrant was issued for the arrest of William

Shakespeare and others for threatening one William Wayte (Public Record Office, Court of King's Bench, Controllment Roll, Michaelmas Term 1596, KB 29/234; cited by Samuel Schoenbaum, *Shakespeare: A Documentary Life,* 146). In 1605, Will Kempe, along with Robert Armin and others, were in a complaint filed by the London aldermen to the Privy Council for "derogatorily" representing aldermen onstage at the Blackfriars (John Payne Collier, *Memoirs of the Principal Actors,* 117). In 1611 William Ostler, a player, is mentioned in the epigram of John Davies of Hereford, *Scourge of Folly,* as being in a fight in which he had his head broken (Chambers, 2:331). In 1622, at the Red Bull, a player by the name of Richard Baxter was challenged by a feltmaker's apprentice by the name of John Gill who, while sitting on the edge of the stage, had been injured by Baxter in a stage sword fight performed by the latter (Gurr, *Playgoing,* 133; 19). In 1627, Richard Errington, the leader of a provincial company on tour in Ludlow was involved in a fracas while doing money collection for an ongoing performance of his company (John Tucker Murray, *English Dramatic Companies, 1558–1642,* 2:326; cited in Bentley, *Profession,* 96).

59. In 1596 a warrant of "attachment" "for fear of death" was issued against Shakespeare, Francis Langley, his wife Dorothy Spear, and Anne Langley on behalf of one William Wayte. William Wayte "swore before the Judge of Queen's Bench that he stood in danger of death, or bodily hurt," from "William Shakspere" and three others. "The magistrate then commanded the sheriff of the appropriate county to produce the accused . . . who had to post bond to keep the peace, on pain of forfeiting the security" (Public Record Office, Court of King's Bench, Controlment Roll, Michaelmas Term 1496, K.B. 29/234; cited by S. Schoenbaum, 146). This may be the same incident mentioned by Ivor Brown on 124. If so, both Ivor Brown and Schoenbaum add that the judge was a corrupt character named William Gardiner, who was later exposed as a swindler. Ivor Brown's mention makes it unclear whether the complaint was brought by Gardiner himself, or whether he issued the orders against Shakespeare on behalf of Wayte whom Ivor Brown doesn't mention. Schoenbaum identifies Langley as a money broker involved in the building of the Swan playhouse, and observes that "Somehow Shakespeare was drawn into this feud."

60. "'Othello Was a White Man,'" 199.

61. Cited by Eldred Jones, "Physical Representation," 19–20

62. For instance, Fenton typically laments "the corruption of the willes of the players and the assistauntes . . . [as] such disguised plaiers given over to all sortes of dissolucion . . . [have not] a wil to do good . . ." (*A Forme of Christian Policie,* in Chambers, 4:285–86); Gosson argues "In Stage Plays for a boy to put one the attyre, the gesture, the passions of a woman; for a meane person to take upon him the title of a Prince with counterfeit porte, and traine, is by outwarde signes to shewe them selves otherwise than they are . . ."; (*An Apologie of the School of Abuse,* in Chambers, 4:207, and *The Confutation of Plays,* in Chambers, 4:215–17); Stubbes asks, "Do they [players and plays] induce whoredom & unclennes? . . . For proofe thereof, but marke the flocking and running to Theatres & curtens . . . Then thee goodly pageants being done, every mate sortes to his mate, every one bringes another homeward . . . verye friendly, and in their secret conclaves (covertly) they play the *Sodomits* or *worse*" (*Anatomie of Abuses,* in Chambers, 4:223–24); Munday asserts, "And as for those stagers themselves, are they not commonlie such kind of men in their conversa-

tion, as they are in profession? Are they not as variable in harte, as they are in their partes? Are they not as good practisers of Bawderie, as inactors? . . . doth not their talke on the stage declare the nature of their disposition?" (*A Second and Third blast of retrait from plaies and Theatres,* in Chambers, 4:212); Northbrooke insists, "in playes you shall learne all things that appertayne to crafte, mischiefe, deceytes, and filthiness . . . shall not you learne, then, at such interludes howe to practise them?" (*A Treatise, wherein Dicing, Dauncing, Vaine Playes &c commonly used on Sabboth day are reproved,* in Chambers, 2:198–99).

63. Mentioned by Field himself in his letter, "Field the Players Letter to Mr. Sutton, Preacher at St. Mary Overs," in 1616, protesting what he implies is the preacher's attempt to "hinder the Sacrament and banish me from myne owne parishe Churche"; see Chambers 4:259. Callaghan cites this incident without elaboration in "What's at Stake in Shakespeare Studies?" 21–22. Of course, the incident could have had reasons other than displeasure with Field's acting career as well, but that reason is also a good probability.

64. Jacqueline Rose in Sachs, 46.

65. Because *Antony and Cleopatra* involves a boy actor playing what to the Elizabethans was historically a colored, "tawny" woman, the psychological dynamics of racial impersonation in that performance must have been extremely complex. For a summary discussion of the Elizabethan belief about Cleopatra as a colored woman, see my book *Shakespeare and Race,* 165–66.

66. The nineteenth-century comment is by J. H. Friswell, "The National Gallery Exhibition, 1866," 116. The contemporary responses are by James Adams, "This one is (probably) Will, portraiture expert says," A3, and by Sue Bond in her review of Stephanie Nolan's *Shakespeare's Face.*

67. I am indebted to the editor of *Medieval and Renaissance Drama in England,* Susan Cerasano, for pointing me toward the insights offered by the Chandos portrait for my argument in this essay.

68. Ingram, 64; Weimann, *Author's Pen,* 111–12.

69. There is a possibility that Shakespeare and Peele may have collaborated in the writing of *Titus Andronicus;* see the essay by MacDonald P. Jackson.

Works Cited

Acts of the Privy Council of England (1542–1604). Edited by John Roche Dasent. 32 vols. London: H. M. Stationer's Office, 1890.

Adams, James. "This one is (probably) Will, portraiture expert says," *Globe and Mail,* February 17, 2006, page A3, available at http://www.theglobeandmail.com/servlet/Page/document/v4/sub/MarketingPage?user_URL = http://www.theglobeandmail.com%2Fservlet%2Fstory%2FLAC.20060217.SHAKESPEARE17%2FTPStory%2F%3Fquery%3Dchandos%2Bportrait&ord = 1151273875962&brand = theglobeandmail&force_login = true.

Africanus, John Leo. *A Geographical Historie of Africa.* London: John Bishop, 1600.

Alexander, Catherine M. S., and Stanley W. Wells, eds. *Shakespeare and Race.* New York: Cambridge University Press, 2000.

Bartels, Emily C. "Imperialist Beginnings: Richard Hakluyt and the Construction of Africa." *Criticism* 34 (1992): 517–38.

———. "Making More of the Moor: Aaron, Othello and Renaissance Refashionings of Race." *Shakespeare Quarterly* 41.4 (1990): 433–54.

Barthelemy, Anthony Gerard. *Black Face, Maligned Race: The Representation of Blacks in English Drama from Shakespeare to Southerne.* Baton Rouge: Louisiana State University Press, 1987.

Bentley, Gerald Eades. *The Jacobean and Caroline Stages.* 2 vols. Oxford: Clarendon Press, 1949.

Best, George. "Discourse (1578)." In *The Principal Navigations, Voyages, Traffiques and Discoveries of the English Nation,* 7:262–64.

Bond, Sue. Review of Stephanie Nolen, *Shakespeare's Face,* API Review of Books, 43 (2006). Electronic essay, available at http://www.api-network.com/cgi-bin/reviews/jrbview.cgi?n = 1877008346.

Brown, Ivor. *Shakespeare and the Actors.* Toronto: Bodley Head, 1970.

Callaghan, Dympna. "'Othello Was a White Man': Properties of Race on Shakespeare's Stage." In *Alternative Shakespeares,* edited by Terence Hawkes, 2:192–215. New York: Routledge, 1996.

———. *Shakespeare without Women: Representing Gender and Race on the Renaissance Stage.* New York: Routledge, 2000.

Chambers, E. K. *The Elizabethan Stage.* 4 vols. Oxford: Clarendon Press, 1997.

Coleridge, Samuel Taylor. *Shakespearean Criticism.* Edited by Thomas M. Raysor. London: J. M. Dent, 1960.

Collier, John Payne. *Memoirs of the Principal Actors of the Plays of Shakespeare (1846).* New York: AMS, 1971.

The Compact Edition of the Oxford English Dictionary: Complete Text Reproduced Micrographically. 3 vols. Oxford: Oxford University Press, 1971.

Cox, J. Charles. *The Parish Registers of England.* Totowa, NJ: Rowman and Littlefield, 1974.

Eden, Richard. *The Decades of the New World and West Indies.* London: Guilhelmi Powell, 1555.

———. *The History of Travel.* Edited by Richard Willes. London: R. Iugge, 1577.

Efron, Bradley, and Ronald Thisted. "Estimating the Number of Unseen Species: How Many Words did Shakespeare Know?" Biometrika 63.3 (1976): 435–47.

Elliott, Ward E. Y., and Robert J. Valenza. "Glass Slippers and Seven-League Boots: C-Prompted Doubts About Ascribing *A Funeral Elegy* and *A Lover's Complaint* to Shakespeare." *Shakespeare Quarterly* 48.2 (1997): 177–207.

Elton, G. R. *Policy and Police: The Enforcement of the Reformation in the Age of Cromwell.* Cambridge: Cambridge University Press, 1972.

Erickson, Peter. "The Moment of Race in Renaissance Studies." *Shakespeare Studies* 26 (1998): 27–36.

Erickson. Peter. "Representation of Blacks and Blackness in the Renaissance." *Criticism* 35.4 (1993): 495–527.

Florio, John. *A Worlde of Wordes, or Most Copious Dictionarie in Italian and English.* London: A. Hatfield for E. Blount, 1598. In *Early Modern English Dictionaries Database (EMEDD),* electronic database at: http://www.chass.utoronto.ca/english/emed/emedd.html.

Forbes, Thomas. *Chronicle from Aldgate: Life and Death in Shakespeare's London.* New Haven: Yale University Press, 1971.

Foreman, Simon. *Medical Casebooks.* Unpublished manuscripts. Ashmole Collection, Bodleian Library, Oxford.

Foster, Donald. *SHAXICON '95.* 1995. http://shakespeareauthorship.com/shaxicon .html. (last accessed June 24, 2006).

Friswell, J. H. "National Portrait Exhibition, 1866." *Notes and Queries,* 3rd. ser., 9 (1866): 116.

George, David. "Shakespeare and Pembroke's Men." *Shakespeare Quarterly* 32.3 (1981): 305–23.

Greenblatt, Stephen. "The Improvisation of Power." In *William Shakespeare's Othello,* edited by Harold Bloom, 37–59. Modern Critical Interpretations. New York: Chelsea House Publishers, 1987.

Greg, W. W. *Dramatic Documents from the Elizabethan Playhouses.* 2 vols. Oxford: Clarendon Press, 1931.

Gurr, Andrew. *Playgoing in Shakespeare's London.* Cambridge: Cambridge University Press, 1987.

———. *Playgoing in Shakespeare's London.* 3rd ed. Cambridge: Cambridge University Press, 2004.

———. *The Shakespearean Stage, 1574–1642.* Cambridge: Cambridge University Press, 1970.

Gurr, Andrew, and Mariko Ichikawa. *Staging in Shakespeare's Theatres.* Oxford: Oxford University Press, 2000.

Habib, Imtiaz. "'Hel's Perfect Character' or the Blackamoor Maid in Early Modern English Drama: The Postcolonial Cultural History of a Dramatic Type." *Literature Interpretation Theory* 11 (2000): 277–304.

———. "Othello, Sir Peter Negro, and the Blacks of Early Modern England." *Literature Interpretation Theory* 9.1 (1998): 15–30.

———. "Reading Black Women Characters of the English Renaissance: Colonial Inscription and Postcolonial Recovery." *Renaissance Papers 1996* (1997).

———. *Shakespeare and Race: Postcolonial Praxis in the Early Modern Period.* Lanham, MD: University Press of America, 2000.

———. "Shakespeare's Spectral Turks: The Postcolonial Poetics of a Mimetic Narrative." *Shakespeare Yearbook* 14 (2004): 237–70.

Hakluyt, Richard, ed. *The Principal Navigations, Voyaiges, Traffiques and Discoveries of the English Nation.* 12 vols. Glasgow: J. Maclehose and Sons, 1904.

Hall, Kim. *Things of Darkness: Economies of Race and Gender in Early Modern England.* Ithaca: Cornell University Press, 1995.

Hawkes, Terence. *Shakespeare's Talking Animals: Language and Drama in Society.* London: Edward Arnold, 1973.

Haynes, A. *Invisible Power: The Elizabethan Secret Service.* New York: St. Martin's Press, 1992.

Hendricks, Margo and Patricia Parker, ed. *Women, Race and Writing in Early Modern England.* New York: Routledge, 1994.

Henslowe's Diary. Edited by W. W. Greg. 2 vols. London: A. H. Bullen, 1904.

Henslowe's Diary: Edited with Supplementary Material Introduction and Notes. Edited by R. A. Foakes and R. T. Rickert. Cambridge: Cambridge University Press, 1961.

Honigmann, E. A. J. "Shakespeare's Life." In *The Cambridge Companion to Shakespeare,* edited by Margreta De Grazia, 1–12. Cambridge: Cambridge University Press, 2001.

Ingram, William. *The Business of Playing: The Beginnings of the Adult Professional Theatre in Elizabethan London.* Ithaca: Cornell University Press, 1992.

Jackson, MacDonald P. "Shakespeare's Brothers and Peele's Brethren: *Titus Andronicus* Again." *Notes and Queries* 44.4 (1997): 494–96.

Jameson, Fredric. *The Political Unconscious: Narrative as a Socially Symbolic Act.* Ithaca: Columbia University Press, 1981.

Jones, Eldred. *The Elizabethan Image of Africa.* Charlottesville: University Press of Virginia, 1971.

———. "The Physical Representations of African Characters on the English Stage During the 16th and 17th Centuries." *Theatre Notebook* 17.1 (1962): 17–21.

Kathman, David. in Shaxicon, Part 7 of "Critically Examining Oxfordian Claims." 1996. http://shakespeareauthorship.com/ox7.html.

King, T. J. *Casting Shakespeare's Plays: London Actors and Their Roles.* Cambridge: Cambridge University Press, 1992.

Knutson, Roslyn L. "A Caliban in St. Mildred Poultry." In *Shakespeare and Cultural Traditions,* edited by Tetsuo Kishi, Roger Pringle, and Stanley Wells, 110–26. Newark: University of Delaware Press, 1991.

Koch, Mark. "Ruling the World: The Cartographic Gaze in Elizabethan Accounts of the New World." *Early Modern Literary Studies* 4.2 (1998): 111–39.

Leggatt, Alexander. *Jacobean Public Theatre.* New York: Routledge, 1992.

Liebler, Naomi. *Shakespeare's Festive Tragedy: The Ritual Performance of Genre.* New York: Routledge, 1995.

Loomba, Ania. *Gender, Race, Renaissance Drama.* Manchester, UK: Manchester University Press, 1989.

———. "Shakespeare and Cultural Difference." In *Alternative Shakespeares, edited by Terence Hawkes,* 2:164–91. London: Routledge, 1996.

———. *Shakespeare, Race, Colonialism.* New York: Oxford University Press, 2002.

Mandeville, John. *The Travels of John Mandeville (1324).* edited by A. W. Pollard. New York: Dover, 1964.

Matar, N. I. "The Renegade in English Seventeenth Century Imagination." *Studies in English Literature* 33 (1993): 489–502.

Maxwell, J. C., ed. *Titus Andronicus.* The Arden Shakespeare. London: Methuen, 1968.

Meyers, Charles. *Elizabethan Marranos Unmasked.* Available at http://www.kulanu.org/unmasked.html.

———. "Lawsuits in Elizabethan Courts of Law: The Adventures of Dr. Hector Nunez, 1566–1591; A Precis." *Journal of European Economic History* 25.1 (1996): 157–68.

Miller, W. E. "Negroes in Elizabethan London." *Notes and Queries* 206 (1961): 138.

Nagler, A. M. *Shakespeare's Stage.* New Haven: Yale University Press, 1981.

William S. Niederkorn. "A Scholar Recants on His 'Shakespeare' Discovery." *New*

York Times, June 20, 2002. Online edition, available at http://www.nytimes.com/2002/06/20/books/20SHAK.html?ex = 1025580532&ei = 1&en;eq1d40a5527b5c6bda.

Neill, Michael. "'Mulattos,' 'Blacks,' and 'Indian Moors': *Othello* and Early Modern Constructions of Human Difference." In *Putting History to the Question: Power, Politics, and Society in English Renaissance Drama,* 269–84. New York: Columbia University Press, 2000.

———. "Unproper Beds: Race, Adultery and the Hideous." *Shakespeare Quarterly* 40.4 (1989): 383–412.

Newman, Karen. "'And Wash the Ethiop White': Femininity and the Monstrous in *Othello.*" In *Shakespeare Reproduced: The Text in History and Ideology,* edited by Jean E. Howard and Marion F. O'Connor. New York: Routledge, 1993. 143–62.

Orgel, Stephen. *Impersonations.* Cambridge: Cambridge University Press, 1996.

Orkin, Martin. "*Othello* and the Plain Face of Racism." *Shakespeare Quarterly* 38.2 (1987): 166–88.

———. *Shakespeare against Apartheid.* Craighill, S. Africa: A. D. Donker, 1987.

Patrides, C. A. "'The Bloody and Cruell Turke': The Background of a Renaissance Commonplace." *Studies in the Renaissance* 10 (1963): 126–35.

Plowden, Alastair. *The Elizabethan Secret Service.* Hemel Hempstead, Herts: Harvester Wheatsheath, 1991.

Price, Diana. "Shaxicon and Shakespeare's Acting Career." *Shakespeare Newsletter* 46.3 (1996): 57–58.

Purchas, Samuel. *Hakluytus Posthumus, or Purchas His Pilgrimes: Contayning a History of the World in Sea Voyages and Land Travells by Englishmen and Others.* 20 vols. Glasgow: J. Maclehose and Sons, 1905–7.

———. *Purchas His Pilgrimage, or, Relations of the World . . .* London: Printed by William Stansby for Henrie Fetherstone, 1613.

Roper, David L. *Henry Peacham's Chronogram: The Dating of Shakespeare's* Titus Andronicus. 2001. Electronic essay at http://www.dlroper.shakespearians.com/henry_peacham.html.

Ridley, M. R., ed. *Othello.* London: Methuen, 1977.

Rutter, Carol Chillington, ed. *Documents of the Rose Playhouse.* New York: Manchester University Press, 1999.

Sachs, Wulf. *Black Hamlet.* Johannesburg: Witwatersrand University Press, 1996.

Schoenbaum, Samuel. *William Shakespeare: A Documentary Life.* New York: Oxford University Press, 1975.

Shakespeare, William. In "Titus Andronicus." *The Riverside Shakespeare,* edited by G. Blakemore Evans. Boston: Houghton Mifflin, 1997.

SHAKSPER Global Electronic Shakespeare Discussion list at http://www.shaksper.net/editor.html.

Tate, W. E. *The Parish Chest: A Study of the Parochial Administration in England.* Cambridge: Cambridge University Press, 1969.

Taussig, Michael. *Mimesis and Alterity: A Particular History of the Senses.* New York: Routledge, 1993.

Thomas, Sidney. "On the Dating of Shakespeare's Early Plays." *Shakespeare Quarterly* 39.2 (1988): 187–94.

Thomson, Peter. *Shakespeare's Professional Career.* Cambridge: Cambridge University Press, 1999.

Towerson, William. "Voyage to Guinea in 1555." In *A General History and Collections of Voyages and Travels,* edited by Robert Kerr. Edinburgh: n.p., 1824.

Vickers, Brian. *"Counterfeiting" Shakespeare: Evidence, Authorship and John Ford's Funerall Elegye.* Cambridge: Cambridge University Press, 2002.

Wells, Stanley. "The Year's Contribution to Shakesperiean Study." *Shakespeare Survey* 40 (2002): 224–30.

———, Gary Taylor, William John Jowett, eds. *William Shakespeare: A Textual Companion.* New York: W. W. Norton, 1997.

Yungblut, Laura Hunt. *Strangers Settled Here among Us: Policies, Perceptions, and the Presence of Aliens in Elizabethan England.* New York: Routledge, 1996.

Weimann, Robert. *Author's Pen and Actor's Voice.* Cambridge: Cambridge University Press, 2000.

The Folly of Racism:
Enslaving Blackface and the
"Natural" Fool Tradition

ROBERT HORNBACK

In April 1566, signs of strain appeared in the relationship between Elizabeth I and her longtime visitor, Princess Cecilia of Sweden, when, after an extended visit in England, the Swedish princess abruptly left the country to rejoin her husband. Once a favorite at the English court, Cecilia had overstayed her welcome there through her extravagant freeloading. She was unwilling to accept any blame for the rift, however, and instead presented a retaliatory list of complaints to her brother John, newly become Swedish king, who then forwarded it to Queen Elizabeth's secretary Cecil. Beyond its revelation of fractured diplomatic relations, by far the most peculiar grievance here is Cecilia's statement that, "beinge bydden to see a comedye played, there was a blackeman brought in, . . . full of leawde, spitfull, and skornfull words which she said did represent . . . her husband."[1] Certainly, this reference to a comic depiction of a "blackeman," apparently "represent[ed]" by an actor in blackface, raises a number of questions (e.g., Why should Cecilia's husband have been represented as black at all? Or, at least, why would she *think* that he had been? Was blackface a mechanism for ridicule? If so, why? What would such blackness have symbolized in a "comedye"? And, how many black people were living in England at the time? Does this knowledge shape our understanding of such comedy?), but the scant critical tradition addressing the episode focused only on one, determining the particular work to which Cecilia referred.[2] Ironically, such a narrow scope contributed to a continued ignoring of a much more far-reaching revelation; whatever play she described, it was hardly the period's lone instance of blackness being associated with a comic figure.

Given that many scholars are currently reexamining the origins of racism and slavery in Western tradition,[3] an exploration of such comic associations with blackness is especially timely. The subject is all the more so in that, because evil is virtually the only symbolic aspect of blackness that medieval and Renaissance scholars have recognized, recent research has too narrowly focused on Judaism, Christianity, and Islam to find origins of racism solely in theological associations of the color black and evil.[4] In this regard, Dympna Callaghan sums up current scholarly consensus when she observes that slavery "had comparatively weak ideological foundations, relying on fairly inchoate connections between black skin and the Prince of Darkness. . . ."[5] Undoubtedly, even though the origins of such a religious connection are surprisingly ambiguous since there is no biblical source,[6] "The association of blackness with evil," Anthony Gerard Barthelemy and others have noted, "has a long history on the English stage" as "the tradition goes back at least to early medieval drama" where Lucifer and other devils "were represented by actors painted black."[7] As Virginia Mason Vaughan has recently found in her study, *Performing Blackness on English Stages, 1500–1800,* "the association between black skin and damnation [also] permeated early modern English culture."[8] Yet, scholars have locked on so exclusively to this color symbolism of evil that they have yet to attend to a more demeaning, buried tradition of early blackface comedy, one that associated blackness with degradation, irrationality, prideful lack of self-knowledge, transgression, and, related to all of these, folly. With disturbing consistency, blackface served as one commonplace mark of foolishness in the iconography of the so-called "natural" fool—in medieval and Renaissance English parlance, a butt, laughed at because he was mentally deficient (whether ignorant, dull-witted, or mad) and often physically different as well (for example, "hunchbacked," dwarfish, lame, deformed, ugly, or blackfaced).[9]

In what follows, I want to interrogate this long-overlooked tradition, to examine some of its roots and its bitter fruit alike, and to suggest its importance not only in understanding medieval and Renaissance drama but in dismantling subsequent constructions of baffling racist stereotypes. Ultimately, I argue, previously ignored fool iconography forged early links in the enslaving fiction of the "Great Chain of Being," adumbrating, if not originating, later racist notions, since it was the blackface tradition that underwrote early slavers' inexplicable assumption that Africans were utterly irrational and, hence, could be treated as beastlike.

The Descent into Racism: The Devil as Fool

As an illustration of the prevalent and long-standing inattention to this range of buried symbolic associations, consider the mystery plays, the most frequently cited instances of blackness being identified with evil in the English theater tradition. The Wakefield mystery cycle's *The Creation, and the Fall of Lucifer* (ca. 1460), for example, depicts the fallen angels lamenting: "Alas, alas and welewo! . . . / We, that were angels so fare, / and sat so hie aboue the ayere, / *Now ar we waxen blak as any coyll* [coal]. . . ."[10] While these lines seem merely to suggest, as most critics have observed, that the fallen angels are now black, the quote actually continues: "Now ar we waxen blak as any coyll / *and vgly, tatyrd as a foyll [fool]*" (ll. 136–37; emphasis added).[11] These fallen angels are not just black devils, then, but black *fools,* suffering degradation. While steering clear of a discussion of blackness, Martin Stevens and James Paxson have demonstrated that, here and elsewhere, "Evil in the Wakefield plays . . . depends . . . on the demon/fool, whose conversion from the angelic . . . develops into a range of personifications of folly."[12] But even Paxson and Stevens finally resist the implications of their own findings, insisting instead that "the Wakefield playwright . . . created a devil who is quite different from his counterparts in the other extant cycles," one "[u]nlike any other cycle."[13]

And yet, contrary to such notions of exceptionality, the Chester *Fall of Lucifer* features a similar focus on folly. In the Chester play,[14] Deus warns Lucifer of the requirement that he remain wise with "Loke that you tende righte wisely" (l. 71). Of course, Lucifer soon ignores the warning, foolishly speculating that if he were in the throne "the[n] shoulde I be as wise as hee" (l. 131). As he begins to plot usurping the throne, he is again warned, this time by another angel: "My counsell is that you be wise" (l. 148). But his companion Lightborne urges him on, saying, "yee may be as wise withall / as God himselfe" (ll. 160–61). After the fall, when Lightborne rebukes him, the blackened Lucifer responds: "Thy witt yt was as well as myne" (l. 246). Clearly, a lack of wit and wisdom is meant to be one primary characteristic of the Chester Devil as well.

The York pageant of *The Fall of the Angels* (ca. 1460s) features black devils that have even more clearly fallen into folly. Here, where the devils ultimately find themselves made "blackest," it is again God who introduces the theme of folly as he warns the newly created angels that they will enjoy all only "To-whiles [they] are stable in thought,"[15] that is, so long as they remain rational and wise. As the Cherubim prudently recall God's warning that they will have "All bliss . . . To-whiles we are stable in thought" (ll. 61–62) and the Seraphim devoutly proclaim "With all the wit we wield we worship thy will" (l. 73), Lucifer not only vainly preens and remarks that he is "fairer by far than my feres [companions]" (l. 53), "featous [elegant] and fair" (l. 55), and the very "form of all fairhead" (l. 66), but he also foolishly boasts that he is superior by virtue of "my wit" (l. 67) and gloats about being "deft" (l. 92) or clever—immediately before his fall and his crying out "Oh, deuce! all goes down" (l. 93). Then, having discovered his sudden blackness ("My brightness is blackest . . . now" [l. 101]), the prideful Lucifer, somewhat humorously, accuses Second Devil: "ye smore me in smoke" (l. 117). Traditionally, the word "smore" has been glossed nonsensically as "smother,"[16] but it appears perhaps more likely that the line could read as "you *smeared* me with smoke" or soot, consistent with *The Oxford English Dictionary*'s

"To smear, bedaub" ([*OED* 3] as in "1530 Pals[grave]. . . . 'where have you ben, you have all to smored your face'"), precisely because it is the devils' blackness that is at issue. More importantly, finding himself "brent" or burnt (1. 107) and "lorn" of "light" (1.108), and being no longer stable in thought, Second Devil laments, "Out, out! I go wood [i.e., mad] for woe, my wit is all went now" (1. 105), with both madness and lost wits—and, apparently, blackness—being conventional attributes of "natural" folly. Finally, the devils' comically childish bickering over the cause of their new state prompts God to call these mad, black devils "Those fools" (1. 129). Therefore, while it is partly true, as Vaughan believes, that "the visual code of the cycle plays was a simple binary: salvation versus damnation,"[17] that binary was far more subtle than simply good versus evil. Blackness in these mystery plays was instead associated less with evil (at least as we know it) than with folly, madness, and an absence of that divine gift, the "light" of reason. The overtly foolish Devil of the mystery play tradition contained, then, what was surely a significant development in the history of racism; here was not simply a black devil's fall into the depths of hell but, more significantly, a very particular depiction of his descent into the degradations of folly via blackness. It would later be a stereotype of irrationality that was, ironically, most damning, lingering on inexplicably well after African American "Negro spirituals," churches, and temperance societies had long since belied an evil stereotype.

Although the blackness of early devils was perhaps, typically, not *expressly* linked to race—even though devils *were* "often compared to Ethiopians"[18]—the irrationality associated with blackfaced devils was nonetheless to have an enduring influence on notions of blackface and thus blackness. In particular, the specter of madness already observable, especially in the York pageant, haunted the blackface tradition from early to late, something evident in illustrations of the rolling-eyed, deranged-looking "Jim Crow" in the 1830s, in Crow originator T. D. Rice's farce *Bone Squash Diavolo* in which a stage direction reads "*Enter* Bone Squash, *crazy,*"[19] or in a newspaper's charges that blackface entertainer George Washington Dixon, famed for singing "Zip Coon," was "wanting in his upper story," via what Dale Cockrell has described as implications that he was "crazy and degenerate enough that he might really *be* black."[20] In one way or another, antebellum whites were determined to "prove" a connection between blackness and irrationality, especially when "the Negro" was left to his own devices. So it was that dubious methods and proslavery zeal led to an 1840 census purporting to have found a rate of insanity and idiocy eleven times greater among freed blacks than among slaves.[21]

Even long after emancipation, the long-standing symbolic association between blackface and madness or irrationality more generally was still evident in a twentieth-century African American blackface performer's explanation of why not all of the black actors blacked up in the minstrel movie *Pitch a*

Boogie Woogie (1928): "We put on blackface when we had something *crazy* to say."[22] One critic has recently celebrated such blacking up in minstrelsy, proclaiming, "I want to figure out a history of blackface that can account for that eager spirit of licensed madness" within it,[23] but this particular association of blackness with irrationality was anything but liberating for people of African descent, not only because "the 'Jim Crow' that meant white male liberation on the minstrel stage later designated the 'Jim Crow' discrimination laws that successfully kept blacks in a state of de facto slavery,"[24] but because it assumed mental debility. After all, as Enid Welsford put it, the natural fool's "mental deficiencies" often "deprived him both of rights and responsibilities."[25] Thus, the short-term license established through blacking up in comic, irrational contexts was, paradoxically, actually limiting over the long haul, perpetuating a stereotype of irresponsibility and irrationality that underwrote systematic slavery and the stubborn denial of meaningful freedom for African Americans until the Civil Rights Act of 1964 and the Voting Rights Act of 1965. Previously, the New York State Constitutional Convention of 1821, which denied the franchise to black New Yorkers through prohibitive property requirements, did so on the grounds that, as one convention member maintained, "The minds of blacks are not competent to vote."[26] As we shall see, it was the rationally impaired Devil and blackfaced fool type more generally who first embodied such an association between blackness and mental incompetence.

To begin to appreciate fully the enormous influence of the Devil's folly on constructions of blackness, therefore, we must first recognize that the foolish black devils of the mystery cycles are anything but anomalous, in spite of John D. Cox's recent provocative claim that the Devil in English drama was noted above all for his "seriousness."[27] Peter Happé has demonstrated rather that in Tudor moral interludes the Devil "is essentially a comic figure" whose appearance is ridiculously ugly.[28] Notably, he is so "evill favoured" in *All for Money* (ca. 1577) that Ill Report comments, "You neuer saw such a one behynde / As my Dad is before," and in Garter's *The Comedy of the Most Virtuous and Godly Susanna* (ca. 1577), Sinne mocks a "snottie-nosed Sathan," threatening, as Happé notes, "to hit him on the snout and to pull it off."[29] Happé concludes that the range of visual characteristics of the Devil usually "appears to have been reduced in the interludes to the large, black-masked head."[30] Other evidence suggests that early devils could appear either in black masks/heads or in painted blackface, as in the records of Coventry, where one finds numerous payments "for blakyng the Sollys [souls'] fassys," for "peynttyng of the demones hede," for "the devyls hede," and for "the devells facys."[31] In their study of early English masks, Meg Twycross and Sarah Carpenter have argued that "the wearing of masks and the painting of faces . . . seems to have been considered very much as equivalents" in the Middle Ages and early Tudor period.[32] In any case, while finding that the black-masked Devil is "irredeemably foolish" and "most frequently seen as a butt . . . inviting ridicule,"[33] Happé seems puzzled by his discovery. "Perhaps out of fear," he muses, "the Devil is usually made ridiculous," for he is noted for "simplicity."[34]

Evidently, I would argue, the cycles' and interludes' masked Devil was a type of natural fool whose blackness connoted not simply (or even primarily) evil, as critics assume, but folly.[35] Such a conclusion is supported by historian of theology Jeffrey Burton Russell who notes that the medieval Devil, though sometimes clever, was also "a total fool," "the personification of . . . our own foolishness," "at bottom a fool who understands nothing."[36] In antiquity, theologians had likewise explained that the Devil's rational powers and intellect were impaired—"darkened by folly," as Augustine would have it— after the fall.[37] We have seen that the Devil was mad as a result, a belief that informs widespread medieval and Renaissance assumptions that madness itself was due to demonic possession or punishment for sin. The prevalence of the Devil's assumed mental impairment is further reflected in Stith Thompson's inclusion of a devil in connection with the category "Absurd Ignorance" in the *Motif-Index of Folk-Literature*.[38] Moreover, the Devil, being foolish, "could be overcome by man's . . . laughter,"[39] and the devil-fool figure was a popular icon that carried over into Elizabethan and Jacobean devil plays, such as Greene's *Friar Bacon and Friar Bungay* (ca. 1589), Haughton's *Grim the Collier of Croydon* (1600), Dekker's *The Merry Devil of Edmonton* (1602) and *If This Be Not A Good Play The Devil Is In It* (1611), and Jonson's *The Devil is an Ass* (1616), the later title being proverbial.[40]

In considering the popularity of the devil-as-fool, we should also take note of the pan-European favorite Tutivillus (spelled variously). In the *Judicium,* from the aforementioned Wakefield mystery cycle, Tutivillus "was clearly conceived of as a comic devil,"[41] as was "Titivillus" in the morality play *Mankind*. The vices build up his initial appearance in *Mankind*, collecting money from the audience in anticipation of the "man wyth a hede that ys of grett omnipotens" (1. 461)—the proverbial "big head" of the foolishly vain is here symbolized in the conventional large black head mask identified by Happé. And, in the *Judicium* and in sermon exempla and Continental drama, Tutivillus appears as "the recording demon" of mankind's folly, either in the form of an assiduously scribbling, cataloging demon who "records in writing the idle words of churchgoers" or as "a sack-carrying devil" who collects the many omitted and mumbled syllables of carelessly recited Latin prayer.[42] Likewise, in the *Judicium* he recites senseless dog-Latin such as "*ffragmina verborum tutiuillus colligit horum*" and "*Balzabub algorum, Belial belium doliorum*" (ll. 251–52). And, his very name is apparently pretentious nonce Latin. In illustrations, Tutivillus often appears as a writing monkey or as "apelike," being described as "*in specie symee*" or "*quasi vultu simie*."[43] But whether appearing as a vain devil with a ridiculously large black head or as a simian devil imitating monks and collecting the idle Latin words of sloth-ful believers, Tutivillus was decidedly a fool "aping" flawed Christians.

Just as the Devil was so often foolish, foolishness in turn could be seen as diabolical and sinful. In the morality plays, sin itself is repeatedly associated with transgressive folly. Thus, in *The Castle of Perseverance* (ca. 1425), fea-turing the Devil in the guise of "Belyal the blake,"[44] Avaricia urges the other vices/sins:

> . . . ye must, what-so befall,
> Feffyn hym wyth youre foly,
>
> .   .   .   .
>
> For whanne Mankynd is kendly koveytous
> He is proud, wrathful, and envyous;
> Glotons, slaw, and lecherous
>
> .   .   .   .
>
> Thus every synne tyllyth in othyr
> And makyth Mankynde to ben a foole.
>
> (ll. 1030–38, on p. 119)

Here, the Seven Deadly Sins are explicitly associated with "foly" as it is "synne" that makes Mankynde a "foole." Or, to take a later example, in *Mundus et Infans* (ca. 1520–22), when Manhode asks Conscyence "what thyng callest thou folly?" (l. 457), Conscyence answers, "pride, wrath, and envy, / Sloth, covetise, and gluttony,— / Lechery the seventh is" (ll. 458–60), concluding, "These seven sins I call folly" (l. 461).[45] In both plays, sin and folly are treated as synonymous, just as the word "folly" itself some-times had definite wicked connotations: "Wickedness, evil, mischief, harm" (*OED*, 2.a.); "A wrong-doing, sin, crime" (*OED*, 2.b.); and "Lewdness, wan-tonness" as in the French *folie* (*OED*, 3.a.). In 1604, Shakespeare was still able to employ precisely such wanton-wicked connotations when Othello be-lieved Desdemona had "gone to burning hell" (5.2.127) because she "turned to folly; and she was a whore" (5.2.130).

What "the fool said in his heart": Toward an Incorrigible Stereotype

The understandings of folly we have just seen are much elaborated upon in William Wager's moral interlude *The Longer Thou Livest the More Fool Thou Art* (ca. 1560–68), where the natural fool is Moros, whose name is de-rived from the ancient Dorian mimic fool, *moros* (μωρός). Moros is appar-ently black, since he calls to mind not only a "monster" (l. 1693) and "a devil of hell" (l. 1698) but is, simultaneously, immediately recognizable as a fool by his face alone—"Have you seen a more foolish face? / I must laugh to see how he doth look" (ll. 699–700)—and since he has "*a foolish counte-nance*" (s.d., following l. 70). He is also damned, ultimately, because God is angry that "such fools in their hearts do say, / That there is no God, neither heaven, nor hell" (ll. 1783–84). In fact, Moros "hath said there is no God in his heart" (l. 1767), echoing the opening verse of Psalm 52 in the Vulgate: "The fool said in his heart, 'There is no God.'" Wager's allusions to the psalm draw upon the iconography established in the illuminated tradition, in which the historiated "*D*" that introduces this psalm in Latin (*Dixit insipiens in corde suo: non est Deus*) often contains "the portrait of a fool."[46] When Wager refers to Moros as an "insipient" (e.g., ll. 844, 1125), he even more overtly links him to the iconography of Psalm 52, illuminations of which often depict a devil or devils (in lieu of a fool), the fool with devils, the fool as diabolical, the fool possessed by the Devil, or even the fool as Antichrist (as in the Evesham Psalter [ca. 1250], where Antichrist holds a bladder).[47]

The fool Moros, then, by virtue of his folly, is already damned even before he is piggybacked off to hell. The Psalter fool's denial of God's existence was, after all, likewise pridefully satanic so that, as the archetypal *insipiens,* the Devil was on some deep level less a trickster than a natural. Thus, in the early fifteenth century Lydgate could write of satanic disbelief: "The chief of foolis, as men in bokis redithe . . . Is he that nowther lovithe God ne dredithe."[48] Moreover, Psalm 52 itself continues: "Are they so ignorant, these evil men. . . ?"[49] Equally important, in terms of emergent racial con-structions, St. Augustine's *Enarrationes in Psalmos* "established the central theme of Psalm 52—the 'non est Deus'—which is the rejection of the Chris-tian faith and the denial of Christ by individuals, infidel sects, Jews, and pa-gans."[50] The insipient fool is, as a result, often depicted as foreign, dark-faced, or even as black, as is the leaping and shirtless black man wearing a leopard-spotted conical cap and Turkish pants in the famed ninth-century Stuttgart Psalter,[51] not coincidentally, I suggest, the work also noted for the devil's "first clear [illustrated] appearance as black."[52] Not only is the Devil repeatedly depicted as black in the Stuttgart Psalter, and not only is the *insi-piens* himself black, but when the *Dixit* verse repeats later, the letter *D* is represented, atypically, with even its center blackened so that the color black alone connotes folly.[53] We know that such symbolism survived not simply from Wager's play from the 1560s but because dark-faced *insipientes* are not uncommon. One example of an *insipiens* as "a Fool with blackened face" is MS Bodley Liturg. 153.[54] More to the point, this particular striking early fifteenth-century illumination appears in a portable psalter that was produced in Britain and was found in the diocese of Norwich,[55] a fact that leads one to presume that Wager himself saw one like it. By the ninth century, then, devil and fool alike were on their way in their descent into the blackfaced folly that was to prove so damning in constructions of blackness that rationalized slavery. In one measure of such logic, western European serfs were commonly portrayed as actually black from sun, soil, and manure and as spiritually simple, naturally stupid, and even subhuman.[56]

Moros's blackness does not merely mark him as a foolish *insipiens,* however, since for the "staunch Calvinist" Wager it also marked Moros as inherently reprobate from birth.[57] Here we must recognize that Calvin, referring to Jeremiah's question at 13:23 ("Can the Ethiopian change his skin? Or the leopard his spots?"—a query notably altered in the Geneva Bible favored by English Puritans to the more contemporary, "Can the blacke More change his skin?"), likened what he referred to in *Commentaries on the Book of the Prophet Jeremiah* as the "Blackness . . . inherent in the skin of the Ethiopians" to something "corrupted" and "enslaved," as well as to being lacking in "discernment" or reason, that is, to being out of one's "right mind":

> Blackness is inherent in the skin of the Ethiopians, as it is well known. Were they to wash themselves a hundred times daily, they could not put off their blacknesss. . . . We now then see what the prophet means—that the Jews were so corrupted by long habit that they could not repent, for the devil had so *enslaved* them that they were *not in their right mind; they no longer had any discernment,* and could not discriminate between good and evil.[58]

For Calvin, Carolyn Prager shows, blackness connoted "the fixed nature of the sinful state" and stood "for the accrued stain of sin which has become as permanent as an 'incurable' disease"[59]—and, I would add, a state of sin that affects primarily the "mind" and "discernment." In keeping with this Calvinist view, the black fool Moros has an "evil nature . . . past cure" so that, we are told, "nothing can [his] crookedness rectify" (ll. 46–48); he "can not convert" (l. 1805).

Nor, it would seem, can he learn. When Piety tells Discipline, "Let us lose no more labor about this fool, / For the more he is taught the worse he is" (ll. 397–98), Wager alludes obliquely to another bigoted proverb, "To wash an Ethiope is a labor in vain," which *Biblioteca Eliota* (1545) defined as follows: "Thou washest a Mooren, or Moore, A proverb applied to him that . . . teacheth a naturall foole wisdome." The play's emphasis on Moros's inability to learn thus draws upon traditions of iconography, theology, and proverb alike connecting blackness and inherent, incorrigible "folly," in varying senses. Remarkably, it was just such assumptions about blackness that slavers like John Barbot, writing in *A Description of the Coasts of North and South Guinea* (1732), subsequently held in justifying slavery: "it must be owned, [Africans] are very hard to be brought to a true notion of the Christian religion . . . being *naturally* very stupid and sensual"—*not evil*—"and so apt to continue till their end."[60] Similarly, when Wager emphasizes that Moros is reprobate in terms of his inability to learn due to his "nature" (e.g., ll. 44,

46), he puns on "natural" fool, so that Moros "*naturally* play[s] the part" (l. 60; emphasis added) of "such as had lever to folly and idleness fall" (l. 53). Moros is so "naturally" a fool that, we are told before he first appears, he is "[r]epresented" as the very "image of such persons" (ll. 51, 50). Unfortunately, part of that "image" of folly was apparently blackness.

Equally disturbing, in terms of the formation of racist stereotypes, the reprobate Moros is attended by the vices Ignorance, Idleness, Wrath, and, eventually, Confusion, the latter being the humiliating "portion of fools" who "abideth with them forever" (ll. 1817–18) as a shameful "companion" (l. 1814) and as "the reward of such . . . foolish ass[es]" (l. 1813). Confusion enters "*with an ill-favored visure and all things beside ill-favored*" (s.d. 1806) as a perpetual sign of Moros's "shame and confusion" (l. 1807). Consistent with Renaissance symbolism, Confusion, like the foolish and wicked Moros himself, would probably have been black, since the conventionally black Satan in Wager's own *Like Will to Like* is similarly described as having an "ill face" (l. 96) and since "ill-favored" was deemed the opposite of "fair."[61] God's Judgment then commands: "Confusion spoil him of his array; / Give him his fool's coat for him due" (ll. 1819–20). The irony here is that Moros, mocked for his looks by the vices fooling him throughout the play, is subsequently a double to the fool Confusion, but, being vain and lacking self-knowledge, he is unable to recognize his masked mirror image, preferring to be carried off straight to the Devil, another double, rather than to be seen with such an "ill-favored knave" (l. 1851). Worse still, in terms of subsequent racial stereotyping, God's Judgment curses Moros's descendants (almost as if he were Cain or Ham) in a manner that disparages all those of his supposed "nature," here, all who are black: "Thy wicked household shall be dispersed, / Thy children shall be rooted out to the fourth degree / Like as the mouth of God hath rehearsed" (ll. 1792–94). In the end, Moros's story serves as a propagandistic myth of origin endorsing proslavery views about Africans that we will see were already current in Wager's day.

The Play of Wit, the "Marke" of Idleness, and the Imposition of Sameness

The kind of connection between blackface and "natural" folly that I am suggesting was at work in the Devil's irredeemable folly or Moros's incorrigible foolishness appears even more clearly in three Tudor moral interludes, the "Wit" marriage plays. In each of these, a vice lulls the youth or everyman figure Wit to sleep, blackens his face, and leaves him to be discovered a fool, after which Wit is restored to whiteness and set finally on a path to redemption, ascent, and union with either Science or Wisdom. In the first of these

plays, John Redford's *Play of Wit and Science* (ca. 1534), the vice Idleness—
appearing associated with blackness as in Wager's later interlude—sings Wyt
to sleep, proclaiming, "whyle he sleepeth in Idlenes lappe / *idlenes marke on
hym shall I clappe.*"[62] After marking Wyt and then dressing him in the
"fooles cote" (l. 598) of her attendant, "Ingnorance" [*sic*], Idlenes observes,
"so [he] beguneth to looke lyke a noddye" (l. 587), using one of several synonyms for both a fool and a black bird.[63] The Cain-like "marke" of Idleness
clapped on Wyt to make him look like a noddy here undoubtedly signifies
blackface, since Wyt subsequently so resembles a "naturall foole" (l. 806)
that Science cannot recognize him: "Who is this?" (l. 732), she asks. Science
then contrasts Wyt's "fayer" (l. 795) portrait to his now "fowle . . . & vglye"
(l. 796) visage. Significantly for the history of racism, it is Science who shuns
a blackened character, just as pseudoscience would be trotted out to condemn
blackness in later centuries. Upon examining his reflection in his "glas of
reson" (l. 824), Wyt exclaims:

> . . . gogs sowle a foole[,] a foole by the mas
>
> . . . .
>
> deckt by gogs bones lyke a very asse
>
> . . . .
>
> & as for this face[, it] is abhominable
> *as black as the devyll.* . . .
>
> (ll. 826, 828, 839–40; emphasis added)

Finally, after examining the audience's reflection in the mirror to test its accuracy ("How loke ther facis heere rownd abouwte?" [l. 833]), he comments
on the contrast: "All fayre & cleere they, evry chone; / & I, by the mas, a
foole alone" (ll. 834–35). Thus, Wyt concludes that he is "a foole alone"
because he alone is "black as the devyll."

The damning symbolism of blackfaced folly in Redford's play is all the
more unavoidable given its depiction of the "foole" Ingnorance as a mirror
image of the folly-fallen Wyt, for, like the reprobate Moros and his double
Confusion, Ingnorance is indeed a black fool from the beginning. Such mirroring is clear, after Wyt's face is blackened and Ingnorance and Wyt have ex-
changed coats, when Ingnorance observes, "He is I now" (l. 599).[64] Idlenes
then asks, "Is he not a foole as wel as thow?" (l. 601), to which Ingnorance
responds, "Yeas" (l. 602). Thereafter, Wyt is taken for "Ingnorance, or his
lykenes" (l. 668). That the now-blackfaced Wyt has been transformed into the
fool Ingnorance's double is apparent when, upon seeing Wyt so unwittingly
disguised, Science mistakes her fiancé for the fool, addressing him with
"What sayst thow, Ingnorance[?]" (l. 737). Emphatically, then, like Wager's
play and the York Pageant, this interlude includes a duo of blackfaced fools.[65]

Significantly, given that Wit essentially temporarily loses himself (i.e., his "wit" or very identity), after having his face blackened, the play suggests that a black face, that is, blackness alone, has the power to erase individuality, marking characters as identical—here identically *ignorant.* Such is the very essence of stereotyping in embryo, if not fully born. Similar assumptions appear, ironically, in arguments dismissing either racial import or effect through "popular masking" in blackface. While maintaining that black-masking represented "simple disguise," merely an "impulse to conceal," since "easily available domestic materials like soot, lampblack, or charcoal" were "all matt monotone black which blanks out the features,"[66] such arguments fail to pursue the consequences of such thinking. That is, the logic of blackface as "simple disguise" alone refuses to acknowledge the damning assumption that blackness erases individuality, producing a stereotypical sameness, the imposed social invisibility explored in Ralph Ellison's *Invisible Man.* After all, the trope that blackness rendered invisibility was actually invited in blackface traditions, whether in minstrel plays in which characters could be described archly with "The rest of the characters are all so dark that they cannot be seen" or in the black-masked Harlequin's ability to "simply point to one of the black patches on his suit and become invisible, a trope that has become central to black literary tradition."[67]

In any case, in scenes imitating Redford's play, such as in *The Marriage of Wit and Science* (ca. 1569–70), performed by the Children of Paul's under Sebastian Westcott's mastership, the connection between blackface and folly seems clearer still, as it is assumed readily with less effort on the author's part.[68] In Westcott's *Wit* play, following the scene in which "Witte" is transformed into the likeness of the black fool Ignorance, Science and her father Reason mistake Witte for a fool and contemptuously refer to his blackness— "Thy loke is like to one that came out of hell" (sig. E.ii.r)—and, when comparing a picture of Witte alongside his altered visage, they report: "[W]hy loke, they are no more like; / . . . then blacke to white" (sig. E.ii.r). Witte then looks in his glass of Reason, remarking in dismay, "By the Masse I loke like a very foole in deede" (sig. Eii.r).

Similarly, the latest of the three Wit plays, Francis Merbury's *The Marriage Between Wit and Wisdom* (1579),[69] includes the stage business: "*Here, shall* [W]*antonis sing . . . him a sleepe . . . then let her set a fooles bable on his hed . . . colling* [coaling] *his face.*" In the song, Wantonnes announces her intention to

> trick this prety doddy
> & make him a noddy
>
> . . . .
> & now of a schollar
> I will make him a colliar. . . .

(ll. 431–38)

After Wit's face is "collied," that is, begrimed or blackened, apparently either with coal or by one of several other methods available to render the face black (but this time without benefit of Ignorance or a fool's coat),[70] a character enters crying, "o god . . . the company made the[e] a foole / that thou of late wast in" (ll. 464–66), after which appears the stage direction: "*He washeth his face and taketh off his bauble*" (l. 475). Evidently a fool's coat and some double's assistance were no longer required to mark folly in this scene because blackface and bauble were now sufficient. The connection between natural folly and blackface may, then, have become even stronger over the course of the sixteenth century, not coincidentally one that witnessed the expansion of the African slave trade. It is also significant that, as we learn in Anthony Munday's *Sir Thomas More* (ca. 1590), *The Marriage Between Wit and Wisdom* was an especially familiar play, indeed a byword, when it was included, along with plays such as *The Play of Four P's, Dives and Lazarus* (a play about damnation), and *Lusty Juventus* (which includes a comic devil), as part of the old-fashioned repertoire of the small wandering troupe, the "Lord Cardinal's players" (3.2.50).[71] Therefore, the blacking episodes of the "Wit" plays and others like them would likely have been seen through much of England.

From Childs' Play(s) to Slavery

Rather than the "Wit" plays being isolated anomalies, a marked association between blackface and folly was fairly widespread in late medieval and Renaissance drama. In addition to appearing in the entertainment featuring the comic "blackeman" that offended Cecilia in 1566 or in Wager's interlude, it is also extant in a number of other plays, including, I believe, John Rastell's *The Nature of the Four Elements* (ca. 1520; printed ca. 1527), a work known to have influenced Redford's *Wit and Science*.[72] Here, a blacking episode probably appeared during a mysterious gap of eight missing leaves (sigs. D 1–8) in the copy since, after the missing leaves, the vices Yngnoraunce and Sensuall Appetyte find the everyman Humanyte, now a "mad fole" (l. 1183), "clene out of [his] mynde" (l. 1202), down on the ground, while his "tayle totyth out behynde" (l. 1195) and his head is, somewhat curiously, initially concealed ("Why, what is cause thou hydest the[e] here?" [l. 1200]). Looking upon his transformed head, Yngnoraunce jests: "Hit were evyn great almys / To smyte his hed from his body" (ll. 1185–86). The point of the joke and the surprise appearance of the everyman's head seems to be that the newly transformed Humanyte now has the large black head of a fool. Moreover, Sensuall Appetyte immediately explains that Humanyte's now-foolish face/head is the result of a temporary disguise:

Nay God forbed ye sholde do so.
For he is but an innocent, lo,
In maner of a fole.

(ll. 1187–89; emphasis added)

As Trevor Lennam observes, "Whatever action has occurred . . . the lines indicate that Humanity is degraded as a fool."[73] Even though we can only conjecture here as to what happened in the missing leaves to make Humanyte degraded, ugly, and foolish, a blacking or masking episode would certainly explain the many curious details in the scene that follows the gap because blackness had become an emblem of degradation, madness, folly, and ugliness alike.

More definitely, blacking occurs in a different context in boy company author John Heywood's *Johan Johan* (printed 1533), when the cuckold Johan is tricked into chafing wax at the fire to mend a leaky pail while his wife Tyb and a cuckolding priest eat up all his dinner. While working at length before the fire, Johan is blackened with smoke, as we learn when he complains that "the smoke puttyth out my eyes two. / I burne my face, and ray my clothes also" (ll. 509–10), and when he afterward repeats for emphasis, "For the smoke put out my eyes two, / I burned my face, and rayed my clothes also" (ll. 637–38). That the smoke that has blackened his clothes and face makes him a fool is evident when this poor "wodcok" (l. 488) is subsequently called an "ape" (l. 514) and a "dryvyll" (l. 655), both synonyms for fool.[74]

Cuckolds like Johan and other foolish old men seem frequently to have had their faces blackened in token of their folly; this is the case with the foolishly arrogant, gulled cheat Grim the Collier of Croyden in Richard Edwards's boy company play *Damon and Pithias* (printed 1571 and performed by the Children of the Chapel), the laughable old would-be cuckolder Lorenzo in boy company author George Chapman's *May Day* (1601; printed 1611), and the foolish cuckold and cowardly braggart John Swabber in *Acteon and Diana* (printed ca. 1655, the year of England's conquest of Jamaica as part of Oliver Cromwell's "Western Design"). The Swabber farce was also subsequently reproduced word for word as *The Humour of John Swabber* in Francis Kirkman's famous collection of popular farcical drolls, *The Wits, or, Sport, being a Curious Collection of Several Drols and Farces* (1673), a work that seems likely to have made its way to British North America thereafter.

As with the rise of the black-masked clown Harlequin in Italy, according to Dario Fo, during "a revival of slavery" when commedia originated, the tradition of the blackfaced fool in England became especially pronounced aside the expanding slave trade in Europe, particularly with the development of an *English* slave trade.[75] The Mediterranean slave trade based in Italian cities like Venice and Genoa had collapsed by the end of the fifteenth century, as Black Sea slave marketing in Tartars, Circassians, Armenians, Georgians,

and Bulgarians was sealed off by the Turks after their capture of Constantino-
ple.[76] By that time, the Portuguese had already developed a slave trade from
West Africa to fill the void; in fact, in 1444 Portugal had launched the modern
slave trade, taking 225 captives from the Guinea coast.[77] After 1454 Portugal
had a monopoly over Guinea by papal bull, and by 1460, seven to eight hundred captives per year were being taken to Portugal.[78] Over the three decades
following 1444, by one count, roughly 12,500 West Africans were abducted,
whereas from 1450 to 1500 a conservative estimate of 35,000 captives were
taken, via Lisbon, to be slaves throughout Europe.[79] Then, in 1518 Spain licensed Portugal's transportation of 4,000 slaves annually for ten years to His-
paniola.[80] By around 1530, the Portuguese also launched the transatlantic
slave trade to the New World. In 1537, New World traffic in African peoples
was spurred on when Pope Paul II differentiated between American Indians
and Africans by denying the sacraments to any colonist who enslaved the
former, because they were rational and thus capable of Christianity—
Africans were not so deemed.[81] European human trafficking of Africans was
thus already well under way by the time of blackface characterizations such
as those in *The Creation, and the Fall of Lucifer* (ca. 1460), *The Fall of the
Angels* (ca. 1460s), *The Nature of the Four Elements* (ca. 1520), *Johan Johan*
(printed 1533), *Wit and Science* (ca. 1534), *The Longer Thou Livest* (ca.
1560–68), *The Marriage of Wit and Science* (ca. 1569–70), and *The Marriage Between Wit and Wisdom* (1579).

Admittedly, England did not enter the slave trade in any considerable way
for some time after Portugal, but that was not from a lack of trying. Edward
IV (1471–83) unsuccessfully asked the pope to allow English trade in Africa.
And, in 1481, hearing rumors that Englishmen William Fabian and John Tintam were preparing a venture to Guinea, the Portuguese protested on the
grounds of their monopoly and the expedition was stayed.[82] While there were
certainly black people, both free and enslaved, in England before 1530,[83] and
while the earliest recorded presence of Africans in Britain were in the days
of Roman occupation and then again after a number were brought to Ireland
by the ninth century, fifteenth- and sixteenth-century English slave trading
from Guinea is "underdocumented because of its surreptitious nature."[84]
Still, we are able to gather that William Hawkins, father of famous slave
trader and pirate John Hawkins, had begun some sort of trading on the northern Guinea coast by the 1530s, with probable ventures there in 1530, 1531,
1532, likely in 1536 (on behalf of "the English African company"), and,
even more likely, again in 1539–40.[85] We also know that Captain Thomas
Windham made an expedition to Guinea and Benin in 1553. And, we learn
of five Western African "Negroes" taken back to England by trader William
Towrson in 1554 and "kept" there "till they could speak the language," and
brought back to Africa only "to be a helpe to Englishmen" there.[86] Similarly,
in 1554–55, the pirate John Lok brought back from Guinea "certain blacke

slaves whereof some were tall and strong men and could wel agree with our meates and drinkes. The cold and moyst aire doth somewhat offend them."[87] Such efforts likely reflect a determination to expand some ongoing slave trade.

Whereas the Catholic queen Mary had largely respected the papal bulls granting an African monopoly to Portugal, Queen Elizabeth "surreptitiously supported" the slave trade: "Of necessity, Elizabeth's reign was character-ized by official reticence and actual aggression toward the African trade."[88] Indeed, when, in 1561 English ventures, backed by four royal vessels, were determined to establish a fort and trading base on the Guinea coast, which they finally did under John Lok's leadership in 1562, the queen's profits amounted to £1,000. By 1562–63, "being amongst other particulars assured that Negros were very good merchandise . . . and that the store of Negros might easily bee had upon the coast of Guinea," John Hawkins "resolved with himselfe to make triall thereof."[89] On this expedition, the pirate Hawk-ins put an end to the Portuguese monopoly, as we learn from his boast to have "got into his possession, partly by the sword, and partly by other meanes, to the number of 300 Negroes at the least, besides other merchandises."[90] Whereas Queen Elizabeth had officially opposed slavery, stating, "If any Af-rican were carried away without his free consent it would be detestable and call down the vengeance of Heaven upon the undertaking," in 1564 she was investing again, this time in Hawkins's second expedition to Guinea.[91] Then, when Hawkins was granted a coat of arms in 1565, it commemorated his success in such trade, as the patent read: "Sable on a poynte wave a lyon passaunt gould . . . and in token of his victorie against the Moores vpon his helme on a wreth argent and azure, a demy Moore *in his proper color,* bounde in a corde as bonde and captive."[92] We know further from 1569 depo-sitions surrounding Hawkin's third voyage that the English were engaged in slave trade to the New World. According to William Fowler, "the best trade in those places [Vera Cruz and the West Indies] is of Negros."[93] The Crown remained active in slave trading interests; a 1588 patent granted exclusive English trade on the coast of Guinea to merchants of London and Devonshire in order to ward off foreign interference with English trafficking. Not surpris-ingly, by 1619 in Jamestown we learn of "20. and odd Negroes, w[hi]ch the Governor . . . bought . . . at the best and easyest rate," since between 1576 and 1675, some 425,000 Africans were transported to British North America.[94]

By the heyday of Shakespeare's career, there were also "probably several thousand black people in London, forming a significant minority of the popu-lation."[95] As of 1578, George Best could dispute the Climate theory of black-ness by mentioning, in passing, his own firsthand observation: "I my selfe have seene an Ethiopian as blacke as a cole brought into England, who taking a faire English woman to wife, begat a sonne in all respects as blacke as the father was."[96] By 1589, the connection between Africans and slavery was so well established that Richard Hakluyt was calling five Africans brought into England "black slaves."[97] By 1596, referring to "divers Blackamoores brought into these realms," Queen Elizabeth asserted in a letter to the mayor of London that "there are already here to[o] manie."[98]

By 1597 the Privy Council was attempting to *export* "slaves" to Portugal and Spain, and by 1599 and 1601, the slave trade had been substantial enough that Queen Elizabeth now issued proclamations actually decrying "the great numbers of Negroes and blackamoors which . . . are carried into this realm" and encouraging "their masters" to assist her attempts "to have *those kind of people* sent out of the lande."[99] As a result, Elizabeth even licensed sea captain Caspar van Senden to deport slaves and prompted those "possessed of any such blackamoors" to relinquish them upon the captain's demand, while speaking of their condition of "servitude."[100] Although the English did not begin their rise to eventual dominance of the trade until the 1655 seizure of Jamaica from Spain, and though Britain did not finally become the primary slave trader until the late 1700s (with a peak in 1780 of 78,000 slaves transported per year and when half of all African slaves were carried in British ships),[101] and even though we may not yet know the degree to which promotion of the slave trade either motivated or reflected the development of the early blackfaced fool tradition, we can confidently conclude that plays featuring blackface nonetheless proliferate alongside such inhumane trafficking.

Links in a Chain: Transmigration, Transcodification, and Rationalization of Blackfaced Folly

But were the assumptions that rationalized the slave trade and those associated with the blackface tradition actually linked at all in the early modern mind-set? And if so, how? While a direct connection is difficult to prove, looking back, there is no lack of suggestive evidence of such a link in the historical record. Consistent echoes of the characters Wit and Ingnorance surface particularly in English traditions of travel and pseudoscientific literature. Notably, the "Second Voyage of John Hawkins, 1564–1565" from Hakluyt's famed *Principall Navigations, Voiages and Discoveries of the English Nation* (London, 1589) includes a reference to West Africans Hawkins encountered as simply "the ignorant people" who "knewe not" about guns and so were shot; here, their pain is described in comic terms: "[they] used a marveilous crying in their flight with leaping and turning their tayles, that it was strange to see, and gave us great pleasure to behold them."[102] Similarly, an account by Robert Baker of his voyages to the West African coast in 1562 and 1563, also published in Hakluyt's *Principall Navigations* (omitted from the 1598 edition), described inhabitants

> Whose likenesse seem'd men to be,
>   but all as blacke as coles.
> Their Captaine comes to me
>   as naked as my naile,
> *Not having witte* or honestie
>   to cover once his tale.[103]

Here, too, as in the Wit plays (one of which, the latest, was still familiar as late as the 1590s) and the tradition of the Devil as an ass, the connection between blackness and assumed ignorance and lack of wit is clear enough, as it is in Peter Heylyn's claims in his *Little Description of the Great World* (1631) that the sub-Saharan African utterly lacked "the use of Reason which is peculiar unto man; [he is] of little Wit."[104] Of course, Leo Africanus's *History and Description of Africa* (1526; English translation ca. 1600) had also represented "Negroes" as gulls "being utterly destitute of the use of reason, of dexteritie of wit,"[105] and Leo had been surprised when one African with whom he was "acquainted" was not irrational: "[H]e is blacke in colour but most beautifull in minde and contions [conscience]."[106] As Leo's remark suggests, even when commentators remarked on supposed black immorality (here an assumed lack of conscience), they regularly did so with respect to a purported lack of rational powers. For John Boemus in *A Fardle of Facions* (1555), then, Africans "carry the shape of men, but live like beast[s]: they be very barbarous . . . *neither do the[y] discerne any difference betwixt good and bad.*"[107] Though later commentators might sometimes debate about whether such supposed witlessness was "natural" or "ingrained" through the circumstances of "savagery" or slavery,[108] the presumption of defective reason was consistently pronounced in the history of early modern European encounters with Africans. And indeed, the connection between Africans and the terms of natural folly were never far away in the subsequent rhetoric of slavers, as in Barbot's previously noted observation: "it must be owned, they are very hard to be brought to a true notion of the Christian religion . . . being *naturally* very stupid and sensual, and so apt to continue till their end."[109] So also for later slavers in the American South, "a white skin was the distinguishing badge of mind and intellect,"[110] so that blackness was once again the emblematic opposite.

Here, to fully grasp the stakes involved in the blackfaced fool tradition we must recognize the degree to which assumptions about another's inherent irrationality were at the very heart of the Western history of slavery from its beginnings: although the Greeks did not enslave any one race (making slaves of any "barbarians" or non-Greeks), prominent philosophers nonetheless presumed that Greeks were the rational master race and that all slaves were rationally impaired by nature. Plato maintained for instance that God had deprived all slaves of half their reason in order to allow them to bear their wrongs—an anesthetizing notion for the masters. Thus it was that, according to Plato in *Meno,* a slave boy could hold true beliefs but could never *know* that he was right because he was inherently deficient in reason.[111] Similarly, for Aristotle, "From the hour of [his] birth," what he referred to as the "natural slave" was rationally deficient, having no deliberative faculty.[112] In defending the institution of slavery, Aristotle defined the man who was "by nature a slave" as being one who "participates in reason [only] to the extent of apprehending [reason] in another, though destitute of it himself."[113] And, whereas the natural master was the rationally superior Greek "in whom the rule of soul over body is accordingly evident," in the inherently irrational natural slave "the reverse would often appear to be true—the body ruling over the soul."[114] Aristotle ultimately went so far as to identify the term "barbarian" as "only seeking to express that same idea of the natural slave," so that he concluded that "there are some who are everywhere inherently slaves."[115]

Hellenistic philosophers such as Philo subsequently held the "slave indeed" to be an inherently foolish, sensual being. As Philo wrote, "he who with a mean and slavish spirit puts his hand to mean and slavish actions contrary to . . . proper judgment is a slave indeed." Whereas one historian finds the central point here to be that "The slave was, in short, a sinner,"[116] Philo conceived of the natural slave more so as something of a natural fool not ruled by "proper judgment." In fact, it was "folly" that Philo had in mind in describing the essential slave, as he clarified at length in *Quod Omnis Probus:*

> We may well deride the folly of those who think that when they are released from the ownership of their masters they become free. Servants, indeed, they are no longer. . . , but slaves they are and of the vilest kind . . . to the least reputable of inanimate things, to strong drink, to pot-herbs, to baked meats. . . . Thus Diogenes the cynic, seeing one of the so-called freedmen pluming himself, . . . marveled at the absence of reason and discernment. "A man might as well," he said, "proclaim that one of his servants became from this day a grammarian, a geometrician, or musician, when he has no idea whatever of the art." For as the proclamation cannot make them men of knowledge, so neither can it make them free. . . .[117]

Here, Philo could hardly have been clearer in his view that the "slave indeed" was inherently a fool; he was marked by his "folly," that is, his irrational subjection to appetite and his "absence of reason and discernment." And, whereas the truly free were "men of knowledge," the essential slave simply "ha[d] no idea whatever. . . ." In all of these statements on slavery we see ancient philosophers sophistically rationalizing what they had to in order to justify the existence of slavery, that is, insisting that those enslaved were inferior to their masters above all in terms of reason and that they were so by nature, not circumstance. The blackface tradition would disseminate and popularize these anesthetizing assumptions.

If, as Pulitzer Prize–winning historian of slavery, David Brion Davis, has theorized, impositions of "bestialization" were central to the history of slavery since slaveholding societies often compared slaves with domesticated animals,[118] it is irrationality that is once again at issue in slavery and blackface traditions alike. In practice, the leap from an emblematic—and stereotypical—imposition of foolish reasoning to an assumed beastlike irrationality was, unhappily, evidently no great one. Once Africans were viewed as irrational as beasts, partly via the blackface tradition, they could be forced into the most bestial servitude. Such is the case in Richard Ligon's view, following his stay in Barbados in the 1640s, that its residents were "as neer beasts" or in Henry Whistler's account a few years later of African slaves as "apes whou [the planters] command as they pleas."[119] Such a connection may also have been made in prior Hispanic slave-trading cultures of the sixteenth century, via the pejorative word "zambo," one of the possible influences upon the name "Sambo," which apparently "meant a bowlegged person resembling a monkey."[120] Joseph Boskin suggested as much, arguing that "Spanish and Portuguese slavers mocked the Africans by calling them 'zamboes,'" which the "English translated . . . into 'sambo.'"[121]

In the same manner, as Winthrop D. Jordan observed, the assertion of African irrationality and witlessness was made by way of direct or implied appeals to a pseudoscientific "Chain of Being" in which Africans were represented as being less than human, that is, one step up from apes in a supposed ascent toward the white man. Thus, Edward Topsell, author of *The Historie of Four-Footed Beastes* (London, 1607; repr., 1678), asserted that Africans "are Libidinous as Apes that attempt women" and are actually "deemed fools" because they have "thicke lippes, the upper hanging over the neather, . . . like the lips of Asses or Apes."[122] Here too, then, was "zambo." Likewise, "Pigmeys . . . are not men, because they *have no use of Reason, . . .* and although they speak, yet is their language imperfect; . . . and their imitation of man, do plainly *prove them rather to be Apes then Men.*"[123] Topsell's reasoning here meets one standard definition of "racism" as "a rationalized pseudoscientific theory positing the innate and permanent inferiority of nonwhites"—a definition its author, George M. Frederickson, believed applied to racial prejudice only after the early decades of the nineteenth century.[124] Instead, here already we glimpse the "simian imperialism" that Anne McClintock has postulated as a significant link between "scientific" and popular racism.[125] Although Jordan is thus certainly correct in noting early modern Europeans' frequent association of apes with Africans, he is admittedly less clear about *why* they might make such a leap in logic in the first place: "The inner logic of this association . . . rather tenuously . . . connected apes with blackness."[126]

One missing term in Jordan's argument here (and an assumption often either implicit or explicit in early modern rationalizing) is suggested by Topsell's references to apes "hav[ing] no use of Reason" and being "deemed foolish," since both "Asses and Apes" were associated with the irrational natural fool type, who we have seen was often represented as black in the period. In fact, it is fools or "divers[e] Jesters" and "laughter" that Topsell has very much in mind at the outset of his discussion of apes. For example, he tells his readers that the Greeks termed them *"Gelotopoios,* made for laughter," and he cites the authority of *"Anacharsis the Philosopher,"* who remarked that "men do but feign merriments, whereas Apes are *naturally* made for that purpose."[127] Interestingly enough, fools such as Henry VIII's fool Will Somer in Henry VIII's 1545 family portrait and dwarfs such as Henrietta Maria's *"hypopituitaristic* or proportionate dwarf" Geoffrey in Anthony Van Dyck's 1633 portrait are often depicted with monkeys, since court fools traditionally "were put in charge of pet apes."[128] In the same way, Leandro Bassano's "Carnival Banquet" (late 1580s), one of the earliest paintings featuring Harlequin and "one of the few known paintings by a native Italian of the early *commedia dell'arte,"* depicts the commedia clown, in a "black, beast-like mask" that appears apelike, further "aped" in that he dances alongside not only a monkey, but a dwarf wearing a similarly beastlike mask, with both diminutive figures mimicking his dance.[129] Similar disturbing juxtapositions are at work in Daniel Mytens's portrait of Charles I and Henrietta Maria, where the sitters preside over a scene featuring a black groom scantily clad in a leopard skin (suggestive of the leopard and Ethiope of Jeremiah that are unable to change their nature) and holding a horse's bridle, the dwarf Geoffrey holding a dog by a leash, and, on the viewer's lower right, a monkey astride the back of a dog. As Kim F. Hall remarks, "a connection between apes and blacks suggests that these figures represent a . . . marginal humanity."[130] Clearly, such representations were also meant to suggest hierarchical tableaus of a Chain of Being in terms not just of scale but proportions of reason. (Similar hierarchically arranged racist spectacles would one day appear in zoos, natural history museums, and circuses in American cities like New York.)[131]

In addition, the word "ape" itself had a number of long-standing connotations with "fool," as in *OED,* 4, "a fool. *God's ape:* a natural born fool[:] *to make any one his ape, to put an ape in his hood, to befool or dupe him.* c. 1386 CHAUCER *Prol.* 706 'He made the . . . peple his Apes . . .' 1611 SHAKS *Cymb.* 4.2.194 'Jollity for Apes, and greef for Boyes'" and *OED,* 7, as *"adj.* Foolish, silly. *adv.* Foolishly, sillily. 1509 BARCLAY *Ship of Fooles* (1570) 33 'Some are ape dronke, full of laughter and of toyes.'" According to H. W. Janson in *Apes and Ape Lore in the Middle Ages and the Renaissance,* "The concept of the ape as the image of the fool . . . gradually replaced that of the 'simian sinner' in the course of the Late Middle Ages," and in England, "ape" first began to be used as an actual term for "fool" in the fourteenth century.[132] Moreover, it was partly through manuscript illustrations and subsequent prints (by famous Northern European artists such as Israel van Meckenem and Hans Holbein the Younger) of "the mirror-gazing ape as a symbol of *vanitas*" that fools were associated with the mirrors that recur frequently in many plays featuring blackface.[133] Woodcuts likewise linked captive, chained apes to court fools, since "the ape as domestic pet was the exact counterpart of the fool,"[134] at least the natural fool. In such a context we are able to see that Topsell's logic, however grossly faulty, was not a wholly idiosyncratic leap (i.e., from African to Ape), but rather a chain of prevalent, and once closely related, demeaning symbolic associations between African/Blackness, the Blackfaced Natural Fool, and the Ape-as-Natural-Fool by way of the natural fools' conventional association with both blackness and apes. That is to say, in the iconography of the blackface tradition, the early Chain of Being that reflected the logic of a "simian imperialism" was not merely Rational Man over Irrational Man over Ape but rather the following Chain of Being: Rational/*White* Man over Irrational Man/ *Blackfaced* Natural Fool/*African* over Foolish *Black* Ape. Clearly, such a rationalized assumption of reason as the exclusive, natural inheritance of "whites," as against purportedly innately, permanently irrational and beastlike "blacks," who were deemed natural or "born" fools, prefigured and prepared the way for nineteenth-century "scientific" racist discourse on the "nature" of different races that may be traced in part to the natural fool traditions.

After all, the spirit or essence of the folk tradition of blackface experienced many transmigrations into more respected or refined forms of discourse—whether natural history, philosophy, linguistics, pseudoscience, or pseudobiblical theories. In particular, the mixing of an emblem or sign from folk tradition (here, blackface) and scientific discourse (as in Topsell on nature) is an instance of the dynamic of "transcodification," mentioned by Vaughan, by which the codes of one type of discourse transfer to another. Vaughan speculates that such transference of blackface as "a simple sign . . . to other sorts of discourse systems" may have been "widespread,"[135] and, though the sign was not always so simple, my own findings demonstrate that transference in fact occurred between early blackface and emergent racist discourse. For instance, early nineteenth-century articulations of racist scientific theories such as "polygenesis"—the theory of the separate creation of races as distinct species, according to which, to cite an example from 1830, there was a "vast preeminence of the Caucasian in intellect" as a "gift of *nature*"[136]— introduced some (yet surprisingly little) new terminology, but not fundamentally new ideas. That is, the pseudoscientific pose of reason in the nineteenth century was not really essentially different than that of Renaissance science. It was no mere coincidence therefore that early dramatists were staging personifications of "Science" shunning a character in blackface as a fool in the *Wit* plays; such drama was not merely inadvertently foreshadowing future developments, since Renaissance science was *already* being appropriated to slur blackness as an innate mark of congenital folly. Nineteenth-century scientific poseurs reenacting the foolish logic and spirit of the blackfaced fool tradition and the stereotypes it had long promoted may have become more sophisticated—or, rather, sophistic—in their treatment of "nature," but when they based their irrational assumptions on appeals to Nature, the ideas were not new; if the form of discourse seems different, the old code of blackness connoting natural folly was one and the same. Here was the essence of blackface transmigrated into a higher form, or perhaps merely dressed-up in the latest scientific garb, but the old, "tatyrd" medieval-Renaissance fashion of the natural fool shows through all the same.

Before the nineteenth century's scientific poseurs, eighteenth-century thinkers had already attempted to rationalize the codes of blackface folly by applying the philosophical veneer so admired in their day upon what was still finally the dubious old logic underlying a timeworn blackface mask. Henry Louis Gates has demonstrated, for instance, that philosophers such as Hume, Kant, and Hegel, in turn, each conflated a black complexion and diminished intellectual capacity. For example, in "Of National Characters" (1748), "suspect[ing] the negroes . . . to be naturally inferior," and asserting that "There never was a civilized nation of any other complexion than white," Hume dismissed "talk of one negroe as a man of parts and learning," believing that he must "be admired for very slender accomplishments, like a parrot who speaks a few words plainly." Writing in *Observations on the Feeling of the Beautiful and Sublime* (1764), Kant similarly asserted, "so fundamental is the difference between [the black and white] races of man, and it appears to be as great in regard to mental capacities as in color" and, more bluntly, "blacks are lower in their mental capacities than all other races." Kant can thus dismiss a black man's comments through choplogic: "[I]n short, this fellow was quite black from head to foot, a clear proof that what he said was stupid." Subsequently, Hegel, likewise assuming Africans "capable of no development or culture" whatsoever, deemed slavery a necessary "phase of *education*—a mode of becoming participant in a higher" civilization (the very argument enacted through the dramas of the naturally incorrigible Ingnorance and Moros).[137] In each instance, eighteenth-century philosophers found a black complexion less theologically than intellectually damning. Yet again, more than associations of blackness with evil, assumptions derived from the heretofore ignored blackfaced fool tradition were exploited in attempts to legitimize slavery.

The multilayered codes of blackface had also been appropriated, applied, and transferred in prior rationalizations, as they informed the connection between blackness and transgression, another facet of blackfaced folly in the Renaissance that could be exploited to justify slavery. In fact, one of the popular early modern theories of racial difference, a purportedly biblical theory (actually based upon Jewish oral tradition of the story of Ham's disobedience in Genesis 9:18–27),[138] accounts for the origins of blackness as a punishment or curse from God for vaguely defined transgression.[139] Arguing against a then-popular Climate theory that ascribed blackness to "the parching heat of the Sunne," in his *Discourse* (1578), Best claimed that blackness was instead the result of the "wicked Spirite" Satan who tempted one of Noah's three sons (Ham) "*to transgresse and disobey* his fathers commaundment, [so] that after him all his posteritie should be accursed." In Best's inaccurate version of the story, when Noah "straitely commaunded his sonnes and their wives . . . while they remained in the Arke, [that] they should . . . abstaine from carnall copulation with their wives," his "wicked sonne Cham [Ham] disobeyed." In consequence, "as an example for contempt of Almightie God, and disobedience of parents," God ordained the birth of a son, Chus, "who not onely it selfe, but all his posteritie after him should bee so blacke and lothsome, that it might remaine a spectacle of disobedience to all the world."[140] Mixing religious legend and pseudoscience, Best believed that after the curse on Ham, blackness became a "natural infection," indeed an "infection of blood."[141] Alongside a notion of an infection by nature, other toxic assumptions of natural folly appear in the Ham mythologies, as in William Strachey's 1612 remark that "what country soever the children of Cham happended to possess, there biganne both the Ignoraunce of true godlinesse . . . and Ignoraunce of true worship of God."[142] The legends that surround Ham also often include laughter as an otherwise curious element.[143] If in the late eighteenth and nineteenth centuries the Ham story was one foundation myth rationalizing slavery, the blackface tradition had long accomplished similar degradation, and it, too, had long been associated with transgression.

Transgression, after all, Linda Woodbridge notes, pertained to blackness especially in the Renaissance when blackface was "a hallmark of popular rites."[144] A link between blackface and associations with often inversive, festive folly appears, for instance, in corn riots, which, Natalie Zemon Davis demonstrates, were led by women or men dressed as women, who, Woodbridge argues, often wore blackface.[145] C. R. Baskervill cites John Aubrey's *Remains* for the game "Cap Justice," in which, Baskervill explains, "the judge who presides has his face blackened by those who plead before him."[146] Similarly, Barry Reay recounts an early modern tradition in Middleton on Easter Tuesday in which "some unlucky fellow who had got himself so far intoxicated as not to be able to take care of himself," was elected mock-mayor, had his face "daubed with soot and grease," was dressed in every possible "article of adornment and deformity," and was paraded through town on a chair.[147] Of course, blackface was also often assumed by participants in Carnival. In his section, *Von fassnacht narren* (*Of Carnival Fools*), Sebastian Brant spoke contemptuously in his *Ship of Fools* (1495, 2nd ed.) of those maskers who blacked themselves and ran amok, just as

Englishman Alexander Barclay remarks in his free translation *Shyp of Folys:* "The one . . . paynteth his visage with fume in such case . . . / And other some besyde theyr vayne habyte / Defyle theyr faces."[148]

I would suggest that blackface in these customs, in conjunction with popular rites featuring comic butts in blackface, invoked the tradition of the natural fool, whose transgression was both licensed and mocked. After all, "[s]ince he does not comprehend the conventions of society," Walter Kaiser observes, "the natural fool is invariably irreverent of those conventions, not out of any motives of iconoclasm but simply because he does not know any better."[149] As Enid Welsford put it, his "mental deficiencies" can often have the effect of "put[ting] him in . . . [a] position of virtual outlawry"; by his very nature the natural fool "stand[s] outside the law" and tends "to turn the world upside down."[150] A black face became a sign of one marked as both transgressor and butt and thus as a scapegoat, a whipping boy, an *insipiens,* a fool—and also a slave. Here again the license authorized by blackface, which modern scholars have occasionally invoked as liberating, was symbolically and stereotypically limiting.

If since at least the fifteenth century the blackface tradition had the effect of rationalizing slavery, by the nineteenth century it was especially underwriting the myth of the happy but incorrigible plantation slave. Notably, in the 1850s, Thomas R. R. Cobb's influential defense of slavery, *An Inquiry into the Law of Negro Slavery,* rested partly upon the idea that black peoples were "mirthful by nature."[151] Years earlier, writing of Southern slaves, John Pendleton Kennedy was likewise "quite sure" in his *Swallow Barn* (1832) that "never could they become a happier people than I find them here."[152] The black man was, of course, believed innately happy because he was assumed to be simply a natural. In fact, as Boskin argues, his humor was depicted as that of "the fool."[153] Washington Irving thus found the "negroes" he described in *Knickerbocker's History of New York* (1809) as "famous for their risible powers,"[154] while English comedian John Bernard, following a visit to America between 1797 and 1811, termed "the negroes the greatest humorists of the union" because of their "profound simplicity," their "*natural* drollery," which was "*Nature*'s spontaneous product in full bloom."[155] Boskin demonstrates further that "once the conception of the black male as the fool became the primary focus of white imagery, it assumed a centripetal energy of its own, as stereotypes often do."[156] A key in such stereotyping was, once again, the figure of Sambo: "slow-witted, loosely-shuffling, buttock-scratching, benignly-optimistic, superstitiously-frightened, childishly lazy, irresponsibly-carefree, . . . sexually-animated. His physical characteristics added to the jester's appearance: toothy-grinned, . . . slack-jawed, round-eyed."[157] But this description seems as apt for the age-old natural fool as for the more recent blackface minstrelsy of the nineteenth and early twentieth centuries, for Sambo is but the latest name for the natural fool in blackface.

Reduced under such a stereotype to the level of a smiling, dehumanized buffoon, any black male could be deemed impervious to pain and incapable of sorrow, so that real guilt or culpability on the part of slaveholders—as opposed to the maudlin sentimentality and disabling pathos sometimes attached to the natural fool tradition and plantation myth alike—was not only unnecessary but inconceivable. That is, through such a Sambo stereotype, black men were constructed as childishly incapable of caring for themselves, assisting the condescending paternalism and "degraded man-child" stereotype that was "an ideological imperative of all systems of slavery,"[158] but especially of the American South.

Of course, as with other natural fool traditions, the specific plantation stereotype of the irrepressibly childlike Sambo found its origins in ridicule and shame. His name, for instance, in addition to owing a debt to the pejorative Spanish "zambo," also apparently derives from West African cultures, particularly the Mende and Vai communities, among whom "sambo" or "sam bo" meant "to disgrace"; the name, as applied to African slaves, appears at least as early as 1692–93, when the ship *Margarett* included as recorded cargo: "2 Negroes Sambo and Jack."[159] But the origins of Sambo before that, Boskin observes, have always been obscure: "There is no precise date, but Sambo was apparently conceived in the minds of Western Europeans in their early interactions with Africans in the fifteenth and early sixteenth centuries and was born during the early period of the slave trade."[160] Elsewhere, Boskin speculates: "In all probability, the American Sambo was conceived in Europe, particularly in England, and drew his first breath with initial contact with West Africans during the slave-trading years. Sambo was a concept long before assuming a specific identity."[161] But we are presently able to move beyond Boskin's apt conjecture, since we know now that the "concept" he posits was that of the natural fool, and that the enduring type that came to be known finally as Sambo took some of his earliest breaths on the stage under names like Tutuvillus, Ingnorance, Moros, and Harlequin, the latter of whom was already an international icon of popular culture by the late sixteenth century. Subsequently, under the name Sambo, a word of disgrace, the blackfaced fool became "a multipublic figure by the eighteenth century,"[162] and he achieved fame that lasted through the early twentieth century: "No comic figure played to wider audiences, received more thunderous applause, or lasted as long in the popular theatre."[163] Yet, we must now admit as much for the blackfaced fool generally, for "Sambo" was simply one of the most enduring names given to an old fool-type.

Conclusions

Blackness was not a simple sign associated with evil alone, since buried associations between blackface and folly had, as we have seen, numerous reinforcing connections, some subtle, others not. More importantly, though long ignored, associations with folly were, ironically enough, more damning than "evil" associations in the construction of stereotypes that were used to justify racial domination and to rationalize slavery. In Renaissance English drama alone, blackfaced fools or foolish black devils appear in plays by Chapman, Dekker, Drayton, Edwards, Fullwell, Garter, Greene, Haughton, both Heywoods, Ingeland, Jonson, Lupton, Merbury, Rastell, Redford, Wager, Westcote, Wever, and Woodes. Even in *Othello* (1604), the symbolism of blackfaced folly is deployed meaningfully throughout the play. In an allusion to the *Wit* interludes, Shakespeare depicts the noble Moor's wits or "best judgement *collied*" (2.3.202), that is, metaphorically blackened by the vice-like Iago. Bigoted characters such as Iago and Emilia subsequently impose terms suggesting folly upon Othello—"fool" (5.2.231), "credulous fool" (4.1.45), "coxcomb" (5.2.231), "ass" (2.1.307), "gull" (5.2.159), "dolt" (5.2.150), "mad" (4.1.101), "light of brain" (4.1.269), "ignorant as dirt" (5.2.160), and led as easily "[a]s asses are" (1.3.401)—and Othello finally rebukes himself with "O fool, fool, fool!" (5.2.321). And, whether used to mark the *insipiens,* a foolish devil, Johan Johan, Humanyte, a gulled Wit, Ingnorance, the lewd "blackeman" that offended Cecilia, Moros, a participant in any of several European popular rites, Grim the Collier, Harlequin, or Sambo, blackface masks were often emblematic of the natural fool, a butt or gull who was laughed at, scapegoated, and abused while being constructed as mentally deficient, transgressive, and as essentially "other."

Although popular cultures are undoubtedly subject to discontinuities and inventions, the long-ignored early blackface tradition, like much fool custom generally, was especially stubborn and resilient. The iconography of blackface as emblem of folly is the result of the influence and conflation of many old popular traditions, each of which, no doubt, originally had different potential symbolic terms that were distilled over time as emblematic of folly. Whatever its origins, myriad transmigrations, and unconscious transcodifications, the palimpsest that was the blackfaced natural fool tradition had devastating consequences as its codes eventually underwrote dehumanizing racist theories articulated more fully, but often only in slightly different idiom (ranging from religious to philosophical and scientific discourse), in later centuries. Because prior depictions originated some of the racist fantasies staged by blackface minstrels and underwrote otherwise inexplicable racist theories of African inferiority, forging early links in the enslaving fiction of the "Great Chain of Being," the widespread, yet previously overlooked natural fool iconography of blackness warrants examination. In the end, one thing we will find is that racism was/is not only folly, but often the stuff of actual fools' play as well.

Notes

This essay is in part a follow-up to issues first raised in my article, "Emblems of Folly in the First *Othello:* Renaissance Blackface, Moor's Coat, and 'Muckender,'" *Comparative Drama,* special issue, "Reading *Othello,*" 35.1 (Spring 2001): 69–100. I would like to thank Oglethorpe University for support that allowed research at the British Library, the Bibliotheque Nationale, and the Folger Shakespeare Library, the Huntington Library, and the Library of Congress; participants at the Citadel Conference on Literature in 2002, the national convention of the Popular Culture Association, and the Second and Third Blackfriars Scholars Conferences (particularly Ralph Cohen of the American Shakespeare Center, Patrick Spottiswode of the Globe Theatre and the International Shakespeare Center, and Virginia Mason Vaughan) in 2003 and 2005, for their encouragement; and especially Jeanne H. McCarthy, Oscar G. Brockett, Elizabeth M. Richmond-Garza, and Leah S. Marcus for comments at various stages of the project.

1. *State Papers, Foreign, 1569–71,* no. 2149. Quoted in Ethel Seaton, *Queen Elizabeth and the Swedish Princess: Being an Account of the Visit of Princess Cecilia of Sweden to England in 1565 [1566]* (London: Frederich Etchells & Hugh Macdonald, 1926), 21.

2. In *Queen Elizabeth and the Swedish Princess,* Seaton attempted to answer this question and suggested that the play may well have been the Boys of Westminster School's Latin play, *Sapientia Solomonis,* or *The Wisdom of Solomon* (January 1566). After all, at the same time that the play flatters Elizabeth's wisdom, the subject matter and the epilogue both draw unflattering comparisons between the by-then unwelcome Cecilia and Sheba (Seaton, 21). Although this speculation seemed plausible enough, Elizabeth Rogers Payne objected: "But since there is no reason to suppose that Marcolph was represented as a 'blackeman' . . . (even though he was traditionally 'of an evill favored countenaunce'), the cause for Cecilia's offense was probably not the *Sapientia*" (148). On this debate, see Elizabeth Rogers Payne, *Sapientia Solomonis: Acted Before the Queen by the Boys of Westminster School, January 17, 1565/6* (New Haven: Yale University Press, 1938), 148n30.

3. See particularly David Brion Davis, *Inhuman Bondage: The Rise and Fall of Slavery in the New World* (Oxford: Oxford University Press, 2006) and George M. Frederickson, *Racism: A Short History* (Princeton: Princeton University Press, 2002), especially 15–48, where Frederickson locates the descent into racism in the West in religious traditions of the late Middle Ages. Other works are cited below and throughout.

4. See, for instance, David M. Goldenberg, *The Curse of Ham: Race and Slavery in Early Judaism, Christianity and Islam* (Princeton: Princeton University Press, 2003) and Stephen R. Haynes, *Noah's Curse: The Biblical Justification of American Slavery* (Oxford: Oxford University Press, 2002); see also Frederickson's chapter on "Religion and the Invention of Racism" in his *Racism: A Short History,* 15–48.

5. Dympna Callaghan, *Shakespeare Without Women: Representing Gender and Race on the Renaissance Stage* (New York: Routledge, 2000), 93.

6. According to noted historian of the Devil, Jeffrey Burton Russell, "The color

black (as opposed to absence of light) is not a symbol of evil in the Old Testament or in the Apocalyptic period. . . . Even where color symbolism is striking . . . neither red nor black becomes symbolically fixed as evil as both would do in Christian iconography" (*Devil*, 217n95). Likewise, "nowhere does [the New Testament] describe Satan as actually black," and "Only in the later Apocryphal literature is blackness specifically assigned to the Devil" (*Devil*, 247): "As early as about 120 A.D. the Epistle of Barnabas designated Satan as *ho melas*, the black one" (*Devil*, 247n41)—"The equation of evil, darkness, and blackness, a source of later racial stereotypes, occurs here for the first time in Christian literature" (*Satan*, 40). Elsewhere, Russell records that "His first clear appearance as black [in an illustration] . . . was in the ninth-century Stuttgart Psalter" (*Lucifer*, 133). Russell conjectures ("but the connection is uncertain") that there may be some association with the festive, but also ambivalently anarchic and destructive figure of Dionysus, who "was sometimes black" (*Devil*, 253) and "who was sometimes called 'he of the black goat' and portrayed as shaggy" (*Devil*, 141). *The Devil: Perceptions of Evil from Antiquity to Primitive Christianity* (1987; repr., Ithaca: Cornell University Press, 1977); *Satan: The Early Christian Tradition* (Ithaca: Cornell University Press, 1981); *Lucifer: The Devil in the Middle Ages* (Ithaca: Cornell University Press, 1984).

7. See Anthony Gerard Barthelemy, *Black Face, Maligned Race: The Representation of Blacks in English Drama from Shakespeare to Southerne* (Baton Rouge: Louisiana State University Press, 1987); Eliot Tokson, *The Popular Image of the Black Man in English Drama, 1550–1688* (Boston: G. K. Hall, 1982); Jack D'Amico, *The Moor in the English Renaissance Drama* (Tampa: University of South Florida Press, 1991). Here quoting Barthelemy, 3–4.

8. Virginia Mason Vaughan, *Performing Blackness on English Stages, 1500–1800* (Cambridge: Cambridge University Press, 2005), 24. On the blackness of the Devil, damned souls in the medieval cycle plays, and drama inspired by such connections, see 19–25, 34, 39, 62, 75, 81, 82, 87, 89, 91, 120.

9. *The Oxford English Dictionary* defines the noun "natural" as "one naturally deficient in intellect; a half-witted person" (*OED*, 2), providing examples such as the usage by Thomas More in 1533: "It could never be done more naturally, not thovgh he that wrote it were even a very naturall in dede." Likewise, the *OED* defines the adjective "natural," when used in "natural fool," as "one who is by nature deficient in intelligence; a fool or simpleton by birth," offering references that include one from Henry VIII's reign in 1540: "Ideottes and fooles naturall, now remayning . . . in his graces custodye." However, natural folly included connotations of two *OED* definitions of "folly" itself: "the quality or state of being foolish or deficient in understanding; want of good sense, weakness or derangement of mind; also unwise conduct" (*OED*, 1) and "madness, insanity, mania" (*OED*, 4). For criticism on natural fools, see Enid Welsford, *The Fool: His Social and Literary History* (London: Faber and Faber, 1935); Leslie Hotson, *Shakespeare's Motley* (New York: Oxford University Press, 1952); Walter Kaiser, *Praisers of Folly: Erasmus, Rabelais, Shakespeare* (Cambridge, MA: Harvard University Press, 1963); John Southworth, *Fools and Jesters at the English Court* (Thrupp, Stroud, Gloucestershire: Sutton Publishing, 1998), 48–60; and my own articles, "Emblems of Folly in the First *Othello*: Renaissance Blackface, Moor's Coat, and 'Muckender'" and especially "The Fool in Quarto and Folio *King Lear*," *English Literary Renaissance* 34.3 (2004): 306–38.

10. *The Creation,* in *The Towneley Plays,* ed. Martin Stevens and A. C. Cawley (New York: Published for the Early English Text Society by the Oxford University Press, 1994), vol. 1, ll. 132–36, 7; emphasis added. All subsequent references will be cited parenthetically.

11. As Martin Stevens and James Paxson have shown, the word "foyll" certainly means "fool" as elsewhere in the Towneley cycle Jesus's enemies taunt him calling him "a flateryng foyll" and "fond foyll." Stevens and Paxson, "The Fool in the Wakefield Plays," *Studies in Iconography* 13 (1989–90): 48–79; here quoting 48.

12. Ibid., 76.

13. Ibid., 49, 76.

14. *The Chester Mystery Cycle,* ed. R. M. Lumiansky and David Mills, Early English Text Society, Supplementary Series 3 (London: Oxford University Press, 1974), cited hereafter parenthetically by line numbers.

15. *The Creation, and the Fall of Lucifer,* in *Everyman and the Medieval Miracle Plays,* ed. A. C. Cawley (1956; repr., London: Everyman, 1999), l. 101, p. 6 and l. 30, p. 4. Hereafter cited parenthetically by line numbers.

16. Cawley, *Everyman and the Medieval Miracle Plays,* 7.

17. Vaughan, *Performing Blackness on English Stages,* 15.

18. Meg Twycross and Sarah Carpenter, *Masks and Masking in Medieval and Early Tudor England* (Burlington: Ashgate, 2002), 202.

19. W. T. Lhamon Jr., *Jump Jim Crow: Lost Plays, Lyrics, and Street Prose of the First Atlantic Popular Culture* (Cambridge, MA: Harvard University Press, 2003), 204.

20. Dale Cockrell, *Demons of Disorder: Early Blackface Minstrels and Their World,* (Cambridge: Cambridge University Press, 1997), 106; emphasis mine. Surprisingly, Cockrell does not develop the connection.

21. Edward Pessen, *Jacksonian America: Society, Personality, and Politics* (1969; rev. ed.: Chicago: University of Illinois Press, 1985), 42.

22. W. T. Lhamon Jr., *Raising Cain: Blackface Performance from Jim Crow to Hip Hop* (Cambridge: Harvard University Press, 1998), 188. Lhamon does not address madness.

23. Lhamon, *Raising Cain,* 188.

24. Brenda Dixon Gottschild, *Digging the Africanist Presence in American Performance: Dance and Other Contexts* (Westport, CT: Greenwood, 1996), 98.

25. Welsford, *Fool: His Social and Literary History,* 55.

26. Patrick Rael, "The Long Death of Slavery," chapter 4 in *Slavery in New York,* ed. Ira Berlin and Leslie M. Harris, published in conjunction with the New-York Historical Society (New York: New Press, 2005), 140.

27. John D. Cox, *The Devil and the Sacred in English Drama, 1350–1642* (Cambridge: Cambridge University Press, 2000), throughout, but especially on 23, where Cox employs a curiously selective criterion for establishing the "seriousness" of theatrical devils, so that he offers as the one supposed exception proving his rule, the following: "Only N-Town includes the merest suggestion of scatalogical humor in the first play: when Lucifer encounters hell, he exclaims, 'For fere of Fyre a fart I cracke!' (*N-Town Play,* 24/8r)."

28. Peter Happé, "The Devil in the Interludes, 1550–1577," *Medieval English*

Theatre 11.1–2 (1989): 43. For another exception to the tendency to ignore the Devil's foolishness, see Allardyce Nicoll who at least recognized the Devil's comic role across Europe as he observed that "[i]n the mystery plays [the Devil] becomes *almost a comic type*. . . . [I]n the mystery cycles the Devil is continually being dragged in, even where he is not strictly required, and scenes of diablerie are introduced purely for their own merriment." Yet, even Nicoll, unaware of the extent to which fool and devil were often conflated, was puzzled upon finding that "the [devil named] Stultus ('Fool') of the French *Ste Barbe* indicates a possible confusion with the fool tradition." Nicoll, *Masks, Mimes and Miracles: Studies in the Popular Theatre* (New York: Harcourt, Brace, 1931), 187 (emphasis added), 188. See also 187n3 for Nicoll's sources on comic devils in the medieval French and German traditions.

29. Happé, "The Devil in the Interludes," 48–49.

30. Ibid., 51. In Anne Lancashire's *London Civic Theatre,* we learn of such masks already in use in English theatrical entertainments at least by 1377 in a mumming featuring eight to ten mummers with "visers nayrs come debblers" or "black masks like devils." *London Civic Theatre: City Drama and Pageantry from Roman Times to 1558* (Cambridge: Cambridge University Press, 2002), 42.

31. *REED: Coventry,* 224, 230, 237, 464, 474–75. 93; 59, 74, 84, 93, 111, 177 (dating from 1477–1554); and 220, 278, 464, 468, 474.

32. Twycross and Carpenter, *Masks and Masking in Medieval and Early Tudor England,* 330.

33. Happé, "The Devil in the Interludes," 47, 43.

34. Ibid., 45, 47.

35. An additional allusion to a mask as a familiar emblem of shameful folly appears in John Skelton's *Magnyfycence* (ca. 1516), where, after Folly promises Fancy and Crafty Conveyance, "I can make ye both fools" (*Four Morality Plays,* ed. Peter Happé [Bungay, Suffolk: Penguin, 1979], l. 1174, 259), the following exchange occurs:

> *Crafty Conveyance.* In a cote thou can play well the dyser [i.e., fool].
> *Folly.* Ye, but thou can play the fole *without a vyser.*
>
> (ll. 1177–78; emphasis added)

A "vyser" (likely black) seems to have been emblematic of folly, since, ironically, the insult implying Crafty Conveyance's innate or natural folly makes little sense if playing the fool *with* a "vyser" (or at least some face paint) were not conventional in the morality play.

36. Russell, *Lucifer,* 60, 76.

37. Russell, *Satan,* 213.

38. See "J7730 Absurd Ignorance": "D834. . . . Man gets shelter in storm; devil gets wet. Devil gives man magic objects in return for information as to how he kept dry." *Motif-Index of Folk-Literature,* vol. 4. J-K, in *Indiana University Studies* 22 (Sept., Dec., 1934), Studies nos. 105, 106, 151–52.

39. Happé, "The Devil in the Interludes," 95.

40. The stubbornness of comic associations with the Devil—and blackness—is evident in William Mountford's *The Life and Death of Doctor Faustus Made into a Farce With the Humours of Harlequin and Scaramouche* (1697), in which a stage

direction reads: *"Enters Several Devils, who black Harlequin and Scaramouche's Faces, and then Squirt Milk upon them"* (sig. D1v).

41. Stevens and Paxson, "The Fool in the Wakefield Plays," 79.

42. Margaret Jennings, *Tutivillus: The Literary Career of the Recording Demon* (*Studies in Philology,* Texts and Studies, 74.5 [Dec. 1977]: 10–11.

43. Ibid., 35–36, 66.

44. *Four Morality Plays,* 1. 199.

45. *Three Late Medieval Morality Plays,* ed. G. A. Lester (New York: W. W. Norton, 1981), 132.

46. D. J. Gifford, "Iconographical Notes Towards a Definition of the Medieval Fool," in *The Fool and the Trickster: Studies in Honour of Enid Welsford,* ed. Paul V. A. Williams, 18 (Cambridge: D. S. Brewer, 1979). See also Southworth, *Fools and Jesters at the English Court,* 36–37.

47. British Library, MS. Add. 44874, fol. 75.

48. *A Selection from the Minor Poems of Dan John Lydgate,* ed. Hames Orchard Halliwell (London: Percy Society, 1860), 164.

49. Quoted in Southworth, *Fools and Jesters at the English Court,* 37; Southworth is not discussing Moros, however.

50. Ahuva Belkin, "Antichrist as the Embodiment of the Insipiens in Thirteenth-Century French Psalters," *Florilegium* 10 (1988–91): 71–72.

51. See the excellent facsimile edition, *Der Stuttgarter Bilderpsalter Bibl. Fol. 23 Wurrtembergische Landesbibliothek Stuttgart* (Stuttgart: E. Schreiber Graphishe Kunstanstalten, 1965), vol. 1 of 2, sig. 15r. The *insipiens* is on the upper right.

52. Russell, *Lucifer,* 133. Russell makes no reference to the black *insipiens.*

53. For illustrations of devils as black in the facsimile edition of *Der Stuttgarter Bilderpsalter,* see sigs. 10v, 16v, 38r, 70v, 102v, 107r, 107v, and 147v. For the blackened *"D,"* see sig. 65r.

54. Sandra Billington, *A Social History of the Fool* (New York: St. Martin's Press, 1984), 12.

55. Kathleen L. Scott, *Later Gothic Manuscripts, 1390–1490. A Survey of Manuscripts Illuminated in the British Isles* 6, 2 vols. (London: Harvey Miller Publishers, 1996), 2:75, table I; Kathleen L. Scott, "Limning and Book-producing Terms and Signs *in situ* in Late-Medieval English Manuscripts: A First Listing," in *New Science Out of Old Books: Studies in Manuscripts and Early Printed Books in Honour of A. L. Doyle,* ed. Richard Beadle and A. J. Piper, 165n29 (Aldershot: Scolar Press, 1995).

56. Paul Freedman, *Images of the Medieval Peasant* (Stanford, CA: Stanford University Press, 1999), 133–73, 300–303.

57. David Bevington, *Tudor Drama and Politics* (Cambridge, MA: Harvard University Press, 1968), 132.

58. Carolyn Prager, "'If I be Devil': English Renaissance Response to the Proverbial and Ecumenical Ethiopian," *Journal of Medieval and Renaissance Studies* 17.2 (Fall 1987): 262 (emphasis added); Prager is discussing and citing John Calvin, *Commentaries on the Book of the Prophet Jeremiah and the Lamentations,* trans. John Owen, vol. 2 (Edinburgh, 1860), 191.

59. Carolyn Prager, "'If I be Devil,'" 261–62; discussing and citing Calvin, *Commentaries on the Book of the Prophet Jeremiah,* 191–93.

60. Joseph E. Harris, *Africans and Their History,* 2nd rev. ed. (1972; New York: Penguin, 1998), 7; emphasis added.

61. Stephen Booth notes that the meaning of blackness was "established by its contrast to fair: . . . ugly (Shakespeare and his contemporaries regularly use black as if it were a simple antonym for 'beautiful' . . .)." *Shakespeare's Sonnets: Edited with Analytic Commentary by Stephen Booth* (New Haven: Yale University Press, 1977), 434; here commenting on Sonnet 127.

62. John Redford, *Wit and Science,* ed. Arthur Brown (Oxford: Printed for the Malone Society Reprints at the University Press, 1951), ll. 434–35; emphasis added. All subsequent citations refer to this edition and will be cited parenthetically.

63. Associations between both lustful natural folly and blackness and between episodes of trickery and the blacking of a "gulled" comic butt are to be found in several prevalent synonyms for the word "fool" involving black- or black-headed birds. The word "noddy," for instance, which we have seen self-consciously applied in blackface episodes, according to the *OED,* meant not only "A fool, simpleton, noodle" (*OED,* 1), but could also refer to "A soot-coloured sea-bird" (*OED,* 2), that is, the "Black Noddy." Like the noddy, other English names for birds, such as the "jackdaw," a small crowlike bird, the Brown Booby with its dark-cowled head, the dark-headed "loon" (i.e., the Old World species of Arctic Loon [*Gavia arctica*] which has an even darker head in breeding season), and the "gull," particularly the Common or Black-headed Gull (*Larus ridibundus*)—which is familiar all over Europe and on which the breeding plumage on the head becomes dark brown in the summer as it breeds in northern Europe—were all synonymous with fools. Other species of gulls familiar to sailors, such as the Laughing Gull (*Larus atricilla*), whose cry resembles human laughter, share the dark head of the Black-headed Gull. The iconography of blackface would thus help to explain the obscure, "doubtful and perhaps mixed origin" in the sixteenth century of the word "gull": "A credulous person; one easily imposed upon; a dupe, simpleton, fool" (*OED,* 1). As in the case of "gull," the *OED* describes "loon" as "Of obscure origin; the early forms [i.e., spellings] do not favour the current hypothesis of conne[ct]ion with early mod[ern] Du[tch] *loen* 'homo stupidus'. . . ." Yet, at least five words for relatively intelligent black or black-headed bird species (noddy, jackdaw, gull, booby, loon) suggested folly partly via the iconography of blackness. No one, to my knowledge, has previously noted this connection.

64. In stagings of the scene I directed at the Second and Third Blackfriars Scholars Conferences at the Blackfriars Theatre in Staunton, Virginia (2003 and 2005), I prompted the actor playing Ingnorance to closely imitate or mirror both the body language and inflection of Idlenes in the language lesson in which Ingnorance foolishly parrots the vice either syllable-for-syllable, word-for-word, or sentence-for-sentence. Such a staging proved effective, particularly given the heightened symbolic import in the play of mirroring via the "glass of Reason" elsewhere.

65. Despite such emphasis, scholars have generally failed to acknowledge the blacking episode. Reavley Gair, for instance, only tentatively suggests that Wyt's transformation was "effected in part by a visual change and presumably make-up." *The Children of Paul's: The Story of a Theatre Company, 1553–1608* (Cambridge: Cambridge University Press, 1982), 77.

66. Lhamon, *Raising Cain,* 42; Twycross and Carpenter, *Masks and Masking in Medieval and Early Tudor England,* 11 and 316.

67. Alexander Saxton, "Blackface Minstrelsy and Jacksonian Ideology," *American Quarterly* 27.1 (Mar. 1975): 23; see Henry Louis Gates, *Figures in Black: Words, Signs, and the "Racial" Self* (New York: Oxford University Press, 1987), 51.

68. See *The Marriage of Wit and Science,* ed. John S. Farmer (London: Tudor Facsimile Texts, 1909), v. All citations refer to this edition and will be cited parenthetically; see also Gair, *Children of Paul's,* 84.

69. *The Marriage Between Wit and Wisdom,* ed. Trevor N. S. Lennam (1966; repr., Oxford: Printed for the Malone Society Reprints at the Oxford University Press, 1971), ix.

70. For a discussion of such, see Vaughan, *Performing Blackness on English Stages,* 9–14, and Richard Blunt's *Recreating Renaissance Black Make-Up,* MLITT in Shakespeare and Renaissance Literature in Performance (Mary Baldwin College, Spring 2006). Blunt found through experimentation and staged demonstration that the most durable of the methods available for representing blackness in the Renaissance was tempera with walnut pigment, recipes for which appeared in both Ben Jonson's *The Gypsy Metamorphosed* (1612) and Johann Jacob Wecker's book *Cosmetick, or The Beautifying Part of Physick* (surviving edition published in 1660, although Wrecker died in 1586). See 24–25, 37–38.

71. *Sir Thomas More: A play by Anthony Munday and others; revised by Henry Chettle, Thomas Dekker, Thomas Heywood and William Shakespeare,* ed. Vittorio Gabrieli and Giorgio Melchiori (Manchester: Manchester University Press, 1990), 142–43.

72. *Three Rastell Plays: Four Elements, Calisto and Melebea, Gentleness and Nobility,* ed. Richard Axton (Cambridge: D. S. Brewer, 1979), 59. Subsequent citations appear parenthetically by line number.

73. Trevor Lennam, *Sebastian Westcott, the Children of Paul's, and The Marriage of Wit and Science* (Toronto: University of Toronto Press, 1975), 94.

74. *The Plays of John Heywood,* ed. Richard Axton and Peter Happé (Cambridge: D. S. Brewer, 1991), 88 and 91.

75. Note that in the following discussion I do not mean to suggest a direct influence of Harlequin upon the blackfaced fool tradition in England. Although commedia troupes appeared in London in 1573 and 1574, it was not until 1578 that a Drusiano, "an Italian, a commediante, and his companye," performed in London. Drusiano Martinelli was a famous Harlequin and brother to the more acclaimed Tristano Martinelli, the self-styled *dominus Arlecchinorum,* who may also have been traveling with the company. In any case, Harlequin seems not to have appeared in England until well after a number of English plays featuring blackfaced fools. On commedia in Renaissance England, see Richard B. Zacha, "Iago and the Commedia dell'Arte," *Arlington Quarterly* 2.2 (Autumn 1969): 101; Dario Fo, *The Tricks of the Trade,* trans. Joe Farrell (New York: Routledge, 1991), 42.

76. David B. Davis, *The Problem of Slavery in Western Culture* (Ithaca: Cornell University Press, 1966), 43.

77. Elizabeth Donnan, *Documents Illustrative of the History of the Slave Trade to America,* vol. 1 of 4 vols. (1930; repr., New York: Octagon Books, 1965), 1; Ulrich B. Phillips, *American Negro Slavery* (1966; repr., Baton Rouge: Louisiana State University Press, 1990), 12.

78. Donnan, *Documents Illustrative of the History of the Slave Trade to America,* 1:5; Phillips, *American Negro Slavery,* 12–13.

79. Harry Harmer, *The Longman Companion to Slavery, Emancipation and Civil Rights,* (London: Longman, 2001), 3; Harris, *Africans and Their History,* 81.

80. Harmer, *Longman Companion to Slavery, Emancipation and Civil Rights,* 5.

81. Davis, *Problem of Slavery in Western Culture,* 170.

82. Kim F. Hall, *Things of Darkness: Economies of Race and Gender in Early Modern England* (Ithaca: Cornell University Press, 1995), 19n24.

83. See Paul Edwards, "The Early African Presence in the British Isles," in *Essays on the History of Blacks in Britain: From Roman Times to the Mid-Twentieth Century,* ed. Jagdish S. Gundara and Ian Duffield, 9–29 (Aldershot: Averbury, 1992): Sue Niebrzydowski, "The Sultana and Her Sisters: Black Women in the British Isles Before 1530," *Women's History Review* (Great Britain) 2001 10 (2): 187–210.

84. Philip D. Morgan, "British Encounters with Africans and African-Americans, circa 1600–1780," in *Strangers Within the Realm: Cultural Margins of the First British Empire,* ed. Bernard Bailyn and Philip D. Morgan (Chapel Hill: University of North Carolina Press, 1991), 159; Hall, *Things of Darkness,* 21.

85. Donnan, *Documents Illustrative of the History of the Slave Trade to America,* 1:8.

86. Winthrop D. Jordan, *White over Black: American Attitudes Toward the Negro, 1550–1812* (Chapel Hill: University of North Carolina Press, 1968), 6.

87. James Walvin, *The Black Presence: A Documentary History of the Negro in England, 1555–1860* (Surrey: Orbach and Chambers, 1971), 61, 212n1.

88. Hall, *Things of Darkness,* 19.

89. Donnan, *Documents Illustrative of the History of the Slave Trade to America,* 1:45.

90. Walvin, *Black Presence,* 50.

91. Harmer, *Longman Companion to Slavery, Emancipation and Civil Rights,* 6.

92. *On Certain Passages in the Life of Sir John Hawkins, temp. Elizabeth. In a Letter from Captain W.H. Smyth, . . . Director of the Royal Geographical Society of London, &c. to Sir Henry Ellis, K.H., Secretary,* in *Archaeologia or, Miscellaneous Tracts Relating to Antiquity,* published by the Society of Antiquaries of London, vol. 33 (London: J. B. Nichols and Son, 1849), 205, emphasis added. Similar family crests featuring "negro heads" appeared, intriguingly enough, by at least the late fifteenth century, but that their meaning reflects participation in the slave trade, as with Hawkins, has been disputed. See Marika Sherwood, "Black People in Tudor England," *History Today* (Oct. 2003), 4.

93. Hall, *Things of Darkness,* 21.

94. Engel Sluiter, "New Light on the '20. and Odd Negroes' Arriving in Virginia, August 1619," *William and Mary Quarterly,* 3rd ser., 54 (1997): 396–98; John K. Thornton, "The African Experience of the '20. and Odd Negroes' Arriving in Virginia in 1619," *William and Mary Quarterly,* 3d ser., 55 (July 1998): 421–34; and John K. Thornton, *Angolans in the Early Dutch Atlantic, 1615–1650* (Cambridge: Cambridge University Press, forthcoming). See also Harmer, *Longman Companion to Slavery, Emancipation and Civil Rights,* 13–14.

95. Michael Wood, *Shakespeare* (New York: Basic Books, 2003), 251. Long ig-

nored, more and more evidence is emerging supporting Wood's conclusion, notably in parish records indicating that a number of the Africans or "Blackamoors" in Renaissance England were Christian. Among the records of St. Botolph's parish outside Aldgate, for instance, beginning especially in the 1590s, there appear numerous entries for the necessarily Christian burial of Elizabethan "blackamoores" such as "Easfanyyo a neagar servant," "Cassangoe A blacke A moore," and "A Negar whose name was suposed to be Francis . . . servant to Mr Peter Miller a beare brewer" (Wood, *Shakespeare*, 252). Likewise, Marika Sherwood has demonstrated, at "All Hallowes, Barking," in 1599, we find recorded the burial of "a blackamore servaunt to Jeronimo Lopez" and of "Mary a Negra at Richard Woodes," just as at "All Sayntes Stayninges Parish" a "Fardinando, a Blackmore" appears in the records in 1582. Not only were many among the English black population Christian, but some of them were undoubtedly free, as was a "Peter Negro" who received awards for his military service in 1546, knightship in September 1547, and an annuity until he died of the "sweating sickness" in 1551. On the other hand, there are numerous accounts of black women, such as the famous beauty "Lucy Negro," forced into working as prostitutes in London in the 1590s. Often, it seems to have been especially the nobility who had black servants or slaves, suggesting that such attendance was intended to enhance the status and power of the noble master. And so, Leicester's household accounts include awards "to the blackamore" in 1583 and 1584; and Raleigh had a black page (aged ten when he was baptized at St. Luke's in Kensington in 1597) as well as two adult male black servants. Sherwood, "Black People in Tudor England," 2.

96. George Best, *Discourse* (1578), in *The Principal Navigations, Voyages, Traffiques and Discoveries of the English Nation,* ed. Richard Hakluyt (New York: AMS, 1965), 7:262.

97. Jordan, *White over Black,* 60.

98. See Peter Fryer, *Staying Power: The History of Black People in Britain* (London: Pluto Press, 1984), 4–12.

99. *Tudor Royal Proclamations,* ed. Paul L. Hughes and James F. Larkin (New Haven: Yale University Press, 1969) 3:221n and 3:221–22; Errol Hill, *Shakespeare in Sable: A History of Black Actors* (Amherst: University of Massachusetts Press, 1984), 8; Walvin, *Black Presence,* 64.

100. Virginia Mason Vaughan, *Othello: A Contextual History* (Cambridge: Cambridge University Press, 1994), 58; emphasis added; Wood, *Shakespeare,* 251.

101. Harmer, *Longman Companion to Slavery, Emancipation and Civil Rights,* 10–11.

102. Donnan, *Documents Illustrative of the History of the Slave Trade to America,* 1:48.

103. Jordan, *White over Black,* 5, emphasis added. Jordan makes no connection to the blackface fool tradition in his work, but the evidence he cites supports its existence.

104. Gates, *Figures in Black,* 15.

105. Jordan, *White over Black,* 34.

106. Eldred Jones, *Othello's Countrymen: The African in English Renaissance Drama* (London: Oxford University Press, 1965), 23.

107. Here citing the 1611 edition: Johann Boemus, *The Manner, Lawes, and Customes of All Nations* (London: Eld and Burton, 1611), 49.

108. Jordan, *White over Black,* 26.

109. Harris, *Africans and Their History,* 7.

110. Davis, *Inhuman Bondage,* 189.

111. Davis, *Problem of Slavery in Western Culture,* 203, 67.

112. Ibid., 70–71.

113. *The Politics of Aristotle,* trans. Ernest Barker (Oxford: Clarendon Press, 1946), 13.

114. Ibid., 12.

115. Ibid., 16.

116. Davis, *Problem of Slavery in Western Culture,* 81; citing Philo Judaeus, *Quod Omnis Probus* 24 (London: Loeb Classical Library, 1941), 139–42.

117. Ibid., 81; citing Philo, 156–57.

118. Davis, "At the Heart of Slavery," in *In the Image of God: Religion, Moral Values, and Our Heritage of Slavery* (New Haven: Yale University Press, 2001), 123–36; Davis, *Problem of Slavery in Western Culture,* 14; Davis, *Inhuman Bondage,* 2–3, 32.

119. Philip D. Morgan, "British Encounters with Africans and African-Americans, circa 1600–1780," 174.

120. "Sambo," in *Encyclopedia of Southern Culture,* ed. Charles Reagan Wilson and William Ferris (Chapel Hill: University of North Carolina Press, 1989), 1141.

121. Joseph Boskin, *Sambo: The Rise and Demise of an American Jester* (New York: Oxford University Press, 1986), 38.

122. Edward Topsell, *The Historie of Four-Footed Beastes* (London, 1678), 3.

123. Ibid., emphasis added.

124. George M. Frederickson, *The Black Image in the White Mind: The Debate on Afro-American Character and Destiny, 1817–1914* (New York: Harper & Row, 1971), xi. Frederickson generally assumes that racism has no long history, as in his punning title, *Racism: A Short History.*

125. Anne McClintock, "Soft-Soaping Empire: Commodity Racism and Imperial Advertising," in *Travelers' Tales: Narratives of Home and Displacement,* ed. George Robertson et al. (New York: Routledge, 1994), 139.

126. Jordan, *White over Black,* 30.

127. Topsell, *Historie of Four-Footed Beastes,* 2, emphasis added.

128. See Southworth, *Fools and Jesters at the English Court,* 75, 121, 153; H. W. Janson, *Apes and Ape Lore in the Middle Ages and the Renaissance* (London: Warburg Institute, 1952), 211.

129. Paul C. Castagno, *The Early Commedia Dell'Arte (1550–1621): The Mannerist Context* (New York: Peter Lang, 1994), 192, 193.

130. Hall, *Things of Darkness,* 236.

131. See Donna Haraway, *Primate Visions: Gender, Race, and Nature in the World of Modern Science* (New York: Routledge, 1989), and Stephen Jay Gould, *The Mismeasure of Man* (New York: Norton, 1981), 113–45.

132. Janson, *Apes and Ape Lore in the Middle Ages and the Renaissance,* 199, 201–2.

133. Ibid., 212–14.

134. Ibid., 211.

135. Vaughan, *Performing Blackness on English Stages,* 23.

136. Frederickson, *The Black Image in the White Mind,* 73; emphasis added. See also William R. Stanton, *The Leopard's Spots: Scientific Attitudes Toward Race in America, 1815–1859* (Chicago: University of Chicago Press, 1960).

137. Gates, *Figures in Black,* 18–20; for Ignorance as unteachable, see the episode in *The Play of Wit and Science* in which he is depicted in a sort of language "lesson" (1. 452), parroting the vice Idleness, who "play[s] the schoolemystres" (1. 450). Here, Idleness attempts to teach Ignorance to say his own name, breaking it down syllable by syllable and prompting the fool, repeatedly, to say after her the sounds: "Ing-no-ran-hys." In the end, when asked what he has learned, Ingnorance can only reply, "Ich cannot tell" (1. 494).

138. Harris observes: "A collection of Jewish oral traditions in the Babylonian Talmud from the second to the sixth centuries holds that descendants of Ham were cursed by being black" (*Africans and Their History,* 5). See also D. Goldenberg, *The Curse of Ham,* and S. Haynes, *Noah's Curse.* On the English Renaissance tradition, see Scott Oldenberg, "The Riddle of Blackness in England's National Family Romance," *JEMCS* 1.1 (Spring/Summer 2001): 46–62.

139. Davis, *Inhuman Bondage,* 64–68, 187.

140. Best, *Discourse,* 7:261, 263–64, emphasis added. On the modern scientific understanding of the actual evolution of skin color in terms of the proximity of our ancestors to the Equator, the regulation of the body's reaction to sun rays, pigmentation, the making of vitamin D, and the like, see Nina G. Jablonski, *Skin: A Natural History* (Berkeley: University of California Press, 2006), 3, 6–7, 15, 37, 38, 58, 72, 75–85, 89–96, 117, 164, 186n. 2, 192n. 12, 198–99n. 15.

141. Ibid., 7:262, 264. For discussion of such, see Sujata Iyengar, *Shades of Difference: Mythologies of Skin Color in Early Modern England* (Philadelphia: University of Pennsylvania Press, 2005), 8.

142. William Strachey, *The Historie of Travell into Virginia Britania* (1612) (London: Hakluyt Society, 1953), 54–55.

143. See, for instance, Stephen R. Haynes, *Noah's Curse: The Biblical Justification of American Slavery* (Oxford: Oxford University Press, 2002), 24, 26, 29, 32, 32, 33, 87, 94, 95, 96, 97, 193. In the index to this work, "laughter" has more entries than any term under "Ham," except for "and dishonor." The third most relevant term in the index is "transgression." All of these terms are relevant in the natural fool tradition.

144. Linda Woodbridge, *The Scythe of Saturn: Shakespeare and Magical Thinking* (Urbana: University of Illinois Press, 1994), 21.

145. Natalie Zemon Davis, "Women on Top," in *Society and Culture in Early Modern France* (1965; repr., Stanford, CA: Stanford University Press, 1978), 179, 156; Woodbridge, *The Scythe of Saturn,* 21.

146. Charles Read Baskervill, *The Elizabethan Jig and Related Song Drama* (Chicago: University of Chicago Press, 1929), 315.

147. Barry Reay, *Popular Cultures in England, 1550–1750* (London: Longman, 1998), 134.

148. Twycross and Carpenter, *Masks and Masking,* 76, 85.

149. Kaiser, *Praisers of Folly,* 7.

150. Welsford, *The Fool: His Social and Literary History,* 55; Kaiser, *Praisers of Folly,* 129, 284.

151. Boskin, *Sambo,* 54.

152. Ibid., 97.

153. Ibid., 54–55.

154. Ibid., 66.

155. Ibid., 61; emphasis mine.

156. Ibid., 63.

157. Joseph Boskin, "The Life and Death of Sambo: Overview of an Historical Hang-Up," *Journal of Popular Culture* 4 (1971): 649.

158. Orlando Patterson, *Slavery and Social Death: A Comparative Study* (Cambridge, MA: Harvard University Press, 1982), 96, 299–333.

159. Boskin, *Sambo,* 35.

160. Ibid., 43.

161. Ibid., 7.

162. Ibid., 12.

163. Ibid., 10.

Moorish Dancing in *The Two Noble Kinsmen*

SUJATA IYENGAR

I₂ Shakespeare and Fletcher's *The Two Noble Kinsmen,* Gerald, a pedantic schoolmaster, badgers a dozen reluctant countrymen and women (including the crazed Jailer's Daughter as the Madwoman and a "bavian" or baboon, "with long tail and eke long tool [penis]" [3.5.131]), to perform a morris dance for the newly married Duke Theseus and his Amazon wife Hippolyta while they are out hunting.[1] The dance takes place immediately before Palamon and Arcite, the two noble kinsmen of the play's title, fall to blows over which one will marry Emilia, Hippolyta's sister. Emilia wishes to marry neither; one of the play's many ironies is that Emilia, "bride-habited, / But maiden-hearted" (5.1.150–51), would rather remain Diana's priestess and die a virgin.

Fletcher adapted the morris dance in *The Two Noble Kinsmen* from Beaumont and Fletcher's *Masque of the Inner Temple and Gray's Inn,* where it forms the second of two popular antimasques. Some critics and directors have interpreted the fact that the morris dance is a revival as proof that the entertainment is an unwelcome or last-minute interpolation in the play's action, an inappropriately lighthearted digression before the kinsmen begin a course of action that will end in defeat for one man and death for the other. But the dance itself takes place in act 3, scene 5, almost at the center of the play. Its position is highlighted by the significant thematic parallels between the dance and the play, notably the sustained metaphor of the morris (associations picked up by the most recent productions, as Potter and Waith observe).[2]

I want to suggest, however, some other ways in which the morris dance in *The Two Noble Kinsmen* functions within the play as an organizing trope for the frustrations of desire and of heterosexual marriage. In particular, I will argue that the supposed Moorish origin of English morris dancing allows Shakespeare to domesticate dark-skinned exoticism by incorporating it into rural English customs and traditions and Fletcher to employ figures of foreign femininity in the service of an emergent, court-centered, coterie feminism. Let me say at the outset that my claims about the collision of the domestic and the foreign owe more to the late Edward Said's definition of "Orientalism" than to more recent arguments of contemporary postcolonial criticism. That is to say, I am more interested here in the morris dance and the Moorishness that informs it as indices to anxieties within early modern England, rather than in uncovering the material conditions of Moorishness and Moorish dancers in England. There may be no original or authentic "Moorish dance," as it were, hiding behind the hybrid presentation that makes up the English morris. For both Fletcher and Shakespeare, as we shall see, the morris makes the strange familiar; the wild, tame; the antique, modern. Renaissance society uses Moorishness, I will argue, to trope geographical, temporal, and literary alterity *within* that culture. These anxieties circulate around nation-formation, in Shakespeare's case, around female autonomy and rank, in Fletcher's, and around the exoticism of the rural—especially of rural women—in their collaboration, *The Two Noble Kinsmen.* Finally, I suggest that as a collective, cross-cultural production, the morris dance in *The Two Noble Kinsmen* recalls both the collaboration of Shakespeare and Fletcher and the dialogue between *The Two Noble Kinsmen* and *A Midsummer Night's Dream.*

Douglas Bruster argues that during the Jacobean period a number of plays and masques figure rustic pastimes such as morris dancing as exotic and unfamiliar. He attributes this new exoticism in part to the influence of London, whose population was growing at an unprecedented rate. As economic historians such as Fernand Braudel and F. J. Fisher have documented, a significant number of the new London immigrants were country gentry who, "from either boredom or ambition, had abandoned their country seats for permanent residence in the town" (Fisher, 114). Bruster suggests that "The social integration that an Elizabethan tradition had imagined in the country is lacking in the plays of later dramatists like Beaumont and Fletcher, whose social visions are more aristocratic than folk" (155). He finds that Jacobean playwrights portray a greater distance between classes of people than in the Elizabethan era; for example, the mechanicals in Shakespeare's *A Midsummer Night's Dream* talk back to Theseus, while the Jailer's Daughter in Fletcher and Shakespeare's *Two Noble Kinsmen* exchanges not a word with him when she participates in a morris dance in his honor (159). By 1613, he argues, morris dancing and other rural pursuits would seem, like the Jailer's Daughter herself, to represent "the countryside and the Elizabethan past" (160). The Jailer's Daughter, he suggests, is isolated by her madness and by her cross-class desires, seen in the play as too different from her knightly lover to have a chance of success. Surely Bruster's hypothesis is correct. Comic accounts of rural revels in the Renaissance range from Will Kempe's self-conscious, autobiographical account of his morris-dance journey up and down the country in *Nine Dayes' Wonder* (1600) to the patronizing reminiscences of the author of *Old Meg of Hereford-shire, for a Mayd Marian: And*

Hereford Towne for a Morris-daunce (1609), yet both relations seem to suggest the increasingly staged theatricality of country matters.

This process of rendering the familiar exotic corresponds, I suggest, to a process of rendering the exotic familiar on the Jacobean stage, in a kind of chiasmus. Between Will Kempe's epic morris dance from Norwich to London in 1600 and the morris dance portrayed in Shakespeare and Fletcher's *The Two Noble Kinsmen* appeared many entertainments presenting "Moors" or foreigners, of all hues, including Jonson's *Masque of Blackness,* Shakespeare's *Othello,* the masque of *Solomon and Sheba,* and "A Mask of the Knights of India and China" (Harbage). The Jacobean interest in Africana was not limited to courtly audiences; both Middleton's *Triumphs of Truth* and Munday's *Chrysanaleia,* intended for Londoners of all classes, include Moorish kings.

Early in the seventeenth century, the morris dance is at once a quintessentially English tradition and a sharp encounter with the foreign. Will Kempe and the author of *Old Meg* both comment on the tanned skins of the village dancers, but in addition to their suntans, English morris dancers usually darkened their faces with soot, charcoal, or walnut juice. Most sources agree that the English morris dance derives its name from the Spanish *moresca,* or "Moorish dance." In Spain the dance is supposed to represent the encounter between Moors and Christians, and it retains this theme in its name (Moros y Cristianos);[3] Covarrubias's Spanish dictionary (1611) defines "Moriscos" as Moors who have converted to Christianity ("Moriscos. Los convertidos de moros a la Fe Católica"). Gamini Salgado has suggested that the Moorish dance travels to England with the Gypsies and that the dancers blacken their faces in imitation of Moors, but E. K. Chambers proposes that blacking up functions as a symbolic disguise, as do mummers' masks. Annette Drew-Bear connects the ancient practice of face-blackening to the "painted faces" that appear on the stage throughout the early modern period.[4]

Both Salgado's and Chambers's theories of the origin of face-blackening may be correct. Jane Garry agrees with Chambers that darkening the face originated as a village custom, but argues that the burgeoning seventeenth-century interest in Africa led to "court entertainment [that] was not ritualistic disguise but sophisticated charade" and to morris dancers who did indeed masquerade as Moors (224). And John Mason's *The Turke* (1610), which features "Cole black Moores / Dauncing their high Lavoltas to the Sun" (3.4, sig. Gv), proves, Garry argues, "an association between Moors and extravagant dancing" (224).

Thus Jacobean morris dance both alludes to foreign parts and nostalgically reminds the audience of the English folk traditions of medieval mumming and dancing around the Maypole; both the English rural past and recently encountered foreigners are emblems of the exotic. Linked to all kinds of sexual misdemeanors (as Philip Stubbes complains in his *Anatomie of Abuses*

[1585]), the dance usually, but not invariably, includes Robin Hood, Maid
Marian, and a hobbyhorse. It recalls the Mummer plays of St. George, who
fights not only a dragon but also, as in Richard Johnson's sixteenth-century
chapbook, "the black King of Morocco": in a reenactment of the Crusades,
the patron saint of England achieves sainthood in opposition to a pagan king.
Fletcher and Shakespeare engage with all these associations—nationality,
rank, and gender—in their treatments of the morris dance. In other words,
Shakespeare connects the morris dance to Englishness, while Fletcher uses
the dance to figure the struggle between men and women for power.

Alan Brissenden argues that Shakespeare generally uses the morris dance
as a symbol of Englishness, and that Shakespearean dance more largely
serves as a physical emblem of harmony. I want, however, to revisit Shakespeare's references to the dance to argue that the Shakespearean morris uses
the dance's foreign origins to assert a national English identity in the process
of formation. In the *Second Part of Henry VI,* York praises the "stubborn
Cade," the rebellious upstart pretending to the throne, whom he has seen
"caper upright like a wild Morisco, / Shaking the bloody darts as he his
bells" (3.1.360, 365–66). Cade, autochthonic English peasant, turns into a
savage Moor menacing England's kingly line as well as the epitome of native
rural strength and courage. The languid Dauphin of France in *Henry V* mistakenly equates the English love of the "Whitsun morris-dance," with military weakness, just as earlier he has sent Henry a chest of tennis balls in lieu
of treasure (2.4.25). Brissenden suggests that, in addition to jeering at the
English, "the French Prince is lampooning Henry by implying that he is no
more than a mock king in a summer festival" (10). *A Midsummer Night's
Dream,* a play I will discuss again later, uses the morris to trope issues of
gender imbalance and English native customs. The "nine men's morris [that]
is fill'd up with mud" in *A Midsummer Night's Dream* appears to be a common corruption of the name "nine men's morals," or "merelles," a traditional game played either outdoors or with marbles on a wooden board;
presumably the association with the morris came about because of the dancing, interwoven movement of the counters or participant during the game
(2.1.98). In this instance, fairy feuding has interfered with the very rural pastimes the sprites aim to protect. And an oblique reference to face-blackening
and the rites of May-dancing tropes racial difference and English whiteness
in act 3, as Kim Hall has pointed out. Lysander, under the influence of Puck's
mischief, reviles dark Hermia as "an Ethiop," a "tawny Tartar," and Hermia
in her turn traduces tall Helena as a "painted maypole" around which both
young men dance attendance (3.2.257, 263, 296).[5] Whiteness comes into
being through the language of skin color used to evoke its opposite, just as
Englishness comes to life through the activities that perform it. Finally, my
initial point that the morris in these plays evokes Englishness *through* its encounter with the foreign appears perhaps most clearly through an implicit

reference to the morris dance in Cleopatra's first grieving words on the death of Antony:

> O, wither'd is the garland of the war,
> The soldier's pole is fall'n! Young boys and girls
> Are level now with men.

(4.14.64–66)

"[T]he garland of the war" and the "soldier's pole" are the triumphal wreaths of battle borne on a lofty standard, but become in Cleopatra's mind the faded flowers girdling the Maypole after "young boys and girls" have ceased their dancing around it. Throughout Shakespeare's play Cleopatra is clearly and repeatedly identified with her kingdom, "Egypt," yet at the same time her language makes her as familiar, as English, as "the maid that milks/ And does the meanest chares" (4.14.74–75).

Shakespeare employs the morris in the history plays in order to blur the boundaries between English and foreign, but Fletcher employs the morris dance and the Maypole primarily as badges of female and political insurrection, and he figures morris-dancing women as a foreign or sunburned threat. In *The Woman's Prize, or The Tamer Tamed* (1613), his feminist response to Shakespeare's *The Taming of the Shrew,* Katharina, "a foole, / [Who] took a scurvy course," has died as a result of Petruchio's cruelty some time before the action of the play begins (1.2.140–41). Petruchio's feisty second wife, Maria, aided by her cousin Livia (her "Commander in chief") and her sister Byancha, devises "a new daunce . . . and a mad one," to tame Petruchio, the "fearfull . . . first breaker of wilde women . . . / and mold him into a babe again" (1.2.169–73). Having barricaded herself into their new home with enough supplies for a month, she refuses to consummate the marriage until Petruchio should meet her demands. When Petruchio and his male companions attempt to take the house by storm, an army of townswomen rallies to their sisters' defense.

So boisterous are these "Jennets," these rebellious females, complains Jaques, that they would "dare attempt the raysing / Against the soveraigne peace of Puritans, / A May-pole, and a Morris" (2.4.63–65). Jaques equates masculine control with Puritanism, and female rebellion with traditional country pleasures. A "jennet" is a horse; these women have taken the reins of the household into their own hands. One of these angry women, a "Tanners wife," is all the more terrifying because "all sun-burnt Barbary / Lyes in her breech" (2.4.47–48), with a punning association of "tanning" as a profession with dark skin or "sunburn." The tanner's wife is what we might call, adapting Patricia Parker's figure of the "literary fat lady," a "literary *tanned* lady," a female figure whose boundless disobedience can only be figured in corporeal vastness, a geographical metaphor, and dark skin.

"Breech" associates her with sexual impersonation ("wearing the breeches"), sexual incontinence, and sexual deviance, a "breach" of convention.

The reference to "Barbary" puns on the female name "Barbara" or "Barbary" and its etymological links to "barbarian," and associates the "Jennet" with a "Barbary horse." In addition, it suggests that the woman may be uncontrollably lustful. As Kim Hall notes, Leo Africanus's *Historie and Description of Africa* (translated by John Pory in 1600) criticizes the customs of "Barbary" because fathers "keep no recognizable control over their daughters' sexuality" before they are married (Hall, 33). Furthermore, complains Africanus, young men no sooner marry than they seek a new "paramour" (Pory D2r). According to Africanus, men and women in Barbary engage freely in premarital and adulterous sex. Shakespeare seizes upon these connotations of darkened female unruliness when Desdemona recalls her mother's "maid named Barbary" (*Othello*, 3.3.393) the night before her own death, when she is made "black" by Iago's calumnies and Othello's jealous fantasies (4.2.69).

In Pory's account, the African women merely accept their husbands' infidelities after marriage, but Fletcher's barbaric fat lady takes unruliness a step further: the tanner's wife and her colleagues chase down recalcitrant husbands and discipline them. To enforce this marital discipline, women co-opt other traditional English customs, like the play of Saint George and the dragon. In most versions of the legend, the dragon is male, and Saint George rescues a damsel who is menaced by it. The sexualized, male dragon in "An Excellent Ballad of St. George for England" is a kind of reptilian Bluebeard, consuming endless virgins until only the king's daughter remains. Petruchio's father-in-law fears, however, that Maria will effect a gender reversal. Instead of rescuing a woman from a dragon, Petruchio may be made to run like "Saint George at Kingston" from the "furious dragon" that Maria's father identifies as his daughter (*Woman's Prize*, 1.3.19–20). The woman who threatens Petruchio is the only one who can save him; Maria becomes both Saint George *and* the dragon, Petruchio, the damsel in distress.

Fletcher uses the morris dance and country entertainments as metaphors for the struggle between men and women for power. By the end of the play, Livia's newly chastened sweetheart, Rowland, calls their marriage "another morris" (5.4.66) that complements the dance begun by Maria and Petruchio. The men have rehabilitated the morris, or have *been* rehabilitated by it, depending on how one looks at it: either the men have taken over the imagery of the morris in the service of traditional marriage, or the morris has redefined the nature of marriage. The second explanation seems more likely. Whereas Jaques identified the Maypole and the morris dance as the work of "Jennets," opposed to the Puritan tendencies of their husbands, Rowland agrees to "dance" with Livia on equal terms, like those agreed upon by Maria and Petruchio.[6]

The source for the morris dance in *The Two Noble Kinsmen* is, as I have mentioned, Beaumont and Fletcher's *Masque of the Inner Temple and Gray's Inn,* performed by the King's Men in honor of the wedding of the Elector Palatine to Princess Elizabeth, daughter of King James, in February 1613. The masque proper celebrates the marriage of the Rhine with the Thames; the frame is a conflict between Jupiter and Juno over which of them should officiate at the wedding, a conflict that Jupiter wins when Juno "gives happy way/ To what is done in honour of the state." Their messengers, Mercury and Iris respectively, join the competition by vying with each other over which shall produce a better antimasque. Iris calls Mercury's dance of Naiades (water-nymphs) and Hyades (sky-nymphs) a "lifeless dance, which of one sex consists." Mercury responds by adding both male dancers and slapstick: blind Cupids, who collide with the other players, and stiff "Statuas" from the throne of Jove, who, robotlike, cannot keep the measure. Iris, still unimpressed, contends that the marriage must be "blessed with the love of the common people," and orders in a "rural company" consisting of "a Pedant, May-Lord, May-Lady; Servingman, Chambermaid; a Country Clown or Shepherd, Country Wench; an Host, Hostess; a He-Baboon, She-Baboon; a He-Fool, She-Fool." King James, with his taste for broad comedy, asked to see this antimasque, and the dance of the Statuas, once more, "but one of the Statuas by that time was undressed" (380), so he was disappointed.

The second antimasque of the "common people" is the morris dance that reappears in *The Two Noble Kinsmen;* the parallels between the masque and both *The Two Noble Kinsmen* and *A Midsummer Night's Dream,* the other Shakespeare play in which Theseus and Hippolyta appear, are immediately visible.[7] All three pieces dramatize the struggle for power between men and women, solved by the woman's eventual, reluctant capitulation to her spouse's will. In Beaumont and Fletcher's masque, Mercury introduces an all-female dance that proves unsatisfactory, even after the intervention of blind and clumsy Cupid. Jupiter wins a battle for supremacy over Juno in the masque just as Oberon and Titania fight for custody of the "lovely boy stolen from an Indian King" in *A Midsummer Night's Dream* (2.1.22) and in both their Shakespearean incarnations Theseus and Hippolyta have a martial, rather than marital, history.[8] Theseus boasts in *A Midsummer Night's Dream:* "Hippolyta, I woo'd thee with my sword, / And won thy love doing thee injuries" (1.1.16–17), and one of the queens whose impassioned pleas open *The Two Noble Kinsmen* reiterates his claim to Hippolyta:

> Bound to uphold creation in that honour
> First Nature styled it in, [Theseus] shrunk thee into

> The bound thou wast o'erflowing, at once subduing
> Thy force and thy affection.

$$(1.1.82–85)$$

Love between men and women is especially associated with the morris in the subplot that is an addition to the Chaucerian source: the story of the Jailer's Daughter, her unrequited love for Palamon, and her subsequent madness. Palamon cries defiantly, "I'll make ye a new morris!" when the jailer threatens to "clap more irons" upon him, fancying his manacles tinkling like the bells the dancers wear upon their wrists and ankles (2.2.274, 276). The Jailer's Daughter continues this image in her soliloquies, after she lets Palamon escape from prison, remembering his "iron bracelets" and worrying lest "the jingling of his gyves / Might call fell things to listen" (3.3.14–15). After Palamon deserts her and she runs mad, she comes across the rural company waiting to perform for Theseus, and participates in their morris dance, since their own female fool has gone missing. The remaining female dancers include "little Luce with the white legs, and bouncing Barbery," another reminder of the contrast between light and dark and the Englishing of foreign customs that the dance entails (3.5.27).

When the morris dancers find the Jailer's Daughter, she is singing two catches that further connect the dance and its bells with foreign exoticism and with frustrated female desire. First she imagines a ship landing "from the coast of Barbary-a" (3.5.61), second, she imagines three fools deciding how to classify an "owlet" or young owl:

> The one he said it was an owl,
> The other he said nay,
> The third he said it was a hawk,
> And her bells were cut away.

$$(3.5.69–72)$$

To cut off a hawk's bells sets her free from human control but also removes the feature that makes her recognizable as a hawk, rather than as an owl or any other bird. In the same way, the madness of the Jailer's Daughter allows her to speak of her love for Palamon but removes her identity as "Jailer's Daughter"; the countrymen see her only as "a dainty madwoman," limited to her function as she-fool in the dance. Like the hawk, she requires bells to identify her, since the bells are a traditional attribute of the fool. Her relentless emphasis upon the tinkling bells ties her thematically to Jephthah's daughter, that other young girl who greets her father with timbrels and dancing and flies to the mountains to mourn her virginity before she must die (Judges 11:1–2).[9] Unlike Jephthah's daughter, however, the Jailer's Daughter survives to marry her old and stalwart wooer, her dower a wedding gift from Palamon.

The madness of the Jailer's Daughter allows the morris dance within the play to go ahead. Before she appears, the dancers complain that the "scurvy hilding," "Cicely, the seamstress' daughter" has failed to arrive (3.5.43, 45), but when they hear a report of "a dainty madwoman" (73), they rejoice: "A madwoman? We are made, boys!" (77). The mad/made pun makes it clear that these countrymen plan on using the Jailer's Daughter to make money (Bruster, 159), but it also ironizes the practice of presenting morris dances onstage; just as the countrymen will profit from the Jailer's Daughter, so Shakespeare and Fletcher profit from the portrayal of country dances in the theater.

The dance carefully reinforces the social hierarchies of its audience; Gerald describes his "rout" in order of the rank that each peasant is playing, moving from the "Lord" and "Lady" through the domestic servants to the comfortable Host and his wife, the country clown, the madwoman, and finally the beast. Each of these characters is less associated with civilization and more strongly with the wilderness than the one before. The Lord and Lady are served by the Chambermaid and Servingman in a country house; the Host maintains a tavern on a country road; the Clown tends sheep or cattle in the field, the Fool wanders and the Bavian lives altogether in the wild.

There are twelve players in the original dance, but the Schoolmaster mentions only nine by name.[10] Bachinger offers us a different structural parallel when she suggests that "the pairing of the main characters," although present in the source and in other romances, "might be thought of as another Morris Dance analogue in the main play: Theseus and Hippolyta, Palamon and Emilia, Arcite and the Keeper's Daughter form three pairs of matched sexualities, or six dancers. And the combat for Emilia has another Morris Dance formation: three pairs of knights plus Arcite and Palamon." (35). Bachinger's helpful insight emphasizes the play's ritual aspects and the interchangeability of Palamon and Arcite, who seem to exchange places in Emilia's affection just as morris dancers change partners.

Gerald introduces the dance with a strange riddle:

> We are a merry rout, or else a rabble,
> Or company, or, by a figure, chorus,
> That fore thy dignity will dance a morris.
>
> .   .   .   .
> And, dainty Duke . . .
>   . . . help me, thy poor well-willer,
> And with thy twinkling eyes, look right and straight
> Upon this mighty "Morr" (of mickle weight)—
> "Is" now comes in, which being glued together,
> Makes "Morris," and the cause that we came hither
>
>   (3.5.105–19)

The solution to the riddle is "morris," made by combining "Morr" (Moor) with "is." *OED* gives "is" as an alternative spelling for "ice." Most modern editions retain the Folio spelling "morr" and "is"; the Regents editor treats it as a purely verbal riddle rather than an emblematic show (Proudfoot), but the Riverside suggests that perhaps at this point someone brought in an emblem of a "moor" or the word "morr" written out and then another board bearing the syllable "is," to make "morris." Another possibility, and one that seems likely, from the Schoolmaster's emphasis on the "mighty morr," is that he gestures toward two members of the troupe, one habited like a Moor and the other dressed as Winter (Bawcutt). Lois Potter, the play's most recent editor, suggests that the players brought in a Moorish guy, stuffed with straw and paper, like the giant figures carried at the Midsummer Watch; since the figures often bore legends, she suggests, the giant might have carried a label reading "Is," or have made "some sort of hissing sound" (Potter, 359). The 1987 Royal Shakespeare Company production included both villagers who carried letters spelling out the word "morris" (Potter, 359) and a dancer garbed as an Indian Moor in turban and flowing robes.[11]

The Schoolmaster may even be blacked up himself, since he describes himself and his dancers' sport as "rude, and raw, and muddy." "Muddy" begins from the late sixteenth-century onward to carry not just its earlier sense of moral slackness but also "muddled" or unclear thinking, and "dark-colored."[12] *OED* lists Shakespeare's usage in *A Midsummer Night's Dream* as the first example of "muddy," meaning "Not clear or pure in color" (4a); just before Lysander calls Hermia an "Ethiop," Demetrius rhapsodizes that "Crystal is muddy" next to Helena's eyes (3.2.137–39).

If the combination of "moor" and "ice" is correct, the riddle becomes a strange reversal of a tradition that associates Moors or Ethiopians with the sunshine and heat. (Although some early modern writers make a distinction between warlike "white" Moors, savage "blackamoors," and Christian "Ethiops," they frequently use the terms interchangeably.) Since a rich body of critical work over the past decade (by Kim Hall, Joyce Green MacDonald, Arthur Little, and Mary Floyd-Wilson, among others) has addressed these associations of Moorishness, heat, and intensity, and I myself have done so elsewhere, I need revisit them only briefly here. In Shakespeare's *Pericles* the first prince to woo the princess Thaïsa bears upon his shield the image of an Ethiop reaching toward the sun with the motto, "Lux tua vita mihi" (Your light is life to me) (1.2.21). The shield alludes to a cluster of myths associating Ethiopians with the heat of the sun, including the story of Phaëthon, who insisted that he be allowed to drive his father Phœbus's chariot across the sky to prove he was in truth the child of the sun god. Unable to control the sun's fiery horses, however, he veered off the path, burning the Ethiopians black and freezing the poles of the earth, and was ultimately destroyed by Jupiter's thunderbolts when the goddess Ceres begged for aid. As Golding puts it in his translation of book 2 of the *Metamorphoses:*

> The Æthiopians at that time (as men for truth upholde)
> (By reason that their blud was drawne foorth to the outer part
> And there bescorched) did becomme ay after blacke and swart.

> (fol. 20)

The Prince of Morocco in *The Merchant of Venice* wears "the shadowed livery of the burnished sun" (2.1.2). When Cleopatra bids Antony, "Think on me, that am with Phœbus' amorous pinches black, /And wrinkled deep in time" (1.5.29), she refers not only to climatological theories about blackness as a hereditary quality induced by the sun's rays, but also to a body of classical literature suggesting that the action of the sun's fierce heat on the rivers Nile and Niger was responsible for generating life and that the first human beings came into existence in sub-Saharan Africa, "deep in time." Jonson refers to this idea in his *Masque of Blacknesse,* where he describes the daughters of Niger as "first form'd dames of earth" of the river, noting: "[i]t is a conjecture of the old Ethnicks, that they, which dwell under the South, were the first begotten of the earth" (l. 138 note m). And he again associates this primal generation of life with the revivifying rays of the sun.

Palamon refers directly to the myth of Phaëthon in his prayer to Venus before the final battle, when he suggests that her "flames [are] hotter" than those of Phœbus: "the heavenly fires / Did scorch his mortal son, thine him" (5.1.91–92). Gerald's riddle, however, reverses the tradition associating Moors with the sun and with heat, but maintains the associations of Moorishness with excess or surfeit. "Morris" is also "more is": the Schoolmaster's emphasis on the immensity of his "Moor," "this *mighty* 'Morr' of mickle weight" is otherwise unaccountable. The bawdy presence of the "bavian, with long tail and eke long tool" fits into this pattern of excess, while Gerald's earnest warnings that the baboon should bear himself with decency only launch him further into realms of sexual innuendo:

> My friend, carry your tail without offence
> Or scandal to the ladies; and be sure
> You tumble with audacity and manhood,
> And when you bark, do it with judgement.

> (3.5.35–38)

"Tumblers" or acrobats occasionally appeared in morris dances, and the quibble on sexual "tumbling" or falling contributed to the dance's reputation as an excuse for ribaldry. The baboon "barks" because, as Edward Topsell notes in his *Historie of Foure-Footed Beastes,* baboons were called "Cynocephalus," "dog-headed," because they resembled men with dog's heads.

They were thought to exhibit exceptional lasciviousness toward human women; Topsell recounts an anecdote of a baboon at the French court who "above all loved the companie of women, and young maidens," and whose "genitall member was greater then might match the quantity of his other parts" (11). Anatomist Helkiah Crooke, arguing in *Microcosmographia* (1615) that an enlarged prostate gland in man, ape, monkey, or bull indicates satyriasis, similarly proves his point by adducing "the great Baboons which were heere to be seene among vs; for they would in a maner offer violence euen to a woman. It is therefore a very wicked and inhumane thing for Gentlewomen to cherish them in their bosoms yea in their beds, as I haue seene some doe with mine owne eies" (T3). Topsell's illustration of the baboon depicts an animal whose "tail" and "tool" are indeed alike; the one is a mirror image of the other (11).

Although the baboon's unusual presence in this morris dance is directly quoted from the *Masque of the Inner Temple,* in the context of Gerald's punning introduction, it is difficult to avoid associating the baboon's "long tool" with the seventeenth-century equation of Moors or Africans with libidinous apes endowed with hypertrophied sexual organs.[13] In the appendix to his cosmetic ethnography *Anthropometamorphosis* (1653), John Bulwer introduces into his text the myth of excessive black virility and bestiality, comparing the English fashion for large and unwieldy codpieces to the genital organs of dark-skinned races: "Those filthy and Apish Breeches, that so openly shew'd our secret parts, with the vaine and unprofitable modell of a member, which we may not so much as name with modesty . . . was the shadowed imitation of the reall bulke of the great Privy Membred Guineans" (4A3). He ascribes the erstwhile popularity of the codpiece to Englishmen's desire to match the "reall bulke" of the men of Guinea, or the penis-sheath of "the Indians of . . . La Trinidad." The word "Apish" here primarily evokes the idea of mimicry, but with a twist: the "ape" derives its name from its imitation of human beings, but here, Bulwer implies, humans of various origins are imitating the genital displays of apes.

Both the bavian's "long tool" and the Jailer's Daughter's fantasies participate in these fantasies of male sexual potency. After the dance her father finds her wandering the countryside, and she fantasizes a Palamon of legendary sexual prowess, who will ride a horse that can

> dance the morris at twenty mile an hour,
> And that will founder the best hobby-horse,
> And gallops to the tune of "Light o' Love."

> (5.2.51–54)

"Hobby-horse" is of course a euphemism for "prostitute" and a stock property of the morris dance, although it seems to have been, famously, "forgot" by Shakespeare's time (Ringler, 185). Bachinger plausibly reads the Jailer's Daughter as a symbolic "hobby-horse" in the play, regarding the morris dance as a "bisexual" spectacle and the Jailer's Daughter as the representative of a pagan or uninhibited sexuality.

The Jailer's Daughter reportedly imagines "a hundred black eyed maids, that love as I do," dancing an "antic" for Palamon's sake before the Duke (4.1.72, 75). "Antic" picks up the associations between the ancient or "antique" morris dance and the "antics" of madness (Potter, 359). In her own voice, she describes the innumerable offspring fantastically fathered by Palamon:

> There is at least two hundred now with child by him—
> There must be four; . . .
>   . . . and all these must be boys—
> He has the trick on't—and at ten years old
> They must be all gelt for musicians,
> And sing the wars of Theseus.
>
> (128–33)

"This is strange," as one of her father's friends remarks (133); first, why should Palamon bring forth men-children only, and second, why should the boys become castrati? Bruster suggests that her remark reflects anxieties about "what it meant culturally to have boys play women on the stage" (164) and the boy-actor's impotence in the Jacobean theater. The very act of creating so many eunuchs, he argues, removes the possibility of self-representation from "real jailer's daughters," in contrast to the real morris dance, offstage, which might at least present the possibility of employing women (although Bruster himself concedes that Maid Marian was often played by a cross-dressed man [165; see also Pilling]). More usefully, perhaps, we can hear in the Jailer's Daughter's words a reminder that history is written by the winners. She emphasizes Theseus's courtly control over the *ways* in which boys will be allowed to represent his encounter with self-sufficient women, the Amazons.[14]

Palamon's "brown" skin associates him with heat and thus explains his surplus of boys: according to Renaissance theories of sexual reproduction, male children were conceived at a higher temperature than females. He prizes his association with the heat of Venus, the fire of love, rather than the heat of Mars, the blaze of battle that Arcite prefers (4.2.42; 5.1.91–92, op. cit.). As for the hypothetical boys' fantastic castration, perhaps the Jailer's Daughter imagines that these children must pay for the philandering of their father and for his battle with Theseus by becoming not only eunuchs but Theseus's minstrels. Perhaps she is also remembering Gerald's parting wish for Theseus's hunting party to catch a fine stag "and the ladies eat his dowsets," that is,

munch on his testicles, and figuring these unborn boyish multitudes, like herself, as wild wandering forest prey (3.6.156). Perhaps she is even recalling
the lustful baboon and associating two different kinds of sexual surgery,
gelding and circumcision: after all, Topsell wonders, "it is most true (though
strange) that [baboons] are brought forth circumcised, at the least wise in
some appearance; whereunto the Priestes give great heede to accomplish and
finish the work begun" (11).

But the Jailer's Daughter does not find her lover after her trials. Her stalwart Wooer tells us that he finds her singing over and over again,

> Palamon is gone,
> Is gone to th'wood to gather mulberries;
> I'll find him out tomorrow.

$$\text{(4.1.67–69)}$$

To go a-mulberrying is to play truant, like Shakespeare's Prince Hal playing
"the micher [to] eat blackberries" (*1 Henry IV,* 2.4.408). More ominously,
when Chaucer's Pardoner claims that he cares only for gold, not for the souls
of his parishioners, "[t]hough that hir soules goon a-blakeberyed," to go for-
aging for berries is to consign oneself to perdition (line 406). The substitution
of mulberries for blackberries in the Jailer's Daughter's speech perhaps refers
to the mulberry tree's emblematic significance as the tree of wise folly (so
linked because of its name, *morus,* the fool). Alciati's Emblem 210 argues
that the mulberry tree is wrongly named *morus* in Greek because in postpon-
ing its blooming until winter is over, it proves itself not foolish but wise.[15]

More directly, Palamon's mulberrying alludes to a story that Shakespeare
rewrites three times in his career and that prominently features a mulberry
tree: the star-crossed lovers, Pyramus and Thisbe. In *Romeo and Juliet,* Pyramus and Thisbe's cross-purposes lead to tragedy; in *Midsummer Night's
Dream,* the mechanicals' play-within-a-play retells the tale as farce; in *The
Two Noble Kinsmen,* the Jailer's Daughter's involuntary casting as Thisbe
strands her uncomfortably on the border of tragedy and comedy.[16] In his 1632
commentary on the mulberry tree in that myth, George Sandys feminizes and
personifies the tree as an emblem of wisely husbanded virginity: "the Mul-
bery knowing the frost for her enemy, will not sprout till it be utterly subdued
by a more certaine temper" (157). The Jailer's Daughter shares a similar philosophy equating sanity with virginity and folly with sexual availability: "To
marry [Palamon] is hopeless; / To be his whore is witless" (2.4.4–5). In so
doing she paradoxically proves herself a wise fool again, having successfully
predicted her own insanity. When she finds herself ready to become Palamon's whore, she indeed loses her wits, becoming literally *besotted* and par-
ticipating in what is not just in a morris dance but also in a *morus* dance or

fool's dance (an association heightened by Gerald's rhyming "morris" with "chorus" in his introduction to the performance).

The broad comedy of the dance takes on a cast of pathos, just as the technically comic resolution to the subplot (presumably the marriage of the Jailer's Daughter to her old Wooer) conveys instead a wistful sadness. As Bruster points out, even when the Jailer's Daughter agrees to marry her old Wooer, convinced in her madness that he is Palamon, "what is literally her final word in the play responds to pain" (169):

> *Jailer's Daughter.*   And shall we kiss too?
> *Wooer.* A hundred times.
> *Jailer's Daughter.*   And twenty.
> *Wooer.*   Ay, and twenty.
> *Jailer's Daughter.* And then we'll sleep together.
> *Doctor.* [*to Wooer*]   Take her offer.
> *Wooer.* [*to Daughter*] Yes, marry, will we.
> *Jailer's Daughter.*   But you shall not hurt me.
> *Wooer.* I will not, sweet.
> *Jailer's Daughter.*   If you do, love, I'll cry.
>
> (5.2.108–12)

Realizing her wish is equivalent to realizing her fears. As she consents to the marriage, she gives up what little control she has over her own destiny, moving from an imperative ("you shall not") to a conditional ("if you do"), which assumes that her lover will break his vow and force her tears.

The failure of the Jailer's Daughter to find and cherish Palamon emphasizes the inability of romantic love to satisfy women in the play. Perhaps the failings of conventional romantic love explain why the "moor" who introduces the morris dance is coupled not with fire but ice. The play celebrates chastity, not fertility, and within *The Two Noble Kinsmen* there exists an awareness of the paradox of "hot ice and wondrous strange snow" (*Midsummer Night's Dream*, 5.1.58). Whenever "ice" is mentioned elsewhere in the play, it is coupled with its opposite, fire or heat. One of the queens who begs for Theseus's help fears that her words have been too cold, "Set down in ice, which by hot grief uncandied / Melts into drops" (*Two Noble Kinsmen*, 1.1.107–8). Palamon, disillusioned with the rampant corruption in Thebes and resolved to leave, pities

> such most,
> That sweating in an honourable toil,
> Are paid with ice to cool 'em.
>
> (1.2.32–34)

When Arcite returns to Athens in disguise to be near Emilia, his "fiery mind" and "his virtue, like a hidden sun, / Break through his baser garments"; he

shall therefore not "Freeze in [his] saddle" (2.5.22–24, 48). The Jailer's
Daughter in her madness pictures lords and courtiers who have got maids
with child languishing in hell: "in fire up to the navel and in ice up to
th'heart, and there th'offending part burns and the deceiving part freezes"
(4.3.43–45).

Palamon and Arcite are themselves examples of the lustful courtiers who
deserve this Dantean punishment, if we are to believe their bawdy badinage
when they boast of having made the Lord Steward's daughter and the marshal's sister, "a pretty brown wench," "play o'th' virginals," and "groan a
month for't—/ Or two or three or ten" (3.3.39, 34, 35–36). Many editors take
this exchange, in conjunction with Palamon's later, inconsistent denial of any
such escapades when he prays to Venus, as proof of two different and careless
hands at work (Waith, 20), although Donald K. Hedrick argues that this exchange fuels the competitive and collaborative anxieties in the play. Yet figuring Palamon and Arcite as lustful hypocrites seems in no way out of
keeping with its jaded tone.

The trope of "fire and ice" is of course Petrarchan, evoking the sufferings
of the lover who burns with desire yet cannot thaw his icy mistress, as in
Sonnet 134, "I burne, yet freeze withall" (I quote Thomas Watson's *Hecatompathia,* Sonnet 40), or Sonnet 145, in Surrey's version, "Set me wheras
the sonne doth p[a]rche the grene, / Or whear his beames may not dissolue
the ise." It can also evoke the contrast between hot youth and chill age; the
astonished author of *Old Meg* wonders at the elderly morris dancers, "[w]hat
man would not wonder to see fire strucke out of yce?" (B1v). And William
Drummond's adaptation of Petrarch's Sonnet 145 adds a racial element lacking in Petrarch's original or Surrey's translation:

> Place mee where angry *Titan* burnes the *More,*
> And thirstie *Africke* firie Monsters brings,
>
> . . . .
> Place mee where *Neptunes* Quire of *Syrens* sings,
> Or where (made hoarse through Cold) he leaues to roare.
>
> (Sonnet 40)

Angry Titan burns the *more* fiercely in order to burn black the *Moor;* thirsty
Africa's drought cannot be quenched by the creatures generated on the banks
of the Nile by the sun's heat. At the other extreme, the poles either give voice
to Neptune's loudly whistling breakers, or silence them by freezing them into
the stillness of the iceberg. Drummond explicitly racializes the Petrarchan
image in just the way, I have been arguing, *The Two Noble Kinsmen* implicitly associates it with racial and ethnic othering. The "Morr" who introduces
the morris dance functions as a metonym for the burning heat of the sun and
of erotic desire. The "ise" that accompanies him is, however, neither melted

by his heat nor able to cool his warmth. Instead, each cancels out the other, just as the kinsmen's prayers are at once successful and doomed.

Palamon implicitly conjures up the contrasts of fire and ice, youth and age, fair and dark—when he prays to Venus for victory in love, and emphasizes love's madness rather than its beauty. Evoking the world of fabliau rather than of romance, his choicest example of Venus's grace is the May–December story of "a man of eighty winters . . . who/A lass of fourteen brided":

> This anatomy
> Had by his young fair fere a boy, and I
> Believed it was his, for she swore it was,
> And who would not believe her?
>
> (5.1.107–8, 115–18)

His example reverses the genders of an icy mistress and a burning lover and the associations of "fair" skin (emphasized by the near-homonym, "fere") with chastity.

Even the queen, Hippolyta, recognizes that marriage necessitates the surrender of power; the very name Shakespeare gives her, a back-formation from that of her son Hippolytus, rather than the usual "Antiope," evokes her tragic future history, as Kathryn Schwarz has discussed.[17] When Hippolyta scolds Emilia, who has said she is sure she shall not "love any that's called man," the rebuke is more like a concession:

> If I were ripe for your persuasion, you
> Have said enough to shake me from the arm
> Of the all-noble Theseus.
>
> (1.3.85; 91–93)

The world that Emilia has been evoking is the realm of female friendship and equal power. Emilia's nostalgic recollections of her childhood friend Flavina and "the true love between maid and maid" (1.3.81) recall Helena's famous paean to female friendship in *A Midsummer Night's Dream:*

> . . . we grew together,
> Like to a double cherry, seeming parted,
> But yet an union in partition,
> Two lovely berries moulded on one stem.
>
> (3.2.209–11)

But *The Two Noble Kinsmen* recollects this image in a very different context. The Queen, who begs Theseus to avenge her husband without delay in the very first scene of the play, argues that if he waits until his honeymoon,

>   . . . when
> [Hippolyta's] twinning cherries shall their sweetness fall
> Upon thy tasteful lips, what wilt thou think
> Of rotten kings or blubbered queens?
>
>   (1.1.177–80)

Since *The Two Noble Kinsmen* is so concerned with the ironies of enforced heterosexual coupling, the image of the twinning cherries seems to be a revision of the earlier motif that is deliberately grotesque in its juxtaposition of "sweetness" and "tasteful" with "rotten" and "blubbered." We face the ironic recognition that even in the earlier play the shafts of unrequited love very soon part the "double cherry." Laurie Shannon argues that female friendship in *The Two Noble Kinsmen* creates an alternative to the model of tyrannical authority and subordination offered by both marriage and royal prerogative: "friendship gendered female appears to extraordinary effect, linking marriage and tyranny and intensifying the otherwise familiar disapprobation the play registers toward absolute (or unreasoning, unbounded, 'tyrannical') power" (98). In particular, she argues, the construction of chastity as an alternative to marriage allows Emilia and Hippolyta, both Amazons, to voice a critique of "not only tyrannical or coercive marriage, but also tyranny in its plain political sense" (102).[18]

We can also read this forsaken world of maid and maid as a revision of *A Midsummer Night's Dream,* in which Theseus offers Hermia a lifetime of celibacy as a nun instead of the forced marriage propounded by her father Egeus. And I find in the scene with the three kneeling queens—which those critics who still wish to divide up the authorship of *The Two Noble Kinsmen* routinely assign to Shakespeare—a recollection of the show of kneeling female solidarity at the end of *Measure for Measure.* In *A Midsummer Night's Dream,* the resolution of romantic comedy reasserts the power of heterosexual marriage and of Duke Theseus; in the problem play, the women's demonstration of unity only ambiguously reestablishes the desirability of (re)productive, heterosexual marriage and the power of the returned Duke.[19] In *The Two Noble Kinsmen,* Fletcher's voice, and the generic shift from comedy to tragicomedy, offer a critique of martial, masculine rule through a court-centered feminism that comes into being through collaborations and commixtures: the joined labor of the playwrights, the forced labor of the Jailer's Daughter, the yoking of fabliau and romance, and the appearance of Moors (and madwomen) in the English countryside.

Notes

1. I would like to thank Douglas Bruster, Susan Cerasano, and Fran Teague for helpful comments on earlier versions of this essay. All references to the works of

Shakespeare come from the *Riverside Shakespeare* unless otherwise noted. All references to the works of Chaucer come from the *Riverside Chaucer* unless otherwise noted. All references to *The Two Noble Kinsmen* come from Lois Potter's Arden3 edition unless otherwise noted. Most scholarship on the play has addressed the question of authorship, which is one reason why I do not do so here. Eugene Waith's Oxford edition and Lois Potter's Arden3 edition provide useful summaries of the authorship dispute in their introductions (Waith, 4–23; Potter, 6–34). Waith, however, argues that the two styles of Shakespeare and Fletcher can easily be distinguished throughout, where Potter prefers to "refrain from identifying the assumed author of each scene" because of her belief that the final draft of the play was revised by Shakespeare (Potter, 34). In addition, Waith dismisses out of hand Donald Hedrick's theory that the non-Fletcherian parts of the play were composed by Nathan Field, while Potter rejects Hedrick's claim that Shakespeare wrote *none* of the non-Fletcherian parts but concedes that Field "had something to do with" the play (Potter, 33). I have preferred to follow Potter's example and to treat the play as a true collaboration whose seams or inconsistencies can easily be ironed out in performance.

2. There is a rich and helpful secondary literature on early modern dance and dancing. On dancing in general, or dancing and disorder, see Skiles Howard, Bevington and Holbrook, Brissenden, and Sorrell. On specific scenes and dances, see Cohen, Jenkins, and Morris. On the relationship between the term "masque" and dancing in Shakespeare and Fletcher, see Gossett. And for a popular overview and some whimsical illustrations of the dances most frequently alluded to in Shakespeare's plays, see Hoskins.

3. I thank Edmund Campos for this reference and for his account of the dance in Mexico.

4. On the Gypsies and Gypsy dances in England, see Salgado; for Chambers's argument that the morris represents a version of the European sword dance, see *The Medieval Stage*, 1:195–204. On the dance's relationship to other folk festivals, see Chambers, *The English Folk-Play*; and Laroque's compendious volume, passim. On St. George, see Chambers, *Folk-Play*, esp. 170–85.

5. Kim Hall, introduction to *Things of Darkness*.

6. Molly Easo Smith writes, "As in Shakespeare, the central images of the world-upside-down and the woman-on-top in *The Woman's Prize* derive from popular cultural activities such as the charivari; but unlike the conventional charivari or skimmington, as it was known in England, which purported to teach women their place in the ordained hierarchy and men how to impose such order, Fletcher's play targets male tyranny and expectations" (55–56).

7. On the parallels between *Two Noble Kinsmen* and the *Masque of the Inner Temple,* see Blincoe, who argues that *Two Noble Kinsmen* takes the form of a "court marriage masque."

8. On the "Indian boy" and "race" within *A Midsummer Night's Dream,* see Raman's *Framing 'India,'* Hendricks's "'Obscured by Dreams,'" and Parker's forthcoming Arden edition of the play.

9. All scriptural quotations appear in the Geneva Bible unless otherwise noted within the text.

10. Pilling suggests melodies and steps that might have been used in the performance.

11. Potter reproduces an illustration (358).

12. I thank Margo Hendricks for bringing this meaning of the word to my attention.

13. On this connection, see also Fryer, 133–46; Jordan, 24–36; and Hall, "Mr. Moores Revels."

14. On Amazons, see Schwarz, especially her epilogue (236–38).

15. On the complex typological and verbal associations between the Latin "mora," meaning "delay," "morus," meaning mulberry tree, "morus," a fool, and the words "moral" and "mural" in English, see Patricia Parker's forthcoming Arden edition of *A Midsummer Night's Dream.*

16. I owe this insight to a thoughtful question from Patricia Parker.

17. Schwarz, chapter 6.

18. Jo Eldridge Carney connects the ambiguous status of love and marriage within the play to that of war and to Jacobean England's ambivalent feelings toward "peacetime policies" (106): "love is both destructive and irresistible, war is both annihilating and attractive" (105).

19. Verna Foster argues that Shakespeare's "problem plays" are in fact tragicomedies, which she defines as plays that "enabled dramatists to explore the frontiers of known sexual reality" (311).

Works Cited

Alciati, Andrea. *Andrea Alciati Emblemata cum Commentariis.* Patavii, 1621.

Bachinger, Katharina. "Maidenheads and Mayhem: A Morris-Dance Reading of William Shakespeare's and John Fletcher's *The Two Noble Kinsmen.*" In *English Language and Literature: Positions and Dispositions,* edited by James Hogg, Karl Hubmayer, and Dorothea Steiner, 23–38. Salzburg: Institut für Anglistik und Amerikanistik, 1990.

Bawcutt, N. W., ed. *The Two Noble Kinsmen.* By John Fletcher and William Shakespeare. Harmondsworth, Middlesex: Penguin, 1977.

Beaumont, Francis, and John Fletcher. "The Masque of the Inner Temple and Gray's Inn." In *Complete Works of Beaumont and Fletcher,* edited by Alexander Dyce, 377–82. Boston: Phillips, Sampson, 1854.

Bevington, David, and Peter Holbrook, eds. *The Politics of the Stuart Court Masque.* Cambridge: Cambridge University Press, 1999.

Blincoe, Noel R. "The Analogous Qualities of *The Two Noble Kinsmen* and *Masque of The Inner Temple and Grey's Inn.*" *Notes and Queries* 43.2 (1996): 168.

Brissenden, Alan. "Shakespeare and the Morris." *Review of English Studies* 30.117 (1979): 1–11.

Bruster, Douglas. *Quoting Shakespeare: Form and Culture in Early Modern Drama.* Lincoln: University of Nebraska Press, 2000.

Bulwer, John. *Anthropometamorphosis: Man Transform'd, or The Artificiall Changling.* London, 1653.

Carney, Jo Eldridge. "The Ambiguities of Love and War in *The Two Noble Kinsmen.*" In Levin and Robertson, 95–112.

Chambers, E. K. *The English Folk-Play.* Oxford: Clarendon, 1933.

———. *The Medieval Stage.* Vol. 1. Oxford: Clarendon, 1903.

Chaucer, Geoffrey. *The Riverside Chaucer.* Edited by Larry D. Benson. Boston: Houghton Mifflin, 1987.

Cohen, Selma Jeanne. "Dance Images of Shakespeare's Characters." In *Images of Shakespeare: Proceedings of the Third Congress of the International Shakespeare Association, 1986,* 276–81. Newark: University of Delaware Press / London and Toronto: Associated University Presses, 1988.

Covarrubias, Sebastián de. *Tesoro de la Lengua Castellana.* 1611. Repr., Madrid: Turner D. L., 1979.

Crooke, Helkiah. [*Microcosmographia*]: *A Description of the Body of Man.* London, 1615.

D'Amico, Jack, ed. and introd. *Petrarch in England: An Anthology of Parallel Texts from Wyatt to Milton.* Ravenna: Longo Editore, 1979.

Drummond, William. "Place mee where Angry Titan burnes the More." In D'Amico, 109–10.

Fisher, F. J. *London and the English Economy, 1500–1700.* London: Hambledon, 1990.

Fletcher, John. *The Woman's Prize, or The Tamer Tamed.* Vol. 4 of *The Complete Works of Beaumont and Fletcher,* edited by Fredson Bowers. Cambridge: Cambridge University Press, 1979.

Floyd-Wilson, Mary. "Temperature, Temperance, and Racial Difference in Ben Jonson's *The Masque of Blackness.*" *ELR* 28 (1998): 183–209.

———. "Transmigrations: Crossing Regional and Gender Boundaries in *Antony and Cleopatra.*" In *Enacting Gender on the Renaissance Stage,* edited by Viviana Comensoli and Anne Russell, 73–96. Chicago: University of Illinois Press, 1999.

Foster, Verna A. "Sex Averted or Converted: Sexuality and Tragicomic Genre in the Plays of Fletcher." *SEL* 32.2 (1992): 311–22.

Fryer, Peter. *Staying Power.* London: Pluto, 1984.

Garry, Jane. "The Literary History of the Morris." *Folklore* 94 (1983): 219–28.

Golding, Arthur, trans. *The XV Bookes of P. Ovidius Naso, Entytuled Metemorphosis.* London, 1575.

Greenhill, Pauline. "On the Whiteness of Morris: An Illumination of Canadian Folklore." *Canadian Folk Music Bulletin* 28.3 (1994): 16–20.

Gossett, Suzanne. "The Term 'Masque' in Shakespeare and Fletcher, and *The Coxcomb.*" *SEL* 14.2 (1974): 285–95.

Hall, Kim F. *Things of Darkness: Economies of Race and Gender in Early Modern England.* Ithaca: Cornell University Press, 1996.

———. "'Troubling Doubles': Apes, Africans and Blackface in *Mr. Moores Revels.*" In MacDonald, 120–44.

Harbage, Alfred, and Samuel Schoenbaum. *Annals of English Drama.* London: Routledge, 1989.

Hedrick, Donald K. "'Be Rough With Me': The Collaborative Arenas in *The Two Noble Kinsmen.*" In *Shakespeare, Fletcher and* The Two Noble Kinsmen, edited by Charles Frey. Columbia: University of Missouri Press, 1989.

Hendricks, Margo. "'Obscured by Dreams': Race, Empire, and Shakespeare's *A Midsummer Night's Dream.*" *Shakespeare Quarterly* 47 (1996): 37–60.

Hoskins, Jim. *The Dances of Shakespeare.* New York: Routledge, 2005.

Howard, Skiles. *The Politics of Courtly Dancing in Early Modern England.* Amherst: University of Massachusetts Press, 1998.

Jenkins, Harold. "The Ball Scene in *Much Ado About Nothing.*" In *Shakespeare: Text, Language, Criticism: Essays in Honour of Marvin Spevack,* edited by Bernhard Fabian and Kurt Tetzeli von Rosador, 98–117. New York: Olms-Weidmann, 1987.

Johnson, Richard. *The Famous Historie of the Seaven Champions of Christendom.* London, 1596–97.

Jonson, Benjamin. *The Masque of Blackness* [1605]. In *Ben Jonson: The Complete Masques.* Edited by Stephen Orgel, 47–60. New Haven: Yale University Press, 1969.

Jordan, Winthrop. *White over Black.* Chapel Hill: Inst. of Early American History and Culture/University of North Carolina Press, 1968.

Kempe, William. *Kempe's Nine Days Wonder.* London, 1600.

Levin, Carole, and Robertson, Karen, eds. *Sexuality and Politics in Renaissance Drama.* Studies in Renaissance Literature 10. Lewiston, NY: Mellen, 1991.

Little, Arthur L., Jr. *Shakespeare Jungle Fever: National-Imperial Re-Visions of Race, Rape and Sacrifice.* Stanford, CA: Stanford University Press, 2000.

MacDonald, Joyce Green. "'The Force of Imagination': The Subject of Blackness in Shakespeare, Jonson, and Ravenscroft." In *Renaissance Papers: Selected Papers from the Southeastern Renaissance Conference* (1991), edited by George Walton Williams and Barbara J. Baines, 53–74. [N.p.]: Southeastern Renaissance Conference, 1992.

———, ed. *Race, Ethnicity and Power in the Renaissance.* London: Associated University Presses, 1997.

Mason, John. *The Turke: A Worthie Tragedie.* London, 1610.

Morris, Harry. "The Dance-of-Death Motif in Shakespeare." *Papers on Language and Literature: A Journal for Scholars and Critics of Language and Literature* 20.1 (1984): 15–28.

Munday, Anthony. *Chrysanaleia: The Golden Fishing, or Honour of Fishmongers.* London, 1616. Repr., New York: Readex Microprint, 1953.

Old Meg of Hereford-shire, for a Mayd Marian: And Hereford Towne for a Morris-daunce; or Twelve Morris-Dancers in Hereford-shire, of twelve hundred yeares old. London, 1609.

Parker, Patricia. "Literary Fat Ladies and the Generation of Text." In *Literary Fat Ladies: Rhetoric, Gender, Property,* 8–36. London: Methuen, 1987.

———. "Teaching and Wordplay: The 'Wall' of *A Midsummer Night's Dream.*" In *Teaching with Shakespeare: Critics in the Classroom,* edited by Bruce McIver and Ruth Stevenson. Newark: University of Delaware Press / Associated University Presses, 1994.

Pilling, Julian. "The Wild Morisco or the Historical Morris." *English Dance and Song* 46.1 (1984): 26–29.

Pory, John, trans. *The History and Description of Africa, by Leo Africanus.* London, 1600.

Potter, Lois, ed. *The Two Noble Kinsmen.* By John Fletcher and William Shakespeare.

Proudfoot, Richard, ed. *The Two Noble Kinsmen.* By William Shakespeare. Regents Renaissance Drama Series. Lincoln: University of Nebraska Press, 1970.

Raman, Shankar. *Framing "India": The Colonial Imaginary in Early Modern Culture.* Stanford, CA: Stanford University Press, 2002.

Ringler, William. "The Hobby Horse is Forgot." *Shakespeare Quarterly* 4 (1953): 185.

Salgado, Gamini. *The Elizabethan Underworld.* London: Dent, 1977.

Sandys, George. *Ovid's Metamorphosis Englished, Mythologiz'd, And Represented in Figures.* London, 1632.

Schwarz, Kathryn. *Tough Love: Amazon Encounters in the English Renaissance.* Durham, NC: Duke University Press, 2000.

Shakespeare, William. *The Riverside Shakespeare.* Edited by G. Blakemore Evans et al. 2nd ed. Boston: Houghton Mifflin, 1997.

Shakespeare, William, and John Fletcher. *The Two Noble Kinsmen.* Edited by Lois Potter. Arden Shakespeare. Third series. N.p.: Thomas Nelson, 1997.

Shannon, Laurie J. *Sovereign Amity: Figures of Friendship in Shakespearean Contexts.* Chicago: University of Chicago Press, 2002.

Smith, Molly Easo. "John Fletcher's Response to the Gender Debate: *The Woman's Prize* and *The Taming of the Shrew." Papers on Language and Literature* 31.1 (1995): 38–60.

Sorell, Walter. "Shakespeare and the Dance." *Shakespeare Quarterly* 8 (1957): 367–84.

Stubbes, Philip. *The Anatomie of Abuses.* London, 1585.

Surrey, Henry Howard. "Set me wheras the sonne dothe perche the grene." In D'Amico, 107.

Topsell, Edward. *The Historie of Foure-Footed Beasts.* London, 1607.

Waith, Eugene, ed. *The Two Noble Kinsmen.* Oxford Shakespeare. Oxford: Clarendon, 1989.

Watson, Thomas. Sonnet 40. *Hecatompathia.* In D'Amico, 91.

Wickham, Glynne. "*The Two Noble Kinsmen,* or *A Midsummer Night's Dream, Part II?" Elizabethan Theatre* 7 (1980): 167–96.

Articles

Ophelia's "Old Lauds": Madness and Hagiography in *Hamlet*

ALISON A. CHAPMAN

RECENT scholarship on *Hamlet* has established the degree to which this play raises questions about early modern religion. Of course, the presence of a ghost seemingly straight out of purgatory has always put the play's theological cards on the table, as it were, but scholars such as Ramie Targoff, Heather Hirschfeld, Stephen Greenblatt, John Freeman, Jennifer Rust and others have further explored the ways in which the play echoes and queries a range of contemporary theological debates.[1] A survey of this body of modern *Hamlet* scholarship, however, reveals that critics have attached the play's religious questions almost exclusively to the character of Hamlet. Admittedly, Hamlet gives voice to many of the most suggestively theological utterances of the play, as when he alludes to the Diet of Worms or fearfully imagines the "undiscover'd country" awaiting us all after death.[2] And yet Shakespeare does not limit himself to using Hamlet's character when he probes religious questions, for as I will argue here, Ophelia's ravings also display a complex awareness of England's medieval Catholic past.[3] Her descent into grief and madness is marked by a surge of allusions to medieval Catholic forms of piety: St. James, St. Charity, "old lauds," pilgrimage to the shrine of Our Lady of Walsingham, and other pre-Reformation religious folklore.

Despite modern contentions to the contrary, Ophelia's network of religious allusions does not conflict with the sexualized nature of her madness.[4] The critical tendency is to see her erotomania as somehow necessarily excluding or disabling religious allusions, a view epitomized in editorial responses to the "snatches of old lauds" that Ophelia sings at her death (4.7.176). The word "lauds" appears only in the Second Quarto (the Folio reads "old tunes"), and as Harold Jenkins, editor of the Arden, notes, some editors have objected to the idea of Ophelia as singing hymns of praise "as incompatible with her earlier love-songs."[5] The assumption here seems to be that since mad Ophelia has been manifestly thinking about sex, she cannot therefore also be thinking about religion. Such reasoning, however, mistakenly imposes a modern understanding of sex and religion as separate categories onto an early modern worldview that saw them as profoundly connected.[6] From an early modern Protestant viewpoint, Ophelia's mingling of eroticism and Catholicism makes sense: it comes as no surprise that a woman who slides into a debased (i.e., eroticized) madness should simultaneously give voice to a debased (i.e., Catholic) series of religious utterances.[7] Ophelia's allusions to both medieval Catholicism and to sexual activity may allow such a derogatory reading, but this is not the interpretation to which the play seems most wedded. While Ophelia's religious references are sometimes contradictory and cannot be assembled into a coherent, stable whole (she is mad, after all), most of them raise resonant questions about the position of women in England's religious past and thus about the relationship between sexuality and sanctity. Furthermore, they seem charged with nostalgia, and since Ophelia herself dies a sympathetic character, we should not dismiss her "old lauds" as simply the spurious ravings of a madwoman. Ophelia seems to resort to old forms of piety precisely because they offer some solace in her personal wasteland. By showing Ophelia's emotional and imaginative landscape scattered with the debris of old doctrines and ritual practices, Shakespeare uses her final madness to reflect on the costs—especially to women—of the English Reformation.[8]

As Gertrude recounts, Ophelia drowns while "chanting snatches of old lauds / As one incapable of her own distress" (4.7.176–77), and this description suggests that a bygone Catholic form of piety informs her final moments. Although "laud" can be a generic noun denoting any song or hymn of praise, it was typically used in a religious context. Furthermore, it carried specifically Catholic associations. Lauds referred to the morning service in the monastic divine office when participants sang praises to God. Psalms 148, 149, and 150 concluded the service, and the frequency of the word "laudate" in these psalms lent the office its name. Gertrude specifies that Ophelia is "chanting" these lauds, and the religious and especially monastic associations of this verb raise a dark irony: Hamlet, in act 3, commands, "Get thee to a nunnery" (3.1.121), and Ophelia later dies intoning the very chants most associated with nunneries. This suggestion that Ophelia, at the moment of her death, imaginatively inhabits a nunnery is consistent with the other religious allusions that inform Ophelia's ravings, which I will trace below. Pre-Reformation women facing a personal devastation similar to Ophelia's may well have taken refuge in a nearby nunnery and there found solace in a female community devoted to prayer and good works. The tragic irony of the play is that while Hamlet would have Ophelia enter a convent as a means to escape the terrible pressures of Elsinore, this option is not available for her.[9] Many of Shakespeare's plays allude to women entering convents. For example, Theseus in *Midsummer Night's Dream* offers Hermia the option of wearing "the livery of a nun . . . in shady cloister mewed," and the friar in *Much Ado* says that Hero can be concealed "In some reclusive and religious life."[10] These plays, like *Measure for Measure,* ultimately turn away from the con-

ventual life and show their female characters in social (and marital) circulation rather than in the cloister.[11] *Hamlet* similarly forecloses the idea of the
convent but in a more bitterly painful way. Ophelia's marriage crisis is not
resolved comically, unlike Hero's, Hermia's, or Isabella's, and in a further
bleak twist, the putative refuge that Hamlet imagines ("Go thy ways to a nunnery" [3.1.130]) is not, finally, representable on the English Renaissance
stage. With her avenues to both marriage and the female community of a
cloister blocked, Ophelia seems to fall by default into madness. Instead of
reciting lauds in the company of nuns, Ophelia must voice them alone, and
instead of the echoing space of the medieval nunnery, Ophelia sings her lauds
beneath the "hoary leaves" of an old willow (4.7.166).

Ophelia's "old lauds" raise difficult questions: Does Shakespeare invite us
to censure Ophelia for resorting to such suspect forms of Catholic piety? Or
does he invite us to censure a world that has driven her to such extremes and
in which she can only voice such forms of piety in mad isolation and at the
moment of death? Does Ophelia reject Protestant forms of belief because she
is deranged or because they offer her less solace than do the lauds of a bygone religious world? Shakespeare does not provide unambiguous answers,
and Ophelia's end remains susceptible to various readings. Through Protestant eyes, the "old lauds" that allow her to surrender so willingly to death
are brutally deceptive, giving only false assurances of salvation: who but a
madwoman would take recourse to such misguided forms of piety? On the
other hand, although Ophelia's seemingly Catholic death accords well with
Protestant expectations, it simultaneously thwarts them. Gertrude's description suggests that Ophelia's "snatches of old lauds" are indicative of one
"incapable of her own distress," or insensible of her impending death. Her
wording, however, also allows the reading that the "old lauds" help to make
her "incapable" of fear. That is, even as her sodden garments "Pull'd the
poor wretch from her melodious lay / To muddy death" (ll. 181–82), this
same "melodious lay"—a fragment of medieval liturgical practice—has spiritually supported her and provided her with peace and comfort. The fact that
Ophelia dies with such old lauds on her lips invites us to look more closely
at the other religious allusions that fill her madness.

In the middle of her first mad scene, Ophelia abruptly pronounces, "They
say the owl was a baker's daughter" (4.5.42–43), and, like the old lauds she
sings at her death, the folkloric story she seizes on here to express her personal anguish and insanity is deeply expressive of a lost world of medieval
piety. Ophelia refers to a popular tale in which Christ enters a baker's shop
and asks for some bread. The baker's daughter decides that a very small piece
of bread will be ample and puts a bit of dough into the oven to cook. When
it miraculously begins to swell to enormous size, she cries out "heugh,
heugh" in surprise, and because of this owl-like noise and her wicked lack
of generosity, Christ transforms her into an owl.[12] Since this story features

the tragic fate of a daughter, it resonates generally with Ophelia's own circumstances, and the baker's daughter transformed into an owl resembles
Ophelia transformed by madness. This story is characteristic of medieval religion not only in what the Reformation would later deem its superstitious,
extrabiblical element (especially the girl's transmogrification) but also in its
anachronistic depiction of Christ walking into what seems to be a medieval
European shop. This aspect of the story thus recalls medieval paintings of
the apostles dressed as fourteenth-century noblemen or of the Annunciation
occuring in a European-style manor. The development of humanist and especially Protestant historiography in the sixteenth century disabled such visions
by creating a more acute sense of historical progression, one that emphasized
the distance and the difference between the past and the present.[13] Folkloric
scenes like the story of the baker's daughter were shown to be untenable, and
Ophelia's prefatory tag—"*They say* the owl was a baker's daughter" (emphasis added)—may register her flickering awareness that such forms of belief were no longer considered legitimate.

Exposing the fiction of the baker's daughter story, however, also meant
dismantling the fantasy that a Christian in any century or from any nation
could encounter Jesus in his or her own home, that the Savior might walk
into one's own storefront and ask for a bite to eat. The Reformation shifted
the idea of this kind of personal encounter onto strictly spiritual terrain: all
believers could talk to Christ daily in prayer and could witness his providence
at work in their hearts, but they could no longer meet him over a bakery
counter. The tale of the baker's daughter, in contrast, makes the encouter a
very material one, and in this sense, it typifies the "commitment to the partic-
ularity of religious experience" that Gail McMurray Gibson sees as characteristic of fifteenth-century piety.[14] This is not a transcendent vision of Jesus
enthroned in glory, reaching down from heaven to the human soul. Instead,
a very real Christ enters the store, and he is hungry. The scene tacitly asks
listeners to imagine the sound of the door closing behind him, the look of his
dusty clothes, and the smells of the warm bakery. Medieval Catholics were
well aware of the metaphorical nature of this story, but Protestants seeking to
purge the vestiges of popish superstition from English devotional practice
were quick to read such tales as reflecting a simpler, more literal view of the
relations between heaven and earth. Although Protestantism may have gained
in theological coherence by working to debunk such stories, it simultaneously
diminished the possibility of God's concrete presence on earth. The story
may not end happily for the stingy girl, but it is a comforting tale in that it
allows a literal reading in which Jesus really enters an English bake shop. In
her study of Richard Hooker and Lancelot Andrewes, Debora Shuger observes that for Protestant thinkers, the central problem of faith was not an
awareness of one's own sin but instead an awareness of God's absence.[15] Perhaps because of such a pervasive sense of being separated from God, possibly

divorced from his love, Hooker and Andrewes, in Shuger's view, cling all the more to the materiality of the Eucharist. Hooker's "graphically physical" account of how the communicant participates in the host "seems driven by feelings of forsakenness and distance" with "the longing for contact being proportional to the terror of abandonment."[16] Ophelia's reference to the baker's daughter can be read as a similar "longing for contact." Of course, for her, the absentee is not just the Protestant God but also her dead father. In effect, the earthly father's physical absence impels her imaginatively into a bygone world in which the spiritual Father is more physically present. Ophelia's subsequent meting out of flowers, each one representing a separate virtue or vice, also participates in this clinging to physical, material traces of larger, intangible concepts. In a world where grace itself often seems frighteningly unknowable, she instead holds a columbine, an "herb of grace" (4.5.180), and where divine faithfulness is perhaps unsure, she can have a material substitute in the allegorical faithfulness of violets (1. 182).

The question of God's presence or absence on earth was epitomized in the early modern Eucharistic controversies, and Ophelia's allusion to the baker's daughter invokes this complex issue. Doctrinal positions on this question ranged widely from the Catholic Church's doctrine of transubstantiation, to Luther's slightly more guarded view of Christ's real presence in the elements, to the sacramentarian views held by Calvin. The story of the baker's daughter, like these Eucharistic debates, turns on the association between Christ and bread. As in the Communion ceremony, the interaction between the girl and Jesus is mediated through the piece of bread, and had she charitably given him a large piece of bread, he would have, in return, given her generously of the spiritual bread of life. Although the medieval story does not challenge the identification between Christ and the bread in the way that later Reformation debates would, Ophelia's use of it pressures the relationship between spirit and material substance. Ophelia's next comment tightens the connection between the anecdote of the baker's daughter and the doctrinal problem of Christ's presence: "Lord, we know what we are, but know not what we may be. God be at your table" (4.5.43–44). The question of "what we may be" echoes other passages in the play that question what happens after death, both to the spirit and to the body. Hamlet, for example, imagines the body of a king passing through the guts of a beggar, a passage that Stephen Greenblatt argues is an allusion to the Eucharist in which the body of a heavenly king, transubstantiated at that altar, moves through the digestive tract.[17] Ophelia's blessing, "God be at your table," rachets up the Eucharistic associations implicit in the story of the baker's daughter. This phrase occurs nowhere else in Shakespeare's works. Unlike more common religious expressions such as "Zounds" or "Marry" or even Ophelia's earlier benediction "good dild you" at line 42 (a conventional corruption of "God yield [i.e., protect, reward] you"), this anomalous phrase has not been emptied of

spiritual meaning through overuse. Ophelia moves from a generalized blessing (may God yield you), through the anecdote of baker's daughter, to a specific wish for God's presence at table. Since "table" in early modern usage
could refer specifically to the Communion table, Ophelia's benediction supports two readings. Her phrase is simultaneously a generalized hope that the
dining table will be full of food and the joyful sense of God's love, and it
also offers a specific hope that God will be literally present at the holy table.
Indeed, Ophelia's phrase, if rendered as a question, neatly sums up the entire
Eucharistic controversy: to what degree was God, in fact, present at the table?

In addition to invoking contemporary questions about the Eucharist and
the nature of divine presence, the story of the baker's daughter also recalls
the difficult choice of religious allegiances that men and women faced in the
early years of the Reformation, a choice that was often simultaneously a marriage choice. In this story, Christ not only asks the girl for physical food to
allay his hunger but also presents her with a spiritual call. Since this is a male
Christ making a request of a presumably marriageable young girl, the story
has overtones of marriage—not an earthly marriage between a man and a
woman but a spiritual union between the human soul and God. In the Bible,
a man's request for food or water from a young woman is often symbolically
linked to marriage. In Genesis 24, Abraham's servant goes to the city of
Nahor in Mesopotamia, and he has been told by his master that the woman
who draws water for him at the well will marry Isaac. Thus, the servant's
request for water is primarily a symbolic request for Rebekah to become
Isaac's wife and thereby the mother of the Israelite nation. Similarly, Christ
asks a Samaritan woman for a drink of water in John 4, and this request is a
prelude to a discussion of her five husbands and her current adulterous liaison. In asking her for a drink, Christ tacitly calls her to forsake her fallen
sexual congress and accept instead the spiritual marriage he offers. This vision of the conversion process as a marriage call widely informed medieval
piety. As Peter Brown observes, the apostles were frequently seen as calling
wives out of their husbands' beds and drawing women out of normal sexual
traffic.[18] In the baker's daughter anecdote, when Christ enters the store and
asks for food from the daughter working the oven, he presents her simultaneously with a difficult choice: marry Christ or marry the world. In failing to
meet Christ's need for bread, she has also rejected his offer of spiritual union,
and thus she becomes transformed into an owl, a bird associated with darkness and evil.

The baker's daughter's symbolic choice of the world of the father over the
world of the Father may well have acquired particular urgency during the
Reformation. Donald Kelley observes that the early Reformation witnessed
an unprecedented number of children defying parental authority and choosing Protestantism over the family's traditional faith: "The massive defection
of sons and daughters was surely one of the fundamental elements of histori-

cal change in this period."[19] Debora Shuger points out that this religious and generational divide often manifested itself in the question of marriage, for young men and women often opted for partners that their parents found unacceptable on religious grounds.[20] As if the basic question of whether to conform to parental wishes were not difficult enough, the Protestant Reformation raised the ante: now the marriage question could also be a spiritual question, and a marriage decision could also be a public declaration of religious loyalties. Of course, by the time Shakespeare wrote *Hamlet* around 1600, this situation was not as acute a dilemma in England, for Protestantism had proved its dominance over the past decades. However, *Hamlet* features what Stephen Greenblatt calls the "fifty-year effect," in which Shakespeare foregrounds and queries practices of half a century earlier, such as the doctrine of purgatory.[21] This fifty-year effect also characterizes Shakespeare's probing of the painful intersection of marriage and religion in a world where Protestantism and Catholicism were colliding. Both the abolition of purgatory and the pressures of marriage in an increasingly Protestant world placed midcentury women and men in a similar predicament: what to do when the growing religion of the present entails a repudiation of the loyalties of the past?

The story of the baker's daughter and the marriage dilemmas faced by young men and especially women during the rise of English Protestantism give us a new vantage point from which to think about Ophelia's own choices. Circumstances have, in effect, forced her to choose between loyalty to Hamlet and loyalty to her father. Polonius seems gratified that she has chosen daughterly submission, for he boasts that she has "in obedience" handed over Hamlet's letter and "given to mine ear" the story of Hamlet's other "solicitings" (2.2.124, 127, 125). In act 3, Ophelia appears to think that cooperating with her father will help Hamlet's madness and thus secure her future marriage. What she cannot predict is the fact that Hamlet will read that choice of loyalties as an unforgiveable rejection of him ("Are you honest?" he asks, implying that her obedience to her father entails sexual promiscuity [3.1.103]), nor can she know that the choice to submit to her father will only intensify the tragedy of the play. The 3.1 "nunnery scene" has powerful religious overtones. Ophelia, for instance, holds a book which makes her a stereotypical image of female piety (Renaissance audiences would have seen countless images of the Annunciation in which Mary sits book in hand), and upon seeing her, Hamlet asks that she remember his sins in her "orisons," or prayers (3.1.89). Specifically, Ophelia's choice to obey her father echoes the decision that many Catholic young women must have made at midcentury when faced with a Protestant suitor. Shakespeare presents a young man associated with Wittenberg who courts a young woman. She, however, ultimately bends to her father's wishes, and returns the young man's letters; then, in a scene of passionate, angry dismissal, the young man tells her she had best join a nunnery. It is hard not to see in this scenario an echo of the tragic familial and romantic fractures all too common in midcentury England. Hamlet seems to overreact to her filial obedience, characterizing it as moral corruption instead of laudable daughterly submission. The historical parallels here invite readers to think about the response of Protestant suitors who, when faced with female loyalty to the old faith, resorted to denunciation and vilification.

This is not to suggest that Polonius and Ophelia should be read as actual recusants and that Ophelia, in preferring her father's wishes over Hamlet's, has in effect preferred Catholicism over Protestantism. This play has no such allegorical leanings, and Ophelia is not a female version of the the Red Crosse Knight forced to pick between Una/Protestantism and Duessa/Catholicism. Shakespeare instead uses English religious history as a means to represent a character's personal dilemma and vice versa. The example of the Ghost is instructive here. In showing Hamlet encountering a specter seemingly right out of purgatory, Shakespeare uses a kind of doctrinal vocabulary as a means to depict more vividly Hamlet's personal grief. And that very personal grief simultaneously becomes a vehicle to think through larger questions of how the abolition of purgatory disabled the ongoing relationship between the living and the dead. Similarly, Ophelia's personal tragedy becomes all the more compelling and complex through its resonances with the tumult of England's religious history.

Mapping Ophelia's predicament onto the situation of midcentury marriages only throws into relief the painful impossibility of both. Ophelia's choice to obey her father compromises her future, but choosing to disobey her father would scarcely be any better in a world that valued daughterly obedience. Early modern men and women forced to choose between loyalty to a father and allegiance to the new religion were in a similar no-win situation. If we think about Ophelia's dilemma as resembling the midcentury marriage situation, then Shakespeare seems to present a guardedly sympathetic view of those forced to make the hard choices. The story of the baker's daughter is the story of a young woman who, faced with a young man, chose the traditional world of the father over the radical options the young man Christ offers. Hers is also a disastrously wrong choice. The fact that Ophelia, in her final madness, alludes to the baker's daughter suggests that she may sense in retrospect that she, too, has chosen wrongly. Just as the baker's daughter's choices result in her transformation into an owl, Ophelia has, however blamelessly or however much a result of impossible circumstances, taken a course that ends in madness and the "maimed rites" due to a suicide (5.1.212). Early modern men and especially women may have looked back at the conservative marriage choices made in the middle of the sixteenth century and realized, in a now dominantly Protestant world, that they too made the wrong choice and their culture now literally damned them for it.

Only a few lines after her reference to the baker's daughter, Ophelia turns to another fragment of the medieval Catholic past, and this allusion raises questions about the relationship between female sexuality and sanctity. Where the baker's daughter chooses, in effect, not to become a bride of Christ, Ophelia alludes to a saint who made exactly the opposite choice: St. Charity. The second stanza of this second song begins with the oath "By Gis and by Saint Charity" (4.5.58). "Gis" is a common mincing of "Jesus," but the reference to St. Charity appears nowhere else in Shakespeare's works. Although Jenkins asserts that there is no saint by this name, the most popular of all medieval hagiographies does, in fact, contain a St. Charity. In his *Golden Legend,* Jacobus de Voragine recounts that St. Charity was one of three daughters to a mother named Sophia, or Wisdom, and not surprisingly, her two sisters are named Faith and Hope.[22] Richard Verstegan borrowed Jacobus's account for his 1606 "Trivmphe of Feminyne Saintes" in *Odes in Imitation of the Seaven Penitential Psalmes.* Verstegan praises the saints *"Fides* and *Spes* and *Charitas,* / Borne of *Sophia* sage" who, for their faith, "Were whipped, thrust in boyling pitche / And hedded [beheaded] afterward."[23] Whether or not there was a St. Charity, the *OED* notes that charity was often personified in the period, and Jenkins argues that although "by Saint Charity" does not actually refer to a saint, it was "often used in oaths as if it were."[24]

Swearing by St. Charity seems to have been particularly associated with Catholics. For example, in *The Troublesome Raigne of John, King of England* (1591), the First Friar begs "Sweete S. *Withold* of thy lenitie, defend vs from extremetie / And heare vs for S. *Charitie,* oppressed with austeritie."[25] In the May eclogue of the *Shepheardes Calender* (1579), the dissembling fox who represents Catholic rapacity disguises himself as a poor peddler and, to win a credulous young goat's sympathy, falls down as if in pain, crying, "Ah dear Lord, and sweet Saint Charitee."[26] In glossing this oath, E. K. notes, "The Catholiques comen othe [common oath], and onely speache, to haue charitye alwayes in their mouth, and sometime in their outward Actions, but neuer inwardly in fayth and godly zeale."[27] If, as E. K. suggests, calling on St. Charity was a characteristically Catholic practice, then Ophelia's oath— which can seem so innocuous to modern ears—may have been more fraught with meaning for early modern audiences. For these listeners, it probably came as no surprise that a woman who swore by St. Charity should also allude to other forms of old Catholic piety and die singing old lauds.

St. Charity epitomizes the same problem raised by the story of the baker's daughter: to what degree can the sacred be understood as materially present? Just as the Reformation responded to the baker's daughter story by scoffing at the idea that Jesus could literally walk into one's shop, so too Protestants saw Charity as strictly an abstract virtue, not a real person. Edmund Spenser's treatment of Charity in *The Faerie Queene* seems to turn on this issue. In book 1's House of Holiness, Spenser features the three daughters of Caelia:

Speranza, Fidelia, and Charissa. As an actual character who meets, talks with, and assists Red Crosse, Charissa—like St. Charity—is a real presence in the narrative. As an allegorical representation of one of the three theological virtues, however, she simultaneously epitomizes charity's absence from the concrete world of things. A similar allegorical impulse probably gave rise to Charity's medieval legend since there is no historical evidence for a flesh-and-blood St. Charity. The medieval Catholic response was to imagine Charity as a real saint, located in a specific historical era and suffering unique bodily torments as a result of her faith.[28] Protestants, in contrast, preferred the idea of charity over such hagiographic embodiments. E. K.'s critique of the Catholic oath "by Saint Charity" is unintentionally ironic: a glossator of markedly Protestant sympathies, who thus regards charity primarily as an abstract virtue, accuses Catholics (who had the option of regarding the saint as an actual person) of draining all the substance out of Charity.

Ophelia's oath "by Saint Charity" is reminiscent of Hamlet's earlier oath "Yes by Saint Patrick" (1.5.143) after first meeting the Ghost. Both oaths raise the question of to what degree the saints—and by extension the things of the spirit—can substantively inhabit the earth. Ophelia's oath "by Saint Charity" is akin to her blessing "may God be at your table" in that it supports two readings. It can be seen as merely a generalized reference to one of the three theological virtues or it can be read as an invocation of a specific virgin martyr. Both "by Saint Charity" and "may God be at your table" thus raise the same question: is the sacred actually immanent in the present? Hamlet contemplates this same issue. After his encounter with the Ghost, Hamlet swears by St. Patrick in order to affirm the reality of what he has seen, and the saint's name becomes the guarantor that the Ghost is not an imagined figment but a real presence. Far from being meaningless invocations, the references to St. Patrick and St. Charity are also underpinned by a fund of specific iconographic meaning. As Greenblatt points out, Hamlet swears "by Saint Patrick" after seeing the Ghost because St. Patrick was the proverbial keeper of purgatory, and Shakespeare displays here a fine-tuned understanding of how the late medieval world viewed this Irish saint.[29] The details of Charity's legend are similarly relevant to Ophelia's oath in act 4.

Charity's legend, like the stories of all medieval virgin martyrs, focuses on female sexuality. As the quintessential virgin martyr, Charity's piety is made most clear by her triumphant rejection of fallen sexual traffic. In her legend, St. Charity chooses very differently than the baker's daughter. By accepting the martyr's crown, she enters into spiritual marriage with Christ even though this marriage entails not just dying to the world's fallen values but also undergoing a panoply of physical tortures. In Jacobus's legend of Sophia and her three daughters, the beauty of the three girls so enchants the Emperor Hadrian that he wants to adopt them as daughters. Unlike other legends where pagan magistrates, kings, or emperors openly demand sex from Christian maidens, this legend sublimates the emperor's erotic attraction into a desire for surrogate parenthood. The sexualized nature of Hadrian's overtures remains muted in the martyrdoms of Faith and Hope: Faith is martyred for refusing to be adopted, and Hope dies because she will not sacrifice to idols. Charity's temptation, however, is the most eroticized of the three. She refuses to yield to what Jacobus calls "Hadrian's blandishments," a refusal that results in her death.[30] Writing three centuries later, Spenser presents a similarly sexualized image of Charissa in *The Faerie Queene:* "Her necke and breasts were ever open bare, / That ay thereof her babes might sucke their fill."[31] Charity is the theological virtue most linked to giving to others, and female embodiments of charity naturally raise the possibility of sexual giving. Characteristically, Jacobus, the Roman Catholic hagiographer, repudiates this question of sexual generosity by replacing it with virgin martyrdom, while Spenser, the Protestant poet, repudiates adulterous eroticism by showing instead virtuous maternal fecundity.

Charity's legend also lays stress on the female saintly community that enfolds her. Just as the Virgin Mary was often depicted in the company of women like her mother Anne, her grandmother Emerentia, and her cousin Elizabeth, Charity dies in the company of her sisters and mother.[32] She chooses a lethal solidarity with her sisters over a sensuous liaison with the male emperor, and Jacobus posits a clear privileging of these female-female relationships (which, in this case, are the paths to holiness) over the hypothetical female-male relationship (which would here lead to spiritual death). Spenser similarly foregrounds Charissa's place in a female community, so much so that even though she exemplifies pious motherhood (i.e., we know her children are born in wedlock), Spenser never alludes to her husband. Her many children thus seem more an allegorical product of Charissa's interactions with her sisters Speranza and Fidelia than of her interactions with a man.

Charity's place in a female saintly community and her steadfast refusal of illicit sex work in painful tension to the context of Ophelia's lament. In her Valentine's Day song, Ophelia invokes St. Charity to criticize casual sexual relations and especially the brutal callousness of young men, and her song highlights the tragic aftermath of sexual congress. In the song, the female speaker comes to a young man's door because it is Valentine's Day:

> Tomorrow is Saint Valentine's day,
>   All in the morning betime
> And I a maid at your window,
>   To be your Valentine.
> Then up he rose, and donn'd his clo'es
>   And dupp'd the chamber door,

> Let in the maid that out a maid
> Never departed more.

$$(4.5.48–55)$$

Ophelia's rendition of the song then turns to a critique of male behavior, one that uses the example of St. Charity to condemn the actions of the song:

> By Gis and by Saint Charity,
> Alack and fie for shame!
> Young men will do't if they come to't;
> By Cock, they are to blame.

$$(ll. 58–61)$$

This young woman is the opposite of St. Charity, who died rather than submit to Hadrian, for instead of rejecting a man's advances, this young woman has initiated those advances herself. She has celebrated St. Valentine's Day not by acts of special devotion or by acting like St. Charity, but by showing exceptional sexual boldness.

The tension between the girl's sexual wantonness and St. Charity's sexual purity is compounded by the larger tension in this passage between St. Valentine and St. Charity. Of course, in medieval hagiography, there is no such tension, and Valentine displays a piety just as correct and praiseworthy as Charity's. *The Golden Legend* recounts briefly that Valentine was a priest who, because he professed Christianity and refused to worship idols, was beheaded by the emperor Claudius near the end of the third century.[33] In a remarkable historical irony, Valentine's Day became the occasion for sexual couplings, probably because birds began pairing sometime in the middle of February. This association between Valentine's Day and sexual intercourse was well enough established by Shakespeare's day that Duke Theseus, in *Midsummer Night's Dream,* seeing the paired young lovers returned from the forest, remarks "Saint Valentine's is past. / Begin these wood-birds but to couple now?"[34] In Ophelia's song, the girl has acted in a way befitting St. Valentine's Day as popularly celebrated but in a manner diametrically opposed to St. Valentine's and St. Charity's models of a holy life. Ironically, St. Valentine's Day has stimulated her misguided actions instead of deterring them, and the song implicitly questions the kinds of behaviors appropriate on a saint's day, tacitly gesturing toward the ever-widening rift between the idea of the holiday and that of the holy day.

Ophelia has, at this point, alluded to three young girls who make literal or symbolic sexual choices that have deep spiritual implications. On the one hand, the girl of the St. Valentine's Day song actually goes to a man's bed out of wedlock. The baker's daughter makes a similar choice, for she, too, turns away from a standard of high spiritual perfection, preferring the traditional values of the world over marriage with Christ. For both, choosing the world of men over the world of God brings tragedy: the baker's daughter is turned into an owl (a bird proverbially associated with witches and thus linked also to wicked sexual relations), and the girl of the song is now damaged sexual goods. In contrast to these young women, Ophelia offers the model of St. Charity who obeys her Savior's call even to the point of death, cleaving to an all-female community made up of her sisters and her mother. In Jacobus's version of the legend, Hadrian has Charity racked, beaten, scourged, thrown into a furnace, and finally "stabbed with white hot nails," and although this last torture understandably kills her, she ultimately wins the spiritual battle. To emphasize Charity's victory, Jacobus ends his account with the emperor's ugly death: "As for Hadrian, his whole body rotted and he wasted away to death, admitting the while that he had unjustly done injury to the saints of God."[35] The choices of these three young girls might be reduced to the following moral: submitting to the claims of mortal men brings only victimization and powerlessness while resisting these claims can lead, through the paradoxical logic of martyrdom, to the ultimate female triumph.

The fact that Ophelia alludes to these extreme examples of female behavior (tellingly, she offers no happy medium of being a contented wife or a socially revered virgin) indicates her state of mind and her understanding of the dramatic events that have transpired. Trying to submit to her father and to be a good potential wife for Hamlet has brought her nothing. Or rather, it has brought her shattering grief and madness. At the opposite extreme from this pliancy in the face of male demands, Ophelia alludes to the example of St. Charity. Charity's unbending piety might not be an appealing one for modern readers who have a hard time comprehending martyrdom, but for premodern readers, she epitomized empowerment and spiritual triumph. By Ophelia's day, however, St. Charity's model was no longer available to young women since after the Protestant Reformation, virgin martyrs ceased to be the cultural ideal of sanctity. Of course, women (both Protestant and Catholic) had been tragically martyred for their faith in recent English history, but these martyrdoms no longer foregrounded the question of virginity in the same way as in the medieval legends. An important tenet of English Protestant thought was that virginity should no longer be lauded as the highest possible goal of human life but rather be seen as a necessary precondition to marriage, and so dying a virgin could be seen as prideful recalcitrance rather than exemplary piety.

Ophelia is thus caught between two models of female behavior: one, embodied by the girl of the song, is both realistic (women widely entered into sexual traffic with men) and tragic (these women are often betrayed, as when the young man of the song refuses to wed the girl precisely because she has had sex with him). The other, represented by St. Charity, is unrealistic (the Reformation had decisively foreclosed the idea of the virgin martyr) and yet ultimately empowering. The misery of this predicament—being caught between equally untenable options—is only compounded by St. Charity's associations with a female community, for such a community is precisely what Ophelia lacks. As the only other woman in the play, Gertrude acts most like the girl of the Valentine's Day song: she eagerly puts herself into a man's bed even though this act leaves what she calls "black and grained spots" in her soul (3.4.90). In the hagiographic tradition, Charity's defense of her virginity and her consequent martyrdom are validated not only by their self-evident piety but also by the example of other women, and the medieval period held up numerous other virgin martyrs as the consummate ideals of virtue.[36] For Ophelia, however, acting like St. Charity and rejecting the world of men would not bring her into solidarity with other women but would only deepen her isolation. Ruth Vanita points out that the iconoclasms of the English Reformation removed countless images of female figures—both Mary and the female saints—from English churches, leaving female believers without the role models available to them a half century earlier.[37] The Protestant Reformation not only disabled the model of the virgin martyr but also erased the many female pseudodeities who could intercede on humans' behalf, and Ophelia's allusion to St. Charity throws into relief how this solacing female spiritual community has been lost.

St. Charity's associations with madness similarly draw attention to the fact that the medieval saints could no longer be invoked for miraculous cures in an early modern world. As Carol Thomas Neely points out, saints like St. Romauld and St. Ignatius Loyola were popularly believed to heal those possessed by evil spirits.[38] St. Charity was likewise prayed to on behalf of children sick with "the fairy," or displaying the kinds of aberrant behaviors associated with enchantment. For instance, in Cambridgeshire, the healer Elizabeth Mortlock cured children sick with the fairy by saying a series of set prayers, measuring out a piece of the afflicted one's girdle or band along her arm, and "craving God for Saint Charity's sake that if [the child] be haunted with a fairy, yea or no, she may know."[39] Although Mortlock invokes Charity to help with a diagnosis instead of a cure, her impulse to call on St. Charity when confronted with a sick child emerges from an age-old association between saints and healings. Indeed, the majority of miracles done at medieval saints' shrines were thaumaturgic ones.[40] We can usefully contrast Ophelia's allusion to St. Charity with the cure proposed for the Jailer's Daughter in *Two Noble Kinsmen*.[41] The Doctor in *Kinsmen* advises sexual intercourse as the best way to heal the Jailer's Daughter's madness. As he frankly tells the Wooer, "fit her home, and presently."[42] Unlike Ophelia whose madness leads to her drowning, the Jailer's Daughter is both rescued from drowning by the Wooer and implicitly cured by having sex with him. While this ending is technically a happy one, it is hard to be comfortable with either the confidence that a good "fitting" is all the Daughter needs or with the fact that the Wooer only wins his way into her bed by pretending to be Palamon.[43] In contrast to the Doctor's belief that sexual intercourse with a man is the best cure for female insanity, Ophelia's mad allusion reminds listeners of the saints' role in healing madness. Of course, seeking a cure from a saint—like dying a virgin marytr—was no longer a mainstream option by the writing of *Hamlet*. The Reformation had disallowed pilgrimage to saints' shrines in the middle of the sixteenth century (perhaps another instance of Greenblatt's "fifty-year effect" at work in this play), and Protestant apologists had denounced the idea that the saints could be invoked to work miraculous cures.[44] Calling on St. Charity admittedly does nothing to heal Ophelia's madness; however, it reminds us of a time when young women in the grip of insanity could readily turn to holy female role models for assistance instead of being remanded to a man's bed.

The references to going on pilgrimage to a saint's shrine buried in the allusion to St. Charity are more prominent in the very first ballad that Ophelia sings. Ophelia's song opens:

> How should I your true love know
> From another one?
> By his cockle hat and staff
> And his sandal shoon.
>
> (4.5.23–24)

The cockle-shell badge, a staff, and sandals were the characteristic iconographic emblems of St. James, and, since St. James was the patron saint of pilgrims, of all pilgrims themselves. James's shrine in Compostella, Spain, was one of the most important pilgrimage sites in Europe, and Ophelia's song would have conjured up images of pilgrims wearing the clothes characteristic of St. James and streaming piously toward his shrine. Ophelia's song alludes also to another well-known pilgrimage site, one closer to home: the shrine of Our Lady at Walsingham. Her song reprises a late medieval ballad in which a deserted lover, following his lady who has gone on pilgrimage to Walsingham, meets another pilgrim coming from the famous English shrine. The lover asks, "[as] yee come ffrom the holy Land of walsingham / mett you not wt my true loue / by the way as you Came." The pilgrim responds, "how shold I know yor true loue," and the lover answers, "Shee is neither white nor browne / but as the heauens ffaire / there is none hathe their fforme diuine on the earth or the ayre."[45] As Peter Seng notes, this popular ballad produced a number of imitations, and he cites numerous examples, including Old Merrythought's song in Beaumont and Fletcher's *Knight of the Burning Pestle* (1613): "As you cam from Walsingham, from that holy land, / there met you not with my tru-loue by the way."[46]

By featuring a woman who has left her lover to go on pilgrimage, forcing him to follow after her, the Walsingham ballad offers a striking image of female mobility, and it provides a glimpse of a late medieval world in which women, under the pretext of pilgrimage, were at least theoretically more free to move around than their early modern counterparts. It furthermore opens up the possibility that pilgrimage could be an option for women who wished to escape the importunities of men. The song gives no account of the young woman's motives for leaving, but simply by featuring a woman who leaves her male lover behind in the name of pilgrimage, the song depicts a course of action not readily available to early modern women. Shakespeare's revision of this ballad stresses the link between female travel and female self-determination. In his unique version of the song, the man leaves on pilgrimage, and the woman must venture after him, asking passersby if they have seen "his cockle hat and staff / And his sandal shoon." Interestingly, one other Shakespeare play provides an image of a woman hunting down her wayward lover, and here too the female freedom to pursue is linked to pilgrimage. In *All's Well That Ends Well,* Helena goes on pilgrimage to St. Jacques (Santiago de Compostella) with the apparent intent to recover Bertram. Furthermore, she goes entirely unaccompanied, entering Florence alone dressed as a "holy pilgrim."[47] Ophelia's ballad and *All's Well* provide images of deserted women who, rather than weeping helplessly at home, venture out searching for the men who have abandoned them, and the fact that the journey is a pilgrimage legitimizes the search of a lone female for her male. These literary figures are descendents of Chaucer's Wife of Bath whose pilgrimage to Canterbury seems motivated in part by a desire to find a sixth husband. In the instances of these pilgrim women, pilgrimage offers them not only the option to travel but also a means to work actively to acquire (or reacquire) their lovers or husbands. However, two of these pilgrim women (the Wife of Bath and the woman of the Walsingham ballad) are part of a medieval world, and the other one is relatively anomalous in sixteenth- and seventeenth-century literature. Helena's freedom to pursue Bertram cannot be read as indicating that abandoned early modern women could ordinarily venture after their men, and Helena only acquires such mobility by donning the costume of a bygone religious world.

In contrast to such fantasized mobility, most early modern women probably experienced a stasis like that of the female addressee in John Donne's "Valediction: Forbidding Mourning" who must stay pinned to one spot while her lover orbits her fixed center. By closing down the busy network of pilgrimage routes that fanned out across medieval Europe, the Protestant Reformers not only eradicated what they considered popery but also dramatically narrowed the horizons and the options of ordinary women. English Reformers urged their congregations to redirect the money previously used for pilgrimages into good works closer to home, and such calls to keep people and money in a purely local circulation meant that men and especially

women lost the travel opportunities formerly available to them.[48] The association between pilgrimage and female empowerment only makes Ophelia's use
of the Walsingham ballad all the more tragic. Unlike the young woman in the
song, she cannot follow Hamlet to England. Instead, she remains fixed in
place, and, denied the freedoms of pilgrimage, she falls by default into the
unconstrained license of madness. Indeed, the predicament of the grieving
yet highly mobile female pilgrim in the ballad seems ultimately less painful
than Ophelia's place in the frozen, claustrophobic world of Elsinore.

In addition to stressing the bygone practice of pilgrimage, Ophelia's ballad
also calls attention to the loss of the Walsingham shrine itself, a sacred place
that has been described as "incomparably the most important shrine of its
kind in medieval England."[49] By Shakespeare's day, the shrine at Walsingham had been destroyed. When Henry VIII dissolved the monasteries, affection for the Walsingham priory led to a minor local rebellion in 1537. With
characteristic Henrician savagery, the leaders were drawn and quartered right
outside the priory walls, the priory and shrine pulled down, and the famous
statue of the Virgin burned in the streets. This destruction of one of the most
beloved holy spots in the kingdom prompted the popular ballad "A Lament
for Walsingham" which unflinchingly censures Henry's "wronge" in de-
stroying the shrine:

> Bitter, bitter oh to behold the grasse to growe,
> Where the walls of Walsingam so stately did shewe.
> Such were the works of Walsingham while shee did stand,
> Such are the wrackes as now do shewe of that holy land.
>
> . . . .
>
> Oules do scrike where the sweetest himnes lately weer songe,
> Toades and serpents hold their dennes wher the palmers did thronge
> Weepe, weepe O Walsingham, whose dayes are nightes,
> Blessinge turned to blasphemies, holy deeds to dispites.
> Sinne is wher our Ladie sate, heaven turned is to hell,
> Sathan sittes wher our Lord did swaye, Walsingam oh farewell.[50]

This song expresses the keen grief felt when old forms of piety and ritual
observance were demolished by the Reformation, and the devastating sense
of loss provides a subtext for Ophelia's own lament.[51] The reference to Walsingham works like her allusion to the story of the baker's daughter and to
St. Charity: all three invoke a medieval world where the sacred impinged
more directly and more concretely upon a fallen earth. Just as believers could
no longer meet Christ in a bakery or invoke St. Charity's aid, they had similarly lost the ability to travel to Walsingham, kneel on its stones, and piously
pray before the miracle-working statue of the Virgin.

Ophelia's use of the Walsingham ballad also reminds listeners of a medieval world in which a woman was the focus of piety. Walsingham was the

center of Marian devotion in England, and in razing the shrine, English Reformers demolished the place where Christianity was most linked to female power. Walsingham's shrine was originally founded in the eleventh century when a wealthy widow, Richeldis, received a vision from the Virgin Mary instructing her to build a wooden replica of the house in Nazareth where Mary was visited by the angel and conceived.[52] The house came to be known as the "newe Nazareth,"[53] and as such it was specifically a shrine to the miracle of Incarnation, when the Word became flesh and dwelt among us. Gibson writes, "no better example exists of the image theology of the late Middle Ages than the Walsingham shrine, a replica or stage setting that pilgrims saw as proof of the Virgin's accessibility, the place where Mary—particularized, localized, in bodily likeness—had made her house and had heard the angel's message."[54] The early modern "Lament for Walsingham" lays stress on the absence of a benign female divinity in the wake of Reformation iconoclasms: "Sinne is wher our Ladie sate, heaven turned is to hell." Where the story of the baker's daughter shows a male Christ literally standing in an English bakery, the Walsingham ballad recalls the shrine where a miraculous image of Christ's mother sat enthroned on English soil, her statue flanked on either side by images of St. Katherine and St. Margaret.[55] Shakespeare's plays notoriously feature daughters without mothers, and Ophelia's allusion to Our Lady of Walsingham suggests that, in the years before the Reformation, a daughter without a mother could turn to a different Mother for comfort. Ultimately, every aspect of Ophelia's world is diametrically opposed to the world of the Walsingham ballad. Where the young woman of the song goes on pilgrimage, Ophelia is frozen in place; where the young woman can try to seek out her lover, Ophelia's is permanently lost to her; where medieval Walsingham made the sacred immanent in the present, the true things of God cannot be seen or felt in the early modern world of *Hamlet;* where the Walsingham shrine allows a redemptive female spiritual force to suffuse a fallen world, *Hamlet* (like early modern Protestantism in general) privileges male embodiments of power. Mad Ophelia enters the stage in act 4, singing of a bygone religious system that could have offered her everything that she has currently lost.

The nature of Ophelia's death is consistent with the network of medieval Catholic allusions that lace her ravings in 4.5, and her drowning resonates with the highly publicized suicide of the Catholic convert, Sir James Hales in 1560. Although by the writing of *Hamlet,* Hales's sensational death would have been old news, this play is deeply preoccupied with events of half a century earlier. Furthermore, Shakespeare was specifically thinking of the Hales case during the writing of *Hamlet,* for editors of *Hamlet* have long recognized that the Gravedigger's hair-splitting in 5.1.10–12 ("if I drown myself wittingly, it argues an act, and an act hath three branches—it is to act, to do, to perform; argal, she drowned herself wittingly") presents a parody of the legal arguments used at Hales's postmortem trial.[56] Significantly, this allusion to Hales—a Reformer under Edward VI, who converted to Catholicism under duress and later drowned himself—appears right after Gertrude recounts Ophelia's drowning. Gertrude describes Ophelia's garments pulling her "To muddy death" (4.7.182), and roughly twenty lines later (including a scene break), the gravediggers begin the legal cavilling that so clearly recalls the Hales trial. This juxtaposition invites audiences to connect the fictional drowning with the historical one, and Ophelia's allusions to medieval Catholic forms of belief further strengthen the association between her situation and Hales's. I am not suggesting that Hales and Ophelia should be read as exact analogues of one another. Ophelia, unlike Hales, does not convert from Protestantism to Catholicism in a public act of renunciation. And although her abbreviated funeral rites strongly suggest suicide, her drowning is admittedly more ambiguous than Hales's clear and deliberate act of self-slaughter. What I am suggesting is that the Hales case provided a contemporary context for understanding Ophelia's death, one in which drowning results from being caught between two rival religious systems. Hales found himself in the tormented limbo of the traitor: Protestants did not want him since his renunciation of his faith was seen as a cowardly betrayal, and Catholics were suspicious since he recanted only under threat. Ophelia's situation is obviously quite different, and yet there are affinities between her and Hales. She seems imaginatively pinned between the real world of early modern Protestantism and the fantasized world of medieval Catholicism, and like Hales, she finds release only at the bottom of a cold river.

In his depictions of both Hamlet and Ophelia, Shakespeare links madness to England's medieval Catholic past. For Hamlet, the encounter with the purgatorial Ghost triggers a kind of mental derangement, and whether his madness is real or feigned, the extremity of his duress is undeniable. In Ophelia's case, Shakespeare presents a slightly different dynamic since the flood of medieval Catholic allusions seems more the result of her insanity than its catalyst. Shakespeare may be experimenting here with the limits of what he can depict onstage: perhaps recognizably Catholic allusions are allowable in a play if spoken by deranged characters? Shakespeare probes this same question further a few years later in *King Lear,* when Edgar, who is feigning madness, sings about St. Withold. Wandering the hilly countryside, the saint meets the "night mare and her nine-fold" and dismisses the witch with the command "aroint thee." Edgar's ditty imagines a saint who wanders the countryside (he "footed thrice" the hilly terrain) and who retains the power to exorcise witches and their brood.[57] In giving Edgar these verses, Shakespeare echoes his earlier depiction of Ophelia, for in both cases the descent into madness (whether real or feigned) is marked by allusions to the saints' efficacy on earth.

Hamlet shows how death can put pressure on the belief structures of English Protestantism, allowing vestiges of England's Catholic past to irrupt into the Protestant present. The task of accommodating the two irreconcilable religious positions can result in madness. Significantly, Shakespeare shows Hamlet and Ophelia reconciling the past and the present in different ways. Hamlet, by the end of the play, seems to shake free of the specter of Catholic purgatory, which has haunted him in acts 1 through 3. After the Ghost disappears from the stage, Hamlet is calmer, and his trust in "the special providence" that guides all things seems strongly reminiscent of contemporary Protestant theology (5.2.215).[58] In Ophelia's case, unlike Hamlet's, the past does not disappear. Indeed, Ophelia seems to slip entirely into this past since she dies voicing monastic forms of piety. Ophelia's final recourse to bygone forms of piety resonates with Fran Dolan's persuasive claim that early modern women were particularly associated with Catholicism.[59] We should resist, however, the temptation to explain away Ophelia's "old lauds" as simply a function of her gender since such a reading does not do full justice to the terrible pressures that the early modern religious controversies brought to bear on ordinary people of all kinds. In *Hamlet,* Shakespeare seems all too well aware of how tragically unbearable those pressures could be.

Notes

The clarity and coherence of this argument owe much to the helpful attensions of Rebecca Bach, Mimi Fenton, and Elaine Whitaker.

1. For a sampling of recent studies of Hamlet and the question of early modern religious controversies, see Ramie Targoff, "The Performance of Prayer: Sincerity and Theatricality in Early Modern England," *Representations* 60 (1997 Fall): 49–69; Heather Hirschfeld, "Hamlet's 'First Corse': Repetition, Trauma, and the Displacement of Redemptive Typology," *Shakespeare Quarterly* 54 (2003): 424–48; Stephen Greenblatt, *Hamlet in Purgatory* (Princeton: Princeton University Press, 2001); Michael Neill, *Issues of Death: Mortality and Identity in English Renaissance Tragedy* (Oxford: Clarendon Press, 1997); John Freeman, "This Side of Purgatory: Ghostly Fathers and the Recusant Legacy in *Hamlet,*" in *Shakespeare and the Culture of Christianity in Early Modern England,* ed. Dennis Taylor and David Beauregard, 222–59 (New York: Fordham University Press, 2003); and Jennifer Rust, "Wittenberg and Melancholic Allegory: The Reformation and Its Discontents in *Hamlet,*" in *Shakespeare and the Culture of Christianity in Early Modern England,* ed. Dennis Taylor and David Beauregard, 260–86 (New York: Fordham University Press, 2003).

2. *Hamlet,* Arden Shakespeare, ed. Harold Jenkins (London: Methuen, 1982), 3.1.79. All subsequent *Hamlet* citations are to this edition and are supplied parenthetically in the text.

3. Ramie Targoff provides an exception to such Hamlet-centered probings of the play's religious involvements, for she discusses Claudius and his chapel scene in the context of Protestant debates about prayer (see Targoff, "The Performance of Prayer"). To my knowledge, no critic has suggested that the female characters of the

play experience any of the same struggles with belief seen in male characters like Hamlet, Claudius, and even Horatio and the soldiers who confront the Ghost.

4. For a classic discussion of how Shakespeare links Ophelia's madness and her sexuality, see Elaine Showalter, "Representing Ophelia: Women, Madness, and the Responsibilities of Feminist Criticism," in *Shakespeare and the Question of Theory,* ed. Patricia Parker and Geoffrey Hartman, 77–94 (New York: Methuen, 1985).

5. Jenkins discusses such editorial responses in his "Longer Notes" at the end of the Arden *Hamlet;* see his gloss to 4.5.165–82, esp. 546. Although Jenkins himself argues against the view that religion and eros are incompatible in Ophelia's lament, he does so by stressing that "what both have in common is their very incongruity." In other words, he reconciles sex and piety in Ophelia's ravings by pointing out that both are equally out of place.

6. The work of Debora Kuller Shuger (*The Renaissance Bible: Scholarship, Sacrifice, and Subjectivity* [Berkeley: University of California Press, 1994], ch. 5) and Rebecca Ann Bach ("[Re]Placing John Donne in the History of Sexuality," *ELH* 72 [2005]: 259–89) are particularly useful in this regard. See also Benjamin Saunders, "Circumcising Donne: The 1633 Poems and Readerly Desire," *Journal of Medieval and Early Modern Studies* 30, 2 (2000): 375–99, and Leo Steinberg's classic *The Sexuality of Christ in Renaissance Art and in Modern Oblivion* (New York: Pantheon, 1983).

7. My argument about Ophelia's use of medieval Catholic allusions would not be possible without Frances E. Dolan's persuasive claim that early modern women were generally associated with recusancy. See her *Whores of Babylon: Catholicism, Gender, and Seventeenth-Century Print Culture* (Ithaca: Cornell University Press, 1999).

8. In making this claim, I am indebted to what has been colloquially called (and sometimes derided as) the "Catholic turn" in Shakespeare studies. Dympna Callaghan argues cogently that while the recent upsurge of interest in Shakespeare and religion has shown convincingly that "the long-held assumption about Shakespeare as the Protestant national poet is probably wide of the mark," much of this scholarship rejects the theoretical gains made in the past decades in gender, sexuality, ethnic, and racial studies (Dympna Callaghan, "Shakespeare and Religion," *Textual Practice* 15, 1 [Spring 2001]: 2). Callaghan, that is, offers a welcome reminder that we should not be worrying the question "Was Shakespeare a Catholic?" Following Callaghan's lead, my intent here is not to speculate on authorial intention or belief but rather to draw attention to the ways in which religious identity, gendered identity, and questions of madness relate to one another in a post-Reformation world, and to the ways in which Shakespeare reflects on these in his depiction of Ophelia. Any cultural, social, political, and religious movement as massive as the English Reformation inevitably leaves wreckage in its wake (regardless of its various gains). We do not have to assert that Shakespeare is a Catholic or a Protestant or indeed anything other than a careful, compassionate observer of his own world in order to say that *Hamlet* studies this debris. For other studies that challenge the role of orthodox Protestantism as defining the early modern English literary project, see Richard Wilson, *Secret Shakespeare: Studies in Theatre, Religion, and Resistance* (New York: Manchester University Press, 2004); Jeffrey Knapp, *Shakespeare's Tribe* (Chicago: University of Chicago Press, 2002); and Alison Shell, *Catholicism, Controversy and the English Literary Imagination* (Cambridge: Cambridge University Press, 1999).

9. For an in-depth survey of whether early modern usages allowed a reading of "nunnery" as brothel, see Jenkins's editorial discussion of 3.1.121. Jenkins concedes that "we cannot dismiss an inherent ambiguity" and that the reiteration of the word over the course of Hamlet's speech may have allowed its meanings to shift; however, as he points out, the early modern evidence indicates that "nunnery" was hardly a common or widespread synonym for a house of ill-repute (493–96).

10. William Shakespeare, *Midsummer Night's Dream,* in *The Norton Shakespeare Based on the Oxford Edition,* Stephen Greenblatt et al. (New York: W. W. Norton, 1997), 1.1.70–71 and William Shakespeare, *Much Ado About Nothing,* in *The Norton Shakespeare Based on the Oxford Edition,* Stephen Greenblatt et al. (New York: W. W. Norton, 1997), 4.1.240.

11. However, as David Beauregard argues, the depiction of nuns and friars in Shakespeare's work generally, and in *Measure for Measure* especially, remains remarkably sympathetic. David Beauregard, "Shakespeare on Monastic Life: Nuns and Friars in *Measure for Measure,*" in *Shakespeare and the Culture of Christianity in Early Modern England,* ed. Dennis Taylor and David Beauregard, 311–35 (New York: Fordham University Press, 2003).

12. Katherine M. Briggs, *A Dictionary of British Folk-Tales in the English Language* (Bloomington: Indiana University Press, 1970), 124.

13. For a compelling discussion of this phenomenon, see Anthony Kemp, *The Estrangement of the Past: A Study in the Origins of Modern Historical Consciousness* (New York: Oxford University Press, 1991).

14. Gail McMurray Gibson, *The Theater of Devotion: East Anglian Drama and Society in the Late Middle Ages* (Chicago: University of Chicago Press, 1989), 6–7.

15. Debora Shuger, *Habits of Thought in the English Renaissace* (Berkeley: University of California Press, 1990), 71, 70.

16. Ibid., 78.

17. Greenblatt, *Hamlet in Purgatory,* 240–43.

18. Peter Brown, *The Body and Society: Men, Women, and Sexual Renunciation in Early Christianity* (New York: Columbia University Press, 1988), 155. See also Shuger, *The Renaissance Bible,* 152.

19. Donald Kelley, *The Beginning of Ideology: Consciousness and Society in the French Reformation* (Cambridge: Cambridge University Press, 1981), 77–78. Quoted in Shuger, *The Renaissance Bible,* 152.

20. Shuger, *The Renaissance Bible,* 152–53.

21. Greenblatt, *Hamlet in Purgatory,* 248.

22. Jacobus de Voragine, *The Golden Legend: Readings on the Saints,* trans. William Granger Ryan (Princeton: Princeton University Press, 1993), 1:185.

23. Richard Verstegan, *Odes in Imitation of the Seauen Penitential Psalmes* (Antwerp, 1601), E1.

24. *Oxford English Dictionary,* 2nd edition (Oxford: Clarendon ressP, 1989), s.v. "Charity"; Jenkins, *Hamlet,* 351n58.

25. *The Troublesome Raigne of Iohn King of England* (London, 1591), E6v.

26. Edmund Spenser, "The Shepheardes Calender," ed. Thomas H. Cain, in *The Yale Edition of the Shorter Poems of Edmund Spenser,* ed. William Oram, Einar Bjorvand, Ronald Bond, Thomas H. Cain, Alexander Dunlop, and Richard Schell (New Haven: Yale University Press, 1989), 96, l. 247.

27. Ibid., 104n247. This association of Catholics with a purely spoken form of charity perhaps contributed to a written skirmish over whether Catholics fail in charity by asserting that Protestatism is a mortal sin. See, for example, Edward Knott, *Charity Mistaken, with the Want Whereof Catholickes Are Uniustly Charged* (Saint Omer, 1630) and Christopher Potter, *Want of Charitie Justly Charged* (Oxford, 1633).

28. Faith, too, seems to have been readily personified in medieval devotion. In her study of holy wells, Alexandra Walsham records accounts of a well at Hexton in Hertfordshire featuring a statue of St. Faith "trymlye apparelled" with a "velvett tippett." Alexandra Walsham, "Reforming the Waters: Holy Wells and Healing Springs in Protestant England," in *Life and Thought in the Northern Church, c. 1100–c. 1700: Essays in Honour of Clare Cross,* ed. Diana Wood, Studies in Church History (Woodbridge, Suffolk: Ecclesiastical History Society by the Boydell Press, 1999), quoted on 233.

29. Greenblatt, *Hamlet in Purgatory,* 73–101.

30. Jacobus de Voragine, *Golden Legend,* 1:187.

31. Edmund Spenser, *The Faerie Queene,* ed. Thomas P. Roche (New York: Penguin, 1978), 1.10.30.

32. For further discussion of this holy female community, see Ruth Vanita, "Mariological Memory in *The Winter's Tale* and *Henry VIII,"* *Studies in English Literature, 1500–1900,* 40 (2000): 311–12.

33. Jacobus de Voragine, *Golden Legend,* 1:159–60.

34. Shakespeare, *Midsummer Night's Dream,* 4.1.136–37.

35. Jacobus de Voragine, *Golden Legend,* 1:185, 186.

36. For further discussion of these figures, see Karen Winstead, *Virgin Martyrs: Legends of Sainthood in Late Medieval England* (Cornell: Cornell University Press, 1997).

37. Vanita, "Mariological Memory," 311–12.

38. Carol Thomas Neely, *Distracted Subjects: Madness and Gender in Shakespeare and Early Modern Culture* (Ithaca: Cornell University Press, 2004), 94, 95. Neely mentions these saints as part of her convincing discussion of how the "iconography of possession is reiterated and redefined" in a later "iconography of hysteria" (97).

39. Quoted in Keith Thomas, *Religion and the Decline of Magic* (New York: Charles Scribner's Sons, 1971), 184.

40. Ronald Finucane, *Miracles and Pilgrims: Popular Beliefs in Medieval England* (Totowa, NJ: Rowman and Littlefield, 1977).

41. It is worth pausing here to note that both madwomen think not just of sex but also of religion: Ophelia alludes to the world of medieval piety while the Jailer's Daughter imagines instead the pagan afterworld (viz., her references to Charon, Proserpine, and Dido) and the punishments of a Dantean hell (4.3). I stress this point because the editors of *The Norton Shakespeare* highlight eroticized speech as the common denominator in these stage instances of madness. For example, in glossing the Daughter's desire for "a prick" to lean against, the editors note the allusion to the nightingale but also provide the following: "'Prick' also carried a sexual meaning; compare the sexual punning here with that in Ophelia's 'mad' speeches in *Hamlet"* (William Shakespeare, *Two Noble Kinsmen,* in *The Norton Shakespeare Based on the*

Oxford Edition, Stephen Greenblatt et al. [New York: W. W. Norton, 1997], 3.4.26n3).
Certainly, both madwomen speak lewdly, but they are equally similar in their insane
recourse to a bygone religious world.

42. John Fletcher and William Shakespeare, *The Two Noble Kinsmen,* Arden
Shakespeare, ed. Lois Potter (Surrey: Thomas Nelson and Sons, 1997), 5.2.11.

43. For discussion of how the Daughter's delusion echoes early modern case histories of female melancholia, see Neely, *Distracted Subjects,* 83–91. Although Neely
points out that the Jailer's family, the Wooer, and the Doctor all treat the Daughter
with gentleness and compassion, she acknowledges the many ways in which "the ending of this story . . . is bitter, not comic" (90).

44. Of course, the fact that Protestantism officially disallowed such practices did
not mean that they disappeared, and historians like Robert Scribner and Alexandra
Walsham have demonstrated the degree to which aspects of "traditional religion"
were quietly preserved and adapted by devout Protestants. See, for example, R. W.
Scriber, *Popular Culture and Popular Movements in Reformation Germany* (London:
Hambledon Press, 1987), 323–53, and Alexandra Walsham, "Holywell: Contesting
Sacred Space in Post-Reformation Wales," in *Sacred Space in Early Modern Europe,*
ed. Will Costner and Andrew Spicer, 211–36 (Cambridge: Cambridge University
Press, 2005).

45. Reproduced in Peter Seng, *The Vocal Songs in the Plays of Shakespeare: A
Critical History* (Cambridge, MA: Harvard University Press, 1967), 137.

46. Seng, *Vocal Songs,* 139, 130.

47. William Shakespeare, *All's Well That Ends Well,* ed. G. K. Hunter, Arden
Shakespeare (London: Methuen, 1969), 3.5.39. Edmund Spenser also imagines pilgrimage as a reasonable option for an abandoned woman. In book 2 of *The Faerie
Queene,* Amavia tells Sir Guyon that having been deserted by Sir Mordant, "Weake
wretch I wrapt my self in Palmers weed, / And cast to seeke him forth through
daunger and great dreed." Spenser, *The Faerie Queene,* 2.1.52.

48. Eamon Duffy, *The Stripping of the Altars: Traditional Religion in England, c.
1400–c. 1580* (New Haven: Yale University Press, 1992), 398.

49. J. C. Dickinson, *The Shrine of Our Lady at Walsingham* (Cambridge: Cambridge University Press, 1956), 14.

50. Reproduced in Dickinson, *Shrine,* 67–68.

51. In speaking of a sense of nostalgia for abolished forms of piety, I do not intend
to claim—with such revisionist historians as Christopher Haigh and even Eamon
Duffy—that the majority of the English populace remained stubbornly resistant to the
new faith that was forcibly imposed upon them from above. As various historians have
noted, this revisionist view does not account for the remarkable success of Protestantism at all levels by the end of the seventeenth century (for challenges to the revisionist
position, see the essays collected in Nicholas Tyacke, ed., *England's Long Reformation, 1500–1800,* Neale Colloquium in British History [London: University College
London Press, 1998]). My claim here is simply that whatever the pace of the Reformation and whatever the level of popular support, it is likely that even early modern
conformists would have preserved a quiet sense of what was being lost, even as they
applauded what was being gained.

52. Dickinson, *Shrine,* 24.

53. Ibid., 129. Dickinson both discusses the ballad's provenance and reproduces it in full: see 124–30.

54. Gibson, *The Theater of Devotion,* 142.

55. Duffy, *Stripping of the Altars,* 171.

56. Jenkins, *Hamlet,* 377n10–20. Roland Mushat Frye also summarizes relevant scholarship on Shakespeare's knowledge of the Hales trial in his *The Renaissance Hamlet* (Princeton: Princeton University Press, 1984), 363n15.

57. William Shakespeare, *King Lear,* Arden Shakespeare, ed. Kenneth Muir (New York: Methuen, 1972), 3.4.117–21.

58. See R. Chris Hassel, "The Accent and Gait of Christians: Hamlet's Puritan Style," in *Shakespeare and the Culture of Christianity in Early Modern England,* ed. Dennis Taylor and David Beauregard, 287–310 (New York: Fordham, 2003).

59. Dolan, *Whores of Babylon.*

"'Now wole I a newe game begynne": Staging Suffering in *King Lear,* the Mystery Plays and Grotius's *Christus Patiens*

BEATRICE GROVES

THE mystery plays put the Passion at the heart of their drama and their concept of dramaturgy. They did not flinch from staging pain and death, and showed the persecutors of Christ reveling in violence and performing tortures as elaborate games. This article will explore the influence of this attitude to dramatic violence on *King Lear* through the coincidence of another Passion play that was published in the same year as Shakespeare's play. Hugo Grotius's *Christus Patiens* is written in a classical style, and it is fundamentally classical in its approach to the violence at its center. Grotius does not stage any part of the torture or Crucifixion of Christ. The scourging is not mentioned and the Crucifixion is only related through messengers. In *King Lear* however, the blinding of Gloucester is not mediated but presented to the audience in its full horror. Shakespeare's source, Sidney's *New Arcadia,* relates the blinding as a story-within-a-story, so that even in this nondramatic context, the reader is shielded from the atrocity by means of enfolded narratives.[1] Shakespeare, however, chooses that his audience shall see it. In Grotius's *Christus Patiens,* as in the *Arcadia,* the audience are not direct witnesses— the violence takes place offstage—and their response is conditioned by the pity of those who respond to it onstage. In *King Lear* by contrast, the onstage reaction to Gloucester's pain ranges from the excitable satisfaction of Regan to the silent complicity of the servants who hold him, with only one character daring openly to voice his opposition. Grotius, because he cannot rely on the sympathy roused by visible agony, does not dare to leave open such a multiplicity of response. However, earlier performers of Christ's Passion had dared to do so. In the mystery plays, as Jesus is beaten and humiliated in the halls of the high priests, the ordinary men—the citizens and the soldiers—are drawn into casual abuse of him through the premeditated vindictiveness of the Sanhedrin. As in *King Lear,* only the occasional character, such as the beadle who lays his coat under Jesus's feet in the York cycle, has the bravery to exhibit the proper response to the suffering victim.

The connection between the ludic portrayal of violence in the mystery plays and *King Lear,* which this article will explore, is not, I hope to show, a purely coincidental one. There are a sufficient number of small correlations between the punishments inflicted on Christ and the blinding of Gloucester to make it likely that Shakespeare's staging of this scene is influenced by the drama of his youth.[2] But there is a wider inference to draw from this case study, that despite the importance of classical texts—such as Ovid and Plutarch, on Shakespeare—his mature dramaturgy is inspired primarily not by Sophocles, Seneca, or Plautus, but by his native English tradition. In both classical and medieval drama, physical suffering is suffused with authority, but in Shakespeare, as in the mysteries, this authority is communicated through the spectacle of the broken body of the victim. Few Greek tragedies have onstage deaths, whereas in the mystery plays the Crucifixion was the climactic stage spectacle of the whole cycle. Like death, violence against the body (such as Oedipus's self-blinding) is generally committed offstage in classical drama, but the scourging and beating of Christ's body, and his agonized death on the cross, were vividly enacted in the mystery plays. In Shakespeare the violent power of medieval theater, rather than the decorum of classical, is revived in drama, which forces the sight of Lear's death, Gloucester's blinding, Desdemona's suffocation, Antony's mangled suicide, and the gang murders of Hector, Caesar, and Cinna upon its audience. In Shakespeare, as in the mystery plays, in direct contrast to the verbosity of Senecan (and Grotian) drama, "The terribleness of what is happening is conveyed by the *in*adequacy of the language."[3]

As the death of Christ was the climax of the action in mystery cycles, medieval drama centered on strategies for staging bodily pain and controlling the audience response so that empathy was elicited for the sufferer. This article will argue that the staging of suffering was something bequeathed to Shakespeare by the earlier English dramatic tradition. It will explore not only Shakespeare's inherited emphasis on a graphic approach to the body in pain, but also one of the strategies he shares with the mystery plays in presenting horrific violence as aesthetically acceptable and emotionally compelling. In both Shakespeare and the mystery plays the rituals of violence and the rituals of games coincide, and in both the staging of suffering as sport increases its theatrical power and empathetic effect.

Only fourteen miles from Stratford-upon-Avon the most famous and popular mystery cycle in Tudor England, the Coventry cycle, was staged. This cycle remained an important annual event until 1579, when Shakespeare was fifteen.[4] The excitement generated by cycle plays, even in the Elizabethan era, is demonstrated by the distances people were willing to travel to see them: a

Shropshire man went to Chester in 1577 because "he heard of the plays [t]here."[5] It seems likely, therefore, that a young man interested in theater would have traveled the short road between Stratford and Coventry to see the most famous dramatic presentation of his day, and his plays support the supposition that Shakespeare caught firsthand what "out-Heroding Herod" (*Hamlet,* 3.2.14) looked like. The pressure of mystery play staging is discernable in many of Shakespeare's scenes, as critics have argued since Glynne Wickham's persuasive discussion of the similarities between the *Harrowing of Hell* and the porter scene in *Macbeth.* There are many other scenes in which Shakespeare's staging seems to be drawn from the mysteries: the killing of Macduff's children has echoes of *The Slaughter of the Innocents,* the groundless jealousy of Leontes may show the influence of *Joseph's Doubts about Mary,* the reviving of Hermione's statue has close connections with *The Resurrection,* and York's sitting on his king's throne in the first scene of *Henry VI Part 3* seems to reference the dramatic opening of the mysteries in which Satan usurps God's seat.[6]

The circumstantial similarities between the scenes of *Christ before Annas and Caiaphas* and Gloucester before Regan and Cornwall are likewise quite striking. In both an innocent man is brought before two people who treat his charitable deeds as treason, and after the sham trial, they torture him. In both cases the interrogation and torture seem gratuitous because the questioners have nothing really to learn from the accused.[7] Cornwall orders his men to "Go seek the traitor Gloucester. / Pinion him like a thief" (3.7.21–22), and the insult offered to Gloucester resonates with Jesus's arrest, at which such force is likewise unnecessary: "Bee ye come out as vnto a theefe, with swords and staues?" (Luke 22:52).[8] In the N-town play of the arrest, Jesus rebukes the soldiers:

> Ye don vnryth
> So vnkendely with cordys to bynd me here,
> And thus to falle on me by nyth,
> As thow I were a thevys fere.[9]

Gloucester and Jesus are both apprehended during the night, bound, and brought forcibly before their accusers as if they were dangerous ruffians.

The scene shows a mystery play parallel in its characterization as well as its action. Although the high priests are virtually interchangeable in the Gospels, the playwrights of the mysteries, in particular the York and Towneley plays, are at pains to differentiate them. One is excitable and voluble in his threats, the other calm but more dangerous in his calculating deliberations.[10] In *King Lear* Regan and Cornwall are similarly characterized. As Gloucester's punishment draws, near the sisters bay for his blood:

> *Regan.* Hang him instantly.
> *Goneril.* Pluck out his eyes.

> *Cornwall.* Leave him to my displeasure . . .
> Pinion him like a thief; bring him before us.
> Though well we may not pass upon his life
> Without the form of justice, yet our power
> Shall do a curtsy to our wrath, which men
> May blame but not control.

(3.7.1–26)

The sisters are instinctively vicious, but Cornwall's deliberate, understated threats are more menacing. Both the punishments suggested by the sisters—hanging and blinding—are penalties that the Towneley Caiaphas likewise longs to inflict, but Annas, like Cornwall, takes over the proceedings with an ominous calm, insisting on legal form:

> *Cayphas.* Nay, bot I shall out-thrist
> Both his een on a raw.
> *Anna.* Syr, ye will not, I tryst,
> Be so vengeabyll;
> Bot let me oppose hym.
> *Cayphas.* I pray you—and sloes hym!
> *Anna.* Sir, we may not lose hym
> Bot we were dampnabill. . . .
> *Sed nobis non licet*
> *Interficere quemquam.*
> Sir, ye wote better than I
> We shuld slo no man.[11]

The insistence of both Cornwall and Annas that they cannot kill their victims—is strongly expressed, but in each case it is slightly surprising. Cornwall has absolute power, and if he can blind Gloucester with impunity, it seems unlikely anyone would dare to take him to task for executing him. Annas's pronouncement is taken directly from the Gospel of John: "then the Iewes sayde vnto him, It is not lawfull for vs to put any man to death" (John 18:31).[12] The Towneley playwright quotes directly from the Vulgate, but the statement is surprising because it is historically odd that the Sanhedrin should have had no jurisdiction in capital cases. Whether or not the high priest's remark is historically accurate has been cause of much debate among New Testament scholars.[13] In the fourth Gospel the remark seems to have an anti-Semitic purpose, making the Jews guilty of Jesus's death despite the historical fact that he was crucified by the Romans. Theatrically however, it performs a different task. Annas, like Cornwall, acquires menace by parading his legalism (which is in fact a veneer for his abuse of his victim). His apparent fair play is the prelude to greater violence—the transfer of judicial murder to the Romans.

Caiaphas's proposed blinding of Christ in the Towneley play—"bot I shall out-thrist / Both his een on a raw"—is one of the specific, recognized connections between this scene and the blinding of Gloucester.[14] It has no basis in the Gospels and is drawn instead from a medieval interpretative tradition known as the secret Passion. This was an account of Christ's Passion that grew up in the fourteenth century in response to a desire for more affecting narratives about his suffering, which were embellished with details culled from Old Testament prophecies.[15] In these stories every punishment inflicted on Old Testament prefigurements of the messiah were also described as suffered by Jesus. The blinding of Christ became part of the secret Passion sufferings because of the connections that were recognized between Samson and Christ. Samson was a ubiquitous type of Christ, and from the fourteenth to the seventeenth century almost every event in his life—from his miraculous birth to his triumphant death—could be understood as a prefiguration of the redeemer.[16] The deep connections perceived between Samson and Jesus led to the belief that Christ too might have been blinded as one of his torments. James Marrow suggests that the juxtaposition of illustrations of the crowning with thorns and the blinding of Samson prepared the way for the merging of the two in the secret Passion. Marrow relates that during the crowning with thorns, "the majority of Netherlandic Passion tracts report that the thorns pierced Christ's eyes, or at least His eyelids or brows."[17] Likewise Samson was shorn of his hair and hence, as one source for the mystery plays phrased it: "whan Iewes had dampned hym [Christ] deth for to haue, / Shamely berde and hede gun they shaue."[18] This interpretation retained its popularity beyond the Reformation because two Isaiahan prophecies likewise suggest that the messiah would suffer the indignity of having his hair and beard pulled out: Isaiah 53:7—"as a sheepe before her shearer is dumme, so he openeth not his mouth"—and Isaiah 50:6: "I gaue my backe unto the smiters, and my cheekes to the nippers" (the Geneva Bible glossed "nippers" as "those who pull out the beard").

Gloucester in act 3, scene 7 shares his blinding with the Christ of the secret Passion, and he likewise suffers the indignity of having hairs pulled out of his beard:

> *Gloucester.* By the kind gods, 'tis most ignobly done,
> To pluck me by the beard . . .
> These hairs which thou dost ravish from my chin
> Will quicken and accuse thee.

>   (3.7.33–38)

Despite the frequency of this torment in pictorial illustrations, however, it has been thought that there is no evidence for its occurrence in the mysteries.[19] The text of the N-town plays, however, may record a staging of this part of the secret Passion while the Jews are playing hot cockles with Jesus:

> *Quartus Judeus.* A, and now wole I a newe game begynne
> That we mon pley at, all that arn hereinne:
> Whele and pylle, whele and pylle,
> Comyth to halle hoso wylle—
> Ho was that?
>
> (*N-Town play,* 29.185–92)

The "newe game" that the Jews are playing with Jesus is hot cockles, which involves someone being blindfolded and then being hit or buffeted by the other players. He can only free himself by guessing the identity of his assailant. This was a popular medieval game, and it has a basic similarity with the humiliation of Jesus before his Crucifixion, during which he was blindfolded, struck, and then his tormentor's jeered at him to prophesy who struck him (Mark 14:65). The connection between Christ's torment and this game, which the Gospel writers themselves may have intended, was revived by a number of medieval writers who made deliberate attempts to imbue popular diversions with religious significance.[20] As Rosemary Woolf has argued, the game in the play is elaborately worked out and "preserves the kind of rhyming nonsense (such as 'whele and pille') and the simple incantatory questions (e.g., 'ho was that?'), which are characteristic of children's games throughout the centuries."[21] "Whele and pylle," however, is not simply nonsense: it is a cry that describes what the Jews are doing. "Whele" presumably means they are turning him round and round (as children still do in blindman's buff), and "pylle" that they are pulling out his hair (a meaning that is retained in the word "depilatory").[22] This suggests that, in the N-town version of the buffeting at least, the Jews plucked out Jesus's hair and beard.

The tormentors are here playing a game at Jesus's expense, and throughout the mystery plays there is a strong emphasis on Christ's suffering as a game. This connection between games and plays was played to the hilt by the theater's detractors. The author of *The Treatise of Miracles Pleying* (ca. 1380–1425), for example, clearly felt that the mystery plays were little better than games: "sithen thes miraclis pleyeris taken in bourde the ernestful werkis of God, no doute that ne they scornen God as diden the Jewis that bobbiden Crist, for they Iowen at his passioun as these Iowyn and japen of the miraclis of God."[23] The metaphor resurfaces over two hundred years later in the writings of another denigrator of biblical theater, William Prynne, who excoriates the blasphemy of those who "turne the most *serious Oracles of Gods sacred word into a Play,* a Iest, a Fable, a Sport, a May-game."[24]

The scorn of Prynne and the *Treatise of Miracles Pleying* grew out of the way that the mystery plays embraced the association between theater and games. Sports, games, and plays about Christ's Crucifixion are often so closely connected that it can be difficult to assess whether a medieval record is describing a game or a play.[25] A description of fashionably dressed gallants as being "degised as turmentours that comen from clerkes plei," for example, seems to be a simile drawn from a spectacle that is on the cusp between the two.[26] It is in some sense theatrical, because the tormentors have costumes, but having a character wandering away from the "plei" still wearing his costume does not sound like a fully fledged theatrical event. It is possible, indeed, that the shared ground between plays and games at this time was so extensive that in some cases it is misguided to try and place them in rigidly defined genres: games involved plots, impersonations, and costumes; plays shared game structures and unscripted play. The deep indebtedness of the mysteries, in particular, to games is evident in the way in which "game" became an overarching metaphor for theatrical productions in the medieval period. When the Chester banns announce "a memoriall / of that death and Passion which *in play* ensue after shall," the metaphor inherent in *ludus* becomes vivid.[27]

The games that are central to medieval performance as a whole reach a climax in the mysteries at Jesus's torture and death. In medieval narrative accounts of the Passion, the mocking of Christ on the night before his Crucifixion and the throwing of dice for Christ's robe are commonly described as games.[28] But the playwrights of the mystery plays, and in particular the authors of the York and Towneley cycles, extend the Gospel accounts, and turn almost all Christ's torments and humiliations into games.[29] In the Towneley *Play of the Dice,* which follows the *Crucifixion* play, the second torturer gives a detailed description about the "newe play" he taught Christ at Calvary:

> The Play, in fayth, it was to rowne
> That he shuld lay his hede downe,
> And sone I bobyd hym on the crowne—
> That gam me thoght was good!
>
> (24.144)

The York soldiers inform the high priests that "we haue bourded with this boy" (29.380) and Caiaphas shares in the naked enjoyment of his subordinates. He calls the flagellation of Jesus a "sporte" (30.205) and tells Annas that he has sent for Jesus partly for amusement: "halfe for hethyng" (29.33). Herod is likewise delighted at the prospect of sporting with Jesus:

> O, my harte hoppis for joie
> To se nowe this prophette appere.
> We schall haue goode game with this boy.
>
> (*York Plays,* 31.163–65)

In Chester, after playing hot cockles with Jesus (16.90–109), the Crucifixion is made into a game, of which the Primus Judeus notes "this poplard never past / so perrelous a playe" (16A.167–68). Once Jesus's feet are nailed down the Secundus Judeus is satisfied that "this gamon went on right" (16A.203).

Cornwall and Regan do not exhibit the same naked enjoyment as the tormentors in the mystery plays—the second Towneley torturer tells Jesus: "Bot the more sorow thou hase, / Oure myrth is incresyng" (Towneley, 22.85–86)—but Regan's reasoning likewise trivializes Gloucester's pain: "One side will mock another; th'other, too" (3.7.68). The mocking of the victim is yet another correspondence between the blinding of Gloucester and the buffeting of Christ in the mysteries. Fundamentally, however, it is in the dignity of suffering that the strongest bond between the scenes lies, a dignity that is strengthened by the mockery of the tormentors.

King Lear is rich with gaming metaphors, and in this context Gloucester's entreaty to Cornwall and Regan to "do me no foul play, friends" (3.7.29) points uneasily to the origins of the expression "unfair conduct in a game."[30] The scene is often played in modern productions with this undercurrent of playful malice painfully visible: Jonathon Miller's 1982 production for the BBC had the sisters laugh as they suggested Gloucester's torments.[31] Shakespeare's torture scene is much less knockabout than the mysteries, but he has retained the essence of the medieval staging in which the playfulness of the tormentors heightens the pathos of suffering.

One of the primary sports played with Christ by his tormentors in the mystery plays involves treating him like an animal: in Towneley the first torturer goads Christ as they enter the high priests' hall: "Do io furth, io! / And trott on apase!" (21.1–2, cf. 621–24). In York Caiaphas tells a soldier who is striking Christ that it is no fun to beat a bound animal: "Itt is no burde to bete bestis that are bune" (29.243). In the Towneley *Buffeting* play Jesus is surrounded by allusions to "cokys in a croft" (21.513–14)—a reference either to cockfighting or the Shrovetide game of throwing sticks at a tethered cockerel, who has to dodge the missiles to survive. Regan, like the torturers in the mystery plays, attempts to dehumanize her victim. She addresses him as an "Ingrateful fox" (3.7.27) and Gloucester recognizes his position as one powerless, bound, and tormented for sport like an animal: "I am tied to th'stake, and I must stand the course" (3.7.52). Gloucester describes himself as a bear using the word "course," which only remains in modern English in the coursing of hares.[32] Theaters sometimes doubled as bear pits and many of the same people patronized both, as attested by the Privy Council ruling in 1591 that forbade theaters to open on Thursdays because they drew away the people from "the game of bearbaiting."[33] Shakespeare's original audience, therefore, are likely to have recognized a particularly unsavory version of bearbaiting, which has a painful resonance with Gloucester's suffering: the tormenting of a blinded bear.[34] A frisson is created in the connection between Gloucester's words and this popular version of the sport, which creates an aptness for his metaphor that Gloucester does not yet recognize.[35]

By showing his tormentors as sporting with Gloucester, Shakespeare is not only echoing medieval drama but also finding the same solution as it did to the problem of staging violence. Unconvincing death scenes can come perilously close to farce, but if laughter has been preempted by the playwright and placed in the mouths of torturers, the audience is discouraged from ridicule. In the blinding of Gloucester "sport" and "game" perform the same dramatic function as they did in the mystery plays. The body in pain has a dignity that the mocking intensifies.

Critics and editors have long expressed their uneasiness with Gloucester's blinding, and many pre-twentieth-century directors, such as Macready, Garrick, Kean, and Irving, either cut the scene or transferred it offstage. The customary solution in the early twentieth century was to place Gloucester's chair a long way upstage and facing away from the audience. It was only with Peter Brook's famously graphic 1962 production (in which Cornwall blinded Gloucester with the spur of his boot), that directors ceased to be hesitant about staging the full horror of the scene.[36] Likewise the first modern productions of the mysteries shied away from graphic staging of the Passion. In the 1951 York Festival production, the scourging took place offstage and the nailing on the cross was shielded from the audience by the soldiers. In the 1951 production of the Chester cycle the director even chose not to stage the Crucifixion. It was not until the professional production of the Towneley plays in the Mermaid Theatre, in London in 1961, a year before Brook's *Lear,* that the Crucifixion was performed in full view of the audience.[37]

The classically trained sensibilities of critics and directors, which shied away from the portrayal of such graphic scenes of violence, were shared by the Dutch theologian and dramatist, Hugo Grotius, whose play *Christus Patiens,* despite being identical to the mystery plays in content, and identical to *King Lear* in date, shrank from staging extreme physical suffering. Grotius was a Dutch lawyer and theologian, famous throughout Europe for his legal and theological treatises. In the Netherlands he was also a respected dramatist. He was strongly influenced by Seneca and, for his *Christus Patiens,* may also have drawn on *Christos Paschon,* a fourth-century Greek play attributed to Gregory of Nazianzus.[38] These classical influences are drawn attention to and celebrated in Grotius's introduction to the reader in which he states that he has attempted to keep his play within the style "which tragedy has made its own." He is anxious to note that his apparent departures from classical decorum (change of scene, two choruses) have precedent. He also alerts the reader to the fact that his play takes no longer than the twenty-four hours recommended by Aristotle; a decorum he chooses to observe despite the problem that it means the Resurrection can only be foretold. This introduction, despite its dedication "to the reader" makes it clear that Grotius intended his play to be performed—he lists the large number of nonspeaking parts he has included—nine apostles, priests, counselors, attendants, elders, and Galilean women—in order to create the complex series of visual tableaux fashionable in Dutch theater at the time. Performance, however, brings its pitfalls, which he solves in typical, classical manner: "There was also this substantial problem: the fact that much had to be represented through messengers: for it was not allowed by the laws of tragedy to represent on stage either the notable miracles of Christ's capture, nor his punishment of hanging on the cross."[39] The influence of Seneca and the *Christos Paschon,* however, have made *Christus Patiens* into a static play in which the central events occur offstage. It is now widely thought that Seneca was intended for declamation rather than performance, and Gregory's play was a byword in the Renaissance for the decorous play-poem, which was not meant to be staged.[40] In Grotius's play, as in both Seneca and Nazianzus, rhetoric takes the place of affective spectacle, and action is replaced with long speeches.

The English translation of Grotius's play, however, is even more resolutely nondramatic. The Dutch stage was much more friendly to religious subjects than the English theater, and *Christus Patiens* was in fact part of a vogue for biblical drama in this period.[41] George Sandys's translation of Grotius's play, however, was not intended to be performed. Theater, biblical theater in particular, was subject to much more severe censorship in England than in Holland, and no new English play had put Christ on the stage since Lewis Wager's *Life and Repentaunce of Marie Magdalene* in the 1560s. Sandys's second edition of *Christ's Passion* (1687) advertises itself as "with Annotations" and "illustrated with Scvlptures": an archaic term for engraving, which suggests that it is only in the illustrations that this play will be bodied forth. Such paratexts make the reading of the play a fuller experience and cement the impression that this was not a text to be played.

Jesus's death is related to the chorus by a relay of messengers, and his sufferings are graphically described because they are not seen:

> *I Nvncivs.* The Steel now bor'd his feet, whose slit veins spout
> Like pierced Conduits; both his Arms stretcht out.
> His Hands fixt with two Nails. While his great Soul
> These Tortures suffer'd, while the rising Bole
> Forsook the Earth, and Crimson Torrents sprung
> From his fresh Wounds, he gave his Grief no Tongue.[42]

In this speech Sandys has borrowed the visually unstageable simile of veins spouting like pierced conduits from Ovid rather than Grotius.[43] The stresses on the graphic verbs ("bor'd," "slit," "spout," "pierced") express what is not seen, in an attempt to communicate its horror to the reader. The striking, lurid rhetoric is highly reminiscent of Seneca. Grotius's play shares the linguistic texture, as well as the formal characteristics of classical drama, because he, like them, needs a solution to staging violence that the audience cannot see.

Shakespearean violence, however, is much closer to the medieval conception than the classical, even as interpreted by his direct contemporary, Grotius. Shakespearean theater replaces the rhetorical descriptions of pain found in Senecan drama, with the physical presence of the wounded body. Rhetoric does not create the same emotional response as seeing pain and death, a truism that Elaine Scarry has theorized by arguing for the inexpressibility of pain: not merely that it is difficult to define but that because "it takes no object it, more than any other phenomenon, resists objectification in language."[44] Instead of the decorum of classical theater, Shakespeare inherited the violent power of the mysteries, whose devotional focus made the emotional potency of the visual fundamental to their dramaturgy. It is in *King Lear* that some of Shakespeare's clearest echoes of the Passion as staged in the mystery plays can be seen. It is in *King Lear* that Shakespeare describes suffering as a "side-piercing sight" (4.5.85), an image that insists on the power of what is seen to transmit an understanding of pain to the spectator, and hints at the devotional origins of such an empathetic gaze.

Notes

My grateful thanks are due to Imogen Black, Karen Junod and Jane McLeod for their help with this article.

1. Sir Philip Sidney, *The Countess of Pembroke's Arcadia,* ed. Maurice Evans (Harmondsworth: Penguin Books, 1987), 278.

2. See Michael O'Connell, *The Idolatrous Eye: Iconoclasm and Theater in Early Modern England* (Oxford: Oxford University Press, 2000), 87–88; Cherrell Guilfoyle, *Shakespeare's Play within Play: Medieval Imagery and Scenic Form in Hamlet, Othello and King Lear* (Kalamazoo, MI: Medieval Institute Publications, 1990), 118; Helen Cooper, "Shakespeare and the Mystery Plays," in *Shakespeare and Elizabethan Popular Culture,* ed. Stuart Gillespie and Neil Rhodes, 39, in the Arden Shakespeare (London, 2006). My grateful thanks are due to Helen Cooper for giving me a copy of this piece prior to publication.

3. Helen Cooper, "Shakespeare and the Mystery Plays," 39.

4. R. W. Ingram, ed., *Coventry,* Records of Early English Drama (Manchester: Manchester University Press, 1981), 294; Lawrence M. Clopper, *Drama, Play, and Game: English Festive Culture in the Medieval and Early Modern Period* (Chicago: University of Chicago Press, 2001), 282, 293.

5. A. L. Beier, *Masterless Men: The Vagrancy Problem in England, 1560–1640* (London: Methuen, 1987), 75.

6. Glynne Wickham, *Shakespeare's Dramatic Heritage: Collected Studies in Mediaeval, Tudor and Shakespearean Drama* (London: Routledge & Kegan Paul, 1969), 214–31; Michael O'Connell, "Vital Cultural Practices: Shakespeare and the Mysteries," *Journal of Medieval and Early Modern Studies* 29, no. 1 (1999): 149–68; Cynthia Marshall, *Last Things and Last Plays: Shakespearean Eschatology* (Carbondale: Southern Illinois University Press, 1991), 122–26; John D. Cox, *Shakespeare and the*

Dramaturgy of Power (Princeton: Princeton University Press, 1989), 82–103. There is also a possible verbal echo of the mysteries in Shakespeare's nonbiblical ascription of "All Hail!" to Judas on greeting Christ in the garden of Gethsemane; Naseeb Shaheen, *Biblical References in Shakespeare's Plays* (Newark: University of Delaware Press, 1999), 335–36.

7. As Foakes points out, Edmund and Oswald have already informed Cornwall that Lear has been sent to Dover: R. A. Foakes, *Shakespeare and Violence* (Cambridge: Cambridge University Press, 2003), 146.

8. All Shakespeare references are from *William Shakespeare: The Complete Works,* ed. Stanley Wells and Gary Taylor (Oxford: Oxford University Press, 1986). All biblical references are from the Geneva Bible. For Shakespeare's detailed knowledge of this version, see Shaheen, *Biblical References in Shakespeare's Plays,* 38–40. The Chester cycle echoes Luke 22:52 closely: "As to a theeffe you came here/ with sword and staves and armerye"; *The Chester Mystery Cycle,* ed. R. M. Lumiansky and David Mills, Early English Text Society, *Supplementary series* 3 and 9 (London: Early English Text Society, 1974–86), 15.351–52. See also ll. 319, 323.

9. *The N-Town Play: Cotton MS Vespasian D.8,* ed. Stephen Spector, Early English Text Society, *Supplementary Series* 11 and 12 (Oxford: Early English Text Society, 1991), 28.133–36.

10. In the Towneley plays it is Caiaphas who is excitable, and Annas who is calm; in the York plays this characterization is reversed.

11. *The Towneley Plays,* ed. Martin Stevens and A. C. Cawley, Early English Text Society, *Supplementary series* 13 and 14 (Oxford: Early English Text Society, 1994), 21.279–92, 330 (Caiaphas's threat to hang him).

12. See also *N-Town Play,* 30.97–98; *Chester Mystery Cycle,* 16.247–50; *The York Plays,* ed. Richard Beadle (London: Edward Arnold, 1982), 30.432.

13. For an overview of the argument, see Paul Winter, *On the Trial of Jesus* (Berlin: Walter de Gruyter, 1961), 14–15, 76, 88–89; J. Duncan M. Derrett, *Law in the New Testament* (London: Darton, Longman & Todd, 1970), 166n3.

14. O'Connell, *The Idolatrous Eye,* 87–88.

15. James H. Marrow, *Passion Iconography in Northern European Art of the Late Middle Ages and Early Renaissance: A Study of the Transformation of Sacred Metaphor into Descriptive Narrative* (Kortrijk: Van Ghemmert, 1979), 196, and passim; F. P. Pickering, *Literature and Art in the Middle Ages* (London: Macmillan, 1970).

16. For sixteenth- and seventeenth-century examples of this typology, see *Certaine Sermons or Homilies Appointed to be Read in Churches in the Time of Queen Elizabeth I (1547–71),* ed. Mary Ellen Riches and Thomas B. Stroup (Gainesville, FL: Scholars' Facsimiles and Reprints, 1968), 191; Joseph Hall, *Contemplations Vpon the principal passages of the holie Historie* (London, 1615), 191, 280; Lancelot Andrewes, *XCVI Sermons* (London, 1629), 473.

17. Marrow, *Passion Iconography,* 141–42, fig. 85.

18. John Bonaventure, *Meditations of the Supper of Our Lord, and the Hours of the Passion, versified by Robert Manning of Brunne (1315–1330),* ed. J. Meadows Cowper, Early English Text Society, o.s., 60 (London: Early English Text Society, 1875), ll. 965–72; Marrow, *Passion Iconography,* 71, figs. 21, 23, 31–3, 36–38, 49–51, 54, 69, 82, 106, 144. For evidence that this aspect of the secret passion was still

known in Shakespeare's day, see: Richard Bancroft, *A Sermon Preached at Paules Crosse the 9 of Februarie, being the first Sunday in the Parleament, Anno. 1588* (London, 1588), F6v–F7r. My thanks to Dr. Peter McCullough for this reference.

19. W. L. Hildburgh, *English Alabaster Carvings as Records of the Medieval Religious Drama* (Oxford: Society of Antiquaries of London, 1949), 78.

20. G. R. Owst, *Literature and Pulpit in Medieval England: A Neglected Chapter in the History of English People* (Oxford: Oxford University Press, 1961), 510.

21. Rosemary Woolf, *The English Mystery Play* (London: Routledge & Kegan Paul, 1972), 255.

22. *Middle English Dictionary,* ed. Hans Kurath, Sherman M. Kuhn, and Robert E. Lewis (Ann Arbor: University of Michigan Press, 1952–), s.v. "pille"; *The Oxford English Dictionary* (Oxford: Oxford University Press, 1989), s.v. "pill."

23. *A Treatise of Miracles Pleying,* ed. Clifford Davidson (Kalamazoo, MI: Medieval Institute Publications, 1993), 97. Most critics are agreed that this is an antitheatrical document (see ibid., 2), but Clopper has argued that critics have confused drama with *ludi inhonesti;* cf. Clopper, *Drama, Play and Game,* 69–74.

24. William Prynne, *Histrio-mastix* (London: Michael Sparke, 1633), 111. Although Prynne is speaking of biblical theater in general here, he seems to have mystery plays in his thoughts shortly afterward when he writes of the blasphemous theatrical productions of popish priests (112, 115).

25. Siegfried Wenzel, "*SomerGame* and Sermon References to a Corpus Christi Play," *Modern Philology* 86.3 (1989): 274–83; Clopper, *Drama, Play and Game,* 74.

26. Thomas Wright, ed., *The Political Songs of England, from the reign of King John to that of Edward* II (London: Camden Society, 1839), 336 (line 285).

27. V. A. Kolve, *The Play Called Corpus Christi* (Stanford, CA: Stanford University Press, 1966), 13.

28. Ibid., 186.

29. Games are also central to continental Passion plays: Woolf, *English Mystery Play,* 254; Jody Enders, *The Medieval Theater of Cruelty: Rhetoric, Memory, Violence* (Ithaca: Cornell University Press, 1999), 175–77.

30. *Oxford English Dictionary,* s.v. "foul." The games alluded to in *King Lear* include bowls (2.2.145), football (1.4.84), handy dandy (4.5.149), primero (1.1.123–24), and tennis (1.4.82).

31. James P. Lusardi and June Schlueter, *Reading Shakespeare in Performance: King Lear* (London: Associated University Presses, 1991), 82. See also Carol Rutter, "Eel Pie and ugly Sisters in *King Lear,*" in *Lear: From Study to Stage; Essays in Criticism,* ed. James Ogden and Arthur H. Scouten, 201–5. (London: Associated University Presses, 1997).

32. Macbeth uses almost the same words for his predicament: "They have tied me to a stake. I cannot fly, / But bear-like I must fight the course" (*Macbeth,* 5.7.1–2).

33. Quoted in S. P. Cerasano, "The Master of the Bears in Art and Enterprise," *Medieval and Renaissance Drama in England* 5 (1991): 196. For other contemporary descriptions of bearbaiting as "play" and "game" see ibid., 199; C. L. Kingsford, "Paris Garden and the Bear-baiting," *Archaeologia* 20 (1920): 168.

34. Cf. *Satiromastix,* in *The Dramatic Works of Thomas Dekker,* ed. Fredson Bowers (Cambridge: Cambridge University Press, 1953), 5.2.244; John Brand, *Observa-*

tions on Popular Antiquities: Chiefly Illustrating the Origin of our Vulgar Customs, Ceremonies and Superstitions (London: Chatto and Windus, 1877), 533; Kingsford, "Paris Garden and the Bear-baiting," 162; Walter W. Greg, ed., *Henslowe Papers: Being Documents Supplementary to Henslowe's Diary* (London: A. H. Bullen, 1907), 106. My thanks are due to Tiffany Stern for alerting me to this final example.

35. The quarto's Gloucester has a stronger sense of the connection between human suffering and the situation of hunted animals. He suggests that humans are baited like tethered animals when he says, "As flies to wanton boys are we to the gods; / They bitt us for their sport" (4.1.35) (Cf. *Oxford English Dictionary,* s.v. "bitt"). And when he accuses Regan of bestial treatment of her father—"In his annointed flesh rash boarish fangs"—he uses a hunting term from the stroke made by a wild boar with his tushes.

36. *A New Variorum Edition of Shakespeare: King Lear,* ed. Horace Howard Furness (Philadelphia: J. B. Lippincott, 1880), note to 3.7.66; *Plays in Performance: King Lear,* ed. J. S. Bratton (Bristol: Bristol Classical Press, 1987), 157. Modern critics have felt very differently to Coleridge about the importance of staging this scene: cf. Richard Strier's excellent discussion of the staging of Gloucester's blinding as essential to gaining the audience's sympathy for the action of the servant; Richard Strier, "Faithful Servants: Shakespeare's Praise of Disobedience," in *The Historical Renaissance: New Essays on Tudor and Stuart Literature and Culture,* ed. Heather Dubrow and Richard Strier, 119–20 (Chicago: University of Chicago Press, 1988).

37. John R. Elliott, *Playing God: Medieval Mysteries on the Modern Stage* (Toronto: University of Toronto Press, 1989), 77, 103, 112.

38. Grotius cites Gregory's play as a prototype for all dramatic representations of the Passion: Hugo Grotius, *Tragoedia: Christvs Patiens* (Leiden, [1608]),*vi*[v.] The two plays, however, are not similar, although they share a reliance on choruses and messenger speeches to ensure that violence takes place offstage; Grégoire de Nazianze, *La Passion du Christ: Tagédie,* ed. André Tuiler (Paris: Les Éditions du Cerf, 1969), ll. 657–69. For the influences of Seneca, see Reinder P. Meijer, *Literature of the Low Countries: A Short History of Dutch Literature in the Netherlands and Belgium* (Cheltenham: Stanley Thornes Ltd., 1978), 129.

39. Habuit & hoc molestiae nonnihil quod multa per internuntios repraesentanda fuerunt: neque enim per leges Tragoediae licuit, aut capturam Christi miraculis insignem, aut cruce pendentis supplicium in scenam producere. Grotius, *Christus Patiens,-*[*vi*v–vii[r]] (my translation).

40. For the likelihood that Seneca was intended for declamation only, see Norman T. Pratt, *Seneca's Drama* (Chapel Hill: University of North Carolina Press, 1983), 132–63; John G. Fitch, "Playing Seneca?" in *Seneca in Performance,* ed. George W. M. Harrison (London: Duckworth, 2000), 9–10. For the Renaissance belief that *Christos Paschon* was not intended for the stage, see Stephen Gosson, *Playes Confuted in fiue Actions . . .* (London, 1582), E5v–6r.

41. For the popularity of biblical subjects in the plays of Grotius's contemporaries, see Meijer, *Literature of the Low Countries,* 134–36. For the opposition to religious subjects on the stage, see ibid., 133, 137; *Theatre in Europe: German and Dutch Theatre, 1600–1848,* compiled by George W. Brandt and Wiebe Hogendoorn, ed. George W. Brandt (Cambridge: Cambridge University Press, 1993), 398–400.

42. George Sandys, *Christ's Passion, A Tragedy; with Annotations* (London, 1687), Fr.

43. In the *Metamorphoses* Pyramus's blood is famously described as spouting like water from a burst pipe, and Arthur Golding, like Sandys, uses the word "Conduite" in his translation: "The bloud did spin on hie / As when a Conduite pipe is crackt"; Geoffrey Bullough, ed., *Narrative and Dramatic Sources of Shakespeare* (London: Routledge and Kegan Paul, 1964–75), 1.407.

44. Elaine Scarry, *The Body in Pain: The Making and Unmaking of the World* (Oxford: Oxford University Press, 1985), 5.

Curtains on the Shakespearean Stage

FREDERICK KIEFER

Although the only surviving drawing of a theatrical interior contemporaneous with Shakespeare (Johannes De Witt's sketch of the Swan) shows an unadorned theater, we know that textiles not only decorated the stages but also figured in the action of Renaissance plays. Dialogue and stage directions sometimes employ one or more of these terms: curtain, arras, hanging, and canopy.[1] Collectively, they constitute what Glynne Wickham has called "soft furnishings."[2] Because we lack pictures or verbal accounts of almost all plays in their original productions, we are left wondering exactly where the "soft" accoutrements of the stage were located and how the actors made use of them. If we cannot resolve with certainty such issues, we can at least enumerate the ways that curtains functioned and speculate about their location. Accordingly, I shall here examine the following topics: bed curtains, discovery curtains; traverse and curtain, arras and hanging, action above and window curtains, and canopy.

Anyone investigating the subject of curtains on the Renaissance stage needs to begin by noticing that the subject is a good deal more problematic than we like to think. Consider, for example, Ben Jonson's *Volpone,* performed by the King's Men at the Globe in 1606. The Folio version of the play begins by naming the characters onstage: "Volpone, Mosca."[3] Modern editors, however, commonly suppose that Volpone is in bed since his day is just beginning. Hence R. B. Parker inserts several words into the opening direction: "[*Enter*] Mosca [*and discovers*] Volpone [*in his bed*]" (1.1.0).[4] Parker explains in a note: "Volpone's bed would probably be a four-poster on the main stage, whose curtains Mosca could open."[5] Such curtains hanging from testers, or four-posters,[6] were a feature of substantial beds in Elizabethan and Jacobean homes and served the practical purpose of keeping warmth from being dissipated and reducing cold drafts at night. Mosca could "discover" Volpone by pushing back the bed curtains. Robert N. Watson's edition, like Parker's, inserts explanatory words in that first stage direction, making more explicit what Parker consigns to a note: "[*Enter*] Mosca, [*pulling back the curtains to discover*] Volpone [*in bed*]."[7] Watson comments that Mosca enters, "perhaps opening the curtains around Volpone's bed, or opening curtains to admit the morning sun." Here the issue seems a little less certain: are the curtains that Mosca handles covering a window rather than a bed? If so, where exactly are such curtains located onstage? And if they are pulled back, what do they reveal? The issue of staging at the beginning of Jonson's play is at least twofold. Does Volpone recline on a bed with or without curtains or on some other kind of furniture?[8] Exactly what curtains, if any, does Mosca open upon his entry? Neither the 1607 quarto nor the 1616 Folio allows us to answer these questions with confidence; no stage directions appear in the scene, only the names of the two characters. We need, therefore, to proceed cautiously, acknowledging the extent to which the theatrical use of curtains remains terra incognita.

Bed curtains

The title page of *The Vow Breaker* by William Sampson, acted ca. 1625–26, contains a woodcut illustrating four incidents in the play, and one section of the print depicts a tester with curtains; the bed's occupant is the chief female character, Anne, who, although pledged to Bateman, covets greater wealth and marries German instead. Bateman in despair hangs himself and, as a ghost, visits Anne. In the illustration the fearful Anne says to her attendants, "Hees come, watch mee or I am gone" (sig. A2r).[9] R. A. Foakes observes that the picture of Anne in bed "may have some relevance to the staging of the play."[10] If so, what does it tell us? George Reynolds conjectures that such a bed "must have been a pretty sizable and cumbersome property."[11] It's entirely possible, however, that carpenters could have assembled a bed that was considerably less weighty and unwieldy than one constructed for, say, a prosperous merchant. After all, some beds were actually carried out or drawn onto the stage, as in Thomas Heywood's *The Golden Age,* first acted by Queen Anne's Men at the Red Bull ca. 1609–11:[12] "*Enter the foure old beldams, drawing out* Dana[e]'s *bed: she in it*" (sig.I1v).[13] And Sasha Roberts observes that simple beds could be furnished to look opulent: "Even if the beds used by theatrical companies were constructed on a much simpler basis than the bed depicted in *The Vow Breaker*'s title page, those stage-beds might still have produced the *impression* or *effect* of a state bed, especially through the display of sumptuous fabrics."[14] In other plays beds were sufficiently light in construction for stagehands or actors to push the furniture out onto the main playing area. A stage direction in Middleton's *A Chaste Maid in Cheapside,* performed by Lady Elizabeth's Men at the Swan in 1613, is explicit: "*A bed thrust out upon the stage,* Allwit's *wife in it.*" (3.2.0.s.d.).[15] This bed, according to Richard Hosley, was presumably "a small curtained four-poster."[16]

In the theater the closing of bed curtains is commonly associated with sexual activity, as in Juliet's metaphoric appeal to the "fiery-footed steeds" of the sun god's chariot to hurry across the sky: "Spread thy close curtain, love-performing night" (3.2.1, 5).[17] When she speaks these lines, Juliet anticipates her wedding night with Romeo. Bed curtains have the advantage of protecting sleepers from prying eyes, as the staging of Heywood's *The Golden Age* illustrates. The playwright dramatizes Jupiter's proclivity for philandering, in this instance with Danae. The god enters *"crown'd with his imperiall robes,"* and *"He lyes upon her bed"* (sig. I2r). Then "Jupiter *puts out the lights and makes unready"* (sig. I2v). Danae says to him, "If you will needs, for modesties chast law, / Before you come to bed, the curtaines draw," adding, "Well I'le even winke, and then do what you will." Curtains, then, afford privacy to lovers on the stage as in ordinary life.

Closed bed curtains may create an air of expectation and suspense preceding sexual activity, as they do in Thomas Heywood's *The Rape of Lucrece,* first acted by Queen Anne's Men at the Red Bull in 1607: *"Lucr[ece] discoverd in her bed"* (sig.G1v).[18] The bed is equipped with curtains, which are probably closed as Sextus Tarquinius approaches, saying to himself, "Heere, heere, behold! Beneath these curtaines lyes / That bright enchantresse that hath daz'd my eies." The curtains he refers to must be bed curtains, for the "enchantresse" lies *beneath* those curtains; Tarquin's pulling back of the curtains reveals the sleeping woman.

The rape of Lucrece becomes a prelude to her demise. In Heywood's play, as elsewhere, curtained beds are associated with death. When, for example, in *Romeo and Juliet* Juliet takes the potion allowing her to counterfeit death, she is preparing for bed; her mother has just said, "Good night. / Get thee to bed" (4.3.12–13).[19] The Q1 stage direction at the end of Juliet's soliloquy, which expresses her fear of awaking in the tomb, reads: *"She fals upon her bed within the curtaines"* (sig. I1r).[20] The potion will, of course, later contribute to her actual death in the Capulet tomb when she awakes to find her husband dead, thereby prompting her suicide. The conflation of bed and death also characterizes *Tancred and Gismund,* probably acted in 1591 by the gentlemen of the Inner Temple, presumably in their hall. The tragedy is precipitated when Tancred goes to his daughter's bedroom, finds it empty, and lies down on her bed to await her return: "And thereupon I (wearie) threw my selfe / Upon her widdowes bed (for so I thought) / And in the curten wrapt my cursed head" (act 4, lines 984–86).[21] The dumb show preceding this act allows us to see what Tancred describes: *"Tancred commeth forth, & draweth Gismund's curtens, and lies down upon her bed."* Thus concealed, he witnesses his widowed daughter embrace her lover when they enter the bedroom through a hidden door; following the discovery of the illicit relationship, a jealous Tancred slays the man, triggering Gismund's suicide.

In Shakespeare's England, as in our own time, beds were typically sites of death. When last we see John of Gaunt in *Richard II,* he says, "Convey me to my bed, then to my grave" (2.1.137). The demise of Falstaff, narrated in

Henry V, also takes place in bed, for the Hostess reports, "I saw him fumble with the sheets" (2.3.13–14). In Shakespeare's *2 Henry IV,* the ailing King asks, "I pray you take me up, and bear me hence," and is apparently moved to a bed; he directs, "Set me the crown upon my pillow here" (4.5.5). Moments later the King is described as "Exceeding ill" (line 11) and "dispos'd to sleep" (line 17). To the Prince, who subsequently enters the room, the sleeping king appears dead; for this reason young Henry takes the crown from the pillow and sets it on his own head.

Beds sometimes become the sites not only of natural death but also of murder. In *The Battle of Alcazar,* originally performed 1588–89 and, in a revised version, 1598–99, we find this stage direction: "*Enter the Moore and two murdrers bringing in his unkle Abdelmunen, then they draw the curtains and smoother the yong princes in the bed*" (line 26.s.d.).[22] The contrast between the cold-blooded murderers and the sleeping princes, who are likened to "poore lambes" (line 24), could scarcely be greater. Their place of death seems to intensify the princes' vulnerability. In *The First Part of the Contention* (i.e., *2 Henry VI*), first staged ca. 1591, Shakespeare dramatizes another murder in bed: "*Then the Curtaines being drawne, Duke Humphrey is discovered in his bed, and two men lying on his brest and smothering him in his bed*" (sig. E2r).[23] Because a bed is ordinarily a place of repose and safety, the horror of the murder is underscored; curtains offer no protection for the man described in the play's full title as "good." Similarly, in Marlowe's *Massacre at Paris,* acted by Lord Strange's Men at the Rose in 1593, murderers sent by the Guise "*enter into the* Admiral's *house, and he in his bed*" (5.24.s.d.);[24] they proceed to stab the man who lies helpless, wounded in an earlier assassination attempt. Finally, in *Othello* bed curtains conceal the victim of murder, and here too the victim is an innocent. At the beginning of 5.2, we find this stage direction: "*Enter* Othello, [*with a light*] *and* Desdemona *in her bed* [*asleep*]" (5.2.0.s.d.). Later in the scene, after he has murdered his wife, Othello hears Emilia knocking at the door and says, "I had forgot thee. O, come in, Emilia. / Soft, by and by, let me the curtains draw" (5.2.103–4). The curtains must be those of a bed, as E. A. J. Honigmann observes in his gloss.[25] Othello closes them to hide the body of his wife. Honigmann adds this direction when Emilia hears Desdemona cry out as she momentarily revives: "[*She draws the bed-curtains*]" (5.2.118). In other words, Emilia opens the curtains of Desdemona's bed and finds the body.

Thomas Heywood dramatizes the nexus of violence and beds in *The Iron Age, Part 2,* performed by Queen Anne's Men at the Red Bull in 1612–13. Aegisthus, described in the dramatis personae as "a favorite to Queene Clitemnestra," visits the queen's bedchamber: "*Enter* Egistus *with his sword drawne, hideth himselfe in the chamber behind the bed-curtaines: all the kings come next in, conducting the generall and his queene to their lodging, and after some complement leave them, every one with torches ushered to their severall chambers, &c."* (sig. H3v).[26] There must be a real bed onstage, curtains and all, for otherwise Agamemnon's subsequent references to "doune" and "sheetes" would make no sense. The stage direction seems to mean that Aegisthus is either actually on the bed behind the curtains or behind the bed whose curtains are closed. When the suspicious Agamemnon hears a sound while speaking to his wife, he expresses apprehension, making explicit the conflation of bed and death: "Beds resemble graves, / And these me-thinkes appeare like winding sheetes, / Prepar'd for corses" (sig. H4r). Scarcely has Agamemnon spoken these words when Aegisthus emerges from his hiding place and, together with Clytemnestra, fatally wounds the King.

In addition to the curtains of a bed, other curtains sometimes figure in the dramatic action when beds appear onstage. For example, in Heywood's *Rape of Lucrece,* we find this stage direction, cited above: *"Lucr[ece] discovered in her bed."* How exactly was this discovery accomplished? Possibly by drawing back a curtain to reveal the bed with the sleeping woman. Some stage directions, after all, suggest that beds are revealed within a curtained space. For example, Nathan Field's *Amends for Ladies,* acted by the Queen's Revels Children at the Whitefriars in 1611, contains this direction: *"A curtaine drawne, a bed discover'd,* Ingen *with his sword in his hand, and a pistoll, the* Ladie *in a peticote, the* Parson" (5.2.180–82.s.d.).[27] Although we don't know whether this bed is equipped with its own curtains, it seems clear that the bed is revealed when a curtain is drawn back. Similarly, in *Lust's Dominion* by Dekker, Haughton, Day, and Marston, acted in 1600 at the Rose by the Admiral's Men, the King of Spain lies in bed: *"The courtains being drawn there appears in his bed King* Phillip, *with his Lords, the Princesse* Isabella *at the feet;* [Cardinal] Mendoza, Alvero, Hortensio, Fernando, Roderigo, *and to them Enter Queen* [Mother] *in hast"* (1.2.0.s.d.).[28] Alan Dessen and Leslie Thomson believe that the stage directions "imply" not the curtains of a bed but rather curtains hanging on the wall of the tiring-house.[29] Possibly the doors opening onto the stage were opened 180 degrees so that they were flush with the tiring-house wall, and then the opening was covered with a curtain. Andrew Gurr has suggested that the curtain "could have hung in the doorways behind the doors, so that when the doors were open the hangings would be visible to conceal a 'discovery,' and when they were closed the hangings would be hidden and so would not impede the normal use of the doors."[30] Tiffany Stern observes that "Thomas in his *Dictionarium [Linguae Latinae et Anglicanae,* 1587] defines 'cortina' as 'the covered place in a stage, whence the players come out'; and numerous other texts suggest the regular use of curtained areas that gave straight from the tiring-house to the stage, the famous references to clowns peeping between curtains . . . being the most obvious."[31] In whatever way the discovery in *Lust's Dominion* was managed, playgoers would likely behold the recumbent figure of the King in his bed, surrounded by family and friends, when the curtain was drawn back, revealing an interior acting space.

The suggestion by Dessen and Thomson about *Lust's Dominion* is attractive, especially because the stage direction apparently specifies a sequence: a curtain is drawn and *then* the bed is seen by the playgoers. But would a so-called discovery space be large enough to contain both a bed and the number of characters specified in the stage direction? Most discoveries reveal only one, two, or three characters and no furniture larger than a chair, table, stool, or bench.[32] According to Richard Hosley's estimate, the discovery space at the Globe was "some 7 ft. or 8 ft. wide" and no more than 4 ft. deep.[33] The curtain, then, conceals a shallow space for acting. Hosley explains, "In a Shakespearian discovery the actor or actors are simply *posed,* in what is essentially a *tableau vivant.*"[34] Typical is the scene in *The Tempest* where Prospero "*discovers* Ferdinand *and* Miranda *playing at chess*" (5.1.171.s.d.). Similarly, *The Wisdom of Doctor Dodypoll,* acted by Paul's Boys in 1600,[35] begins with this discovery: "*A curtaine drawne, Earle* Lassingbergh *is discovered (like a painter) painting* Lucilia, *who sits working on a piece of cushion worke*" (sig. A3r).[36]

Conceivably the discovery of the bed in *Amends for Ladies* could have been managed within such a limited space. But the discovery in *Lust's Dominion,* with its various lords and family members, could not. Nor could the death scene of Zenocrate, also initiated by drawing back a curtain, in *Tamburlaine the Great, Part 2,* acted by the Admiral's Men in late 1587: "*Zenocrate lies in her bed of state,* Tamburlaine *sitting by her; three physicians about her bed, tempering* [i.e., mixing] *potions.* Theridimas, Techelles, Usumcasane, *and the three sons*" (2.4.0.s.d.). This stage direction indicates the presence of no fewer than eleven characters, which makes for a very crowded discovery scene.

The problem of accommodating both a bed and a sizable group of characters in a discovery space may be resolved, however, if we posit such a space at the center of the tiring-house wall,[37] a space wider and deeper than those that could be created in the left and right doorways.[38] Admittedly, the De Witt drawing fails to indicate a central opening onto the Swan stage. But even if the Swan theater had no such opening, other theaters did. A sketch by Inigo Jones, thought to represent the Cockpit in Drury Lane, depicts a stage with three entrances.[39] Some plays, moreover, indicate three points of entry onto the stage rather than the two depicted in the De Witt drawing. For example, in Greene's *Alphonsus, King of Aragon,* perhaps first performed by the Queen's Men ca. 1587–88, this direction suggests a central alcove: "*Let there be a brazen head set in the middle of the place behind the stage, out of which, cast flames of fire*" (lines 1246–47.s.d.).[40] More specifically, in *The Four Prentices of London,* probably performed by the Admiral's Men at the Rose in 1594, the prologue begins: "*Enter three in blacke clokes, at three doores."*[41] And in *Eastward Ho,* acted by the Queen's Revels Children at the Blackfriars in 1605, the first stage direction reads: *"Enter* Master Touchstone *and* Quicksilver *at several doors. . . . At the middle door, enter* Golding *discovering a goldsmith's shop and walking short turns before it"* (1.1.0.s.d.).[42] William Percy's *Arabia Sitiens,* written ca. 1601 for Paul's Playhouse, contains a stage direction anticipating the use of a "midde doore."[43] On the basis of such directions, Andrew Gurr and Mariko Ichikawa suggest that stages featured three entrances, and that a wide central alcove was used "for special displays and shows."[44] Such a discovery space may have been larger at some theaters than others and therefore better able to accommodate both a number of characters and a large piece of furniture like a bed.

Let us assume the existence of such an alcove. Was it ordinarily covered with a curtain? Andrew Gurr reports that Richard Hosley "voiced the conjecture to me" in the early 1980s but "never chose to publish it"; Gurr continues, "the possibility that the Swan did have hangings across its *frons* has festered quietly in my mind ever since he mentioned it."[45] If Hosley was right in his conjecture, then why does Arend van Buchell's copy of the De Witt sketch fail to depict such a central curtain? Perhaps because curtains covered the entire wall of the Swan. Gurr explains: "What if, when De Witt went to see his play at the Swan, he found that the performance he was seeing required the whole of the *frons scenae* to be concealed behind hangings? That is certainly a possibility, and would explain the blankness of the *frons* wall [in the drawing]."[46] That hangings existed at the Swan we know from the report of a trickster who advertised a performance at the theater and then absconded with the money, failing to present the promised entertainment: the crowd "revenged themselves upon the hangings, curtains, chairs, stooles, walles, and whatsoever came in their way."[47]

Hosley and Gurr's suggestion about a central alcove is not universally accepted. Tim Fitzpatrick and Wendy Millyard have argued that the tiring-house wall in London theaters was not straight but angled, or "multifaceted," that the angles of the wall allowed for what they call a "concealment space," that a curtain was rigged up in front of the wall to create that space, which was about two feet deep, and that there was no central opening onto the stage.[48] Their thesis is based on the 1989 excavation of the Rose theater, which has led historians to conclude that the *frons* was not straight, but rather followed the polygonal shape of the theater.[49] Even if this supposition is accurate, the design cannot have been imitated at all of the London theaters. After all, the only graphic evidence we have of a theatrical interior during a performance, the De Witt drawing of the Swan, clearly shows a flat wall. Fitzpatrick and Millyard also claim that "there is some textual evidence" for an angled wall. That evidence consists chiefly of Caesar's remark in Shakespeare's *Antony and Cleopatra* about a "three-nook'd world" (4.6.5). Most Shakespeareans, however, interpret Caesar's remark not as an architectural description of "three obtuse angles or junction points,"[50] but rather as a characterization of the world as three-sectored, consisting of Europe, Asia, and Africa.[51] In the absence of compelling verbal evidence from the plays, and in the absence of a full archaeological dig at Shakespeare's theater, it seems imprudent to assume that the wall behind the actors at the Globe and at other public theaters like the Red Bull was angled. And even if it was, nothing would preclude the construction of an alcove in the tiring-house wall.

Discovery Curtains

In addition to bed curtains, other curtains figure in dramatic action, especially in discovery scenes.[52] Consider Jonson's *Volpone* once more. Volpone directs Mosca: "Open the shrine that I may see my saint" (1.2.2).[53] At this point Alvin Kernan inserts a stage direction: "[*Mosca opens a curtain disclosing piles of gold*]."[54] The speech that follows indicates that the revelation has made visible objects that represent Volpone's wealth: "let me kiss, / With adoration, thee, and every relic / Of sacred treasure in this blessed room" (lines 11–13). How exactly does Mosca open that shrine? Helen Ostovich imagines the treasure as located in a "cupboard."[55] In many productions, however, Mosca, instead of opening a cabinet or other piece of furniture, simply draws back a curtain. Thus R. B. Parker supplies a stage direction: "[*Mosca draws a curtain to disclose Volpone's treasure*]" (1.1.2.s.d.). Parker adds, "any alcove or discovery space would do."[56] Similarly, David Cook inserts a stage direction following line 2: "Mosca *draws a curtain, and reveals piles of gold, plate jewels, etc.*"[57] If there is such a curtain, where is it? The most logical place for the curtain would be at one of the two doorways onto the stage depicted in the De Witt drawing or at a central alcove, which the stage directions of various plays seem to imply. The "shrine," then, may consist simply of a table, revealed by moving aside a curtain covering an entrance into the tiring-house.[58]

Another such discovery occurs in *The Merchant of Venice* when suitors arrive in Belmont to woo Portia. They are required to choose between three caskets, one of which contains Portia's picture. When each suitor prepares to make his choice, the caskets, which have been concealed from view, are made visible by drawing back a curtain, revealing them, probably, on a table. When, for instance, the Prince of Morocco arrives, Portia directs: "Go, draw aside the curtains and discover / The several caskets to this noble prince" (2.7.1–2). The opening of the curtains adds to the sense of expectation on the part of both Morocco and the playgoers. The closing of the curtains signals the respective suitor's failed attempt and its finality: following the prince's errant choice, Portia directs, "Draw the curtains, go" (lines 78–79). As in *Volpone,* the simplest and most economical way of accomplishing the discovery would be to have an actor or stage attendant draw back a curtain that stretches across an entryway onto the stage.[59] Drawing a curtain would obviate the need to bring onstage a piece of furniture.

The tragic counterpart of such discoveries occurs in John Webster's *The White Devil*, acted by Queen Anne's Men at the Red Bull in 1612. Behind a curtain lies a poisoned painting. Webster describes the action in a dumb show: "*Enter suspiciously,* Julio *and another, they draw a curtaine where* Bracciano*'s picture is, they put on spectacles of glass, which cover their eyes and noses, and then burn perfumes afore the picture*" (2.2.23.s.d.).[60] Then Isabella enters, "*kneels down as to prayers, then draws the curtain of the picture, does three reverences to it, and kisses it thrice, she faints and will not suffer them to come near it, dies.*" John Russell Brown observes that "pictures were often protected by curtains,"[61] and he cites these lines in *Twelfth Night*: "Wherefore have these gifts a curtain before 'em? Are they like to take dust, like Mistress Mall's picture?" (1.3.125–27); later Olivia says, "We will draw the curtain, and show you the picture" (1.5.233). How did Queen Anne's Men stage Webster's dumb show? The poisoned painting could have been set on an easel or stand covered with a small curtain of the kind used today in art museums to shield precious artifacts from light. Or perhaps an easel with the painting was placed behind a curtain covering one of the entrances onto the stage. Either method of staging would entail a minimum of preparation and expense.

The parting of curtains may, of course, reveal people as well as artifacts, and, when it does, the staging implies ongoing activity. In Shakespeare's *Henry VIII*, acted by the King's Men in 1613, we find this stage direction: "*the King draws the curtain and sits reading pensively*" (2.2.61.s.d.). Gordon McMullan observes, "The King is revealed to be sitting inside the 'discovery space,' concealed by a curtain which is drawn to reveal him."[62] Busy reading, Henry initially seems unaware of anyone else: he certainly is not meant to hear Suffolk's words: "How sad he looks! Sure he is much afflicted" (line 62). Only at this point does the King signal cognizance of others, and when he does, it is to reprimand them for trespassing on his privacy: "How dare you thrust yourselves / Into my private meditations?" (lines 64–65). The imaginative line represented by the discovery curtain signals a division between the personal space of the King and what might be called the more public space of the larger play. Thomas Dekker's *Satiromastix,* performed by Paul's Boys in 1601, employs a curtain for essentially the same purpose: "Horrace *sitting in a study behinde a curtaine, a candle by him burning, bookes lying confusedly: to himselfe*" (1.2.0.s.d.).[63] A twenty-line soliloquy follows in which the moody poet seeks inspiration. Only when another character enters and engages him in conversation does the preoccupied Horace emerge from his private meditation and, perhaps, from the discovery space as well. Immediately the tone of the scene changes, becoming jaunty and humorous where earlier it was rarefied, concerned with "Things abstruse, deep and divine" (line 5).

A discovery scene may furnish not merely the prospect of characters engaged in a characteristic activity but a catalyst for dramatic action, as in Thomas Middleton's *Hengist, King of Kent,* acted ca. 1619–20 at an undetermined venue. To the sound of music a dumb show unfolds: "*ffortune is discovered upon an alter, in her hand a golden round full of lots.*" The statue of the goddess, having been revealed when a curtain is pulled back, becomes the genesis for a flurry of developments: "*Enter Hengist and Hersus with others they draw lotts and hang them up with joy, soe all departs saveing* Hengist: *and* Hersus *who kneeles and imbrace each other as partners in one fortune, to them enter* Roxena: *seemeing to take her leave of* Hengist *her ffather; but especially privately and warily of* Hersus *her lover. She departs weepeing: and* Hengist: *and* Hersus *goe to the doore and bring in their souldiers with drum and coullers and soe march forth*" (lines 261–70).[64] Were it not for the pantomime, considerable dialogue and stage time would be required to represent the complicated action, precipitated by revealing the statue. The ensuing exegesis by Ranulph Higden, the presenter, endows the dumb show "with a sense of compacted significance that invites explication."[65]

Perhaps the most theatrically stunning instance of a discovery revealing an artifact or person appears in *The Winter's Tale,* acted by the King's Men, presumably at the Globe and Blackfriars, in 1611. Near the end of the play Paulina displays to Leontes the treasures of her gallery. When she says, "Behold, and say 'tis well" (5.3.20), she evidently draws back a curtain to reveal the statue of Hermione, for when Leontes reacts emotionally to what he sees, Paulina tells him, "If I had thought the sight of my poor image / Would thus have wrought you . . . / I'ld not have show'd it" (lines 57–59); Leontes interjects, "Do not draw the curtain" (line 59). The actor counterfeiting the statue presumably stands either in a doorway of the tiring-house or in a central alcove, a curtain drawn across the opening.[66] That curtain intensifies the mood of enchantment that envelops the characters: it is as though Leontes and his courtiers are being initiated into a religious mystery. David Bevington comments, "The drawing back of the curtain before the statue of Hermione . . . is a recognition that brings with it grace, wonder, and forgiveness."[67]

What sets the revelation of Hermione in *The Winter's Tale* apart from many other discovery scenes is that the object behind the curtain, the supposed "statue," interacts with the characters on the other side of the curtain. In other words, the parting of the curtain does not simply reveal an inert artifact or a figure engaged in some characteristic activity. What appears to begin as a relatively conventional discovery becomes something extraordinary. The presentation of Hermione, who conflates statue and living person, art and nature, initiates the emotionally powerful reconciliations of husband and wife, mother and daughter.

A particularly complex use of curtains, one that advances the plot and generates surprise, occurs in Barnabe Barnes's *The Devil's Charter,* acted in 1606–7 by the King's Men at the Globe. This stage direction begins a scene: "Alexander *unbraced betwixt two cardinalls in his study looking upon a booke, whilst a groome draweth the curtaine*" (5.4.3283–85.s.d.).[68] The curtain having opened, three figures walk out of a discovery space onto the main playing area; the cardinals "*place him in a chayre upon the stage*" (line 3294) and they exit. Left alone, Alexander reflects that "my soule is damn'd, / I damn'd undoubtedly" (lines 3312–13). At some point during his soliloquy, the curtain covering the discovery space must be closed by an unspecified figure, though a stage direction is missing, for, following his meditation on damnation, Alexander turns back to his study and "*draweth* [i.e., opens] *the curtaine of his studie where hee discovereth the divill sitting in his pontificals*" (lines 3539–41). The same curtain is opened twice in this scene, and the second discovery creates an intense effect. The shock of finding the devil sitting in his chair causes Alexander to "start" at the sight.

When curtains open in *Grim the Collier of Croyden, or The Devil and His Dame,* probably first performed by the Admiral's Men ca. 1600, we confront another unusual discovery: a conclave of devils who initiate the action of the play. Immediately before the curtains are drawn back, Saint Dunston announces his return to this world "after many hundred years" (1.1.3).[69] Feeling sleepy, "*He layeth him down to sleep; lightning and thunder; the curtains drawn, on a sudden* Pluto, Minos, Æacus, Rhadamantus *set in counsell, before them* Malbecco *his ghost guarded with Furies*" (1.1.42.s.d.). With the parting of the curtains, playgoers witness a kind of dream vision in which the devils parley and give this charge to Belphagor: "go into the world, / And take upon thee the shape of a man; / In which estate thou shalt be married" (lines 125–27). This business having been set in motion, Dunston rises from his sleep: "What, dream'st thou *Dunston?* yea I dreamt indeed. / Must the Devil come into the world? / Such is belike the infernal kings decree" (lines 154–56). The synod of devils creates a frame for the ensuing play,[70] and in the final scene we return to those devils, who hear a report of Belphagor's unhappy adventures on "vile Earth" (5.3.7).

As the dramatic actions recounted here attest, playwrights create discoveries for a variety of purposes. Most correspond to Richard Hosley's description of a discovery as "a sudden revelation of an important or interesting person or object, in a significant situation or at a characteristic activity."[71] What makes that revelation sudden is, of course, the use of a curtain.

Traverse and Curtain

In Ben Jonson's comedy we encounter an enigmatic direction: "*Volpone peeps from behind a traverse*" (5.3.8.s.d.).[72] This is usually interpreted as referring to a curtain behind which the character hides so that he can spy on others (Corvino, Lady Would-Be, Corbaccio) while remaining visible to the audience. It is, however, possible that the "traverse" is some sort of screen, for the *OED* defines the term as "a curtain or screen placed crosswise, or drawn across a room, hall, or theatre; also a partition of wood, a screen of lattice-work, or the like." The *OED* goes on to list the stage direction in *Volpone* as one of its examples. In her comment on Jonson's stage direction, Helen Ostovich conjectures that such a screen "would allow the audience a better view of Volpone's reactions, rather than a conventional curtain."[73] In the previous scene, however, Volpone speaks specifically of watching the legacy hunters from behind a *curtain:* "I'll get up, / Behind the curtain, on a stool, and harken; / Sometime peep over; see how they do look" (5.2.83–85). Are we to understand that the *traverse* specified in the stage direction is synonymous with the *curtain* mentioned in the dialogue?

Because the term appears so rarely in the drama, it is difficult to know exactly what *traverse* means. We find the word in a single moral interlude, *Godly Queen Hester,* acted ca. 1529, where a marginal stage direction reads: *"Here the kynge entreth the travers & Aman goeth out"* (sig. A4v); later, *"Here the kynge entreth the traverse"* (sig. D1v).[74] E. K. Chambers observes that the term "does not appear again in any play for nearly a hundred years,"[75] and when it does, it shows up in *Volpone* where, for Chambers, it designates "a low movable screen, probably of a non-structural kind."[76] W. W. Greg imagines the traverse in *Godly Queen Hester* as "a curtain, opening in the middle, which hung across the stage."[77] But Richard Southern objects that there is not "the slightest indication of anything being used in Interludes which was called a stage."[78] Instead, he envisions the use of a traverse at an indoor performance in a great hall, which features two large doorways in the "screens": the traverse is "a fairly small two-part curtain, perhaps some eight feet high and some six to ten feet wide in all, hung on a rod supported on two uprights, and set up on the floor about a couple of feet in front of the centre element of the screens."[79] In other words it would look like a small version of the booth made of curtains for a (temporary) booth stage. This speculation would seem more compelling were it not for Alan H. Nelson's finding: "Genuine evidence for the use of hall screens in play production has, to my knowledge, not been produced, and in fact seems flatly contradicted by evidence from Cambridge and elsewhere."[80]

Perhaps other instances of an onstage traverse, closer in time to the staging of *Volpone,* may help clarify Jonson's meaning.[81] In *The White Devil* when Flamineo speaks to Francisco (who wears a disguise), Francisco reports that Flamineo's mother grieves over the corpse of Marcello. Flamineo resolves, "I will see them. / They are behind the traverse. I'll discover their superstitious howling" (5.4.63–65). The traverse is then moved in order to reveal the lamentation over Marcello's body: "Cornelia, [Zanche] *the Moor and three other ladies discovered, winding* Marcello'*s corse*" (line 65.s.d.). Surely the easiest and quickest way to accomplish such a revelation would be for the actor playing Flamineo to draw back a curtain rather than to move a screen. After all, a screen that could conceal both the corpse and five mourners would need to be rather large and thus somewhat unwieldy, even if portable. Hence John Russell Brown's conclusion, in the form of an inserted stage direction: "[*Draws the traverse curtain*]." Another of Webster's plays, *The Duchess of Malfi,* performed by the King's Men both at the Globe and Blackfriars, also employs a traverse: "*Here is discovered, behind a traverse, the artificial figures of Antonio and his children, appearing as if they were dead*" (4.1.55.s.d.).[82] My guess is that the traverse here, as in *The White Devil* and *Volpone,* is a curtain, if only because it could more easily and quickly be moved than a freestanding screen, which might require the assistance of one or more attendants.

If the traverse is a curtain, it is, however, perhaps not the same curtain that hangs on the wall of the tiring-house and used for most discovery scenes. Rather, it may take the form of a curtain, high enough to conceal a standing figure, rigged somewhere else onstage.[83] William Poel's nineteenth-century speculation may prove helpful: namely, that the traverse is a curtain set up away from the tiring-house wall but parallel to it.[84] Such a curtain, possibly suspended between the two stage pillars, would create two spaces for acting: one between the tiring-house wall and the traverse; the other, between the traverse and the front edge of the stage. In the case of Webster's plays, there would be a distinct advantage in bringing the figures who are discovered close to the beholder. What the traverse allows for in *The Duchess of Malfi* is the creation of particular theatrical effects: first, a feeling of suspense and dread before the traverse is moved, then sudden shock when Duchess and playgoers experience simultaneously the sight of husband and children, apparently dead. By moving the bodies downstage, the company makes their impact more immediate, for the figures are no longer contained within the usual discovery space.

Curtains in various plays function like the traverse in Webster's plays. That is, curtains, when opened, reveal an unexpected and sometimes startling view. For example, in *A Looking Glass for London and England,* first acted ca. 1587–88 at an undetermined venue and then at the Rose in 1592, the King, hearing thunder and seeing lightning, asks Radagon to "ope ye foldes where queene of favour sits, / Carrying a net within her curled locks, / Wherein the Graces are entangled oft" (lines 544–46).[85] What they actually behold, however, is not the beautiful Romelia they expect to see, but her corpse: "*He drawes the curtaines and findes her stroken with thunder, blacke*" (lines 552–53). A thunderbolt has transformed Romelia into charred flesh.

Although a curtain in other plays may not generate the striking effect we experience in *Looking Glass,* a curtain may at least create a marked discrep-

ancy between the tone of the principal dramatic action and that of action revealed in discovery. Stage directions in such plays refer to a curtain rather
than a traverse, and that curtain almost certainly covers either a doorway onto
the stage or a central alcove. But the principle of staging is essentially the
same, for the revelation establishes a disparity between the chief dramatic
action in front of the curtain and the secondary action behind it. At its simplest we see this in Anthony Munday's *The Downfall of Robert, Earl of Huntingdon,* first acted in 1598 by the Admiral's Men at the Rose. Fitzwater
enters *"like an old man"* and proceeds to lament all that he formerly possessed: "Fitzwater once had castles, townes, and towers, / Faire gardens, or-
chards, and delightfull bowers" (lines 1476–78).[86] Now he has nothing:
"Only wide walkes are left mee in the world, / Which these stiffe limes wil
hardly let me tread" (lines 1480–81). Before he leaves this world, the melancholy father would see his "faire lucklesse childe," and just then a stage direction signals the opening to view of that very daughter previously hidden
from his (and our) sight: *"Curtaines open,* Robin Hoode *sleepes on a greene
banke, and* Marian *strewing flowers on him"* (lines 1490–91.s.d.). Fitzwater
then invites us to appreciate the significance of what we behold: "Looke how
my flower holds flowers in her hands, / And flings those sweetes, upon my
sleeping sonne" (lines 1494–95). The contrast between disheartened father
and blissful daughter, oblivious of being watched, gives this scene its special
poignancy.

Robert Greene's *Friar Bacon and Friar Bungay,* possibly first performed
by the Queen's Men ca. 1589–90, also uses a curtain to create a marked contrast. A stage direction signals both a development of the plot and change of
mood: *"Enter Frier Bacon drawing the courtaines with a white sticke, a
booke in his hand, and a lampe lighted by him, and the brasen head and
Miles, with weapons by him"* (lines 1561–63).[87] The character moving the
curtains is a magician who carries a conjuring stick, and behind those curtains lies the astonishing sight of the brazen head. The act of drawing aside
the curtain ushers us into the world of the marvelous: Bacon intends to coop-
erate with the brazen head in order to surround England with a wall of brass.
The curtain, then, becomes a line of demarcation separating the quotidian
world from the world in which magic flourishes.

Dumb shows also posit a contrast between principal and secondary dramatic action. Although characters in those shows normally enter through the
same doors as other characters, the drawing of a curtain occasionally initiates
the pantomime, as for example in *Tom a Lincoln,* acted ca. 1611–16 by the
gentlemen of Gray's Inn: *"Time drawes a curtaine & discovers Angellica in
her bed a sleep, the infant lyinge by her, then enters the kinge & the Abbesse
whispering together the Abbesse takes the childe out of the bed & departs,
the kinge alsoe after a litle viwinge of Angellica at an other doore departs,
Angell: still sleepinge he being gone drawes the curtaynes & speaks"* (lines

150–55).[88] Contrary to ordinary practice, the actors have assumed their places out of view of the playgoers. This has the effect of investing the mimed action with an enhanced status. Angelica and King Arthur have already appeared onstage and conversed with one another. But their participation in the stylized action of the dumb show, revealed by a personified figure, creates a sense that we are watching something especially meaningful. Personified Time also initiates a dumb show in Thomas Dekker's *The Whore of Babylon,* performed by Prince Henry's Men at the Fortune in 1606: Time *"drawes a curtaine, discovering* Truth *in sad abiliments; uncrowned: her haire disheveld, and sleeping on a rock . . ."* (dumb show preceding scene 1, lines 27–28).[89] Here the contrast between the action of the dumb show and the larger play is even greater, for all of the figures in the pantomime are personified symbols. As Dieter Mehl observes, the action performed when the curtain opens gives "the drama an extra dimension by adding to the scenes of ordinary dialogue something in the nature of a morality play."[90] The curtain, then, creates a separation between the more stylized world of the dumb show and the wider world of the play.

A curtain functions as a dividing line between a make-believe world and an everyday world in *The Spanish Tragedy* when Hieronimo prepares his entertainment for the court: *"Enter* Hieronimo; *he knocks up the curtain"* (4.3.0.s.d.).[91] Unfortunately, the stage direction fails to specify precisely where that curtain is located. Philip Edwards in his Revels edition offers this hypothesis about the curtain, "Probably a hasty hanging in a prepared place"; and he goes on to connect the curtain with Hieronimo's revelation of his son's corpse later in the scene: "the best suggestion is that it hung over one of the doors, so that Horatio's body could conveniently be brought behind it."[92] Similarly, J. R. Mulryne in the New Mermaids edition suggests that "Hieronimo probably hangs a curtain over one of the large entrance-doors at the rear of the Elizabethan stage."[93] D. F. Rowan supposes that the curtain covers a theatrical property, the arbor in which Horatio was earlier hanged: "If then the arbour covered with the curtain must be placed against the back wall so that it can load its deadly freight the courtly audience 'above' cannot see Hieronimo's gruesome revelation."[94] Whether Hieronimo's curtain is located in a doorway leading from the tiring-house or stretched across a theatrical property (the arbor) and thus probably at the center of the tiring-house wall, Horatio's body could easily be placed behind the curtain that the grieving father "knocks up." When Hieronimo, having accomplished his revenge in the playlet, reveals Horatio's corpse to the spectators, he likely does so by opening the curtain, though there is no specific stage direction to this effect except for these four words: *"shows his son's body"* (4.4.88.s.d.). The spectacle of the bloody, unburied corpse is as unexpected as it is shocking, creating a disparity between, on the one hand, the fictive world of the play-within-the-play, enjoyed by the King, Viceroy, and other courtly playgoers, a realm of make-believe where death is merely apparent because "acted," and, on the other hand, the actual Spanish court, where intrigue, injustice, and murder prevail. Parting the curtain to reveal his son's body, the knight marshal collapses the distinction between the world of the play-within-the-play and the world of pain he inhabits.

Arras and Hanging

An arras was a customary furnishing in prosperous Elizabethan and Jacobean homes. According to the *OED, arras,* which originated in the name of a French city renowned for its tapestries, had entered the language with this meaning as early as ca. 1400: "A rich tapestry fabric, in which figures and scenes are woven in colours." The word, which may have a number of meanings, need not refer to a textile hanging on a wall; *arras* can also refer to a textile of the kind placed atop tables when meals were not being served. For instance, in Thomas Dekker's *The Bloody Banquet,* acted ca. 1617–39 by an unidentified company, we read: "*A table with lights set out. Arras spread*" (line 1051.s.d.).[95] A character entering at the beginning of the scene sees the preparations for a meal and comments: "Ha! the ground spread with arras?" (line 1066). This line suggests that the arras covers "the ground," or floor, not a wall; perhaps it has been moved from the tabletop as preparations for the meal are made. Ordinarily an arras was too valuable to be used as a carpet. Pride in Marlowe's *Doctor Faustus* suggests its status as a luxury by saying, "I'll not speak another word, except the ground were perfumed and covered with cloth of arras" (2.3.115–17).[96] Most references to an arras in plays, however, designate textiles hung on walls. Such furnishings, which provide delight for the eye as well as protection from drafts, are evoked in *Cymbeline* when Jachimo, emerging from his hiding place in a trunk, takes an inventory of Imogen's bedroom: "Such and such pictures; there the window; such / Th' adornment of her bed; the arras, figures" (2.1.25–26).[97] When he speaks these words, the actor is probably looking at a textile decoration on the wall of the tiring-house; the arras would have hung on that wall, probably in the middle.

An arras typically features the representation of human figures, as Jachimo's line seems to imply. In John Day's *Law Tricks,* performed ca. 1606–8 at the Whitefriars, Emilia urges Count Lurdo to "scape behinde the arras" (sig. D4v).[98] When Polymetes, upon entering, asks, "What storie is this?" Emilia answers, "Why my lord? the poeticall fiction of Venus kissing Adonis in the violet bed." In other words, by its design the textile represents a liaison between Venus and Adonis. Similarly in William Heminges's *The Fatal Contract,* performed by Queen Henrietta Maria's Men at Salisbury Court in 1638–39, the Queen inquires about recent visitors, "You know them not?" A servant replies: "No dearest lady, for th'appear'd to me / Like to the silent postures in the arras, / Onely the form of men with stranger faces" (sig. B3v).[99]

Because such furnishings were "placed round the walls of household apartments, often at such a distance from them as to allow of people being concealed in the space between," according to the *OED*, an arras could provide a convenient hiding place. In *Much Ado About Nothing*, for instance, Borachio tells Don John, "I whipt me behind the arras, and there heard" the Prince say that he would woo Hero for himself (1.2.60–61). This action is only recounted; we do not actually see Borachio hide himself. But playgoers had ample opportunities to behold the kind of action described here. In *The Merry Wives of Windsor*, for instance, Falstaff hides from Mistress Page: "She shall not see me, I will ensconce me behind the arras" (3.3.89–90). In the revised Riverside edition Evans inserts this stage direction: "[*Falstaff stands behind the arras.*]" The arras here must refer to whatever textiles hang on the wall of the tiring-house. Similarly, in *1 Henry IV* Falstaff conceals himself from the sheriff. Hal tells his friend, "Go hide thee behind the arras" (2.4.500); later Poins finds him "fast asleep behind the arras, and snorting like a horse" (2.4.528).[100]

The darker counterpart of these comic actions appears in *The Duchess of Malfi* when the Duchess tells Cariola: "Leave me: but place thyself behind the arras, / Where thou mayst overhear us" (1.1.357–58). The context is filled with menace, for the Duchess means to woo her steward and embark upon a clandestine marriage to which Cariola will serve as witness. Although weddings are ordinarily happy occasions, this one, conducted without benefit of clergy, will evoke hostility in the Duke and Cardinal and eventually culminate in the deaths of both the Duchess and her husband. Even the Duchess concedes that she is "going into a wilderness" (line 359) when she sets out to woo Antonio. Another dramatic action involving an arras and a concealed character occurs in *Hamlet* when Polonius proposes to Claudius that they spy on the Prince: "I'll loose my daughter to him. / Be you and I behind the arras then, / Mark the encounter" (2.2.162–64). Later in the play Polonius conceals himself behind the same furnishing in Gertrude's chamber so that he may eavesdrop on her conversation with her son: "Behind the arras I'll convey myself / To hear the process" (3.3.28–29). Subsequently, Hamlet, hearing a sound behind the arras, slays Polonius by plunging a sword through it (3.4.24). We have no conclusive evidence that a gap existed between the textile and the tiring-house wall, as it apparently did in homes and palaces. But the lack of such space might actually prove an advantage in the theater, for a person hiding behind the arras would be more readily observable to someone standing before it. Of course, the actor playing Polonius would be less conspicuous if he stood behind an arras that was drawn across one of the openings onto the stage.

Eavesdropping from behind an arras need not imply perfidy. In Thomas Heywood's *The English Traveller*, acted by Lady Elizabeth's Men at the Phoenix in 1624, Old Lionel, a merchant who fears having been outwitted by a servant, sees the crafty Reignald approach; Lionel and his aides then "*withdraw behind the arras*" (4.6.155.s.d.).[101] After hearing Reignald confess a guilty conscience, the old man steps forward and engages the recreant in conversation, finally calling out, "Appear, gentlemen, / 'Tis a fit time to take him" (lines 193–94). The ensuing stage direction reads: "*They all appear with cords and shackles*" (line 208.s.d.). In Lewis Sharpe's *The Noble Stranger*, acted by Queen Henrietta's (II) Men at Salisbury Court, 1638–40, the King and Callidus conceal themselves "*behind the arras*" in order to eavesdrop on those suspected of defying the King's will. When he hears evidence of treachery in the ensuing conversation, the King reveals himself: "I am no longer able to contain— / Out traytors" (sig. F2r).[102]

Nevertheless, when characters conceal themselves behind an arras, their action is at least potentially suspect, for often they mean to exploit the vulnerability of others, as Polonius and the King do in *Hamlet*. In other plays such concealment may be synonymous with sexual transgression. For instance, in *Cynthia's Revels*, acted by the Children of the Queen's Chapel at the Blackfriars in 1600, Moria says: "I would wish to be a wisewoman, and know all the secrets of court, citie, and countrie. I would know what were done behind the arras, what upon the staires, what i' the garden, what I' the *Nymphs* chamber, what by barge, & what by coach" (4.1.140–43).[103] And in Dekker and Webster's *Northward Ho*, acted by Paul's Boys in 1605, Doll says, "I will discover it . . . softly as a gentleman courts a wench behind an arras" (3.2.3–5).[104] On the strength of these and other such references, Colin Gibson concludes, "the dominant Jacobean and Caroline association of the phrase [i.e., 'behind the arras'] is with court lechery."[105]

Is the arras cited in various stage directions and dialogue to be distinguished from the curtains that we have already considered? C. Walter Hodges contends that they are essentially different: "an arras usually suggests a fixed hanging, or a tapestry, which cannot be drawn aside like a curtain."[106] The *OED* definition of *arras* would seem to support Hodges's view: "a rich tapestry fabric, in which figures and scenes are woven in colours" (a curtain may be simply a textile of a single color and need not display any pictorial design). But did a true arras of the kind that decorated the homes of the wealthy hang on the tiring-house wall of London theaters? John Ronayne believes that the public stages were more likely to have used a painted cloth,[107] defined by the *OED* as "a hanging for a room painted or worked with figures, mottoes or texts"; in other words it served as a substitute for a more substantial arras, or tapestry. Falstaff distinguishes between the two in *2 Henry IV* when he bids Mistress Quickly pawn a tapestry and replace it with something cheaper: "the German hunting in waterwork, is worth a thousand of these bed-hangers and these fly-bitten tapestries" (2.1.145–47); here Falstaff refers to "boar-hunting scenes painted in distemper on imitation tapestry."[108] Ronayne observes that woven cloths and tapestries "would be vastly more expensive" than painted cloths, and such woven materials "would be at some risk in use on an outdoor stage."[109] Genuine tapestries would also be bulkier and therefore more difficult to store. We know, too, that acting companies owned and used painted cloths; the inventory of the Admiral's Men in Henslowe's *Diary* lists several, including "the clothe of the Sone & Mone," "Tasso picter," and "the sittie of Rome."[110] Painted cloths also figure in the dialogue of various plays. For example, in *The Knight of the Burning Pestle,* acted by the Children of the Queen's Revels at the Blackfriars in 1607, the Citizen's Wife asks, "Now, sweet lamb, what story is that painted upon the cloth?" (interlude II, lines 11–12).[111] When she asks the question of her husband, they are almost certainly looking at a painted cloth on the wall behind them.[112]

What are the implications for staging? If we imagine that the arras of the stage was not an expensive tapestry but rather a cheap painted cloth, the distinction between arras and curtain begins to disappear. A stage direction in Chapman's *Bussy D'Ambois,* first performed in 1604 by Paul's Boys, supports the assumption that curtain and arras function in essentially the same manner. In the last act of Q2 we find this direction concerning Montsurry: "*He puts the Frier* [Comolet] *in the vault and follows, she* [Tamyra] *raps her self in the arras*" (sig. I2r).[113] Although it is difficult to imagine a person "wrapping" herself in a true arras, which would be a fairly thick textile and thus not especially pliable, one can easily envision Tamyra drawing around herself a curtain or painted cloth that hung on the wall of the tiring-house. In their stage directions, moreover, Renaissance plays provide evidence that a theatrical arras could be easily "drawn." For example, in a deathbed scene of *Tamburlaine the Great, Part 2,* we find this direction: "*The arras is drawn, and* Zenocrate *lies in her bed of state*" (2.4.0.s.d.). Similarly, in the anonymous *Claudius Tiberius Nero,* "*They draw aside the arras, and banquet on the stage*" (sig. K3r).[114] Both of these stage directions treat the arras as if it were a curtain.

If the terms *arras* and *curtain* seem virtually interchangeable in their use onstage, so too do *arras* and *hanging.* In the anonymous *Tragedy of Nero,* acted ca. 1619–23, a character conflates the two in the expression "arras hangings" (2.1.4).[115] In John Day's *Law Tricks,* performed at the Whitefriars, Emilia advises Count Lurdo to hide: "Behinde the arras; scape behinde the arras" (sig. D4v). Julio then enters the room, praising the "verie faire hangings," and Polymetes comments, "Passing good workmanship." This dialogue suggests that *arras* and *hangings* describe the same furnishing. And as we have seen above, the hangings behind which the character hides feature a pictorial representation of Venus and Adonis. Characters also use hangings as a means of concealment in *The Jews' Tragedy,* by William Hemings; at one point Zareck says, "I will withdraw myself," and the stage direction in the margin reads: "*Zareck stands behind the hangings*" (sig. G1v);[116] moments later when three other characters have entered, the stage direction reads: "*A table set, and Zareck stands behind the arras*" (sig. G2r). It seems unlikely that Zareck has moved; rather he remains behind the same furnishing. Similarly, in *Philaster* Galatea exits "*behind the hangings*" (2.2.56.s.d.),[117] so that she may overhear a conversation between two others; when those two exit, Galatea returns from her hiding place "*behind the hangings*" (line 140.s.d.). In Arthur Wilson's *The Swisser,* performed by the King's Men in 1631, Andrucho hides himself in order to eavesdrop: "I'le borrow / The shelter of this hanging" (4.2.5–6).[118] And in Brome's *The Northern Lass,* performed by the King's Men at the Globe and Blackfriars in 1629, a character "*withdrawes behind the hanging*" (4.3.47–48.s.d.).[119]

If an arras may be "drawn," so too may a hanging, though Irwin Smith believes otherwise; he writes of hangings: "Unlike curtains, they could not be drawn back; instead, they were lifted if a person had to pass through them,"[120] and he cites an instance in Henry Killigrew's *The Conspiracy* [*Pallantus and Eudora*]: "Pallantus *goes out, and returnes presently again, and holds up the hanging for* Eudora" (sig. P1v).[121] But may we reasonably conclude from a single stage direction that hangings could not be drawn? Even Smith concedes that in Davenant's *The Unfortunate Lovers,* acted at the Blackfriars in 1638, the prologue speaks of player who "Through th'hangings peep'd to see how th'house did fill" (sig. A3),[122] and this "can only have meant the curtains at the front edge of the rear stage."[123] In the same play a character "*drawes the hangings*" and then "*drawes the hangings further*" (sigs. G2v and G3r). This evidence flatly contradicts Smith's claim. What's more, Smith neglects to acknowledge that the stage direction about "holding up the hanging" in *The Conspiracy* is not to be found in the original 1638 quarto; it appears only in the 1653 edition, published eleven years after the closing of the theaters and some fifteen years after the first performances.

Ben Jonson's dedication to the reader of *The New Inn,* performed by the King's Men in 1629, closely links the terms *hangings* and *arras* when he scornfully characterizes theatrical audiences:

> "What did they come for, then?" thou wilt ask me. I will as punctually answer: "To see, and to be seen. To make a general muster of themselves in their clothes of credit, and possess the stage against the play. To dislike all, but mark nothing. And by their confidence of rising between the acts, in oblique lines, make affidavit to the whole house of their not understanding one scene." Armed with this prejudice, as the stage-furniture or *arras-cloths,* they were there, as spectators, away. For the faces in the *hangings* and they beheld alike.[124]

Michael Hattaway glosses *arras-cloths* as "painted cloths hung against the tiring-house façade."[125] Here the meanings of *arras, painted cloth,* and *hang-*

ing converge. Similarly, James Shirley, in *The Lady of Pleasure,* performed by Queen Henrietta Maria's Men at the Phoenix in 1635, identifies *arras* and *hanging.* Celestina asks, "What hangings have we here?" The Steward says, "They are arras, madam," and Celestina replies, "Impudence, I know't. / I will have fresher and more rich, not wrought / With faces that may scandalise a Christian, / With Jewish stories stuffed with corn and camels" (1.2.11–15).[126] Once again, the meanings of *arras* and *hanging,* textiles either painted with or worked with human figures, merge in the dialogue. The issue is perhaps best summed up by Dessen and Thomson in their entry on *hangings:* "an infrequently used alternative for the *curtain* or *arras* that hung just in front of the tiring-house wall."[127]

It is possible, perhaps likely, that the textile in the middle of the tiring-house wall differed from textiles elsewhere on that wall or at the doorways. That is, the dialogue in *Law Tricks, The Fatal Contract,* and *The Lady of Pleasure,* cited above, strongly suggests that the center of the *frons* was covered with an arras/hanging/painted cloth/curtain representing human figures in much the way it is today at the rebuilt Globe theater in London.[128] (The curtain on the tiring-house wall in the frontispiece of *Messalina* also depicts various figures, one of whom seems to be Cupid.)[129] But that central "soft furnishing" was handled and employed in essentially the same manner as the curtains covering the two principal doorways onto the stage.

Did that textile have any specific significance for the nature of the dramatic action performed in front of it? Stage directions in Massinger's *The City Madam,* acted by the King's Men at the Blackfriars in 1632, suggest that it may have: *"Musicians come down to make ready for the song at aras"* (5.1.7–11).[130] Evidently the musicians exit their customary location above the tiring-house and descend to stage level, where they proceed to take their places, probably at the center of the arras/hanging. What explains this unusual staging? Richard Hosley persuasively suggests that the action performed *above* in this scene, the discovery of two "statues," necessitates clearing the musicians from their music room so that actors might replace them.[131] When the statues "come to life" through the application of "magic," the actors exit the playing area above, and descend to stage level, to the accompaniment of music played behind the arras. Let us suppose that Hosley's supposition is correct. Why should a stage direction specify an *"arras hung up for the musicians"* (4.4.160.s.d.) if, as I have argued, the central section of the tiring-house wall was already covered by arras/hanging/painted cloth? The arras newly hung up probably portrays a figure or scene or colors in keeping with the dramatic action: the wondrous animation of the statues.

Even though Renaissance theaters did not employ painted scenery in the modern fashion and certainly did not seek to achieve scenic illusion, the acting companies must have varied the hangings in order to match the mood of the action, as in *The City Madam.* After all, we have evidence that the hang-

ings varied, depending upon the occasion. A tragedy, for example, would require colors suitable for the subject. Thus in *A Warning for Fair Women,*
acted by the Lord Chamberlain's Men ca. 1595–99, personified History tells
Comedy: "The stage is hung with blacke; and I perceive / The auditors prepared for *Tragedie*" (induction, lines 82–83).[132] Later Tragedy comments:
"now we come unto the dismall act, / And in these sable curtains shut we
up, / The comicke entrance to our direful play" (lines 777–79). Similarly, in
Northward Ho, a character who claims to be writing a tragedy says that "the
stage [is] hung all with black velvet" (4.1.53).[133] And in Marston's *The Insatiate Countess,* a character announces, "The stage of heav'n is hung with
solemn black, / A time best fitting to act tragedies" (4.4.4–5).[134] All of these
citations suggest that black hangings were the customary accoutrement for
tragedies.[135] Comic action would necessarily require something else. The induction of Jonson's *Cynthia's Revels* refers to "fresh pictures that use to
beautifie the decaied dead arras, in a publike theatre" (lines 150–52). R. A.
Foakes comments: "The Jonson allusion suggests that the 'arras' or heavy
tapestry may have been a permanent feature, and that painted cloths were
hung over this when desired."[136] If that central textile were a painted cloth
rather than a genuine tapestry, as I have suggested, it would have been a fairly
simple matter to replace one with another.

Action Above and Window Curtains

Although action *aloft* or *above* occurs with some frequency in Renaissance
drama, the use of curtains on the upper playing level is rare. Shakespeare and
Fletcher, however, call for them in *Henry VIII* when the King, along with his
physician, spies on a meeting of noblemen and clergy: "*Enter the* King *and*
Butts *at a window above*" (5.2.19.s.d.). The position of the King, vis-à-vis
the other characters, signals superior power and knowledge. A suspicious
Henry tells Butts: "By holy Mary, Butts, there's knavery. / Let 'em alone,
and draw the curtain close; / We shall hear more anon" (5.2.33–35). Having
drawn the curtain, the men proceed to eavesdrop on the Privy Council. In the
Riverside edition G. B. Evans introduces a stage direction: "[*Curtain, above,
partially drawn, but the King and Butts remain listening*]" (line 35.s.d.). Depending on how far the curtain is closed, the staging may allow the King and
Butts, in view of the playgoers, to register on their faces a reaction to the
overheard remarks. Later in the scene, having exited the "window," the King
in effect reveals himself by reentering, this time on the main stage: "*Enter*
King *frowning on them; takes his seat*" (line 148.s.d.). Armed with the
knowledge gained through eavesdropping, Henry surprises the Bishop of
Winchester and Archbishop of Canterbury: "I had thought I had had men of

some understanding / And wisdom of my Council; but I find none" (lines 170–71).

Philip Massinger twice incorporates curtains *above* in his staging. In *The Unnatural Combat,* acted by the King's Men at the Globe before 1622, the principal action on the main stage involves Theocrine, who has been ravished by Montrevile. As she dies, her father Malefort expresses his vengeful impulse: would that Montrevile would "appeare" and defend his act or "Shew some compunction for it" (5.2.236, 238).[137] At this point the quarto supplies a stage direction: "Montrevile *above, the curtaine suddenly drawn*" (line 238.s.d.). The guilty man has apparently been eavesdropping on the conversation between father and daughter. Confronting Malefort, Montrevile looks down and laughs contemptuously, "Ha, ha, ha." "My daughter's dead," cries the distraught father, and Montrevile replies, "Thou hadst best follow her" (line 240). Montrevile's location *above* suggests the superiority of his might and the vulnerability of others to his whim. His use of the curtain, moreover, dramatizes his capacity for spying with impunity, and thus for gaining the advantage of surprise. Another overheard conversation figures in Massinger's *The Emperor of the East,* acted by the King's Men at the Globe and Blackfriars in 1631. The pagan princess Athenais seeks help from Pulcheria, who acts as "protectress" until her younger brother becomes emperor: "By these teares by which I bath 'em, I conjure you / With pitty to looke on mee" (1.2.150–51).[138] Pulcheria obliges: "Pray you rise, / And as you rise receive this comfort from mee" (lines 151–52). When Pulcheria subsequently banishes from court those who have oppressed others in order to claim their estates, this stage direction appears: "*The curtaines drawne above,* Theodosius, *and his* Eunuches [*and* Philanax] *discover'd*" (line 288.s.d.). Although he does not interact with the characters below, as Montrevile does in *The Unnatural Combat,* the authority of Theodosius, soon to become emperor, is implicit both in his position *above* and in his ability to see and hear others who are unaware of his presence. In both of Massinger's plays a powerful figure, initially hidden by a curtain, observes a vulnerable woman below. Presumably, the actors playing Montrevile and Theodosius occupy a space corresponding to one of the "boxes," or compartments, above the tiring-house in the De Witt drawing.

In *The Thracian Wonder,* acted ca. 1611–12, another action *above* bespeaks superior authority. A priest, who seeks to know "how or when" a "noisome sickness" afflicting Thrace will cease, stands on the stage floor and, looking upward, propitiates the goddess Pythia (2.3.3–4).[139] Following his speech, a stage direction appears: "*Pythia above, behind the curtains*" (line 7.s.d.). The goddess then announces: "for the time when plagues shall end, / This schedule to the king I send," and "[She] *Throws down a paper*" (lines 14–15, 17.s.d.). The location *above* dramatizes the power of the deity, and the curtain, which must be at least partially opened so that she may toss the paper down to the priest, underscores her mystery. A marginal direction in the 1661 quarto, "Pythia *speaks in the musick-room, behinde the curtains*" (sig. D1v),[140] suggests that the actor playing the deity occupies the same compartment, above the tiring-house occupied, respectively, by Henry VIII and Butts, Montrevile, and Theodosius. In other words, the music room doubles as the site of action *above* or *aloft*. It would have been a simple matter for the musicians to vacate their usual space, to replace them with an actor (or actors), and to part the curtain that ordinarily blocked a view of the musicians.

The reference to a music room in *The Thracian Wonder* alerts us to another use of curtains *above:* concealing from view those who supply musical accompaniment during the performance of plays. It is not entirely clear why those musicians should have been made invisible to playgoers. Richard Hosley proposes that "the attention of a theatrical audience would have tended to be diverted from players to musicians if the latter were visible during the action of a play."[141] Only when musicians played between the acts at private theaters were musicians in view of the spectators.[142]

If curtains *above* are comparatively rare on the stage, so too is dramatic action involving windows with curtains. Possibly curtains were used, even when they are not specifically mentioned, in scenes featuring windows *above* as, for example, in Celia's appearance at her window in Jonson's *Volpone* (2.2.229.s.d), or Juliet's at hers (2.2.1), or Brabantio's in *Othello:* "[Enter] *Brabantio at a window*" (1622 Q, sig. B2r). An explicit use of a window curtain occurs in William Heminges's *The Jews' Tragedy,* acted at an undetermined venue after 1622: Lady Miriam tells Eleazar, "Patience my lord I pray; and you shall see/ That Miriam has reserv'd a part for you" (sig. K2r). The stage direction printed in the margin reads: "*She drawes her window curten.*" Miriam is presumably on the main stage along with the other characters in this scene, but where exactly is the curtain that she draws? The window curtain could be represented by a curtain covering a door into the tiring-house or by a curtain covering a central alcove. But there is another possibility, suggested by *The Shoemaker's Holiday,* performed by the Admiral's Men at the Rose in 1599: Simon Eyre commands, "Open my shop windows!" (4.9).[143] Later Simon Eyre refers to his windows, saying, "my fine dapper Assyrian lads shall clap up their shop windows and away" (17.53–55). Shop windows typically "had wooden shutters hinged at the top and bottom which formed a counter when they were open during the day and an excellent protection against thieves when closed at night."[144] Smallwood and Wells offer this speculation about Dekker's staging: "One possibility that seems not to have been suggested is that one or more of the stage doors was fitted with practicable shutters."[145] It is even possible that the tiring-house wall was itself outfitted with shutters. R. A. Foakes speculates: "probably hinged shutters were made that could serve as windows, and also opened out to form a board or counter. But when the shops were closed up, the stage became a street, or a rural place."[146] Although the references to windows in Dekker's comedy fail to mention curtains, it's possible that curtains were located within shutters that opened outward.

In Thomas Middleton and William Rowley's *The Spanish Gypsy,* performed by Lady Elizabeth's Men at the Phoenix in 1623 and, later, at Salisbury Court, a character refers specifically to window curtains. In the play's first scene Roderigo seizes Clara and carries her off to rape her. When Clara next appears, she is presumably in a bedchamber (though it's not clear whether there is a bed onstage); she says, "What's here, a window curtaine?" (sig. B2v).[147] The room is almost certainly meant to be above the ground floor of a house, for she goes on to say that she can see the garden: " 'tis a garden / To which this window guides the covetous prospect, / A large and a fair one; in the midst / A curious alabaster fountaine stands." Elizabethan and Jacobean gardens, like those on the Continent, were meant to be admired from above; that is, observers could appreciate the garden's intricate design by looking down from an upper floor. What's unusual in *The Spanish Gypsy* is the window at stage level. The window is referred to again later (3.3) when a seated Clara says, "Yon large window / Yields some faire prospect; good my lord, look out, / And tell mee what you see there." Pedro replies, "Easie suite: / Clara it over-viewes a spacious garden, / Amidst which stands an'alabaster fountaine, / A goodly one" (sig. F2r). The dialogue suggests that the characters are above the ground floor of their dwelling, but the actors are not above the main stage of the theater. The "window," therefore, must be imagined as located somewhere on the wall of the tiring-house, possibly in one of the entrances onto the stage.

Canopy

We need to consider one other "soft furnishing," the canopy, which appears in Shakespeare's *King Henry VIII:* "*Enter . . . four* Noblemen *bearing a canopy, under which the* Duchess of Norfolk" (5.4.0.s.d.). In George Peele's *Edward I,* acted in 1595 by the Admiral's Men at the Rose, we read: "*Enter the nine lordes of Scotland, with their nine pages, Gloster, Sussex, king Edward in his sute of glasse, Queene Elinor, [Jone,] Queene Mother, the King and Queene under a canopie*" (line 630.s.d.).[148] This canopy corresponds to the first meaning recorded in the *OED:* "a covering or hangings suspended over a throne, couch, bed, etc., or held over a person walking in procession." In this instance, the textile has the function of signaling the status of king and queen. Similarly, a canopy serves as a processional cover in Thomas Dekker's *The Whore of Babylon,* acted at the Fortune by Prince Henry's Men in 1606: "Empresse *of* Babylon: *her canopie supported by four cardinals: two persons in pontificall roabes on either hand, the one bearing a sword, the other the keies: before her three kings crowned, behinde her friers, &c."* (1.1.0.s.d.).[149] And in Massinger's *The Picture,* performed by the King's Men at the Globe and Blackfriars in 1629, we read: *"Lowd musicke,* Honoria *in state under a canopy, her traine borne up by* Silvia *and* Acanthe" (1.2.128.s.d.).[150]

A fixed, rather than a handheld, canopy would seem to be called for in James Shirley's *The Humorous Courtier,* performed by Queen Henrietta Maria's Men at the Phoenix in 1631: *"Loud musicke, then enter Depazzi, Giotto, Dutchess, Laura, attendants. Dutchesse sits under her canopy"* (5.3.102.s.d.).[151] A few moments later the Duchess *"descends"* (line 148.s.d.), suggesting that she has been sitting on a chair, which in turn rests atop a dais, commensurate with her rank; the canopy may be attached to the back of the chair, allowing it to be easily brought onstage. In Dekker and Webster's *Satiromastix,* a *"chaire is set under a canopie"* (5.2.22.s.d.). Similarly, Nathan Field's *A Woman Is a Weathercock,* acted by the Children of the Queen's Revels at the Whitefriars in 1609, has this stage direction: *"Scudmore passeth one doore, and entereth the other, where Bellafront sits in a chaire, under a taffata canopie"* (3.2.68–70).[152] Dessen and Thomson believe that this stage direction suggests "the use of a recessed space in the tiring-house wall,"[153] though there is no specific evidence in the scene to make this conclusion persuasive.

These instances of canopies onstage are straightforward enough. Less clear is the theatrical property that appears in Sir William Davenant's *Albovine, King of the Lombards,* possibly acted ca. 1626–29: *"A canopy is drawne, the king is discover'd sleeping over papers"* (sig. L2v).[154] Paradine wakes the king, they quarrel, and the king is killed. Paradine then *"puts him behind the arras, opens the doore; enter Rhodolinda"* (sig. M1v). She asks, "Is it done?" and he shows her the king's body: *"He opes the arras."* Do these stage directions signify that *canopy* and *arras* represent the same textile? I am inclined to think so for two reasons. First, it is hard to imagine that the canopy named in the stage direction refers to the kind of portable canopy carried in processions. Second, it is equally difficult to imagine that the king would be sleeping under a canopy above a chair since such a freestanding fixture could, presumably, not be "drawn." I conclude that *canopy* and *arras,* terms used within the same scene of Davenant's play, are essentially equivalent. Support for the notion that *canopy* and *arras* designate a similar furnishing is found in Chapman's *Bussy D'Ambois.* In Q2 Tamyra *"raps her self in the arras"* (sig. I2r) following her torture. In Q1 the Friar's ghost later appears to Tamyra: *"Intrat umbra, Camolet to the Countesse, wrapt in a canopie"* (sig. I1v).[155] Nicholas Brooke, in the Revels edition, concludes, "It is clear that Arras and Canopy are identical."[156]

Almost a century ago E. K. Chambers, in *The Elizabethan Stage,* discussed the nature of a theatrical canopy, arguing that at the back of the Blackfriars stage was "a curtained recess, corresponding to the alcove of the public theatres, and known at Paul's as the 'canopy.'" "Above the canopy," according to Chambers, "was a beam, which bore the post of the music-tree. On this post was a small stand, perhaps for the conductor of the music, and on each side of it was a music-house, forming a gallery." [157] A stage direction in Marston's *Sophonisba,* a Blackfriars play, would seem to support this suggestion: "*A treble viol and a bass lute play softly within the canopy*" (4.1.200.s.d.). [158] MacDonald P. Jackson and Michael Neill, in their edition of *Sophonisba,* comment on the last phrase of this direction: "presumably the curtained 'discovery' space in the centre of the tiring-house façade." [159] In other words, the canopy may be imagined as covering a central opening onto the stage, to be distinguished from the curtains over the doors on either side of the stage when they are being employed for discovery scenes. Scholars as disparate as William J. Lawrence and Andrew Gurr have suggested the existence of a central discovery space the interior of which was entirely curtained. [160] Perhaps the "canopy" that appears in stage directions consisted of a single textile that covered the ceiling of the central alcove, rising to a peak, and that tapered downward and outward to the floor in the way Gerard ter Borch depicts a bed canopy in his painting *Woman Writing a Letter* (1655). [161] In William Heminges's *The Fatal Contract,* a Salisbury Court play, we find in the stage directions a clue as to how such a canopy might work: "*Enter the* Eunuch . . . *and solemn'y drawes the canopie, where the* Queen *sits at one end bound with* Landrey *at the other, both asleep*" (sig. H3r). If we imagine the interior of the discovery space as completely covered with a larger version of the canopy that appears in Gerard ter Borch's painting, we understand that the Eunuch has opened that part of the canopy that hides the captives from the playgoers. In the same scene when the Eunuch has poisoned both Landrey and the Queen, he turns to her, saying: "I will be bold to gag your ladyship; / I'l leave a peeping hole through which you shall / See sights shall kill thee faster than thy poyson" (sig. I1r). The marginal direction reads: "*draws the curtain again.*" The curtain that the Eunuch *again* draws must be part of the larger enveloping canopy.

Conclusion

As the compilation of stage directions by Dessen and Thomson attests, curtains were a common feature of staging in Shakespeare's England. Bed curtains are typically associated with a sense of expectation, with sex or death or both. Other curtains could be drawn across one of the entrances onto the stage for discovery scenes, or, less often, employed on the upper level of the stage in one of the "boxes," or compartments, depicted in the De Witt drawing. [162] If there was a central opening onto the stage from the tiring-house at the Globe and other theaters, it was in all likelihood wider than the others, and it was covered with a textile, usually referred to as an *arras* or *hanging;* this textile was probably decorated with one or more figures drawn from history or mythology. Onstage the chief functions of curtains are concealment and revelation. In addition to making visible artifacts and characters that figure in the subsequent staging, the opening of curtains in discovery scenes may create a significant contrast between the principal and the secondary dramatic action. In most cases curtains have implications for the emotional temperature of a scene: they tend to intensify theatrical effects. When closed, curtains may create suspense: for example, we wait for a character to emerge from a hiding place. Opened, those curtains may create surprise, shock, and even wonderment by the spectacle they reveal.

Notes

1. I wish to acknowledge my gratitude to Leslie Thomson for commenting on an early draft of this essay, written for the meeting of the Shakespeare Association of America in 2004.

2. Glynne Wickham, *Early English Stages, 1300 to 1660,* vol. 2, *1576 to 1660,* part 1 (New York: Columbia University Press, 1963), 282.

3. *Volpone, or The Fox,* in *The Workes of Benjamin Jonson* (London, 1616), 450.

4. Ben Jonson, *Volpone, or The Fox,* ed. R. B. Parker, Revels Plays (Manchester: Manchester University Press, 1983). I cite the plays in modern editions when they are available as here. When no such editions are at hand, I quote from the earliest publications. For the sake of consistency, I have eliminated random capital letters from both original and modern texts.

5. Ibid., note to 1.1.0. In the Revels Student Edition of *Volpone,* ed. Brian Parker and David Bevington (Manchester: Manchester University Press; New York: St. Martin's Press, 1999), Parker's 1983 remark about the four-poster bed is deleted. In its place is this gloss on "discovers": "i.e. draws back the bedcurtains." The revised note goes on to say: "Volpone could begin the scene by entering with Mosca rather than rising from bed, but the bed is certainly needed later in the act."

6. Ivan G. Sparkes, in *Four-Poster and Tester Beds* (Haverfordwest, Dyfed: Shire Publications, 1990), observes, "The term *four-poster* was not used until the nineteenth century" (6). For photos, illustrations, and discussions of beds in the Renaissance, see Victor Chinnery, *Oak Furniture: The British Tradition* (Woodbridge, England: Antique Collectors' Club, 1979), 384–96; Peter Thornton, *Seventeenth-Century Interior Decoration in England, France, and Holland* (New Haven: Yale University Press for the Paul Mellon Centre for Studies in British Art, 1978), 154–77.

7. Robert N. Watson, ed., *Volpone,* 2nd ed., New Mermaids (New York: W. W. Norton, 2003), 1.1.0.s.d.

8. In her paper for the Shakespeare Association of America, 2004, Leslie Thomson argued that the play fails to support the notion that Volpone is in bed as the play begins. She observed that, later in the play, Volpone is said to recline on a couch

(3.5.32, 3.7.138.s.d.). It is possible, of course, that Volpone reclines on a bed in the play's first scene and later on a different piece of furniture, a couch.

9. William Sampson, *The Vow Breaker, or The Fair Maid of Clifton* (London, 1636).

10. R. A. Foakes, *Illustrations of the English Stage, 1580–1642* (Stanford, CA: Stanford University Press, 1985), 141.

11. George Fullmer Reynolds, *The Staging of Elizabethan Plays at the Red Bull Theater, 1605–1625* (New York: Modern Language Association, 1940), 65.

12. Eva Griffith provides a valuable summary of information about this theater in "New Material for a Jacobean Playhouse: The Red Bull Theatre on the Seckford Estate," *Theatre Notebook* 55.1 (2001): 5–23.

13. Thomas Heywood, *The Golden Age* (London, 1611).

14. Sasha Roberts, "'Let me the curtains draw': The Dramatic and Symbolic Properties of the Bed in Shakespearean Tragedy," in *Staged Properties in Early Modern English Drama,* ed. Jonathan Gil Harris and Natasha Corda, 159 (Cambridge: Cambridge University Press, 2002). See also Roberts's "Lying among the Classics: Ritual and Motif in Elite Elizabethan and Jacobean Beds," in *Albion's Classicism: The Visual Arts in Britain, 1550–1660,* ed. Lucy Gent, 325–57 (New Haven: Yale University Press for the Paul Mellon Centre for Studies in British Art, 1995).

15. Thomas Middleton, *A Chaste Maid in Cheapside,* ed. R. B. Parker, The Revels Plays (London: Methuen, 1969).

16. Richard Hosley, "The Playhouses," in *Revels History of Drama in English,* vol. 3: *1576–1613* (London: Methuen, 1975), 173.

17. *Romeo and Juliet,* in *The Riverside Shakespeare,* ed. G. Blakemore Evans, 2nd ed. (New York: Houghton Mifflin, 1997). All citations of Shakespeare are from this edition unless otherwise indicated.

18. Thomas Heywood, *The Rape of Lucrece* (London, 1608).

19. James N. Loehlin, in *Romeo and Juliet,* Shakespeare in Production (Cambridge: Cambridge University Press, 2002), writes: "Juliet's bed, which appears in 4.3 and 4.5, was either brought out from the tiring house, in which case it must have had its own curtains, or it was located in the discovery space in the tiring-house façade, and so curtained off; the former seems more likely, given sight-line constraints" (4).

20. *An Excellent conceited Tragedie of Romeo and Juliet* (London, 1597). Q2 (1599) omits the stage direction.

21. Robert Wilmot, *The Tragedy of Tancred and Gismund,* ed. W. W. Greg, Malone Society Reprints (Oxford: Oxford University Press, 1914). This play represents a thorough recasting of *Gismond of Salerne;* see A. R. Braunmuller, "Early Shakespearian Tragedy and its Contemporary Context: Cause and Emotion in *Titus Andronicus, Richard III,* and *The Rape of Lucrece,*" in *Shakespearian Tragedy,* ed. David Palmer and Malcolm Bradbury, Stratford-upon Avon Studies 20, 97–128 (London: Edward Arnold, 1984).

22. *The Battle of Alcazar,* ed. John Yoklavich, in *The Dramatic Works of George Peele,* in *The Life and Works of George Peele,* gen. ed. Charles Tyler Prouty, 3 vols. (New Haven: Yale University Press, 1961), vol. 2.

23. William Shakespeare, *The First Part of the Contention betwixt the Two Famous*

Houses of Yorke and Lancaster, with the Death of the Good Duke Humphrey (London, 1594).

24. Christopher Marlowe, *The Massacre at Paris,* in *"Dido Queen of Carthage" and "The Massacre at Paris,"* ed. H. J. Oliver, Revels Plays (London: Methuen, 1968).

25. E. A. J. Honigmann, ed., *Othello,* Arden Shakespeare, 3rd ed. (Walton-on-Thames: Thomas Nelson and Sons, 1996), 313.

26. Thomas Heywood, *The Second Part of The Iron Age* (London, 1632).

27. *Amends for Ladies,* in *The Plays of Nathan Field,* ed. William Peery (Austin: University of Texas Press, 1950).

28. *Lust's Dominion, or The Lascivious Queen,* in *The Dramatic Works of Thomas Dekker,* ed. Fredson Bowers, 4 vols. (Cambridge: Cambridge University Press, 1953–61), vol. 4.

29. Alan C. Dessen and Leslie Thomson, *A Dictionary of Stage Directions in English Drama, 1580–1642* (Cambridge: Cambridge University Press, 1999), 62.

30. Andrew Gurr, *The Shakespearean Stage, 1574–1642,* 3rd ed. (Cambridge: Cambridge University Press, 1992), 135.

31. Tiffany Stern, "Behind the Arras: The Prompter's Place in the Shakespearean Theatre," *Theatre Notebook* 55.3 (2001): 112.

32. For a list of plays featuring discoveries and a treatment of this convention, see T. J. King, *Shakespearean Staging, 1599–1642* (Cambridge, MA: Harvard University Press, 1971), chapter 4.

33. Richard Hosley, "The Discovery-Space in Shakespeare's Globe," *Shakespeare Survey* 12 (1959): 46.

34. Hosley, "Shakespearian Stage Curtains: Then and Now," *College English* (April 1964): 490.

35. For a valuable summary of information about this theater, see Roger Bowers, "The Playhouse of the Choristers of Paul's, c. 1575–1608," *Theatre Notebook* 54.2 (2000): 70–85.

36. *The Wisdom of Doctor Dodypoll* (London, 1600).

37. Some scholars doubt the existence of a central entrance onto the stages of public theaters. See, for example, Tim Fitzpatrick, "Stage Management, Dramaturgy and Spatial Semiotics in Shakespeare's Dialogue," *Theatre Research International* 24.1 (Spring 1999): 12–14.

38. See Andrew Gurr, "Staging at the Globe," in *Shakespeare's Globe Rebuilt,* ed. J. R. Mulryne and Margaret Shewring, 161–62 (Cambridge: Cambridge University Press in association with Mulryne & Shewring, 1997).

39. See John Orrell, *The Theatres of Inigo Jones and John Webb* (Cambridge: Cambridge University Press, 1985), fig. 7. John Webb's plan for the Cockpit-in-Court shows five entrances onto the stage (fig. 17).

40. Robert Greene, *"Alphonsus King of Aragon" 1599,* ed. W. W. Greg, Malone Society Reprints (Oxford: Oxford University Press, 1926).

41. *Thomas Heywood's "The Four Prentices of London": A Critical, Old-Spelling Edition,* ed. Mary Ann Weber Gasior (New York: Garland, 1980), 4.

42. George Chapman, Ben Jonson, John Marston, *Eastward Ho,* ed. R. W. Van Fossen, Revels Plays (Baltimore: Johns Hopkins University Press, 1979).

43. Reavley Gair, *The Children of Paul's: The Story of a Theatre Company, 1553–1608* (Cambridge: Cambridge University Press, 1982), 61.

44. Andrew Gurr and Mariko Ichikawa, *Staging in Shakespeare's Theatres,* Oxford Shakespeare Topics (Oxford: Oxford University Press, 2000), 7.

45. Andrew Gurr, "Stage Doors at the Globe," *Theatre Notebook* 53.1 (1999): 18n16.

46. Ibid., 14.

47. Quoted by E. K. Chambers, *The Elizabethan Stage,* 4 vols. (1923; repr., Oxford: Clarendon Press, 1951), 3:79.

48. Tim Fitzpatrick and Wendy Millyard, "Hangings, Doors and Discoveries: Conflicting Evidence or Problematic Assumptions?" *Theatre Notebook* 54.1 (2000): 2–23.

49. John Orrell and Andrew Gurr, in "What the Rose can tell us," *Antiquity* 63 (September 1989): 421–29, report: "No sign has been found that the *frons scenae* at the rear of the stage was constructed as a straight chord across the polygon: both stages, the earlier and the later, seem to have been backed by a wall that followed the polygonal line of the main frame" (427).

50. Fitzpatrick and Millyard, "Hangings, Doors and Discoveries," 23n9.

51. In his edition of Shakespeare's *King John* (New York: Oxford University Press, 1988), A. R. Braunmuller notes that the term "three-nooked" may "refer to an outmoded (for the Elizabethan audience) three-continent world (as at *Tamburlaine, Part 1* 4.4.78)" (270).

52. "To 'discover' has a technical meaning in the Elizabethan theatre: to expose something to the actors' and audience's view." See Hugh Macrae Richmond, *Shakespeare's Theatre: A Dictionary of His Stage Context* (New York: Continuum, 2002), 144.

53. Jonson, *Volpone,* ed. Parker.

54. Alvin B. Kernan, ed., *Ben Jonson: "Volpone"* (New Haven: Yale University Press, 1962), s.d. following line 2 of the first scene.

55. Helen Ostovich, ed., *Volpone,* in *Jonson: Four Comedies* (New York: Longman, 1997), 76. Ostovich goes on to say that such a cupboard "may merely have been suggested at the Globe by one of the stage doors or the discovery-space."

56. Parker, ed., *Volpone,* 95.

57. David Cook, ed., *Volpone* (1962; repr., London: Methuen, 1967), 61.

58. Andrew Gurr, in *The Shakespearean Stage, 1574–1642,* noting that the De Witt drawing fails to depict curtains covering entry into the tiring-house, speculates: "The hangings might either have been omitted by de Witt because they would have obscured the location of the stage doors, or possibly they could have hung in the doorways behind the doors, so that when the doors were open the hangings would be visible to conceal a 'discovery,' and when they were closed the hangings would be hidden and so would not impede the normal use of the doors" (135).

59. "At Cuckfield in Sussex . . . there is a discovery-monument which illustrates in some detail how curtains might be suspended or drawn back; it shows curtains sewn over a pole, and pulled back along it, enclosing a small discovery-space, such as might have been set up either within an entrance-door or within a specially-constructed space on a tiring-house façade." See Jean Wilson, *The Shakespeare Leg-*

acy: The Material Legacy of Shakespeare's Theatre (Godalming, Surrey: Bramley Books, 1995), 93.

60. John Webster, *The White Devil,* ed. John Russell Brown, 2nd ed., Revels Plays (1966; repr., London: Methuen, 1968).

61. Ibid., 56n.

62. Gordon McMullan, ed., *King Henry VIII (All is True),* Arden Shakespeare, 3rd series (London: Thomson Learning, 2000), 283.

63. *Satiromastix,* in *The Dramatic Works of Thomas Dekker,* vol. 1.

64. *"Hengist, King of Kent, or The Mayor of Queenborough" by Thomas Middleton,* ed. Grace Ioppolo, Malone Society Reprints 167 (Oxford: Oxford University Press, 2003). This edition reproduces the Portland Manuscript in the University of Nottingham's Hallward Library; the play was first published in 1661.

65. Julia Briggs, "Middleton's Forgotten Tragedy *Hengist, King of Kent,*" *Review of English Studies* 41 (November 1990): 485–86.

66. David Carnegie writes: "it seems to me clear from the intensity of the dialogue, and from Paulina's protective proximity to Hermione, that she controls the curtain herself." See "Stabbed through the Arras: The Dramaturgy of Elizabethan Stage Hangings," in *Shakespeare: World Views,* ed. Heather Kerr, Robin Eaden, and Madge Mitton, 193 (Newark: University of Delaware Press; London: Associated University Presses, 1996).

67. David Bevington, *Action is Eloquence: Shakespeare's Language of Gesture* (Cambridge, MA: Harvard University Press, 1984), 116.

68. *"The Devil's Charter" by Barnabe Barnes: A Critical Edition,* ed. Jim C. Pogue (New York: Garland, 1980). Pogue observes that "since it does, more often than not, state explicitly how the action is to be staged, *The Devil's Charter* is especially valuable in the study of staging practices in Renaissance drama and at the Globe" (34).

69. *Grim the Collier of Croyden,* in *A Choice Ternary of English Plays: Gratiæ Theatrales (1662),* ed. William M. Baillie, Medieval and Renaissance Texts and Studies (Binghamton, NY: Center for Medieval and Early Renaissance Studies, 1984).

70. Baillie, ed., *Grim the Collier,* comments: "although the induction characters do not sit onstage as spectators, their expectation of a report from Belphagor upon his return from earth creates a kind of unseen stage audience, as if the devils were peeping from behind the curtain during the main action to follow Belphagor's progress" (181).

71. Richard Hosley, "Shakespearian Stage Curtains: Then and Now," 490.

72. Jonson, *Volpone,* ed. Parker.

73. Ostovich, ed., *Volpone,* in *Ben Jonson: Four Comedies,* 196.

74. *Godly Queen Hester* (London, 1561). Paul Whitfield White speculates that this play was written "for chapel performance under the auspices of Henry VIII's court," that transepts and side chapels "provided points for entrances and exits and for costume changes," and that "curtained traverses could easily be erected to close off these areas to the spectators." See *Theatre and Reformation: Protestantism, Patronage, and Playing in Tudor England* (Cambridge: Cambridge University Press, 1993), 146. White goes on to suggest of this interlude, "The stage directions call for a 'traverse' to be used exclusively for King Assuerus' entrances and exits, which might have been

the same as 'her Majestes Travess' in Queen Elizabeth's chapel at St. James Palace to curtain off a particular area from the rest of the sanctuary" (148–49).

75. Chambers, *The Elizabethan Stage,* 3:26.

76. Ibid. More recently the traverse in *Godly Queen Hester* has been interpreted as "probably a screen at the back of the stage." See Darryl Grantley, *English Dramatic Interludes, 1300–1580* (Cambridge: Cambridge University Press, 2004), 131.

77. W. W. Greg, ed., *"A New Enterlude of Godly Queene Hester,"* edited from the *Quarto of 1561,* Materialien zur Kunde des älteren Englischen Dramas 5 (Louvain: A. Uystpruyst, 1904), 50.

78. Richard Southern, *The Staging of Plays before Shakespeare* (London: Faber and Faber, 1973), 267.

79. Ibid., 270.

80. Alan H. Nelson, "Hall Screens and Elizabethan Playhouses: Counter-Evidence from Cambridge," in *The Development of Shakespeare's Theater,* ed. John H. Asting-ton (New York: AMS Press, 1992), 71.

81. Glynne Wickham, in *Early English Stages, 1300 to 1660,* vol. 1: *1300 to 1576* (London: Routledge and Kegan Paul, 1959), observes that a description of arrangements for the wedding of Katharine of Aragon at St. Paul's identifies the word *traverse* with the word *curtain* (92).

82. John Webster, *The Duchess of Malfi,* ed. John Russell Brown, Revels Plays (1964; repr., London: Methuen, 1969).

83. Peter Thomson, in *Shakespeare's Theatre,* 2nd ed. (New York: Routledge, 1992), speculates that the traverse was a curtain that could be deployed anywhere onstage: "traverse curtains were always in stock, to be draped across the stage doors, on the mobile platforms, or even slung between the pillars for climactic scenes such as the masque of *The Revenger's Tragedy,* or the play-within-the-play in *Hamlet*" (52).

84. See Robert Speaight, *William Poel and the Elizabethan Revival* (London: William Heinemann, 1954), 84, 107–8.

85. *"A Looking-Glass for London and England,"* by Thomas Lodge and Robert Greene, 1594, ed. W. W. Greg, Malone Society Reprints (Oxford: Oxford University Press, 1932).

86. *"The Downfall of Robert Earl of Huntingdon"* by Anthony Munday, 1601, ed. John C. Meagher and Arthur Brown, Malone Society Reprints (Oxford: Oxford University Press, 1965).

87. *"Friar Bacon and Friar Bungay,"* by Robert Greene, 1594, ed. W. W. Greg, Malone Society Reprints (Oxford: Oxford University Press, 1926).

88. *Tom a Lincoln,* ed. G. R. Proudfoot, H. R. Woudhuysen, and John Pitcher, Malone Society Reprints (Oxford: Oxford University Press, 1992).

89. *The Whore of Babylon,* in *The Dramatic Works of Thomas Dekker,* vol. 2.

90. Dieter Mehl, *The Elizabethan Dumb Show: The History of a Dramatic Convention* (London: Methuen, 1965), 21.

91. Thomas Kyd, *The Spanish Tragedy,* ed. Philip Edwards, Revels Plays (1959; repr., London: Methuen, 1969).

92. Ibid., 110.

93. J. R. Mulryne, ed., *The Spanish Tragedy,* 2nd ed., New Mermaids (1989; repr., New York: W. W. Norton, 1997), 112.

94. D. F. Rowan, "The Staging of *The Spanish Tragedy*," *The Elizabethan Theatre* 5 (1975): 122.

95. [Thomas Dekker], *"The Bloody Banquet," 1639*, ed. Samuel Schoenbaum and Arthur Brown, Malone Society Reprints (Oxford: Oxford University Press, 1962 [for 1961].

96. Christopher Marlowe and His Collaborator and Revisers, *"Doctor Faustus": A- and B-texts (1604, 1616)*, ed. David Bevington and Eric Rasmussen, Revels Plays (New York: St. Martin's Press, 1993). The lines quoted here are from the A-text.

97. Several scenes later, Jachimo, describing Imogen's bedchamber, says that "it was hang'd / With tapestry of silk and silver; the story / Proud Cleopatra, when she met her Roman" (2.4.68–70).

98. John Day, *Law Tricks, or Who Would Have Thought It* (London, 1608).

99. William Heminges, *The Fatal Contract* (London, 1653).

100. Hosley, in "Shakespearian Stage Curtains," writes that "Falstaff is asleep, either seated in a chair or reclining on a bench" (489).

101. *The English Traveller*, in *Thomas Heywood: Three Marriage Plays*, ed. Paul Merchant, Revels Plays Companion Library (Manchester: Manchester University Press New York: St. Martin's Press, 1996).

102. Lewis Sharpe, *The Noble Stranger* (London, 1640).

103. *Cynthia's Revels*, in *Ben Jonson*, ed. C. H. Herford and Percy and Evelyn Simpson, 11 vols. (Oxford: Clarendon Press, 1925–52), vol. 4.

104. *Northward Ho*, in *The Dramatic Works of Thomas Dekker*, vol. 2.

105. Colin A. Gibson, "'Behind the Arras' in Massinger's 'The Renegado,'" *Notes and Queries* 214 (August 1969): 296.

106. C. Walter Hodges, *The Globe Restored: A Study of the Elizabethan Theatre* (1953; repr., New York: W. W. Norton, 1973), 17.

107. John Ronayne, "Totus Mundus Agit Histrionem: The Interior Decorative Scheme of the Bankside Globe," in *Shakespeare's Globe Rebuilt*, ed. J. R. Mulryne and Margaret Shewring, 121–46 (Cambridge: Cambridge University Press, 1997).

108. Giorgio Melchiori, ed., *The Second Part of King Henry IV* (Cambridge: Cambridge University Press, 1989), 88. The *OED* defines "waterwork" as "A kind of imitation tapestry, painted in size or distemper."

109. Ronayne, "Totus Mundus," 136.

110. *Henslowe's Diary*, ed. R. A. Foakes, 2nd ed. (Cambridge: Cambridge University Press, 2002), 319–20.

111. Francis Beaumont, *The Knight of the Burning Pestle*, ed. Sheldon P. Zitner, Revels Plays (Manchester: Manchester University Press, 1984), 103.

112. For a useful discussion of painted cloths, see Arthur H. R. Fairchild, *Shakespeare and the Arts of Design (Architecture, Sculpture, and Painting)* University of Missouri Studies 12.1 (Columbia: University of Missouri Press, 1937), 147–50. According to Fairchild, painted cloths "were hung in the streets for pageants and used as signs for shows; they decorated the interior of temporary buildings that were erected for entertainments; and they were used on the stage; but by far their most common use was as hangings for rooms, especially of the more ordinary type" (147).

113. George Chapman, *Bussy D'Ambois* (London, 1641).

114. *The Tragedy of Claudius Tiberius Nero, Rome's Greatest Tyrant* (London, 1607).

115. *The Tragedy of Nero,* ed. Elliott M. Hill (New York: Garland, 1979).

116. William Heminges, *The Jews' Tragedy* (London, 1662).

117. Francis Beaumont and John Fletcher, *Philaster, or Love Lies a-Bleeding,* ed. Andrew Gurr, Revels Plays (London: Methuen, 1969).

118. Arthur Wilson, *The Swisser,* ed. Linda V. Itzoe (New York: Garland, 1984).

119. *A Critical Edition of Brome's "The Northern Lasse,"* ed. Harvey Fried (New York: Garland, 1980).

120. Irwin Smith, *Shakespeare's Blackfriars Playhouse: Its History and Its Design* (New York: New York University Press, 1964), 342.

121. Henry Killigrew, *Pallantus and Eudora* [*The Conspiracy*] (London, 1653). The 1638 quarto is entitled *The Conspiracy.*

122. William Davenant, *The Unfortunate Lovers* (London, 1649).

123. Smith, *Shakespeare's Blackfriars Playhouse,* 342–43.

124. Ben Jonson, *The New Inn,* ed. Michael Hattaway, Revels Plays (Manchester: Manchester University Press, 1984), 48–49.

125. Ibid., 49.

126. James Shirley, *The Lady of Pleasure,* ed. Ronald Huebert, Revels Plays (Manchester: Manchester University Press, 1986).

127. Dessen and Thomson, *A Dictionary of Stage Directions,* 110.

128. See Carnegie, "Stabbed Through the Arras," in *Shakespeare: World Views,* 181–99.

129. See the reproduction in Foakes, *Illustrations of the English Stage,* no. 70.

130. Massinger, *The City Madam,* in *The Plays and Poems of Philip Massinger,* ed. Philip Edwards and Colin Gibson, 5 vols. (Oxford: Clarendon Press, 1976), vol. 4.

131. Hosley, "Was There a Music-Room in Shakespeare's Globe?" *Shakespeare Survey* 13 (1960): 116.

132. *"A Warning for Fair Women": A Critical Edition,* ed. Charles Dale Cannon (The Hague: Mouton, 1975).

133. *Northward Ho,* in *The Dramatic Works of Thomas Dekker,* vol. 2.

134. John Marston and others, *The Insatiate Countess,* ed. Giorgio Melchiori, Revels Plays (Manchester: Manchester University Press, 1984).

135. Andrew Gurr, in *The Shakespeare Company, 1594–1642* (Cambridge: Cambridge University Press, 2004), argues that "this tradition of signalling how a play would end seems to have vanished when tragicomedy entered the repertory" (46).

136. R. A. Foakes, "Playhouses and Players," in *The Cambridge Companion to English Renaissance Drama,* ed. A. R. Braunmuller and Michael Hattaway, 20 (Cambridge: Cambridge University Press, 1990).

137. *The Unnatural Combat,* in *The Plays and Poems of Philip Massinger,* vol. 2.

138. *The Emperor of the East,* in *The Plays and Poems of Philip Massinger,* vol. 3.

139. *"The Thracian Wonder" by William Rowley and Thomas Heywood: A Critical Edition,* ed. Michael Nolan (Salzburg: Institut für Anglistik und Amerikanistik, Universität Salzburg, 1997).

140. *The Thracian Wonder* (London, 1661). The title page attributes the play to William Rowley and John Webster; Nolan attributes the play to Rowley and Heywood.

141. Hosley, "Was There a Music-Room in Shakespeare's Globe?" 114.

142. The curtains in the middle of the "boxes" above the stage, pictured in the fron-

tispiece of *The Wits* (1662), may conceal musicians. See Hosley, "The Playhouses," 231.

143. Thomas Dekker, *The Shoemaker's Holiday,* ed. R. L. Smallwood and Stanley Wells, Revels Plays (Baltimore: Johns Hopkins University Press, 1979).

144. Trudy West, *The Timber-frame House in England* (n.d.); quoted by Smallwood and Wells, 45.

145. Smallwood and Wells, ed., *The Shoemaker's Holiday,* 46. Anthony Parr, in his New Mermaids edition of *The Shoemaker's Holiday,* 2nd ed. (New York: W. W. Norton, 1990), endorses this suggestion: "given the frequency of shop scenes in the drama of this period such a device might have become a shorthand convention obviating the need for elaborate settings to indicate location" (xxviii).

146. R. A. Foakes, "Playhouses and Stages," 21.

147. Thomas Middleton and William Rowley, *The Spanish Gypsy* (London, 1653).

148. Peele, *Edward I,* ed. Frank S. Hook, in *The Dramatic Works of George Peele,* in *The Life and Works of George Peele,* vol. 2.

149. *The Whore of Babylon,* in *The Dramatic Works of Thomas Dekker,* vol. 2.

150. *The Picture,* in *The Plays and Poems of Philip Massinger,* vol. 3.

151. *James Shirley's "The Humorous Courtier,"* ed. Marvin Morillo (New York: Garland, 1979).

152. *A Woman is a Weathercock,* in *The Plays of Nathan Field.*

153. Dessen and Thomson, *A Dictionary of Stage Directions,* 41.

154. William Davenant, *Albovine, King of the Lombards* (London, 1629).

155. George Chapman, *Bussy D'Ambois* (London, 1607).

156. Brooke, ed., *Bussy D'Ambois,* 121.

157. Chambers, *The Elizabethan Stage,* 3:144. William A. Armstrong, in "'Canopy' in Elizabethan Theatrical Terminology," *Notes and Queries* 202 (October 1957): 433–34, notes the two possible meanings of canopy: as a covering above a chair of state and as a curtained recess.

158. *Sophonisba,* in *The Selected Plays of John Marston,* ed. MacDonald P. Jackson and Michael Neill (Cambridge: Cambridge University Press, 1986).

159. Ibid., 460.

160. William J. Lawrence, *The Physical Conditions of the Elizabethan Public Playhouse* (Cambridge, MA: Harvard University Press, 1927), 47.

161. Reproduced in *Gerard Ter Borch, Zwolle 1617, Deventer 1681* (Munich: Landesmuseum für Kunst und Kulturgeschichte, 1974), plate 34.

162. Andrew Gurr, in *The Shakespearean Stage,* notes: "All three extant illustrations of stages in use between de Witt's Swan and 1642 . . . show the whole tiringhouse façade curtained off. This practice, which must have derived from the curtained booth of the street theatres, was probably fairly general" (151).

Imagining the Actor's Body on
the Early Modern Stage

JEREMY LOPEZ

THIS essay is a prolegomenon to a larger study of the relationship between casting, dramaturgy, and theatrical rhetoric on the early modern stage. The last decade or so has seen an increased interest in the importance of the acting company (rather than the playwright) as the fundamental unit of the early modern theater. Theater historians such as Roslyn Knutson, Scott McMillin and Sally-Beth MacLean, Andrew Gurr, and Tiffany Stern have focused our attention on the relationship between the structures of repertory playing and the creation of theatrical meaning.[1] My goal is to build upon the methods and discoveries of these scholars and to combine them with more literary, formal analysis in order to develop a critical method that attempts to imagine the way early modern acting companies, and their playwrights, might have used actors' bodies as formal devices not distinct from dramaturgical elements such as verse style, subject matter, and staging habits. Such a critical method might, I suggest, help put early modern plays into vivid and as yet unfamiliar dialogue with one another.

Much of the work of such a project is and will remain necessarily speculative, and the first word of this essay's title is intended to insist upon the value of speculation. Caesar and Polonius were *probably* played by the same actor, as probably were Brutus and Hamlet. The grim joke Polonius and Hamlet share about Polonius playing the part of Caesar at University (3.2.101–2) is *probably* the first half of an intertextual rhyming couplet that is completed when Hamlet kills Polonius in 3.4.[2] We do not, of course, have anything like evidence to support the claim that this cross-casting actually occurred. Nor do we have evidence to support the idea that Shakespeare was writing for a company in which there were two particularly strong boy actors, of notably different height and temperament (it doesn't help that he often seems unable to decide which is which) as he created the wonderful pairs of female characters in the stretch of plays through the mid-1590s: Helena and Hermia, Rosalind and Celia, Portia and Nerissa, Beatrice and Hero, Mistress Page and Mistress Ford. Criticism at least since Gerald Bentley has been reluctant to pursue intertextual rhyming of this kind in large part because we cannot attach actors' names to roles (much less physical appearance or personalities to names). I think it is important not to be overly cautious about identifying particular bodies to the extent that we simply go on forgetting that *some* bodies did in fact inhabit these roles in the late sixteenth century.[3] Thinking about actual pairs of boy actors on Shakespeare's stage in the mid-1590s—whether the same or different pairs from play to play—creates a productive position from which to view the point of entry for particularly Shakespearean fantasies about love and language into literary and theatrical culture. A discussion, for example, of the convention of the witty but submissive woman from Hermia to Beatrice would be richly filled out by an attempt to imagine the way in which these roles might represent the career of a single actor (or even several different actors), and the way in which the ethics of the convention might have become tied to, and/or authorized in, an actor's body.[4]

I return to this point in more specific detail later in the essay. For the moment I want simply to say that the methodology I am trying to develop is not one of identifying likely role-rhyming or specific actors across plays and authors and companies; rather, it is one of imagining early modern characters as actors and actors as necessary agents of theatrical meaning—much as we might think of words or scenes or props—so that we can begin to think more specifically about the effects of acting on an early modern audience. In "Personations: *The Taming of the Shrew* and the Limits of Theoretical Criticism."[5] Paul Yachnin argues that "the semantic unit—the quantum of theatrical meaning-making in Shakespeare's playhouse—comprised the person. . . . [M]eaning was produced on the early modern stage through personation rather than by developing systems of ideas abstracted from the dramatic action" (7). Not theater history, but rather a critique of traditional theoretical approaches to theatrical problems such as the submission of Katherina in *Shrew,* Yachnin's article is concerned to demonstrate the way in which particularly literary critical models—materialist, rationalist, new historicist— anachronistically limit the possibilities for meaning that inhere in a theatrical text. In its insistence that the body of the actor in the theater allows a spectator to comprehend a wealth of complexity and contradiction (see 31), Yachnin's essay is a call for the development of a critical imagination that perceives the theater as a locus for the refraction of multiple systems of meaning through the prism of physical, speaking, thinking human bodies— and not only the bodies onstage, but those in the audience as well. A small polemical goal of my own essay, as it moves from a discussion of Shakespeare to a discussion of acting companies to a discussion of early modern drama "in general," is to suggest that theater history's disciplinary imperative to differentiate is occasionally in danger of limiting the possibilities for meaning that inhere in theatrical texts, and that a focus on playing companies and their different repertories and styles will only take us so far; given the state of the documentary evidence in the field, there is a point at which imagination must take over where evidence leaves off.[6]

In the particular and unique case of Shakespeare, the performance tradition and the critical tradition of performance studies allows us to see quite clearly the relationship between specific actors, audiences, and the reception and dissemination of a multiplicity of theatrical and interpretive conventions. It is easy to imagine how an influential company (like the Royal Shakespeare Company [RSC]) performing *Hamlet* and *Coriolanus* in the same season might draw out the echoes between Hamlet and Gertrude and Coriolanus and Volumnia, and might quite explicitly seek to frame those echoes within the critical tradition.[7] Companies frequently perform *Measure for Measure* and *All's Well That Ends Well* in repertory, using cross-cast actors to underscore the intertextual echoes between the Angelo-Isabella-Mariana triangle in the former and the Bertram-Helena-Diana triangle in the latter. Possibly, though certainly less frequently, one might be fortunate enough to see repertory performances of *Pericles* and *Cymbeline,* two plays (possibly written and performed in succession) in which an actor must emerge, surprising audience and characters alike, from a trunk. It is very unlikely that one might also get to see, at the same theater or even a different one, a production of the nearly contemporaneous *Family of Love* (Barry) and start to think about what might have been so interesting to acting companies about boy-sized trunks in the first decade of the seventeenth century.[8] As far as I know, no modern company has presented in the same season the three perverse and chaotic families that burst onto the Globe stage in the remarkable 1606–7 season: Lear, Cordelia, Goneril, and Regan; Vindice, Hippolito, Gratiana, Castiza; Volpone, Mosca, Dwarf, Eunuch, Fool.[9] My point here is that the methodology I am attempting to sketch out is valuable, and perhaps essential, for allowing ourselves to imagine more fully the relationships between Shakespeare and other playwrights, and between other playwrights and other playwrights. It is valuable and perhaps essential for developing a vocabulary with which to discuss the dramaturgy of a large number of obscure plays whose coexistence with the works of Shakespeare, Marlowe, and Jonson can all too frequently seem merely coincidental.

In 4.2 of Shakespeare's *Cymbeline,* Cloten's body becomes a prop. Dressed in Posthumus's garments and deprived of his head, Cloten has gone from animate to inanimate, from subject to object. Like all the best props he is an object whose history and meaning are open to multiple levels of interpretation. When Imogen comes upon him she misreads the forms of his body for those of her beloved Posthumus: "this is his hand," she says (309), and there is a sly echo here of what Cloten said earlier when he wrested from Pisanio

the letter directing Imogen to Milford Haven: "It is Posthumus's hand" (3.5.108). Like a letter—or a bracelet or a ring or a bloody cloth—Cloten's body is a visible, tangible marker of the distance between stage and audience; it is, to borrow Fran Teague's phrase, a "speaking property,"[10] an inanimate object lent by the stage a heightened capacity to signify.

Cloten had put on Posthumus's clothes because Imogen told him that Posthumus's "meanest garment" was worth more than Cloten's whole person. Raping and kidnapping Imogen while wearing her husband's clothes would, Cloten thought, have a certain satisfying irony. That irony never comes to fruition, but the "garments" do create the extravagant irony of Imogen mistaking Cloten for her husband. There is a close relationship here between language and staging: what starts as a purely rhetorical moment—"you're not worth his meanest garment"—turns into a moment where the garments and the body they adorn have an urgent physical significance on the stage. This process is analogous to the process whereby Posthumus's "hand"—his penmanship—in 3.5 leads to Imogen's misreading of Cloten's hand in 4.2. In *Cymbeline* Shakespeare pushes to their very limits the conventions of disguise comedy and theatrical romance: in 2.5, dramatic irony causes us to heap scorn upon Posthumus for his acceptance of Iachimo's description of the "mole cinque-spotted" as evidence against Imogen; that irony and that scorn are converted by the final scene into the generically motivated goodwill that allows us to accept the "sanguine star" on Guiderius's neck as proof of his royal identity. The headless, silent, but also extremely communicative body of Cloten is only the most vivid example of the way in which, in the world of *Cymbeline,* it is difficult to distinguish what is said about bodies from the bodies themselves.

The syntax of the first scene of *Cymbeline* is notoriously convoluted and one function of the convolution is to confuse, in a spectator's mind, Cloten and Posthumus. This is a habit of the play's: even once we have seen both characters, Posthumus's behavior goes only some little way to distinguish him from his belligerent rival. The culmination of the confusion is the scene of Cloten's decapitation. But Shakespeare's interest in blurring the lines between distinct bodies, or between bodies and language, is not exclusively thematic. Sometimes it tends, as Renaissance dramatic poetry and structure will, toward the merely ludic, toward a form of communication that does not signify so much as it creates unlikely unions. At the beginning of 2.2, Imogen is tired from reading. "To bed," she says, "Sleep hath seized me wholly" (4–7). She sleeps, at which point Iachimo rises out of the trunk he had put in her room. Much later, in 4.2, Lucius and some Roman soldiers come upon Imogen and Cloten's corpse. "Soft, ho, what *trunk* is here?" Lucius says. Then he notices Imogen: "How, a page? / Or dead or *sleeping* on him? But dead rather, / For nature doth abhor to *make his bed* / With the defunct or sleep upon the dead" (353–57, emphasis mine). Imogen is twice in the position of sleeping next to an importantly ambiguous trunk. Cloten's body has and resonates with multiple levels of meaning in a way we might more customarily think of as limited to words or images. Cloten's body is not only a prop. It is also a pun.

At the risk of stating the obvious I would like to suggest that one of the most important attractions of the theater for an early modern audience was the chance to see the bodies of actors on display, in motion, and in improbable positions. To put this another way, I want to argue that some of the most significant imaginative energy of the early modern repertory theater would have flowed from the way in which it allowed an actor's body to participate in the elaborate systems of punning and mirroring that we understand to be characteristic of early modern dramatic structure, language, and form. I suggest that if we allow ourselves to think of early modern play texts as inhabited by the bodies—even by many different bodies, and kinds of bodies—of early modern actors, we may find our way into a liberating and liberated imagining of the early modern theatrical world, where plays, familiar and unfamiliar alike, come unmoored from the categories to which we have confined them. In the pages that follow I will elaborate upon this proposition first with reference to the works of Shakespeare, and then with reference to a couple of lesser known works of his anonymous contemporaries.

Dromio of Ephesus's girlfriend Nell never appears onstage in *Comedy of Errors,* but her enormous body is referred to repeatedly. First, there is the lengthy description of her by Dromio of Syracuse in 3.2. Then, at the end of 4.1, Dromio S., being sent away by the arrested Antipholus E. to get bail money says, "To Adriana—that is where we dined, / Where Dowsabel did claim me for her husband. / She is too big, I hope, for me, to compass. / Thither I must, although against my will" (108–11). And finally, at the end of 4.4 Antipholus S. and Dromio S. scare away the Ephesians with their swords and head for the ship that will bear them away from Ephesus. Dromio says, "Methinks they are such a gentle nation that, but for the mountain of mad flesh that claims marriage of me, I could find in my heart to stay here still, and turn witch" (155–57). I think the first of these instances probably creates the expectation that Nell is going to appear onstage and interrupt (perhaps violently) the comic routine Dromio and Antipholus are performing. That expectation is thwarted: Nell does not appear. I think that the second instance creates the expectation that when Dromio S. gets back to the house where he's been sent, the first person he will encounter will be Nell. That expectation is also thwarted—in 4.3 we see him come to the house, but he only interacts with Luciana and Adriana. In the third instance, I think we might be meant to expect that Dromio and Antipholus, having frightened away all whom they believe to be Ephesian witches, will now be spooked by the sudden entrance of Nell. But again this expectation, if it is there, is thwarted. There is a close parallel to this scene in 3.1 of *Two Gentlemen of*

Verona, where Launce and Speed catalog the virtues and vices of Launce's unseen beloved—a milkmaid with no teeth, more hair than wit, and more faults than hairs. These scenes are both similar to the first half of *Taming of the Shrew,* 3.2, where Petruchio's fantastical wedding attire is described in great detail by Biondello in advance of the groom's arrival: in all cases a very specific, hyperbolical physicality is invoked to heighten the audience's desire to see. The scene in *Shrew* differs from the other two, of course, in that the described body does in fact appear onstage—and it is the actor's privilege and challenge at that point to exceed the expectations that have been created by the language. It is conjectural, but not I think implausible, to suggest that Shakespeare and his audience probably had in mind a specific physical body, a specific actor or actors, who could have played the part of Nell or of Launce's milkmaid—and that part of the pleasure of those thematically pertinent but extradiegetic comic routines derived from the audience's ability to imagine, as it could with Petruchio in *Shrew,* 3.2, the specific ways in which one actor or another might embody the hyperbole.

Disappointment is a vital element of theatrical experience, because it creates desire. What you don't see is as important as what you do. Biondello spends at least as much time describing Petruchio's horse as he does Petruchio himself, but it's unlikely that the horse ever appeared onstage. The vivid but absent horse has the effect of suggesting that what happens onstage is part of a world more extensive and populous than the stage can adequately represent, and this creates a satisfying verisimilitude. But there would be something satisfying about seeing the horse as well, just as there would be something satisfying about seeing the marriage of the lovers at the end of *Love's Labour's Lost,* or Viola turned back into a girl at the end of *Twelfth Night.*[11] If an audience can imagine the actor who might play Dromio's Nell—possibly even sees that actor playing another role in the play—and the play keeps presenting opportunities for that actor to appear as Nell, only to pass them up, the audience is caught in a delightfully sad place between imagination and the stage. The most elaborate traps of this kind Shakespeare laid for his audiences—and here we can be sure he and his audience had a specific actor in mind—had to do with Falstaff. Falstaff's ability to resurrect himself at the end of *1 Henry IV* surely made audiences believe he could rebound from disgrace at the end of *Part 2,* and indeed all the signs point that way. Even the ruthless Lancaster is given some rather mawkish lines that seem intended to get the audience in the mood to applaud after the shock of Hal's rejection: "I like this fair proceeding of the king's. / He hath intent his wonted followers / Shall all be very well provided for, / But all are banished till their conversations / Appear more wise and modest to the world" (5.5. 97–101).[12] There is much virtue in *till.*

There seems to be no consensus on what to make of *2 Henry IV*'s epilogue, textually or as something to be performed, but the lines in which he describes himself as a debtor and the audience as his "gentle creditors" has always made me think that it was meant to be spoken by the Falstaff actor. Falstaff's tantalizing, offstage nonappearances in 2.1 and 2.3 of *Henry V* would have been all the more cruel, and all the more affecting, if that actor had given the epilogue to *2 Henry IV* and in doing so given the audience the chance to right the wrong done by the new king himself. That seems, at least to me, to be the point of the epilogue's line "here I commit my body to your mercies." In anticipation of *Volpone* the protean prodigal relies on the conventions of the theater—applause after epilogue—to overturn the judgment against him. The 1598 audience, nothing "too much cloyed with fat meat" forgave the knight and was rewarded with the final image of him—actor and character at once—dancing till his legs were tired. It's a nicer view than that afforded Mistress Quickly. It is hard to imagine that the Lord Chamberlain's Men would have performed *Henry V* in 1599 without this obviously magnificent actor, but I like to think that he was simply given a day off.[13]

Falstaff's resurrection at the end of *1 Henry IV* is a conventional trick of the early modern theater, of which Fletcher in particular would make frequent and extravagant use. The audience sees an actor fall down and thinks of the character as "dead." Then the actor, whom we always knew was alive, jumps up and the audience is put in the enjoyably ridiculous position of thinking "He's alive!" But Falstaff's resurrection is, I think, somewhat unusual for Shakespeare in that Falstaff is a male character. Resurrection, even if only temporary, tends to be a female phenomenon in Shakespeare's plays. When male actors fall down on the stage they tend to stay down: Romeo and Antony die more or less on the first try, while their wives, variously presumed dead, return long enough to witness the spectacle of their husbands' deaths. This is not to say it is always clear what we are meant to think when male actors play dead. Prince Arthur in *King John,* Enobarbus in *Antony and Cleopatra,* and even Lear at the end of *King Lear* are all characters whose deaths are either improbable or uncertain at the moment they occur. We might put Mercutio and Timon of Athens in this group as well. The case of Enobarbus makes most explicit Shakespeare's interest in exploiting the power of the theater to change an audience's perception of the physical body even in an instant. "O sovereign mistress of true melancholy, / The poisonous damp of night dispunge upon me, / That life, a very rebel to my will, / May hang no longer on me," says Enobarbus in 4.9. If we have read Plutarch, perhaps the invocation of night's poisonous damp makes us think of the ague that killed Domitius, the source-character for Enobarbus, but more probably this speech sounds rhetorical and hyperbolic. Eight lines later Enobarbus falls down and the three witnesses are no more certain than we are about what has happened to him: "He sleeps," says the second watchman; "Swoons rather," says the sentry, who a line or two later changes his mind: "The hand of death hath raught him." Second Watchman is not convinced: "Come on then. He may recover yet." And that's the last we see of Enobarbus. The actor's body in this scene works to mystify rhetorical, dramatic language: the uncertainty of how we are supposed to interpret the body being carried offstage— pretending to be sick? pretending to be dead? pretending to pretend to be dead?—imbues Enobarbus's self-curse with the kind of power tragic characters generally seem to hope language can have.

Something like the inverse of Enobarbus are Emilia and Desdemona— bodies that are quite clearly "dead" and that spring back to life at moments that are not merely opportune, but downright theatrical. "Sure he hath killed his wife" is Gratiano's diagnosis after Iago stabs Emilia, and he repeats himself before pursuing the villain: "He's gone, but his wife's killed." Othello is left onstage with the two dead women and wonders, "why should honor outlive honesty?" Half a line later Emilia rises with a question of her own: "What did thy song bode, lady?" and then she dies, like Desdemona's mother's maid, singing *Willow*. Some two-hundred lines earlier Desdemona, heretofore presumed smothered, finds her voice at the exact moment Othello discovers Cassio is still alive: "falsely, falsely murdered!" It is the theater's prerogative to resurrect the dead at weightily meaningful moments, and the effect is at once satisfying and disturbing: it plays our sympathy for the characters (on some level we want Desdemona to live) against understanding of generic form (Desdemona must die if this is to be a proper tragedy). In *Othello*'s cousin-play, *Winter's Tale,* our understanding of generic form is perhaps never quite so certain as it is in *Othello,* and our sympathy for the character of Hermione is allowed to fade away or be redirected after we do not see her body for two acts. I imagine Shakespeare's audience would have been expecting that body to reappear—possibly in the form of the lost daughter, just as that audience might very possibly have seen the body of the stricken daughter of Antiochus reappear in the form of Marina a couple years earlier in *Pericles.* The longer the Hermione-actor stayed out of sight, the more intensely the audience might have looked forward to the role that allowed him to return. *Winter's Tale,* like its slightly later contemporary *Henry VIII,* is hugely self-conscious about *not* showing you things, and that is why both are able in the end to show you the last thing you could have hoped to see: the dead-now-living body of Hermione, the infant body of the great sovereign Elizabeth. The actor's body becomes a fetish and seeing is a privilege.

Theatrical time, *Winter's Tale* teaches us, is a great resurrecter: the longer you stare at a stone the more likely it is to come to life. The tremendous energy Shakespeare finds and unleashes in the actor's perfectly still body at the end of this late romance can be seen, still latent, in the daring death scenes of *Hamlet* and *Julius Caesar* ten or so years earlier, where Polonius and Caesar are required to lay onstage, bleeding and still, 192 and 223 lines, respectively, after their murders. I think that when you have to look at the motionless body of an actor for 200 lines, you start to envision the possibility that he's going to start moving again, no matter how much historical or narrative context tells you otherwise. And of course Caesar does get up again—in 4.2, when he haunts the wakeful Brutus. There is something theatrically exuberant about making live bodies seem extravagantly dead, and also about representing ghosts with indisputably corporeal actors: these were secrets Shakespeare discovered early in his career, as the examples of *Titus Andronicus* and *Richard III* show. The audience must quite consciously decide to see something other than it is seeing. We might see an inversion of Caesar in the character of, and actor for Hotspur: introduced unnecessarily and quietly in *Richard II,* he is allowed to emerge larger than life in *1 Henry IV,* only to end up rather abruptly lying on the ground, a perverse mirror of Falstaff.

There is an analogous exuberance in theatrical doubling, but in a large-scale history-play project like the three *Henry VI* plays, it might have tended to take on a grim, fatalistic cast. I have always imagined, for example, that the same actor played the Duke of York and his son Clarence in *3 Henry VI.* Clarence doesn't appear till after York is dead and York's early death in *Part 3* suggests he would stick around to play another part. Clarence replays the reckless ingratitude, though without the competence or the sympathy, that characterized his father's revolt.[14] At the same time I think we can see the subversive, necromantic side of theatrical doubling at work in the *Henry VI* trilogy—Shakespeare's delighted indulgence in the particularly unnatural power of the theater, which raised such a sense of danger in the Puritan antitheatricalists. In *1 Henry VI*, 1.3, Joan of Arc, discussing the English power, says "Glory is like a circle in the water, / Which never ceaseth to enlarge itself / Till, by broad spreading, it disperse to nought" (112–14). I'm not sure if an audience would have remembered Joan, but I think she is there, in language and quite possibly body, in *2 Henry VI*, 1.2, when Eleanor Cobham, discussing her desire for Henry's crown, says "gaze on, and grovel on thy face / Until thy head be *circled* with the same. / Put forth thy hand, reach at the *glorious* gold" (9–11, emphasis mine). Like Joan, Eleanor is apprehended for sorcery. And as with Joan, everything Eleanor has learned from her demons turns out to be true. The doubled role would be an embodiment of the irony whose significance is made visible by the machinery and the forms of the theater. The stage breeds witches and affirms what they say.

In the final section of this essay, I want to discuss two obscure, textually problematic, anonymous plays of the early 1590s: *A Knack to Know a Knave,* performed by Strange's Men in 1592, and *A Knack to Know an Honest Man,* performed by the Admiral's Men in 1594. My purpose here is to imagine these plays in performance and to imagine them being perceived in performance; my focus, as in the first part of this essay, is on the actor's body as a primary agent of theatrical meaning; and my desire is to make these plays seem less strange, and a more central part of the early modern theatrical landscape, than they have typically seemed.

A Knack to Know a Knave is a kind of morality play and/or estates satire. The legendary King Edgar of Britain travels throughout his land, accompanied by a fellow named Honesty who reveals the knavery of the four sons of the corrupt, then deceased Bailiff of Hexham: a farmer, a courtier, a cony-catcher, and a priest. There is a subplot in which Edgar sends one of his knights, Ethanwald, to woo a common woman on Edgar's behalf; Ethanwald ends up marrying the woman, Alfrida, himself, and must beg for Edgar's mercy. *A Knack to Know an Honest Man* is set in Venice, though it begins in something like an Arcadian forest on the outskirts of the city. There, the main character, Sempronio, seems to be killed by Lelio, who accuses Sempronio (rightly) of trying to seduce his wife. Sempronio does not die, but is nursed back to health by an old hermit and in the process has a conversion experience. He returns to Venice disguised as someone called Penitent Experience and sets about revealing the vices of the Duke's corrupt son and his hangers-on. Lelio, meanwhile, is on the run for the murder of Sempronio and only escapes execution in the final scene when Sempronio removes his disguise.

To the extent that scholarship has made any assumptions at all about the two *Knack* plays together, it has assumed that they are different—that the latter is divergent from or in opposition to the earlier. In the case of Louis Wright, who considers *Knave* a late morality play whose function is to make a specific kind of social commentary, the upshot is somewhat arbitrary and dismissive: "No effort at a really serious treatment of social conditions is evident in [*Honest Man*]."[15] In the case of David Bevington, who sees *Knave* as the seminal text for Puritan satire on the stage, the result is to figure *Honest Man* as an expression of the radical Puritan left and thus, by implicit extension, *Knave* as a forerunner to the conservative crypto-Catholicism of playwrights like Jonson and Chapman.[16]

That *Honest Man* was written with *Knave* in mind is indisputable, but the assumption that the goal was differentiation seems off the mark. Typical of the way in which *Honest Man* specifically invokes its predecessor is the following passage, which occurs in the scene where Fortunio has been brought before his father the Duke and charged with the attempted seduction of Lelio's daughter. He has confessed to his fault—and to being tempted by a flattering courtier—and the Duke forgives him. The disguised Sempronio says: "This likes me well, now growes the world to frame, / Fortunio now hath learnd to know a knaue: / And is expert to prooue an honest man" (G1v). *Honest Man* is concerned to remind the audience of the antecedent *Knave,* but the purpose doesn't seem to be parody or even commentary, merely allusion. Further, there is only the most slender distinction to be made between the knack to know a knave and the knack to know an honest man. As Sempronio says, one leads you to the other. The satisfying joke for the audience would probably have been that Edward Alleyn, the premiere actor in London, has both. I think Alleyn probably played the role of Honesty as well as Sempronio. He had moved from the Lord Admiral's company to the Lord Strange's in 1591, and was with them when they performed *Knave* at the Rose in June 1592 (Henslowe's diary shows Alleyn starting as one of Strange's players in February of that year). The Admiral's company, which Alleyn left in 1591, split apart, as did the Lord Strange's (now Derby's) when Alleyn left and their patron died in April 1594; Alleyn was then made a part of the newly reconstituted, newly powerful Admiral's Men. Henslowe records *Honest Man* at the Rose in October 1594.

It is unfortunate, bordering on tragic, that so much of the Admiral's repertoire has vanished, especially in the crucial years 1594–98 when Shakespeare was writing all those plays starring paired boy actors. It is impossible to say whether Alleyn's knack for exposing knaves and rewarding honest men was a frequent sight on the London stage during this period, but later Admiral's plays seem to provide a compelling clue: Chapman's *Blind Beggar of Alexandria* (1598), Dekker's *Shoemaker's Holiday* (1599), Chettle and Day's *Blind Beggar of Bednal Green,* and Chettle, Dekker, and Haughton's *Patient Grissil* (both 1601) all have a similar exposure-by-disguise structure. It might be unreasonable to make the claim that Alleyn played the lead in all of these, but it is not unreasonable to suggest that the pleasure of going to an Admiral's play at the end of the 1590s was closely bound up with watching your favorite actors become masters of disguise in order to tear away the vicious masks of human nature.[17]

Of course plays attributable to the Admiral's Men are not the only Renaissance plays concerned with the exposure of vice. Playwrights throughout the period are positively obsessed with it. The *Knack* plays are particularly interesting in this regard, however, because, as their titles make clear, the development of a *mechanism* for the exposure of vice is the linchpin on which the whole theatrical apparatus turns. Almost without exception, every episode in these very episodic plays is structured around the theatrical revelation of one or another character's viciousness. These plays make a particularly explicit, governing part of the structure of their action something that is a fundamental and pervasive preoccupation of early modern drama. While it might be productive to talk about this preoccupation in terms of the development of a convention,[18] I am interested in using the *Knack* plays to make some arguments about what is theatrically valuable about the exposure of vice for Renaissance drama broadly considered,[19] and to say something about the relationship between this preoccupation and the early modern acting company's (and playwright's) artistic use of the actor's body.

Because its priest character refers to himself and his brethren as "pure Precisians" (B2v), *A Knack to Know a Knave* has been pigeonholed in its project to expose vice as an anti-Puritan satire.[20] Indeed, a certain amount of theatrical mileage is got out of what Honesty calls the Priest's "mocking the diuine order of Ministery" (G3v), but ultimately the Priest is more similar to than different from the three other sons of the Bailiff of Hexham. All four sons are linked by their participation in what Honesty calls "vndoing . . . the commen wealth" (G2v)—specifically their attempts to export vital commodities (corn, tin, hides, lead, wool) overseas (see D4v–E1r for the Farmer and Perin, G2v for the Priest). Three of the four sons (including the Priest) are ultimately executed for this crime. *A Knack to Know a Knave* is not concerned with satirizing a particular kind of vice—religious hypocrisy—nearly as much as it is with *staging* the exposure of vice in general.

When Cony-catcher is revealed to be a knave, it is in a kind of skit directed by Honesty. Honesty disguises the King as one farmer and Bishop Dunstan as another—the former is supposed to have bought the latter's farm. The King then sets up Cony-catcher:

> I bought a farme of one that dwels here by,
> And for an earnest gaue an hundred pound,
> The rest was to be paid as sixe weekes past,
> Now sir, I would haue you as witnesse,
> That at my house you saw me pay three hundred pound,
> And for your paines I will giue you a hundred pound.

> (C4v–D1r)

The Courtier brother is brought in on the plot as well—disguised as the Judge who will adjudicate the dispute between the two "farmers." Cony-catcher swears as he's been paid to and, in the end, is confronted with the King's wrath. The superfluity of the disguisings is justified by the process of judgment they enable. Similar, but somewhat more bizarre, is the hypertheatrical working out of the Edgar-Ethanwald-Alfrida plot—a plot that criticism has tended to treat as completely separate, but that is as much concerned with the exposure of vice as any other episode in the play.[21] Ethanwald, sent early in the play to woo Alfrida on behalf of King Edgar (A4v–B1r), ends up marrying her himself and making the excuse that she was not fair enough to marry a king. The scene in which Ethanwald decides to "cosen [the King] of his choise" (D2v) structurally connects Ethanwald to the other cozeners in the play: it immediately follows the scene in which Honesty's disguise plot exposes Cony-catcher, and immediately precedes the scene in which the Farmer flouts the ancient laws of hospitality and refuses to invite a Knight, a Squire, and Honesty to dinner. The scene in which Ethanwald's own vice is revealed is a weird combination of the two earlier scenes between which his decision to lie is placed: when Edgar visits Alfrida and Ethanwald at home, Ethanwald instigates a rather extraneous disguise plot (Alfrida and the Kitchen Maid switch identities) that immediately fails, in large part because of the Maid's comically inept attempts to seem hospitable in a way that does not give away her station (F2v–F3r). Above all the Kitchen Maid disguise plot, like the method of Cony-catcher's exposure, is for the audience's sake more than the plot's: costumes, mimicry, and easy dramatic ironies are deployed perhaps unnecessarily and certainly expediently to give the morality of the characters a particularly theatrical form.

This is also true of the bizarre way in which the exposure of Ethanwald occurs. Ethanwald is Bishop Dunstan's nephew, which is why Dunstan pleads on his behalf after Edgar vows to kill him for his "subtiltie" (F3v). Edgar is impervious to the Bishop's pleas and so, once Edgar exits, Dunstan calls forth "Asmoroth," a devil whom he uses to charm Edgar into forgiving Ethanwald. The way in which the scene unfolds (G1r–G2r) is quite unclear in the 1592 text, and only marginally less so in the single widely available modern text of the play, Dodsley's.[22] Dunstan brings before the king "Alfrida disguised with the Deuil" (G1v)—a stage direction that Dodsley's edition augments by saying that the Devil is "disguised as Ethanwald."[23] Dodsley's guess is as good as any, but it still does not clarify what an audience is supposed to see when Dunstan says "Asmoroth away" (G1v) and when "Ethanwald," according to a speech-heading, thanks the King for his mercy. Perhaps the 1592 text leaves out a direction for Ethanwald to enter with Alfrida and the Devil, and what we are meant to see is Alfrida and Ethanwald kneeling before the King while the "Deuill," whom Dunstan has declared "inuisible," indicates that he is charming Edgar into having an abrupt change of heart. Or perhaps the 1592 text leaves out a direction for Ethanwald to enter in the Devil's place—a kind of comic switch that could also be effected while the King was supposedly charmed. Whatever an audience was meant to (or did) see at this moment, the play seems to go to rather unnecessary trouble to achieve it. The reason it goes to this trouble may be to echo another earlier, apparently unrelated moment in the play—the death of the Bailiff of Hexham. In that scene (B3r), the Bailiff's death speech is followed by the direction "Enter Deuil, and carie him away." The echoes are complex. In each scene a devil (possibly the same actor?) appears as one or more characters are exposed for their sins—in the earlier scene the Bailiff suddenly realizes that he is "damned to euer burning fyre" while in the later scene Edgar renounces his adulterous desires for Alfrida; in the earlier scene the Bailiff finds that his "*heart* is hardened, I cannot repent" (B3r, my emphasis), while in the later scene Ethanwald "layes his *breast* wide open to your Grace, / If so it please your Grace to pardon him" (G1v, my emphasis). The moral, formal, and verbal structures of the play are recapitulated, reiterated, metamorphosed as different bodies find themselves in similar situations, familiar situations manifest themselves in new bodies.

What seems to be of consequence in the scenes where the Devil enters, or the disguising scenes involving Cony-catcher and the Kitchen Maid, is not only the educative power of a satire in which vice is exposed, but also the particularly physical, *visual* possibilities that satire of this kind provides. Analogous moments in comparable plays might be the hanging of Sordido in *Every Man Out of his Humour,* the vanishing banquet and harpy Ariel in the *Tempest,* the fight between Lucio and the Duke at the end of *Measure for Measure,* possibly even the seduction of Cressida in *Troilus and Cressida.* A final analogy, to return to Edward Alleyn, would be the apparent death of Sempronio at the beginning of *A Knack to Know an Honest Man,* his Enobarbus-like exit with the Hermit, and his reappearance a scene later—perhaps not immediately recognized by the audience—as the old man, Penitent Experience. One thing that seems to make the trope of the exposure of vice a vital and enduring theatrical commodity is the opportunity it provides for spectacle—not simply spectacle in the narrow sense of exciting things to look at, not simply the spectacle of penance and punishment (as in *Knave*) or of punishment and shame (as frequently in Jonson), but the spectacle of the theater passing judgment. *A Knack to Know a Knave* and *A Knack to Know an Honest Man* are concerned with religious fraud, agricultural fraud, and the subversion of royal prerogative, but the element that links these things—as we see in the devils, the disguise plots, and the highly stagy final scenes—is their identification of the theater as the locus for the knack that Honesty, or Sempronio, has. Perhaps the most productive way of discussing *A Knack to Know a Knave*'s anti-Puritanism then is to say that it is anti-Puritan in the way virtually all Renaissance drama is: judgments on virtue and vice legitimize and are legitimized by the body of the actor, the machinery of the theater.

Notes

I am grateful to Holger Syme, Christopher Warley, Carolyn Sale, and Elizabeth Pentland for their comments on an earlier version of this essay. The earliest version was presented as a talk at the University of Toronto in 2005; I am grateful to my colleagues in the Department of English for their questions and comments, which have shaped my thinking considerably in the process of revision. My mentor and friend, the late Scott McMillin, read and provided invaluable commentary on this essay in draft form, and the debt I owe to his scholarship and his advice is evident on every page; this essay is dedicated to his memory.

1. I am thinking in particular of Knutson, *The Repertory of Shakespeare's Company* (Fayetteville: University of Arkansas Press, 1991) and *Playing Companies and Commerce in Shakespeare's Time* (Cambridge: Cambridge University Press, 2001), as well as her many articles on the early modern repertory; McMillin and MacLean, *The Queen's Men and their Plays* (Cambridge: Cambridge University Press, 1998); McMillin, *The Elizabethan Theatre and the Book of Sir Thomas More* (Ithaca: Cornell

University Press, 1987) and "Shakespeare and the Chamberlain's Men in 1598," *Medieval and Renaissance Drama in England* 17 (2005) 205–15; Gurr, *The Shakespeare Company, 1594–1642* (Cambridge: Cambridge University Press, 2004) and *The Shakespearian Playing Companies* (Oxford: Clarendon, 1996); and Stern, *Rehearsal from Shakespeare to Sheridan* (Oxford: Oxford University Press, 2000). See also Lawrence Manley, "Playing with Fire: Immolation in the Repertory of Strange's Men," *Early Theatre Journal* 4 (2001): 115–29 (an essay, along with one by Knutson on Pembroke's Men and Mark Bayer on the Cockpit, which appears in the "Issues in Review" section, introduced by Scott McMillin, of this journal, 111–48); Mary Bly, *Queer Virgins and Virgin Queans on the Early Modern Stage* (Oxford: Oxford University Press, 2000)—a detailed study of the repertory of the Whitefriars children's company; and Lucy Munro, *The Children of the Queen's Revels* (Cambridge: Cambridge University Press, 2005). The spirit of the latter two are particularly close to my own goals, though Bly's focus is verbal and Munro's generic while mine might be called something more like structural or scenographic. For a review of acting company scholarship, see Paul Whitfield White, "Playing Companies and the Drama of the 1580s: A New Direction in Theatre History?" in *Shakespeare Studies* 28 (2000): 265–84.

2. All references to Shakespeare are from the *Complete Pelican Shakespeare,* ed. Stephen Orgel and A. R. Braunmuller (New York: Penguin, 2002).

3. The work of theater historians such as John Astington, William Ingram, and David Kathman (among others) is invaluable in reminding us that actual persons inhabited the theatrical world of the sixteenth and seventeenth centuries. Scott McMillin has an essay, "The Sharer and his Boy: Rehearsing Shakespeare's Women," in *From Script to Stage in Early Modern England,* ed. Peter Holland and Stephen Orgel, 231–51 (New York: Palgrave, 2005), in which he gives an accounting of Shakespeare's boy actors. The approach is to study the cue-lines of boy actors to see how closely they are tied to one or two master actors, to whom they would have been apprenticed. This piece draws in part on another recent piece that is also important for the study I am proposing here—David Kathman's article in *Shakespeare Quarterly* 55.1 (2004) on freemen and apprentices in the Elizabethan theater. It is nevertheless, and unfortunately, true that there remains virtually no evidence for which of these real persons played which character in any particular play or group of plays. Bentley and the cautious tradition that has followed him was, of course, reacting to T. W. Baldwin, whose methods can still be seen in contemporary scholarship, such as David Grote's *The Best Actors in the World* (Westport, CT: Greenwood, 2002). I think (hope) the differences between the approach I am advocating and that of Baldwin and Grote (who are, ultimately, interested in presenting productive speculation in evidentiary terms) will be fairly evident.

4. For analysis along these lines, see McMillin, "The Sharer and his Boy."

5. *Early Modern Literary Studies* 2.1 (1996).

6. Roslyn Knutson's current ongoing work on the lost plays seems to me a good example of the kind of productive imagining that is necessary to perceive more fully and richly the world of early modern repertory theater.

7. Both plays appeared, for example, in 1953–54 at the Old Vic, both starring Richard Burton, Fay Compton, and Claire Bloom. Toby Stephens was in an RSC pro-

duction of *Coriolanus* in 1994 and ten years later opened that company's season as Hamlet. The reviews of these latter productions were strikingly similar—a relatively weak star performance in an overall strong production—and possibly say something about the RSC's dramaturgical goals and problems over the course of a decade. Surprisingly, modern theater reviews generally do not deal with this subject in any detail. Extended critiques, such as Richard Paul Knowles's essay on the 1993 Stratford, Ontario Shakespeare Festival (*Shakespeare Quarterly* 45.2) and Gary Taylor's essay on the 1998 Stratford, Ontario Shakespeare Festival (*Shakespeare Quarterly* 50.3) are particularly sophisticated theoretical examples of a methodology that could be applied quite readily to even the most basically descriptive reviews of a single Shakespeare festival's or theater's season.

8. *Your Five Gallants,* also from this period, brings a trunk onstage in the first scene, but it's filled with apparel, not a boy.

9. Barnabe Barnes's *Devil's Charter,* another play about a spectacularly dysfunctional family, also probably appeared around the same time as *Volpone, Lear,* and *Revenger's Tragedy.* Its casting does not break down into the same pattern evident in the others, but considering it alongside them, imagining the same group of actors inhabiting the world of Lear and his daughters and the world of the Borgias, certainly gives one a firmer handle on Barnes's hyperbolical theatricality.

10. Fran Teague, *Shakespeare's Speaking Properties* (Lewisburg, PA: Bucknell University Press, 1991).

11. Perhaps an even better example here would be the postponed double-metamorphosis at the end of Lyly's *Gallathea.*

12. There is an interesting, similarly clunky-sounding parallel to this speech at the end of *Richard II,* and its purpose is also to prepare the audience for the introduction of an important character in a subsequent play. Significantly, this character is also one who must be redeemed. At 5.3.1–3 Bolingbroke says: "Can no man tell me of my unthrifty son? / 'Tis full three months since I did see him last. / If any plague hang over us, 'tis he." Hearing from Harry Percy that Hal has been seen going "unto the stews," Bolingbroke says, "As dissolute as desperate! Yet through both / I see some sparks of better hope, which elder years / May happily bring forth" (16–18). The contemporary audience would have known how that story turned out.

13. David Wiles, in *Shakespeare's Clown* (Cambridge: Cambridge University Press, 1987) identifies the Falstaff actor as Will Kemp and suggests that the decision to excise Falstaff from *Henry V* might have played a part in Kemp's departing for Worcester's in 1599, or vice versa. Wiles's book (Cambridge, 1987) is a study very close in spirit to (though narrower in scope than) the one proposed in this essay. It focuses on three major clowns: Tarlton, Kemp, and Armin, identifies some of their roles, and creates taxonomies of the conventions that defined those roles. For Tarlton, "the comedian's skill lies in convincing the audience that he has been outwitted and humiliated. He then judges the timing of his reply carefully, offering a throwaway insult in place of cleverness. He crushes his victim with mimicry, yet continues to present himself as one so stupid that anybody ought to outwit him . . . Tarlton's physical ugliness is essential to a comic persona that invites mockery from the audience" (17). Roles for Tarlton include Derrick in *Famous Victories,* which Wiles sees as a role elaborately reworked by Kemp as Falstaff in the *Henry IV* plays. Kemp speaks

"in the idiom of the 'plain man'" (101), "constructs his audience as a community of peers" (103), and is "adept at extracting comedy from inactivity" (105). This is in contrast to Armin, who "pretends that his utterances are syntactically tight" (101), "does not engage in an implied dialogue with the audience as equals" (103), and "personalizes his slapstick . . . the projection of multiple identities is the staple of Armin's clowning" (139). Roles for Kemp include or may include Peter in *Romeo and Juliet,* Bottom, Dogberry, Pipkin in *How a Man May Choose a Good Wife from a Bad,* Jenkin in *Woman Killed with Kindness.* Roles for Armin include or may include Touchstone, Feste, Lavatch in *All's Well,* Thersites, and Lear's Fool.

14. A similar resurrection and doubling is suggested by Stephen Booth in his discussion of *Macbeth:* Fleance might return to life briefly in the form of the actor playing the "cream-faced loon" who brings Macbeth news of Birnam wood come to Dunsinane. See *King Lear, Macbeth, Indefinition, and Tragedy* (New Haven: Yale University Press, 1983), 140.

15. "Social Aspects of Some Belated Moralities," *Anglia* 54 (1930): 107–48. The quotation is from 144.

16. *Tudor Drama and Politics* (Cambridge: Harvard University Press, 1968) 227–29.

17. There were, of course, other pleasures as well. The list of titles for 1594–98 provided in Harbage's *Annals* indicates that the Admiral's Men were heavily involved in probably quite ambitious history plays of all kinds (legendary, biblical, classical, European, English, etc.)—e.g., *1 and 2 Hercules* (1595), *Nebuchadnezzer* (1596), *Uther Pendragon* (1597), and *1, 2, and 3 Civil Wars of France* (1598).

18. This is the work of David Houser's article, "Purging the Commonwealth: Marston's Disguised Dukes and *A Knack to Know a Knave,*" *PMLA* 89.5 (1974): 993–1006.

19. I should note here the debt this section of the essay owes to Alan Dessen's "The 'Estates' Morality Play," *Studies in Philology* 62 (1965): 121–36.

20. See Mary Grace Muse Adkins, "The Genesis of Dramatic Satire Against the Puritan, as Illustrated in *A Knack to Know a Knave,*" *RES* 22.86 (April 1946): 81–95; E. N. S. Thompson, *The Controversy between the Puritans and the Stage* (New York: Henry Holt, 1903); Wright, "Social Aspects"; Houser, "Purging the Commonwealth"; and Bevington, *Tudor Drama and Politics.*

21. Wright, "Social Aspects," says that *Knave* is "a tri-partite performance [which] has, along with a love-intrigue plot and a clown skit by Will Kemp, a morality play in which Honesty seeks out the knaves in the kingdom and exposes them to the king" (141).

22. Paul E. Bennett edited the play as a University of Pennsylvania doctoral dissertation in 1952.

23. Dodsley 7:583. Bennet suggests that the 1592 text is imperfect at this point and that the Devil is in fact disguised as Alfrida (52–54).

"Ick verstaw you niet": Performing Foreign Tongues on the Early Modern English Stage

ANDREW FLECK

> Gentlemen, this play of *Hieronimo* in sundrie Languages, was thought good to be set downe in English more largely, for the easier understanding to euery publicque Reader.
>
> —*The Spanish tragedie . . .* (1592)

In his *Defense of Poetry,* Sir Philip Sidney praises English, "our mother tongue," for its vitality in poetry and "in other arts."[1] He goes on to celebrate its malleability, "capable of any excellent exercising of it," and recasts charges of the language's impurity and its lack of formal grammar as virtues, concluding that it surpasses Latin in expressing "the conceits of the mind" and should in fact rank "equally with any other tongue in the world" (119). Sidney may have been trying to imagine his English into prominence; he was not alone in praising the language. As Carla Mazzio recalls, Richard Mulcaster had valorized English's ability to domesticate foreign terms to allow them to be made useful, and as Steven Mullaney notes, Richard Carew had reimagined the apparent shortcomings of English as a mark of its great potential.[2] And yet there were others who worried precisely about the debasing that could accompany this vernacular flexibility and capacity to encompass the barbarous. Spenser's participation in Sidney's project evinces just this anxious defensiveness in lamenting that they did not yet have "the kingdome" or mastery over "oure owne Language."[3] Nevertheless, Sidney persisted, defending his language's voracious ability to "tak[e] the best of both the other" and enrich itself (119). English playwrights might have agreed.

Despite the recognition that, for good or ill, the porous English language was likely to absorb exotic terms and grow larger and stronger, the English themselves were notoriously monolingual.[4] Portia's deriding of her English suitor Falconbridge, who "hath neither Latin, French, nor Italian . . . alas who can converse with a dumb show?" embodies this stereotype.[5] The delicious irony of an (perhaps "the") English dramatist creating an Italian character in an Italian setting speaking an English to be understood by an English audience as Italian as she mocks the English for their lack of linguistic facility points to the issue here. For audiences who refused (or were imagined as unable) to genuinely learn a foreign language, could English dramatists in 1600 find a way to present another tongue without turning their stage into an incomprehensible Babel? That playwrights would try to represent linguistic difference—sometimes accurately, sometimes suggestively—demonstrates both the playwrights' and their audiences' appetite for foreignness. London was one of the most important trade centers in Europe; its immigrant population, while comparatively small, did create the likelihood that real Dutch, French, or Spanish might be heard (if not understood) in the public arena: markets, fairs, public houses, theaters. The foreign tongues that non-English characters speak on these stages had to be somewhat comprehensible to English audiences if a play's action was meant to be understood by the paying customers, and the fact that playgoers could make even rudimentary sense of dramatized foreigners would testify to England's significance as a cosmopolitan trade center. And while the English are traditionally derided for their lack of skill with other languages, these strange dialects were a mark of England's prominence in the mercantile arena of early modern Europe. Rehearsing exotic tongues, even if they were not entirely understood, signaled the emergence of England and cosmopolitan London on the metaphorical stage of European events.[6]

Despite anxieties about Englishmen's ability to learn foreign languages, and the fact that an audience of the middling sort was even less likely to have reached the sophistication of a linguist like Sidney, popular playwrights in Elizabethan London persisted in commodifying other languages and bringing them before a broad audience, often for the effect of "jest[ing] at strangers because they speak no English so well as we do" that Sidney had lamented (116). Putting aside the ambivalent xenophobia and nationalist aspects of such rehearsals—the recognizing and cataloging of the strangeness of their Continental neighbors' language and customs—the practical question of the staging of foreign tongues remains. If a character spoke "stage" Welsh, or Dutch, or Latin, how might this exotic language be accommodated to a popular audience, most of whom would not speak the language being staged? Did the playwrights expect audiences to accept a series of incomprehensible sounds that may or may not have been a genuine language as "foreign" or were there ways such languages could be staged that would still signify to this notoriously monolingual audience? Attending to staging clues in several early modern plays, we may discern how playwrights could bring commodified foreign tongues onstage for their audiences' consumption. Several well-known instances of linguistic confusion illustrate three strategies for marking linguistic difference; a survey of the staging of Dutch figures shows how these strategies might have worked in practice.

Responding to the Challenge of Foreign Languages

The linguistic mélange of the late Elizabethan stage might take as its most emblematic moment the playlet in Kyd's *The Spanish Tragedy*. With the plot of the tragedy of *Soliman and Perseda* in hand, the vengeful Hieronimo persuades Lorenzo, Balthazar, and Bel-imperia to join with him in "act[ing] his part / In unknown languages": Latin, Greek, Italian, and French (4.1.173–74).[7] The anonymous note (the epigraph for this essay) that interrupts the printed text of *The Spanish Tragedy* to explain that the printer has translated the play-within from sundry languages into English raises the difficult question of whether the actors actually performed in four exotic languages—two of them scholarly—in addition to English, and if they did so, how they staged the playlet for a public audience, most of whom would not have known Italian or French, let alone Latin or Greek. The note asserts a polyglot performance and a concession to a less linguistically able readership. It makes no mention of how "euery publicque *spectator*"—if they were not polymaths—might have responded to such a play-within-the-play. Placing too much emphasis on the note's veracity, however, obscures evidence elsewhere in the text that a multilingual performance of the play would have been unnecessary and unlikely.

In one scenario, the actors in the playlet actually speak their parts in Greek, Latin, French, and Italian.[8] In such a situation, Kyd does not leave his audience completely in the dark. While casting the playlet, Hieronimo provides Kyd's audience with the basic argument of the plot as he explains the story to the actors, Balthazar and Lorenzo, in extensive detail: "The chronicles of Spain / Record this written of a knight of Rhodes . . ." (4.1.108ff.). Hieronimo's royal audience in 4.4, characters who clearly do not understand the words spoken by their children, have the argument before them, and comment briefly on the action during the performance, reinforcing the audience's understanding of the plot. The Spanish King hands the argument to the Portuguese Viceroy at the play's outset, making him "the book-keeper" and informing him that it contains "the argument of that they show" (4.4.9–10). As the action proceeds, the royal spectators help each other understand what they are watching. Following Balthazar's first speech (perhaps in Latin) the King helpfully tells his Portuguese counterpart, "See, Viceroy, that is Balthazar, your son, / That represents the emperour Soliman" (4.4.19–20) and later when Lorenzo enters as Erasto, the King inquires, "Here comes Lorenzo; look upon the plot / And tell me, brother, what part plays he?" (4.4.33–34). As the murders and suicide of the playlet proceed, the action, if not the words, of *Soliman and Perseda* can be understood by both the royal audience within *The Spanish Tragedy* and the paying audience in the Rose's yard. It can be understood in much the same way as the previous use of dumb show in the play.[9] So, in the first possibility for this linguistically confused playlet, an audience might productively be alienated by hearing a confused assembly of four foreign languages,[10] but the playlet is so brief and the plot so simple, with its argument presented twice—once before and once during the interior performance in lieu of translation—and complemented by action, as in the play's earlier dumb shows, that Kyd's English audience could have comprehended it.

In the more likely possibility, maugre the printed prefatory note, Lorenzo, Balthazar, and the rest of the playlet's actors perform their parts in English, and Kyd uses theatrical conventions to establish which characters can understand what others speak onstage, without requiring a learned audience beyond the stage's edge. After all, *The Spanish Tragedy* is set in Spain, yet Kyd's English audience at the Rose miraculously understands each word spoken by the Iberian characters in the first three and a half acts of the play. Why couldn't *Soliman and Perseda* also be performed in English, with Kyd's audience understanding every bit of it, while Hieronimo's onstage royal audience, with their signs of lacking comprehension,[11] are imagined to be hearing Greek, Latin, French, and Italian, miraculously translated (like their Spanish and Portuguese) into an English only the paying audience can understand? The tragedy, then, offers two possibilities: either that something approaching genuinely foreign languages appeared onstage, or that English could be understood as "foreign" through establishing the conventions of linguistic difference in the staging itself. Although Sheldon Zitner concludes that "we cannot decide these questions of theater history" (89), the careful reading of plays like *The Spanish Tragedy* can at least lead us to two of the strategies available to Elizabethan playwrights who wanted to exhibit exotic cultures and strange tongues on their stage.

The second solution to the dramatic presentation of languages—of asserting that English stood in for a foreign tongue—works when the printer claims to have translated foreign speech into English. What happens when the printed play contains genuinely foreign matter, as in Shakespeare's *Henry V* (1599)? Take, for instance, the "language lesson" between Katherine and Alice.[12] Printed texts of *Henry V* suggest that some French was spoken in performance; the printer captures something approaching phonetic French. In Q1 the princess asks her attendant to teach her how to name the parts of the body in English, beginning "Coman sae palla vou la main en francoy" (C3r).[13] Despite this interesting confusion—why ask how to name "le main" in "francoy" instead of in "Anglois" as happens in F1[14]—the more important issue from a staging perspective is the fact that Shakespeare brings something resembling real French to his new stage at the Globe. Did his audience speak French? Did they turn to others in the audience to ask, "What was that?" And if not, how would they have understood this scene (while so many of our students are left in confusion by the printed text)? The answer, it seems, is that for the benefit of the majority of Shakespeare's audience, who knew no French, the *performance* of the scene itself leads the audience to comprehension. If a princess holds forth her hand for all the audience to see and asks, "Coman sae palla vou la main en francoy," and her respondent, adding an "accented" English word at the end of a French sentence, replies "La main madam de han" (C3v), and then follows the rest of the language lesson by wiggling her fingers, bending her elbow, or pointing to her chin (with as much royal dignity as possible in this comic scene), it is reasonable to assume that the language lesson works not only for a French princess but also for a notoriously thick English audience. The "coarse physicality" of this scene, as Helen Ostovich observes, certainly resonates with thematic aspects of nationalist conquest in the play.[15] But this "coarse physicality" may also be literalized in the body standing on the stage and gesturing to hands, limbs, and neck.[16] The staging of a genuinely foreign language, at least when accompanied by corporeal gestures, is perhaps not impenetrable.[17]

Shakespeare offers other strategies for performing foreign tongues throughout the Henriad. The scene that immediately follows Katherine's language lesson, for instance, also involves French characters, but they use a limited quantity of genuine French. The scene's complex mixture of coarse and abstract subjects cannot be presented in French accompanied by gestures in a way that an English audience would readily understand. The Constable's frustration and surprise, "whence haue they this mettall? / Is not their clymate raw, foggy and colde. / On whom, as in disdaine, the Sunne lookes pale?" (C4r), would not make sense, even with gestures, if presented in French. Instead, the only genuine French in this scene is contained in the handful of angry oaths the French peers utter. If these few phrases surpass the English audience's literal understanding, their brevity and inflection would allow them to convey the sense of French frustration, and would thus serve their purpose. Following hard upon the extended scene of French in the language lesson, the scene might have the aura of French in performance without requiring real French. When Shakespeare makes more extensive use of French in later scenes, he does so in the context of bilingual characters who can translate for other English speakers, both those onstage and those in the Globe's audience. This technique had been adequate earlier in the Henriad, when the monolingual Mortimer married the Welsh daughter of Glendower and had to admit to his coconspirators, "My wife can speak no English, I no Welsh," but could fortunately understand some of her "looks" and could rely on his father-in-law to gloss her more complex speeches.[18] In *Henry V,* such scenes present the opportunity for further comedy, as when Pistol mistakes the language of his French prisoner and requires the boy to translate for him. With an effective translator in the scene, Shakespeare can give Le Fer several substantial speeches in French and allow the boy's faithful translations for Pistol—"He saies . . ."—to translate for the audience as well. After one such sustained speech, the boy's translation builds to the climax "He will giue you 500 crownes," with the scene culminating in Pistol's comic "My fury shall abate" (E3v). Q1 also includes the satisfying measure of Katherine's progress in English as she translates Henry's broken French, phrase by phrase in the play's final scene, in lines typically lacking in modern editions based on F1.

Between the extremes of a foreign language that is merely imagined as foreign while performed in English on the one hand, and genuine foreign speech on the other, a third strategy for staging a foreign tongue remains. English can be made to suggest the foreign through "patois"—English spiced with sounds or small portions of a foreign language—offering the third, more common possibility for marking language or speakers as foreign while not entirely obscuring the meaning. In *Henry V*, we find a nice counterpoint to the linguistic Babel of the *Spanish Tragedy* in the much-remarked scene of the British captains, Gower, Fluellen, Jamy, and MacMorris. Here the F1 scene—in which the printed speech prefixes signal the national identities of the characters (Welsh, Scot, Irish) rather than their names[19]—gives aural signals of cultural difference between them. Thus the overbearing Welsh captain, Fluellen, speaks with *p*s for *b*s, and *Ch-* for *J-* ("by Chesu," he swears) while his Scots counterpart, Jamy, uses vowels that phonetically mark his difference ("vary gud, gud . . . gud Captens bath") and his Irish fellow slurs the ends of words, perhaps suggesting a stereotyped drunkenness ("so Chrish save me," he swears and reminds them that the "Town is beseech'd"). Such signals of dialect may serve merely to differentiate characters, to give a sense of individuality perhaps, though of course there is some humor made of linguistic difference in a later scene over Fluellen's discourse on "Alexander the pig." For the most part, however, it is this final strategy or convention—creating characters who speak an adulterated English, marked by aural markers of difference and an occasional, contextualized foreign word—that marks foreigners on the stage in 1600.

Dutchmen Onstage, English Facility

Because the Dutch signify multivalently on the English stage—the English had a vexed relationship with their Dutch coreligionists and trade rivals—they provide a useful case study for observing how these strategies for staging linguistic foreignness might work. Each of the strategies discussed so far makes an appearance in plays staged in the decade around the turn of the century, though the simple strategy of marking difference through slight changes in consonants in regular English constructions predominates. For instance, William Haughton's *Englishmen for My Money* (1598) portrays three foreign and three English suitors wooing three half-English ladies. Though

their Portuguese father would have them marry the wealthy foreign merchants who pursue them, the willful women mock and deride these aliens,
especially for their lack of linguistic facility: "If needes you marry with an
English Lasse, / Woe her in *English* or sheele call you Asse."[20] The Dutch
merchant, Vandalle, comes in for the worst treatment of the three foreign suitors, just as the Dutch language comes in for extended abuse in the play. Told
that he will recognize a man's ability to speak Dutch if he can say something
like "Haunce butterkin slowpin," Pisaro's servant replies that he too "can
speake perfect *Dutch*" if he can "have my mouth full of Meate first, and then
you shall heare me grumble it foorth full mouth, as *Haunce Butterkin slowpin
frokin*" (183, 186–88). The language of the Dutchman is derided for its associations with gluttony and appetite. This instance of "speaking" is purposely
marked as linguistic nonsense; it is the "sound" of Dutch grunting that is
required here.[21]

English facility is the means of influencing these English maidens, and
Vandalle laments his immanent failure—"if dat ick can neite dese Englese
spreake vel" (1153)—in language that marks his linguistic difference, if not
his incomprehensibility. The markers of linguistic difference—mostly the
substitution of consonants such as *d* for *th* and the use of foreign words such
as "neite" or "spreake" with close English cognates ("not" or "speak")—
are blunt and obvious, but would have little effect of veiling the meaning
behind these characters' words. When the pressure is on and Vandalle fails
to sustain coherent English, reverting to a mixture of English and Dutch—
"de loue tol v be so groot, dat het bring me out of my bed voor you" (1717–
18)—he reveals his identity to the daughters through linguistic difference;
they declare "we know the Asse by his eares; it is the *Dutchman*" (1719–20).
Vandalle's stage Dutch, even at the moment when it is supposed to be most
different, registers as a recognizable English. Haughton stages a London populated by scheming, linguistically unskilled foreigners whose anti-English
plans are foiled. Nevertheless, his staging of foreignness in the Dutch Vandalle and his companions requires very little from the audience; they must
merely mark the patois or the accent and associate it with the mercantile
Dutchman.

Something approaching genuine Dutch makes its way to the Fortune in
Thomas Middleton's *No Wit, No Help Like a Woman's* (1611), but competing
onstage translators accommodate this foreign tongue to comic effect.[22] Sir
Oliver Twilight comes to suspect that Philip, his son, and Savorwit, his servant, have duped him when a Dutch merchant arrives with news that Sir Oliver's wife, whom Philip has convinced him is dead, is languishing in the Low
Countries lamenting his neglect. Moreover, the merchant reports, Grace is
not Oliver's long-lost daughter, but is instead a tavern wench. Having reported this in plain English, the Dutch merchant leaves his son, who can
"speak no English, [but] all Dutch," while he attends to business in Lon-

don.[23] Determined to learn the truth of these allegations, Sir Oliver confronts his unreliable servant, who feigns offense at the accusations. Claiming to speak Dutch, Savorwit interrogates the merchant's son in a series of nonsensical exchanges. Since Sir Oliver cannot speak Dutch, Savorwit "translates" the exchanges to his advantage. Savorwit's "Dutch" is gibberish: "Hoyste kaloiste, kalooskin ee vou, dar sune, alla gaskin" (1.3.143). The boy's responses reflect his confusion, though the audience may not have understood them: "Ick wet neat watt hey zacht; Ick unverston ewe neat" [I know not what thou sayest; I do not understand you] (1.3.144). Since Oliver lacks comprehension as well, Savorwit is free to translate as he sees fit. He claims that the boy has informed him that the merchant is a lunatic who "talks like a madman" (1.3.147). Savorwit proceeds to fabricate "translations" that might clear him and Philip of suspicion. The skeptical Oliver, though, cannot believe that one brief phrase, "Nimd aweigh de cack," can mean "his father came from making merry with certain of his countrymen and he's a little steep'd in English beer," as Savorwit claims, when "I heard him speak but three words" (1.3.178, 181–83, 185–86). Though Savorwit tries to persuade his master that "Dutch is a very wide language. You shall have ten English words for one," he does not press his luck and makes a hasty retreat (1.3.187–88). The Dutch merchant's return allows Sir Oliver to learn the truth of what the Dutch boy has said, as he repeats the questions he posed with Savorwit's "help" and learns the trick his servant has been playing. As in the scene of Pistol and the Boy's exchange with Le Fer, the use of an onstage translator adds to the scene's comic effect, but the competing translations of a genuine speaker of the language and one whom the audience knows is improvising to save his skin add a further layer of linguistic play to Middleton's staging of Dutch.

John Marston wrote *The Dutch Courtesan* (1605) for the children's company at the Blackfriars. The Dutch figure of Marston's title, the inaptly named Franceschina, muddles an Italianate name and manners with a sometimes unintelligible garble of Germanic expressions.[24] Despite this accomplished courtesan's social refinements, she speaks an unpleasing, guttural language, an English with harder consonants inserted to mark her foreignness. In her first appearance on the Blackfriars stage, for example, Franceschina speaks recognizable English, marred by harsher consonants, and mixed with one foreign term: "O mine arderliuer love, vat sall me do to requit dis your mush affection."[25] Though the coterie English audience might not know the Dutch word "arderliver," they might be able to guess from context that it means, "dearest" and modifies "love"; even if they missed this, their comprehension of the line is not seriously compromised. The rest of her lines here are similarly recognizable; spoken with some sort of an accent and occasionally inverted syntax, they would not likely confuse the audience. So, lines such as "A mine art, Sir you bin very velcome" (B2r; 86) and her ardent

"Vill not you stay in mine bosome to night love?" (B2v; 109) would not give the English audience too much pause. In fact, her parting lines in this scene might seem to drop all pretense of foreignness: "Rest to mine deare loue, rest, and no long absence" (B3r; 125). The initial signals of "Dutchness" are fairly transparent in Marston's comedy. The fact that Franceschina has no scenes in which she speaks more than a few Dutch words also helps.

In fact, in the crucial scene in which Franceschina ensnares Malheureux to help her injure Freevill, who has just cast her off, and Beatrice his more acceptable, English beloved, the artifice of the courtesan's foreign language drops almost completely away. Responding to Malheureux's inappropriate effort to take up the cast-off woman in her grief, Franceschina coyly asks, "doe you take mee to be a beast, a creature that for sense onely will entertaine loue, and not, onely for loue, loue? O brutish abhomination!" (C4r; 2.2.130). Nothing in the printed version of this speech marks it as foreign—no foreign words are imported, and not even simple changes of consonants or vowels creep in to mark Franceschina's "Dutch" accent. On the one hand, this might signal that Malheureux knows exactly what he is getting himself into. On the other, it might also be a concession to the audience, to ensure that they know precisely what Franceschina asks Freevill to do. Yet another possibility is that the linguistic signs of foreign speech are so slight that the playwright or the printer neglected to mark these occasional signals. Once the courtesan's plot begins, the casual mix of unaccented English and lightly marked patois again returns as Franceschina exits declaring "Now does my harte swell high, for my reuenge / Has birth and form, first friend sall kill his friend, / He dat suruiues, ile hang; besides de / Chast *Beatrice* ile vexe" (D1r; 2.2.205–8). As "Dutch" markers return to her speech—the return of hard *s* for *sh* and *d* for *th*—the audience does not lose any sense of comprehension but might instead merely mark the foreign feel of this wicked woman.

At the supposed height of her success, Franceschina gloats in the most guttural of her stage Dutch. Though consonants shift and syntax twists, however, the sense is not hard to follow:

> Metre *Frevile* liue: ha, ha, liue at mestre Shatewes:
> Mush at metre Shatews, *Frevile* is dead, *Malhereux,* sall hang,
> And swete diuel, dat *Beatrice* would but run mad, dat
> she would but run mad, den me would dance and sing.
>
> (G4r; 5.1.79–82)

And her final words are a similarly not impenetrable mixing of English with "Dutch" sounds: "Ick vil not speake, torture, torture your fill, / For me am worse then hangd, me ha lost my will" (H2r; 5.3.77–78). Marston's "stage"

Dutch requires little sophistication to present or perform, and little effort for an audience to comprehend, and in this it is typical of the practices required for staging Dutch or other foreign languages in 1600.

While the stage Dutch in Marston's comedy is typically clumsy and blunt, a more complex staging of Dutch, combining several of these strategies, appeared at about the same time. Several scenes in *The Weakest Goeth to the Wall* (c. 1600) take place in the Low Countries, where Lodowick and his family seek refuge under the roof of the lascivious, unscrupulous, and bilingual Yacob van Smelt. A range of linguistic markers pepper Yacob's stage Dutch. Speaking to the whole company, Yacob's Dutch mixes English, accented English words, cognates, and internal translations.[26] Taking stock of the group asking for lodging with him, Yacob observes, "Well, here bene van you vier (four as you seg in English): twea mannikins, twea tannikins; twea mans, twea womans."[27] With Yacob speaking to Lodowick, Bunch, Oriana, and Diana, the audience could probably translate "vier," "twea," "mannikins," and "tannikins" as "four," "two," "men," and "girls," even if Yacob had not reinforced his meaning by explicitly translating his phrases into English, "as you zeg." This complex strategy allows for comic staging as the botcher Barnaby Bunch consistently takes offense at Yacob's words. Having learned that Bunch is a tailor willing to practice his trade to pay for his keep, Yacob tells him, "Ick heb a cleyne skuttell, a little stall, by mine huys dore. Sall dat hebben for a skoppe" (4.70–72). Bunch's suspicious, "'Hebben, habben,' quoth 'a? What shall I 'hebben'?" might have left them at an impasse were it not for Lodowick, who understands Dutch. His explanation placates Bunch who sets to work. More importantly, Lodowick's facility with Dutch permits Yacob to use a foreign language in more complex ways. A combination of props, gestures, interior glosses, and Lodowick's responses to and translations of Yacob's propositions allows the melodrama of Lodowick's poverty and Yacob's designs on the beautiful Oriana to proceed. Confronting Lodowick with "a long board chalked" (7. s.d.) with Lodowick's charges, Yacob demands that he "Betall, betall . . . / Betall, shellam, betall. I mought gelt / heb. Comt, *pay*" (7.4, 10–11; my emphasis). Lodowick's response, "have patience awhile. / I will endeavor to come out of debt" (7.12–13) and Yacob's mixture of Dutch and English, "Ick can niet forbear, niet suffer, / niet spare" (7.19–20) make Lodowick's situation plain as he must leave his wife and daughter as "eane gage, eane pawn" (7.72). Between Yacob's mixed stage Dutch, Bunch's misunderstandings that require explanation from Lodowick, and Lodowick's own translations of and responses to Yacob's scheme, *The Weakest Goeth to the Wall* is capable of creating surprisingly complex emotional tension in a foreign tongue. It is not surprising that the play is often associated with Thomas Dekker, who frequently uses Dutch in his acknowledged body of work.

Dekker's Dutchmen

Thomas Dekker's collaboration with John Webster on *Northward Ho* (1607) at about the same time as Marston's *Dutch Courtesan* similarly relies on English patois, this time sprinkled with a little more genuine Dutch, in the incidents involving Hans van Belch, the Dutch merchant and suitor to Doll. Hans's Dutch is mostly English dressed up with harder consonants, as in his entrance line in 2.1: "Dar is vor you, and vor you," he says, counting out coins to Leverpoole and Chartly.[26] When he does switch to genuine Dutch, counting the coins, "een, twea, drie, vier and viue skilling," the strategy is similar to that employed in the *Henry V* language lesson. Holding up coins and counting them out into his companions' hands, introduces the English audience to some simple Dutch terms. As more "real" Dutch slips into Hans's dialogue, the audience finds assistance in Doll herself, who claims to be "an apt scholler" able to translate the broken sentences of her Dutch suitor.

When the gullible Dutch lover worries about Doll's pander, Jack Hornet, Doll persuades Hans that Jack is actually her father. Anxious to impress him and "call you mine vader ta for Ick loue dis schonen vro your dochterkin" (i.e., call you my father for I love this beautiful woman your daughter), Hans brags about his ships:

Ick heb de skip swim now vpon the vater: if you endouty, goe vp in de little Skip dat goe so, and bee puld vp to Wapping, Ick sal beare you on my backe, and hang you about min neck into min groet Skip.

[I have the ship now swimming upon the water: if you're in doubt, go up in the little Ship that goes so, and be pulled up to Wapping. I shall bear you on my back, and hang you [you may hang?] about my neck into my great Ship.]

(2.1.84–87)

Though Hornet professes to misunderstand, "He Sayes Doll, he would haue thee to Wapping and hang thee," Doll sets him and the audience straight with an indirect paraphrase of the merchant's words: "Nay Father I vnderstand him, but maister Hans, I would not be seene hanging about any mans neck, to be counted his Iewell, for any gold" (2.1.88–92). In this brief incident, as with other foreign tongues in the play, linguistic confusion is not left to stand, but, in a technique hearkening back to Kyd's treatment of the polyglot, it is quickly Englished for the audience—under the guise of clarifying it for onstage auditors—so as to leave no room for confusion.

Such concern for absolute clarity stands in marked difference from Dekker's earlier play, *The Shoemaker's Holiday* (1599), in which more sophisticated use is made of Dutch, with a concomitant trust in the audience's ability either to comprehend it or to suspend their frustration. In the comedy, Lacy disguises himself as a Dutch shoemaker in order to remain in London in pursuit of his beloved Rose. His first entrance in Dutch disguise activates the stereotypes of Dutch drunkards as he literally sings a "Dutch Song":

> Der was een bore van Gelderland
>> Frolick sie byen;
>> He was als dronck he could nyet stand,
> Upsee al sie byen;
> Tap eens de canneken,
> Drincke schone mannekin.[29]

The Dutch here is not so important; rather, the audience's sense that it is a drinking song, reinforced perhaps with gestures and certainly with words they might recognize such as "dronck" "Tap" or "Drinck," would serve to characterize this new character of the Dutch shoemaker.[30] In the play, Dekker most often relies on simple audible signals, such as harder consonants, to signal the foreign language being spoken. Hans introduces himself as a "skomawker" (shoemaker), for instance (4.77). But whereas other playwrights make somewhat simplistic use of a "stage accent" to indicate their speakers of a foreign tongue, such as Dutch, Dekker's characters' accents in *The Shoemaker's Holiday* represent a more sophisticated appreciation for the genuine foreign language. The introduction of the sound *sk* here, for instance, more closely represents the difficult sound of native Dutch's *sch* while the subtle use of *aw* may be an effort to reproduce the long *a* of Dutch's *aa*. The English audience would not necessarily be unable to understand the playwright's more sophisticated appreciation of Dutch—after all, it wouldn't be too difficult to determine that this word "skomawker" means "shoemaker" in a play about shoemakers and in a scene in which the character enumerates the various tools of his trade—and its use does suggest how even more complex use of a foreign language can be staged.

Lacy-as-Hans does occasionally speak accurate Dutch in this play. For instance, he places helping verbs in the second position of sentences, reserving main verbs until the end of sentences. Thus, when he happily agrees to accompany Sybil to service Rose's cobbling needs (and thus to meet his beloved clandestinely), he declares, "Yaw, yaw; ik sal mit you gane" (Yes, yes; I shall with you go) (14.63). Similarly, the Dutch skipper, even when he is most drunk, not only separates helping verbs and main verbs, but uses the characteristic syllable *ge* to indicate the past tense of main verbs. When Eyre asks Hans whether he has "made him drink" the skipper interjects, "Yaw, yaw, ik heb veale gedrunck" (Yes, yes, I have drunk well) (7.139). Both of these instances of grammatically correct Dutch are not so complex as to cause confusion in the English audience, though Firk does enjoy mocking his Dutch comrade in his absence, joking with Margery and Hodge, "Yaw heb veale gedrunck, quotha! They may well be called butter-boxes when they drink fat veal, and thick beer too!" (7.142–43). While this English character may not understand the grammatically correct Dutch he overhears (or may claim to misunderstand it in order to make a stereotyped joke of it), the foreign language here resembles English closely enough that many auditors of the play could understand it or at least piece the meaning together, especially with Firk's mangled assistance.

When Hans/Lacy does speak Dutch that has no English cognate, Dekker proceeds to provide a partial gloss for his English audience, again under the guise of accommodating English characters in the play. Thus, for instance, when Sybil comes to find Lacy disguised as Hans to request his help for Rose—a clandestine meeting of the lovers in the offing—he uses some terms that sound nothing like their English counterparts. Sybil asks for Hans at the shop and Firk calls him forth—"Hark, butter-box, now you must yelp out some spreaken"—larding his speech with a little foreign matter of his own (13.52). Hans/Lacy politely asks the customer, Sybil, "Vat begey you," but before an audience can be thrown off by this uniquely Dutch phrase ("What do you desire?"), he follows the question immediately with an Englished version of it: "Vat begey you, vat vod you?" (13.53). His English interlocutor knows precisely what he has asked—"What would you?"—and responds with a request for him to accompany her to help Rose. He again immediately juxtaposes his "Dutch" reply, "Vare ben your edle fro?" lest the use of another foreign phrase cause any confusion, with a more "English" gloss: "Vare ben your edle fro? Vare ban your mistress?" (13.56). Thus Dekker includes snippets of genuine Dutch in his comedy, but makes concessions to accommodate his English audience, most of whom (though not all) might have no understanding of this foreign tongue.

Other plays of the period make similar use of these staging techniques to signal the foreignness of speech. Between English made to seem foreign (through conventions or slight alterations) and genuinely foreign speech (made comprehensible through its simplicity in combination with gestures or through the use of interpreters for other characters onstage, and by extension for the audience) stands the third and most common staging technique: a combination of sounds and contextualized phrases that would "sound" foreign without taxing an audience's ability to make sense of dialogue. Such techniques allow Elizabethan and Jacobean playwrights to do as Mullaney suggests—to "collect and exhibit . . . other cultures . . . and the pleasures of the strange" (63) as part of the process of extending, reformulating, and coming to understand the evolving new national culture. These staging strategies allow playwrights to gently mock their supposedly dull English audience, though there is generally a sense of fun about linguistic play, so that, finally, when someone like Hans can turn the linguistic confusion around and reply to Firk's interrogation with "ik verstaw you niet" (I understand you not)

(4.89) the layers of linguistic play—an English actor, playing an English aristocrat, disguised as a Dutch cobbler, claiming not to understand the perfectly lucid English of an English actor playing an English journeyman before an English audience—suggest how lively the staging of language on the stage in 1600 could be.

Notes

This essay draws on work I began at the Staunton, Virginia Blackfriars, and the London Globe during an NEH Summer Seminar conducted by Ralph Cohen and Patrick Spottiswoode, "Shakespeare's Theatres: Inside and Out," and first presented in William Kerwin and Ewan Fernie's seminar at SAA, 2003. I thank Paul Menzer and an anonymous reader at the journal for encouraging comments on previous drafts of this essay. The epigraph at the beginning of this essay is from Thomas Kyd, *The Spanish tragedie . . .* (London, 1592), K3r. I quote here from the first printing. Further references will be to act and scene numbers in the New Mermaids edition, Thomas Kyd, *The Spanish Tragedy,* ed. J. R. Mulryne (London: A & C Black, 1989).

  1. Sir Philip Sidney, *Miscellaneous Prose,* ed. Katherine Duncan-Jones and Jan Van Dorsten, (Oxford: Clarendon, 1973), 74.

  2. Carla Mazzio, "Staging the Vernacular: Language and Nation in Thomas Kyd's *The Spanish Tragedy,*" *SEL* 38 (1998): 208; Steven Mullaney, *The Place of the Stage: License, Play, and Power in Renaissance England* (Chicago: University of Chicago Press, 1988), 79. On the status of English, see also Colin Kidd, *British Identities Before Nationalism: Ethnicity and Nationhood in the Atlantic World, 1600–1800,* (Cambridge: Cambridge University Press, 1999), 62.

  3. *The Works of Edmund Spenser: A Variorum Edition,* ed. Edwin Greenlaw et al., vol. 9 (Baltimore: Johns Hopkins University Press, 1949), 16. Although Richard Helgerson recalls that Spenser is more concerned here with the tension between different poetic genealogies, his treatment of Spenser's relationship to his own language is significant. *Forms of Nationhood: The Elizabethan Writing of England* (Chicago: University of Chicago Press, 1992), 2.

  4. Stephen Greenblatt focuses on the importance of appropriating and domesticating exotic terms in both Hal's ability to record the alien voices of the Elizabethan underclass (*Shakespearean Negotiations: The Circulation of Social Energy in Renaissance England* [Berkeley: University of California Press, 1988], 49) and in the exploration of the New World, where the English blithely (or cynically) assumed that their language would be understood by the indigenes, or represented an indigenous yearning to learn English (*Marvelous Possessions: The Wonder of the New World* [(Chicago: University of Chicago Press, 1991], 105).

  5. William Shakespeare, *The Merchant of Venice,* in *The Norton Shakespeare,* ed. Stephen Greenblatt et al. (New York: Norton, 1997), 1.2.58, 61.

  6. Steven Mullaney suggests "Learning strange tongues, or collecting strange things, rehearsing the words and ways of marginal or alien cultures, upholding idleness for a while—these are the activities of a culture in the process of extending its boundaries and reformulating itself" (82). See also P. K. Ayers's comments about city

comedies' presentation of foreign tongues in the context of a "new urban Iron Age." "'Fellows of Infinite Tongue': Henry V and the King's English," *SEL* 34 (1994): 269.

7. Carla Mazzio offers a brilliant reading of *The Spanish Tragedy* "in light of contemporary debates about the heterogenous and intertwined fabrics of language, culture, and nation," but neglects the question of how Hieronimo's playlet would have been *performed* (213).

8. In Sheldon P. Zitner's reading of *The Spanish Tragedy,* the alienating confusion created by performance in sundry languages heightens the drama. Arguing that Kyd "sought strong emotion without much cost of imagining affective language," Zitner concludes that the polyglot performance would reach emotions incapable of linguistic expression, that language is subordinate to drama, and implicitly that a translated printing of the text does Kyd a disservice. *"The Spanish Tragedy* and the Language of Performance," *Elizabethan Theatre* 11 (1990): 90.

9. J. R. Mulryne, who has edited *The Spanish Tragedy,* believes that the playlet was performed in Greek, Latin, French, and Italian. In this case, he argues, the emblematic elements of the play must "stand out even more vividly in a kind of dumb show." "Nationality and language in Thomas Kyd's *The Spanish Tragedy,*" in *Travel and Drama in Shakespeare's Time,* ed. Jean-Pierre Maquerlot and Michele Willems, 93 (Cambridge: Cambridge University Press, 1996). Assuming that such foreign speech would leave an English audience in the dark, Mulryne argues that Kyd made the most of this linguistic confusion for other nationalist purposes in the play. Similarly, Michael Hattaway suggests that Kyd attempted an experiment to determine whether he could create a play that would, "to the unlettered at least, communicate by its mere sound." *Elizabethan Popular Theatre: Plays in Performance* (London: Routledge and Kegan Paul, 1982), 110.

10. See S. F. Johnson, "The Spanish Tragedy, or Babylon Revisited," in *Essays on Shakespeare and Elizabethan Drama in Honor of Hardin Craig,* ed. Richard Hosely, 25 (Columbia: University of Missouri Press, 1962).

11. On the significance of the royal audience's minimal comprehension here, see Kevin Dunn's important consideration of word and action in the tragedy, "'Action, Passion, Motion': The Gestural Politics of Counsel in *The Spanish Tragedy,*" *Renaissance Drama* 31(2002): 49.

12. In the discussion of *Henry V* that follows, my interest is in Shakespeare's *staging* of linguistic difference—the way he embeds the performance of the foreign into his play—rather than the important nationalist implications of that difference. Much excellent work on the nationalist and xenophobic aspect of these scenes has been written since Mullaney's treatment of such rehearsals in the Henriad (79–87) and Greenblatt's interest in Hal's recording and domesticating of other tongues (*Negotiations,* 58–59), but the best and most recent is Margaret W. Ferguson, *Dido's Daughters: Literacy, Gender, and Empire in Early Modern England and France* (Chicago: University of Chicago Press, 2003), 152–60.

13. I cite the text from *Shakespeare's Plays in Quarto: A Facsimile Edition of Copies Primarily from the Henry E. Huntington Library,* ed. Michael J. B. Allen and Kenneth Muir (Berkeley: University of California Press, 1981).

14. Just as Andrew Murphy points to the bibliographic blind spot in treatments of *Henry V* that do not account for their use of heavily edited editions of the play, "an

unproblematized reliance on modern editions of *Henry V*," so critics who do not examine their assumptions about how a play like *The Spanish Tragedy* presents foreign tongues take a good deal for granted. "'Tish ill done': *Henry the Fift* and the Politics of Editing," in *Shakespeare and Ireland: History, Politics, and Culture,* ed. Mark Thornton Burnett and Ramona Wray, 218 (London: St. Martin's 1997). P. K. Ayers occasionally notes the significance of different readings gleaned from the Quarto and the Folio, though his concern is not with the staging of language difference so much as with Hal's characteristic speech practices and his royal claim to lack sophisticated rhetoric (262). For Folio *Henry V,* I cite William Shakespeare, *Henry V: The Life of Henry the Fift,* ed. Nick de Somogyi, Shakespeare Folios (London: Nick Hern, 2001).

15. Helen Ostovich, "'Teach you our princess English?': Equivocal Translation of the French in *Henry V*," in *Gender Rhetorics: Postures of Dominance and Submission in History,* ed. Richard C. Trexler, 153 (Binghampton, NY: MRTS, 1994). These thematic, nationalist issues in the play have been treated at great length elsewhere; my concern here is in exploring the performance strategies of bringing a foreign language before an English audience in the popular theater. On the transformation of the stage's interest in female sexuality in plays at the turn of the century, see Mary Bly, "Imagining Consummation: Women's Erotic Language in Comedies of Dekker and Shakespeare," in *Look Who's Laughing: Gender and Comedy,* ed. Gail Finney, 47 (Langhorne, PA: Gordon and Breach, 1994).

16. Huston Diehl is more interested in the moral and tragic implications of gesture, but argues effectively that an Elizabethan audience could be expected to "read" gesture and other visual rhetoric with great care: "the physical action in a Tudor morality is, for its audience, often charged with iconographic significance . . . [and] on the Elizabethan commercial stage, we find that this visual rhetoric does not radically or profoundly change." "Inversion, Parody, and Irony: The Visual Rhetoric of Renaissance English Tragedy," *SEL* 22 (1982): 200. One excellent discussion of the power of gesture in the Elizabethan theater can be found in Paul Menzer, "That Old Saw: Early Modern Acting and the Infinite Regress," *Shakespeare Bulletin* 22 (2004): 34.

17. Although Frances Teague is interested in a different aspect of stage practice, what she calls "stage synecdoche," in her treatment of the stage's literalization of the trope of taking a bride's hand in marriage, her attention to hands and their importance to stage practice offers an interesting analogue to Katherine's practice here. "'What about our hands?': A Presentational Image Cluster," *Medieval and Renaissance Drama in England* 16 (2003): 219.

18. *King Henry IV, Part 1,* ed. David Scott Kastan, Arden Third Series (London: Thomson, 2002), 3.1.189, 196.

19. On this issue, see Murphy's discussion of Jamy's appearance in the text (221).

20. William Haughton, *Englishmen for My Money,* Malone Society Reprints, ed. W. W. Greg (London: Malone Society, 1912), lines 1125–26. Further references will be to line numbers in this edition.

21. Ton Hoenselaars suggests that derision of foreign tongues in the drama may derive "from a hidden frustration among Englishmen regarding the poor status of their own language" and anxiety about mass immigration into England. "In the Shadow of St. Paul's: Linguistic Confusion in English Renaissance Drama," in *English Literature and the Other Languages,* ed. Ton Hoenselaars and Marius Buning,

DQR Studies in Literature 24 (Amsterdam: Rodopi, 1999), 33. While I would agree that some may have felt that English as a language was under assault, I am more interested in Haughton's effort to present, or represent, the Dutch language on an English stage. On acting styles of the period as more typical than specific, which might suggest the effort to give the appearance of something foreign rather than to genuinely present the foreign, see Hattaway (73).

22. For the dating and staging of the play, see John Jowett, "Middleton's *No Wit* at the Fortune," *Renaissance Drama* 22 (1991): 191.

23. *No Wit, No Help Like a Woman's,* ed. Lowell E. Johnson, Regents Renaissance Drama (Lincoln: University of Nebraska Press, 1976), 1.3.101. A. J. Hoenselaars points to the rarity of Middleton's positive depiction of the Dutch merchant. *Images of Englishmen and Foreigners in the Drama of Shakespeare and His Contemporaries: A Study of Stage Characters and National Identity in English Renaissance Drama, 1558–1642* (Rutherford: Fairleigh Dickinson University Press, 1992), 138. Jonathan Gil Harris suggests that the playwright included this scene of stage Dutch to give a "global accent" to the play's mercantile conventions. *Sick Economies: Drama, Mercantilism, and Disease in Shakespeare's England* (Philadelphia: University of Pennsylvania Press, 2004), 184.

24. Jean Howard calls her speech a sign of her "monstrous hybridity." *Theater of a City: The Places of London Comedy, 1598–1642* (Philadelphia: University of Pennsylvania Press, 2007), 157. Hamilton comments briefly on Franceschina's "irregular mixture of accents," though her interest in the play focuses more on the witty approach to English of the English characters in the play. "Language as Theme in *The Dutch Courtesan*," *Renaissance Drama* 5 (1972): 85. Editors run into great troubles in deciphering Franceschina's language: "perfume my seetes" (4.3.26) has been interpreted as "feetes" or "sweetes," but rarely as "sheetes" as the context would seem to demand. Perhaps the language isn't as transparent as I believe it is.

25. John Marston, *The Dutch Courtezan* . . . (London, 1605), B2r. Line numbers will be to John Marston, "The Dutch Courtezan," in *Four Jacobean City Comedies,* ed. Gamini Salgado (New York: Penguin, 1975), 1.2.82–83.

26. Although he does not mention the language barriers in the play, Jeremy Lopez does notice other staging techniques, including dumbshows, that increase the play's accessibility. *Theatrical Conventions and Audience Response in Early Modern Drama* (Cambridge: Cambridge University Press, 2003), 80.

27. *A Critical Edition of the Anonymous Elizabethan Play The Weakest Goeth to the Wall,* ed. Jill L. Levenson (New York: Garland, 1980), 4.4–6. This edition uses scene and line numbers only. Levenson discusses the likely collaboration of Dekker and others in this play (18).

28. Thomas Dekker and John Webster, "Northward Ho," in *The Works of Thomas Dekker,* ed. Fredson Bowers, vol. 2 (Cambridge: Cambridge University Press, 1953). Further references are to this edition. Bowers does not even "translate" Hans's mixture of English and Dutch, perhaps assuming that it would be transparent to the modern reader as well.

29. Thomas Dekker, *The Shoemaker's Holiday,* ed. Anthony Parr, New Mermaids (New York: Norton, 1990), scene 4, lines 39–44. References will be to scenes and lines in this text.

30. In a mid-Tudor interlude, *Welth and Health,* the Dutch figure, Hance, enters "with a dutche songe," though the song is not specified. *The Interlude of Wealth and Health,* ed. W. W. Greg (London: Malone Society, 1907), s.d. 397. Lacy's evocation of the drunken Hans may thus activate not only a stereotype but an emblem, in the sense of Huston Diehl's analysis of "visual rhetoric" on the Elizabethan stage (201).

Notes and Documents

The Succession of Sots,
or Fools and Their Fathers

JOHN H. ASTINGTON

ONE of the jolly little tales told in the second part of *Tarltons Jests* (entered in the Stationers' Register in 1600) is "How *Tarlton* made *Armin* his adopted sonne to succeed him" (C2r, 1638 edition). Apocryphal as this short anecdote may be—the young Robert Armin, visiting a tavern owned by Tarlton to collect a debt owed to his master, composes four lines of comic verse, and Tarlton matches them with his own—it does not lie outside the limits of possibility.[1] Armin was certainly apprenticed to a goldsmith with a shop in Lombard Street, as the book says he was, from later 1582 onward; if he completed his indenture, as he is likely to have done, since he subsequently took his freedom as a goldsmith, he was there until 1591. Tarlton became a freeman of the Vintners' Company in 1584, and he may have begun his tavern enterprises before that date, as a freeman (of the Haberdashers) and citizen since 1576.[2] The terminus for the waggish encounter, evidently, is Tarlton's death in September 1588. Given that the story tells us that following the meeting Armin "so loved Tarlton after, that regarding him with more respect, he used to his Playes, and fell in a league with his humour" (*Jests,* C2r), we might choose the middle of the six-year span possible for the meeting as a likely date: 1585. In that year Armin was probably in his middle teens and Tarlton in his midthirties, and though a famous entertainer and leading member of the Queen's Men at a time of life when competing talent in the young can be regarded with more equanimity, even by actors. If Armin did indeed become a fan of Tarlton, he would have remembered the older man's performances vividly for the rest of his life. In a theatrical period we know very little about, the art of the mature Shakespearean clown had its fundamental inspiration. If we want to stretch the succession further, we can imagine that another goldsmith's apprentice, Andrew Cane, in London from 1602 and about fifteen years old in 1604, became a follower of Armin "where, at the Globe on the Banks side men may see him" (*Jests,* C2r). Neater still would be the story of the actual apprenticeship of Cane under Armin as goldsmith, but the older man had not taken his freedom by the time Cane began his training (with his older brother as his master).[3] Neither Armin nor Cane served their formal

apprenticeships under actors—nor had Tarlton. History refuses, in such instances, to be the handmaid of romance. The story of sots (not counting
Kemp, of whose origins and early life we still know very little) is that they
all began as provincials from nontheatrical families (like their most renowned
contemporary in the profession), becoming London apprentices in nontheatrical trades, and all of them continuing enterprises in other areas after becoming famous on stage.[4] Perhaps their humor livened up the shops where they
worked, as in *The Shoemakers' Holiday,* but they were not so idle, or uninter-
ested, as not to serve the term of their indentures and take their freedom.

The actual history of Tarlton's encounter with Armin, assuming there is
one, has both a temporal framework and a topography. While he was an apprentice Armin's (second) master was John Kettlewood, a prominent goldsmith (liveryman and Fourth Warden of the company in 1575–76) who since
1566 had leased a shop owned by the Goldsmiths' Company in Lombard
Street. Kettlewood regarded himself a parishioner of St. Mary Woolnoth,
where his children were baptized between 1549 and 1563, where he was
churchwarden in 1563–64, where his wife Mary was buried in April 1583,
and where the young Armin no doubt accompanied him to divine service as
a member of the household.[5] Probably his shop lay at the far western end of
Lombard Street, on the south side, and hence across the neighboring ward
and parish boundaries which marked off the very end of the street. In the
1582 Lay Subsidy, a general civic tax, John Kettlewood was assessed as a
resident of Walbrook Ward, rather than of Langbourn Ward, in which most
of Lombard Street lay, and of the parish of St. Mary Woolchurch.[6] His contribution, of three pounds, indicates a fairly modest economic standing. Yet
both Lombard Street and the church of St. Mary Woolnoth, which stood
nearer the middle of its south side than in the modern layout (these days the
postfire, postblitz church marks the junction with King William Street), were
prosperous sites, frequented by the civic elite: Sir Martin Bowes, alderman,
sheriff, Lord Mayor (in 1545), and chief Tudor benefactor of the Goldsmiths,
was buried at the church (as was the historical Simon Eyre), which the wardens of the company visited annually to hear a sermon in his memory. Bowes
had kept his shop at the sign of the White Lion in Lombard Street; the Vyn-
ers, prominent goldsmiths, lived in the street in the Stuart period.

The young Armin, who had been first apprenticed, for roughly half a year,
to John Lonyson, Master of the Mint (d. 1582), grew up surrounded by all
the signs of wealth and privilege. His father, a tailor from King's Lynn in
Norfolk, seems to have placed him very well in terms of the civic pecking
order and the opportunities likely to arise from his position. (Lonyson himself was a native of King's Lynn and evidently retained contacts with his
birthplace; he left money to its church in his will.) We might therefore read
Armin's conversion to the theater, however it came about, as a romantic ab-
negation of a wealthy bourgeois career, rendering him the more of a true fool

in conventional "citizen" judgment as it is portrayed in contemporary drama: see *The Knight of the Burning Pestle,* for example, in which masters and their apprentices are represented at both initial levels of the fiction. The hard truth probably was that without some family money, or an advantageous marriage (unlikely without the first condition), mere freedom in a company did not take one very far. Becoming a goldsmith was not a license to print money, and there were many "poor" members of the company (and of other Great Companies), Andrew Cane among them.

If Armin had time and permission to go and see Tarlton on the stage, where did he go? As it happens he was living just two or three minutes' walk from a major theater district of the 1570s and 1580s: Gracious or Gracechurch Street, which ran in a northerly line from Eastcheap, continuing the path of New Fish Street north from London Bridge to Bishopsgate; at the intersection with Gracious Street the eastern end of Lombard Street terminated. The Queen's Men did not have a "home" playhouse in London, but in November 1583 they had permission from the city "to play at the Bull in Bishopsgate Street and the Bell in Gracious Street on holidays, Wednesdays, and Saturdays" until the following Shrovetide.[7] Tarlton's name was also associated with playing at the Cross Keys, an inn that stood just around the northern corner of the junction with Lombard Street, on the western side; the Bell was close by, a little further north.[8] The inn Tarlton ran, the Saba, was also in Gracious Street, and perhaps was the site of Armin's encounter with his father in folly; nothing much is known about it (although see note 2), but it too, given its management, may have been used for entertainments of some kind. It is clear that however much stress general histories of the Elizabethan theater have laid on the development of playhouses and on playing outside the walls of the City of London, making fashionable hay with liminality and marginality in the last few decades, a major center of theatrical activity in the high Elizabethan period was not only within the square mile, but immediately contiguous to and mingled in among the property of very rich citizens and their commercial life, close not only to Lombard Street and its goldsmiths, but to the Royal Exchange, Leadenhall, and the halls of various other prominent livery companies. There was not a physical separation, in Tarlton's and James Burbage's days, between theater business and the business of the city, and all the people involved in the latter were potential members of a theatrical audience.[9] Armin grew up, then, close both to prosperity and to playing places; with his master's leave he might have been a playgoing apprentice, and have seen the Queen's Men in their heyday.

There is at least one other overlap between the theatrical career of Tarlton and the commercial world in which Armin began his London career, personified in the leading nobleman who died in the same month and year as Tarlton: Robert Dudley, Earl of Leicester. Leicester's role as a patron of players is not a new story. He seems to have had a particular fondness for fools: in the

1580s he paid for performances by Tarlton, Will Kemp, "Powell the foole," and "Luck the foole of Wickham," as well as by funny men in the Low Countries.[10] At least one of these occasions was a performance by the Queen's Men, at Grafton House in Northamptonshire, one of Leicester's properties, on September 2, 1585, but the account identifies them by their leading player ("in reward to Torellton and hys feallou"). But if Leicester cared for the theater, he also cultivated the London civic elite, for the important practical reasons of financial and political support. A consortium of London merchants underwrote a loan that financed Leicester's expenses in the Netherlands, and shortly before embarking on the expedition, in December 1585, he dined with the Lord Mayor, Sir Wolstan Dixie.[11] His policy had begun early in the reign: for example, Leicester dined with the Mercers' Company in July 1560, and attended the Lord Mayor's feast in the Guildhall on October 29 of the same year, when Sir William Chester (a draper) became mayor; on the latter occasion his followers and horses appear to have been accommodated at Bosom's Inn in Cheapside and the Maiden Head in the Steelyard.[12] As a place for coming and going, these details remind us, London required an extensive hospitality industry, as we now call it. In Leicester's day there was a link between that business and the business of theater— Tarlton was involved in both.

As a man of wealth and fashion Leicester also patronized the luxury market of London tradesmen, particularly in the early Elizabethan years. Among many other records of Leicester's accounts of payments to goldsmiths, haberdashers, mercers, and the like, there appear several to John Lonyson and one to an otherwise unidentified "Kettlewood goldsmith" (but probably John), in 1560, for supplying "one douzen of goold wreathed buttones . . . being wrought in hast"—to cut a suitable dash at some important occasion.[13] If Armin's masters were not exactly "by appointment to her majesty the queen," they could advertise themselves as suppliers to the highest echelons of her court. Yet Lonyson had an even closer relationship with Leicester; he may, in fact, at one time have been a member of his household, since a "Mr Lanyson" appears in a list of people supplied with livery cloth in 1567–68.[14] Some years after this, in 1572, Lonyson received the significant appointment of Master of the Mint, the man in charge of producing the coin of the realm, working in the Tower. Leicester's support or patronage may have been behind the appointment; he had borrowed money from officials of the Mint in the past, and it was in his interest to have a sympathetic incumbent as Master.[15] Lonyson was then in an even stronger position to fulfill a role he already had, as a chief financial guarantor and underwriter of credit for Leicester. Early in 1561 the following item appears in Leicester's account book: "Item paid unto Robotham of the Roobes [Robert Robotham, Yeoman of the Robes] for the discharge of certain obligacions whearin Lanyson goldsmith and other stoode bownd for the payment of CCCCli.[16] This was no small commitment. Lonyson evidently continued to lend money to Leicester in one way or another, and in his will he forgave what was outstanding at his death. Lonyson's close involvement in the Company of Mineral and Battery Works gave him further contact with Leicester, and with other leading figures of the Elizabethan court.[17] Armin's first master was a man of some wealth, prominence, and influence, and a financial, if not political, supporter of one of the most powerful figures in Elizabethan England. If John Kettlewood was of rather less consequence, he certainly belonged to the same world, and probably knew Lonyson fairly well; they had both served as wardens of the Goldsmiths' Company in the 1570s, and would have both had a contemporary place on its Court of Assistants. So Kettlewood had perhaps been nominated to take over the relatively new apprentice in Lonyson's final sickness (Lonyson's will has nothing to say about such obligations).

So what of all this in the context of theater history? Were such circumstances known about the young Shakespeare, one can imagine what would have been made of them in the way of biographical romance. Leicester, told by Tarlton of a young wit who had his start with Master Lonyson, trusted old supporter, takes the lad to court, and there his jests catch the fancy of Good Queen Bess, whose favors . . . your story here. Chris Sutcliffe, in his note on Armin cited above, slips briefly into this mode as he imagines a youthful contact with Mary Hopton (later Lady Chandos), a resident of the Tower when Armin began his work at the Mint (if indeed he did so; Lonyson may have continued concurrently to run a shop in his home parish of St. Vedast Foster Lane).[18] If it seems plausible that Armin met Tarlton—they lived and worked in the same part of London at the same time,[19] and goldsmiths, we've seen, were in the business of moneylending, so the debt-collecting story also has credibility—I think it quite unlikely that Armin knew Leicester, other than as a great lord passing in the streets. The matter of interest, I think, is the overlapping of webs of patronage to do with business, politics, and the arts, to use modern terms. In a recent chapter on Leicester's policy as a patron of players, Sally-Beth MacLean has argued that Leicester directed his troupe to districts where allegiances to him were already strong or where he wished to strengthen his influence; their arrival was a sign of favor from their lord.[20] Given Leicester's financial and political alliances with the wealthy citizens of London, then, we may ask whether this policy extended to the activities of players in or near the city; both of his own troupe and, after 1583, of the Queen's Men particularly. Civic politics are always complex, but there must have been a keen awareness among the rich and powerful upper levels of London government that it would not do to offend national political leaders, particularly when large amounts of money were involved. Large-scale mutual interests override less significant differences of opinion, in those of shrewd and steady judgment. (Such understanding began increasingly to break down after 1625.) Trust and goodwill on both sides were expected, and gift exchange was one way of expressing their spirit: invitations to civic feasts, countervailing offerings of barrels of wine, venison from the country, or visits from players. One sign of civic favor might have been to allow those players to conduct their own business in the London streets. How might we calculate such influences over the thirty years between Elizabeth's accession and Leicester's death? (*Not* the "Elizabethan Theater" whose literature we teach.) The theme of E. K. Chambers's magisterial history is of conflict between court and city interests over the rise of the professional theater; I find it too simple a paradigm, particularly for the period defined above.

The general question I have in mind as regards Armin is how, and why, he made the leap from the relatively rich world of his apprenticeship to the ever-uncertain condition of a player. One answer is that he was starstruck; entranced by Tarlton, he took him as a model, particularly, perhaps, after the famous clown's much-lamented early death, a year or two before Armin's bonds as an apprentice came to an end. "[P]rivate practice brought him to present playing," says *Tarltons Jests* (C2r); however much he may have continued to respect his master's interests his true apprenticeship was conducted in the bathroom mirror, as it were. That his first known theatrical job was with the troupe belonging to Lord Chandos may or may not have significance in terms of the connections examined here; Gyles Bridges, third Lord Chandos (d. 1594, whom Andrew Gurr made famous for his hat), was an associate of Leicester, and a chief mourner at his funeral.[21] Though the Dudley and the Bridges families were on opposite sides of the religious divide in the 1540s and 1550s, Leicester's expanding role as a territorial magnate after 1558 required cooperation with Chandos, who was Lord Lieutenant of Gloucestershire, with a seat at Sudeley Castle. Leicester became a chief figure in the government of the west Midlands and the Welsh borders; he was High Steward of Bristol and Tewkesbury, among other towns.[22] Leicester's players were regular visitors to Gloucester between 1560 and 1588, and might well have visited Sudeley Castle itself, roughly fifteen miles to the northeast;[23] a clear sign of patronage exchange in the other direction is suggested by the entertainment offered to Leicester by Chandos's musicians as he was en route to Oxford early in 1585—they were rewarded with a gift of ten shillings.[24] Chandos's stage players were never a London company, and seem to have had a fairly local range; they were, however, working part of the same circuit as the more famous troupes, and it seems likely that the touring routes served as channels of communication about opportunities in the acting profession as well as about weightier matters. Opportunities may have arisen in 1592, when Armin had completed the term of his apprenticeship as a goldsmith. In September of that year Queen Elizabeth visited Sudeley Castle on progress, and was entertained with speeches, songs, and shows featuring shepherds, Apollo, Daphne, and Cotswold rustics.[25] If Lord Chandos was "hunting for players and such kind of creatures" in preparation for his royal guest,[26] the word may have spread back to London, and Armin have responded to it.

A different kind of speculative question may be posed if we consider the attitudes of such men as John Armin the Norfolk tailor and John Kettlewood the London goldsmith toward the choice the young man Robert Armin made in the early 1590s: to pursue his talent for comic improvisation and playing as a full-time occupation, and to move to the western provinces to do so. One might represent such men as Armin Sr., John Lonyson, and John Kettlewood as hardheaded men of business who would regard a life devoted to professional clowning as a trivial waste of time. Perhaps Armin did need an adopted father, if his true father were to disown him as a wastrel. On the other hand, rich London merchants and craftsmen of the period dealt in an economy that was cultural as well as monetary, and evidently they had close bonds with leading members of the court and the national government, who saw the theater as both valuable in itself—a source of recreation, pastime, and pleasure—but also as a valuable tool of propaganda and opinion formation. Inevitably there were many shades of attitude to players and playing at all levels of society, but the widespread appeal of a popular clown like Tarlton would not have gone unnoticed by thinking people. Talented actors were a special kind of resource, and I think it at least as likely that John Kettlewood would have regarded his unusual apprentice with some pride as that, inevitably, he would have sneered at a secure bourgeois career thrown away. The attitude of the citizens of London to the players who lived and worked among them is a central question, I think. The period I have in mind covers the hundred years from 1550 to 1650. Lacking much direct evidence in the form of written comments, one has to do one's best to gauge the nuances of such social judgment. What will not do, and what has so often been done, is to portray the City of London, as represented by its mayors and aldermen, who came from the ranks of the Great Companies, peers of men like Lonyson and Kettlewood, as implacably and unvaryingly opposed to playing, both as a new economic venture and as an attraction of civic life. The players were closely involved with the vitality of the city at many levels, and particularly so, it seems, during those years of the 1580s when Tarlton passed the torch to Armin.

The adoption story and its factual framework also point out the essential independence of the Elizabethan comic performer. That we have very little trace of Kemp before his arrival in Leicester's troupe around 1585 indicates that he too took up a stage career on his own initiative, without any extensive training in the theater. What Tarlton admired in Armin, according to the story, was the ability to improvise in verse (presumably with some accompanying performative brio), as he himself was able to do. One could, evidently, teach oneself to do this, given the right bent for rhythm and verbal inventiveness, simply by absorbing the style, through listening and reading. Once a reasonably imaginative someone has listened to a certain amount of rap music and its rhyming techniques, he or she will begin to experiment with original composition within the framing convention. Many popular forms of music, particularly, flourish through a combination of imitation and original invention, and since broadcasting and recording became common such copying has proliferated beyond immediate social and cultural contexts.

Singing rhymes, jigs—insofar as these were verbal performances—and ballads are all popular forms that might easily have been absorbed aurally, as well as through reading, and then, given a suitably inventive instinct, reproduced and modified. The essential principles of all such forms are regular simple rhythms and repeated phrases, or refrains, in song or verse. If one is using them to be funny, one looks for surprising or outrageous conjunctions of words, phrases, and ideas, or indeed looks to point the way, so that the audience can see the punch line or clinching rhyme word coming, like the falling anvil in a cartoon. Such techniques were available to anyone, and were employed in lampoons, libels, and mocking games in provincial and rural England as much as on the metropolitan stages.[27]

An aptitude for verbal wit and inventiveness can hardly be taught; Armin's evident possession of such a kind of intelligence partly governed his turn to a stage career, and it was plainly a requirement in any stage comic who regularly or occasionally gave unscripted performances, essentially detached from written play texts, as Andrew Cane, John Shank, and Thomas Pollard, for example, also did in the 1620s and 1630s. Training in improvisation is something of a contradiction in terms; one must absorb the principles, but then be original. The famous Elizabethan fools, it seems, did so on their own account during their formative years, turning to the stage as creative adults. A great deal of developmental activity must have gone on in the teens of Tarlton and Armin in particular, but a good part of it must have depended on their contact with the popular culture of London, which surrounded them, including song, dance, ballad making, and singing, as well as common forms of social humor: jokes, mockery, and irony, both sweet and bitter. The fool's training was rooted in vernacular and communal life, and partly "picked up on a street." As beginning apprentices both Tarlton and Armin would have been required to be literate, and they both lived in a place where reading material was readily available. What they may have read is worth thinking about. Armin's style in his various publications shows some rhetorical sophistication, and Tarlton's range of jesting, so far as we can judge secondhand, included verbal dexterity as well as physical clowning. Both men, finally, were playwrights.

Andrew Cane certainly and John Shank probably had similar paths to the professional stage, Cane as an apprentice goldsmith in London during the first decade of the seventeenth century, and Shank an apprentice weaver, in all likelihood in London, and perhaps roughly contemporary with Armin's apprenticeship.[28] Thomas Pollard, apprenticed to Shank probably at some time around 1612, was the first famous comic actor to emerge from a principally theatrical training in his youth, although Tarlton had bound an apprentice, Richard Hayward, in 1584 who was perhaps destined for the stage (he is otherwise unknown to theater history), while both Armin and Cane in particular took apprentice "goldsmiths" who had stage careers.[29] During the middle Jacobean period, then, it seems as if a transition to a more professionalized system of training for comic performance had been established, although the avenue for untrained, inspired talent was no doubt still open, as it always is in the theater.

In the jestbook story the qualities Tarlton recognized in Armin were those he might have wished for in Richard Hayward, or in any apprentice to be trained in performance. The relationship between masters and younger adolescent apprentices had a firm paternal model, and in making the younger man his adopted son, Tarlton bestowed an honorary apprenticeship, and future freedom, on a promising comic actor. The story, composed after whatever fact it may be based on, is distinctly nostalgic and elegiac, and to that extent suspect. Tarlton's versified prediction is as follows: "Let me divine: As I am, so in time thou'lt be the same,/ My adopted sonne therefore be,/ To enjoy my Clownes sute after me" (*Jests,* C2r). Armin, son of two fathers, servant of three masters, indeed came after Tarlton; how far he was after Tarlton in the stylistic sense is very hard to judge, but his observation of the famous clown's performances and his subsequent memories of them are very likely to have been formative influences on his own art.

Notes

A version of this essay was first presented in the seminar "Plots, Playhouses, and Players" at the Thirty-Third Annual Meeting of the Shakespeare Association of America, in Bermuda, March 2005.

1. E. K. Chambers, *The Elizabethan Stage,* 4 vols. (Oxford: Clarendon Press, 1923), 2:342–45.

2. David Kathman, "Grocers, Goldsmiths and Drapers: Freemen and Apprentices in the Elizabethan Theater," *SQ* 55 (2004): 1–49. The claim made by Simplicity in Robert Wilson's play *The Three Lords and Three Ladies of London,* acted by the Queen's Men after Tarlton's death, that the famous player had been "a prentice in his youth of this honorable city" is true, but not the accompanying story that he had been a waterbearer. Contemporary audiences would have appreciated two jokes: the waterbearers never had the status of a company—Simplicity's professional pride in his wife's calling claims more civic dignity for an essential trade than in fact it had—and Tarlton had handled stronger waters. That "he hath tost a Tankard in Cornehil er nowe" may be a clue to the site of the inn he kept, somewhere near the intersection

of Cornhill and Gracechurch Street. See *The pleasant and Stately Morall, of the three Lordes and three Ladies of London* (London: Richard Jones, 1590), C1v.

3. See my article "The Career of Andrew Cane, Citizen, Goldsmith, and Player," in *MaRDiE* (2003), 16:130–44.

4. Tarlton may have come from Chelmsford in Essex, where he was married; Armin was a native of King's Lynn in Norfolk, and Cane of Windsor in Berkshire. See Kathman, "Grocers," and Astington, "Andrew Cane."

5. John Kettlewood and John Lonyson, Armin's first master (lived 1525–82), were probably contemporaries, but Kettlewood was the longer lived. Chris Sutcliffe reports the burial of a second wife of Kettlewood, Elizabeth, in May 1586 at St. Mary Woolchurch Haw: "Robert Armin: Apprentice Goldsmith," *N & Q* 239 (1994): 503–4. The Lay Subsidy Roll for 1599 records a John Kettlewood living in the parish of St. Mildred Poultry, and assessed at six pounds (with thanks to Alan Nelson's Web transcriptions: http://socrates.berkeley.edu/~ahnelson/). By 1604, when Armin took his freedom, Kettlewood appears to have been dead, since Armin's guarantor was John Moth, a goldsmith who had apprenticed with Lonyson from 1568 to 1577 and who remained associated with his master, and could have reported on the circumstances of Armin's apprenticeship. Whether Kettlewood, in his last years, or Moth himself had seen Armin perform at the Globe is an open question. For these and other facts cited here I am indebted to notes kept in the library of the Worshipful Company of Goldsmiths, and to corresponding entries in the Court Books and Apprenticeship Books. I am grateful to the Company, and to the librarian, Mr. David Beasley, for granting me access to them.

6. *Two Tudor Subsidy Rolls for the City of London, British History Online:* http://www.british-history.ac.uk.

7. Scott McMillin and Sally-Beth MacLean, *The Queen's Men and their Plays* (Cambridge: Cambridge University Press, 1998), 46.

8. For information on the playing inns, see Glynne Wickham, Herbert Berry, and William Ingram, eds., *English Professional Theatre, 1545–1660* (Cambridge: Cambridge University Press, 2000), 295–305. Both the Cross Keys and the Bell yards can be easily identified (and measured) on the Ogilby and Morgan map of 1676 (see *English Professional Theatre,* 296), and Bell Inn Yard survives as a modern thoroughfare.

9. Similarly in the Jacobean period and thereafter playhouses, though they might be outside the walls, were surrounded by populous and fast-growing districts, in the parishes of St. Bride Fleet Street, St. Giles-in-the-Fields, St. James Clerkenwell, and St. Giles Cripplegate.

10. Simon Adams, ed., *Household Accounts and Disbursement Books of Robert Dudley, Earl of Leicester, 1558–1561, 1584–1586* (Cambridge: Cambridge University Press, 1995), 231, 245, 249, 253, 300, 370, 371, 374.

11. Ibid., 341, 385–95.

12. Ibid., 144, 165.

13. Ibid., 127. See also 45, 88, 94, 124.

14. Ibid., 426–27.

15. Thomas Stanley, Under-Treasurer of the Mint until 1571, lent Leicester a hundred pounds in December 1560: ibid., 115.

16. Ibid., 119.

17. See M. B. Donald, *Elizabethan Monopolies* (Edinburgh: Oliver and Boyd, 1961). On Lonyson's work at the Mint, see C. E. Challis, *A New History of the Royal Mint* (Cambridge: Cambridge University Press, 1992).

18. See note 4.

19. Tarlton's residence, which might always have been distinct from his innkeeping business, appears to have been at the other extreme end of the city, at least in the first half of the 1580s. In 1582 "Richard Tarleton" was assessed for a payment of ten pounds—quite a high sum—in the Lay Subsidy collection conducted in the ward of Farringdon Within, in the parish of St. Martin Ludgate (*Two Tudor Subsidy Rolls*). Tarlton's wife Thomasine was buried at the same parish church in late 1585. The Bel Savage Inn, at which Tarlton also performed, lay just to the west of the parish boundary of St. Martin Ludgate, within the parish of St. Bride Fleet Street. See *English Professional Theatre,* 302.

20. "Tracking Leicester's Men: The Patronage of a Performance Troupe," *Shakespeare and Theatrical Patronage in Early Modern England,* ed. Paul Whitfield White and Suzanne R. Westfall, 246–71 (Cambridge: Cambridge University Press, 2002).

21. For the hat, see *The Shakespearean Stage, 1574–1642,* 3rd ed. (Cambridge: Cambridge University Press, 1992), 3.

22. See the entry on Robert Dudley by Simon Adams in *The Oxford Dictionary of National Biography* (Oxford: Oxford University Press, 2004); http://www.oxforddnb .com/view/article/8160.

23. Audrey Douglas and Peter Greenfield, eds., *Records of Early English Drama: Cumberland/Westmorland/Gloucestershire* (Toronto: Toronto University Press, 1986), 259, 447–48. Any visits by players to great houses would have been recorded, if they involved rewards of cash or hospitality, in household account books kept by stewards and similar figures. The rate of survival of such documents since the 1580s has not been high.

24. Adams, *Household Accounts,* 211.

25. Douglas and Greenfield, *REED Gloucestershire,* 259–60, 348–56. The visit was Elizabeth's third; she had been there on previous progresses in 1574 and in 1575 (after the famous visit to Kenilworth).

26. Cf. the letter by Sir Walter Cope to Robert Cecil, ca. 1604, quoted in Chambers, *The Elizabethan Stage,* 4:139.

27. See David Underdown, *Revel, Riot and Rebellion* (Oxford: Oxford University Press, 1985).

28. Astington, "Andrew Cane"; Kathman, "Grocers."

29. See Kathman, "Grocers," 38–39, and Astington, "Andrew Cane." My estimate of Pollard's career is based on the knowledge that he was christened December 11, 1597, at the church of St. Mary, Aylesbury, Bucks., the son of Edward and Elizabeth Pollard. He would have been fourteen in 1612, the age at which Cane was apprenticed, and a common age for stage apprenticeship.

An Early Seventeenth-Century Playhouse in Tonbridge, Kent

JAMES M. GIBSON

ON June 26, 1610, Edward Calverley received a fatal stab wound in the head during a fray in "a certain house called a playhouse" in Tonbridge.[1] After Calverley died some weeks later, an inquest convened by coroner George Pattenden on September 18, 1610, found that Edward Oxley of Tonbridge, yeoman, John Holmden of Tonbridge, butcher, Sidney Francis of Tonbridge, butcher, William Beach of Tonbridge, tailor, Edward Calverley, deceased, of Tonbridge, and various other persons unknown to the jury had assembled at the playhouse, where a fray had broken out on the evening of June 26. Holmden, Francis, and Beach had beaten Calverley about the head and arms with their staves, and Oxley had mortally wounded Calverley above the eye with his dagger. On July 23, 1610, Calverley had died.[2] The defendants were taken into custody, until the case came before the assize court at Maidstone on February 21, 1610/11.[3] The inquisition as originally drafted (mb. 11) was declared void, due to insufficient evidence to convict Holmden, Francis, and Beach for their part in the fray. It was then redrawn (mb. 26) to focus on Edward Oxley, omitting the details of the billets, staves, beatings, blows, and bruises and stating more generally that Holmden, Francis, and Beach had supported, aided, and encouraged Oxley to commit felony and homicide. All four defendants pleaded not guilty. A trial jury was convened (mb. 27), which found Oxley guilty of homicide and the other three defendants not guilty. Oxley was granted the benefit of clergy, branded on his right hand with an M for murderer, and committed to the bishop's custody.[4] Transcription and translation of the assize court original inquest (mb. 11), redrawn inquest (mb. 26), and trial calendar (mb. 27) appear below.

Assize Court Inquest (TNA: PRO ASSI 35/53/5, mb. 11)

kanc*ie sessiones*
Inquisic*io* indentat*a* capt*a* apud Tunbridge in Com*itatu* pre*dic*to xviij° Die Septembris Anno Regni D*omi*ni *no*st*r*i Iacobi Dei gr*ati*a Anglie ffranc*ie* et

hibernie Regis fidei defensoris &c octauo et Scotie xliiij[to] Coram Georgio Pattenden generoso vno Coronatorum dicti Domini Regis Comitatis predicti Super visum corporis Edwardi Calueley ibidem mortui iacentis per sacramentum Nicholai ffarmer generosi Ierratti Gatlin generosi willelmi Harris senioris Iohannis Dann Thome Vnderhill Roberti Bourman Alexandri Rottenbridge walteri Saker willelmi Harris Iunioris Thome Bowle willelmi Harte Thome Hasselden Mosee Hodge Henrici Burden & Petri Harris proborum & legalium hominum Comitatis predicti Qui dicunt super sacramentum suum quod predictus Edwardus Calveley et quidam Edwardus Oxley <yeoman>[5] Sidneus ffraunces <butcher> Iohannes Homden <butcher> willelmus Beache<butcher Tayler> et diuersi alij[6] persone Iuratoribus predictis incognite xxv[to] die Iunij <Anno &c> vltimo preterito in simul convenerunt apud Tunbridge predictam in quodam Domo ibidem vocato a playehowse & predictus Edwardus Calvely Edwardus Oxley Sidneus ffrances Iohannes Holmden & willelmus Beach insultum & quendam affraiam inter se adtunc & ibidem in nocte eiusdem diei fecerunt in qua quidem affraia et insultu predictus idem Edwardus Oxley <yeoman> cum pugione Anglice a dagger valloris xij d. quod idem Edwardus ^ <Oxley> adtunc et ibidem in manu sua dextra habuit prefatum Edwardum Calveley vnum vulnus ^ <mortale> in fronte suo de funditate[7] quartij vnius vncij adtunc dedit & predicti Iohannes Holmden Sidneus ffraunces & willelmus Beache adtunc et ibidem in affraia & insultu predictis existentes cum quibusdam baculis anglice billettes & staues valoris iij d. quos ijdem Iohannes Holmden Sidneus ffraunces & willelmus Beache adtunc in manibus suis habuerunt quosdam ictus ^ <& quassaciones> anglice blowes and bruyses vnacum prefato Edwardo Oxley in & super Caput & humeros predicti Edwardi Calveley adtunc dederunt De quibus quidem vulneribus <quassacionibus> & ictibus idem Edwardus Calveley ab eodem xxvj[to] die Iunij vsque ad septimum diem Augusti tunc proximum sequentem languebat et eodem die apud Tunbridge predictam de eodem vulneribus ^ <vulnere & quassacionibus> & ictibus ^ <predictis> obijt Et sic Iuratores predicti pro dicto domino Rege dicunt quod predicti Edwardus Oxley Iohannes Holmden Sidneus ffraunces & willelmus Beach modo & forma predictis prefatum Edwardum Calveley felonice percusserunt & interfecerunt contra pacem dicti domini Regis nunc Coronam & dignitatem suas &c Et sic Iuratores predicti super sacramentum suum predictum dicunt quod predictus Edwardus Calveley sic ad mortem suam deuenit et non aliter Et quod predicti Edwardus oxley Iohannes Holmden Sidneus ffraunces nec willelmus Beach nulla habuerunt bona seu cattalla in Comitatu predicto tempore felonie superius facte & perpetrate que in manus dicti domini Regis accione predicte capi aut seisiri possunt ad eorum noticiam Et quod predicta pugio & bacculi remanent in custodia cuiusdam willelmi Harris de Tunbridge predicta ad vsum dicti domini Regis In cuius Rei testimonium tam prefatus Coronator quam Iuratores predicti hinc Inquisicioni sigilla sua apposuerunt

die Anno & loco supra*dictis* &c   p*ro* homicidio   ta{m}
su*per* aliud questu*m*   *per* me Georgiu*m* pattenden
Coronatore*m*   vacat quia insufficiens & fit de novo

Kent Sessions
*An indented inquest was held at Tonbridge in the aforesaid county on 18
September in the eighth year of the reign of our lord James by the grace of
God king of England, France, and Ireland, defender of the faith, etc. and in
the forty-fourth [year of the reign of our lord James king] of Scotland before
George Pattenden, gentleman, one of the coroners of the said lord king of the
county aforesaid, upon the view of the body of Edward Calueley lying dead
there, by the oath of Nicholas Farmer, gentleman, Garret Gatlin, gentleman,
William Harris the elder, John Dann, Thomas Underhill, Robert Bourman,
Alexander Rottenbridge, Walter Saker, William Harris the younger, Thomas
Bowle, William Harte, Thomas Hasselden, Moses Hodge, Henry Burden and
Peter Harris, good and lawful men of the county aforesaid. They say upon
their oath that the aforesaid Edward Calveley and a certain Edward Oxley,
yeoman, Sidney Francis, butcher, John Homden, butcher, William Beache,
tailor, and various other persons unknown to the aforesaid jurymen on 25
June in the year &c last past assembled together at Tonbridge aforesaid in a
certain house there called "a playhouse"; and [that] the aforesaid Edward
Calveley, Edward Oxley, Sidney Francis, John Holmden, and William Beach
did then and there make an assault and a certain affray among themselves in
the night of the same day; [and that] indeed in this affray and assault the
same aforesaid Edward Oxley, yeoman, with a dagger, in English "a dagger," of the value of 12d., which the same Edward Oxley then and there had
in his right hand, did give the aforementioned Edward Calveley a mortal
wound in his forehead a quarter of one inch in depth; and [that] the aforesaid John Holmden, Sidney Francis, and William Beache, being then and
there in the aforesaid affray and assault, with certain staves, in English "billets and staves," of the value of 3d., which the same John Holmden, Sidney
Francis, and William Beache then had in their hands, did then together with
the aforementioned Edward Oxley give certains blows and beatings, in English "blows and bruises," on and about the head and arms of the aforesaid
Edward Calveley; [and that] indeed the same Edward Calveley lay ill from
these wounds, beatings, and blows from the same 26 June until 7 August then
next following, and on that day at Tonbridge aforesaid he died from the same
wound and the aforesaid beatings and blows. And thus the aforesaid jurymen
for the said lord king say that the aforesaid Edward Oxley, John Holmden,
Sidney Francis, and William Beach in the manner and form aforesaid did
feloniously beat and kill the aforementioned Edward Calveley contrary to the
peace of the said lord king, his Crown, and dignity etc. And thus the aforesaid jurymen upon their aforesaid oath say that the aforesaid Edward Calve-*

*ley came to his death in this manner and not otherwise; and that to their knowledge neither the aforesaid Edward Oxley, John Holmden, Sidney Francis, nor William Beach had any goods or chattels in the aforesaid county at the time of the felony previously made and perpetrated that can be taken or seized into the hands of the said lord king; and that the aforesaid dagger and staves remain in the custody of a certain William Harris of Tonbridge aforesaid for the use of the said lord king. In witness whereof the aforementioned coroner as well as the aforesaid jurymen have affixed their seals to this inquest in the day, year, and place aforesaid etc.   for murder
so upon another inquest   by me George Pattenden, Coroner
It is void because insufficient, and it should be done anew.*

Assize Court Inquest (TNA: PRO ASSI 35/53/5, mb. 26)

kanc*ie* se*ssiones*
Inquisic*io* indentat*a* Capt*a* apud Tunbridge in Com*itatu* p*re*dic*to* decimo Octauo die Septembris Annis Regni d*omi*ni n*ost*ri Iacobi dei gr*at*ia Angl*ie* ffranc*ie* et hibe*r*nie Regis fidei defensoris &c Octauo et Scotie quadragesimo quarto coram Georgio Pattenden gen*er*oso vno Coron*atorum* d*i*c*t*i d*omi*ni Regis Com*itatis* p*re*di*c*ti sup*er* visum Corporis cuiusdam Edwardi Calvely nup*er* de Tunbridge p*re*dic*to* in Com*itatu* p*re*dic*to* yeoman ^ <mortui> ibi*dem* ^ <iacen*tis*> p*er* sacra*mentum* Nich*ol*ai ffarmer gen*er*osi Gerratti Gatlyn gen*er*osi will*elm*i harrys sen*ioris* Ioh*ann*is dann Thome vnderhill Roberti Bourman Alex*andr*i Rottenbridge walt*er*i Saker will*elm*i harrys Iun*ioris* Thome Bowle will*elm*i harte Thome hasselden Mosee hodge henrici Burden et Petri harrys proboru*m* et leg*alium* hominu*m* Com*itatis* p*re*di*c*ti qui dicunt sup*er* sacra*mentum* suam quod p*re*dic*t*us Edwardus Calvely et quidam Edwardus Oxley nup*er* de Tunbridge in Com*itatu* p*re*dic*to* yeoman Sidneus ffrancis nup*er* de Tunbridge p*re*dic*ta* in Com*itatu* p*re*dic*to* Butcher Iohannes hombden nup*er* de Tunbridge p*re*dic*ta* in Com*itatu* p*re*dic*to* Butcher et will*elm*us Beech nup*er* de Tunbridge p*re*dic*ta* in Com*itatu* p*re*dic*to* Taylor et diu*er*se alie p*er*sone Iur*atoribus* p*re*dic*t*is incognite vicesimo sexto die Iunij Annis Regni d*omi*ni n*ost*ri Iacobi dei gr*at*ia Angl*ie* ffrancie et hibe*r*nie Regis fidei defensoris &c Octauo et Scotie quadragesimo tercio insimul convenerunt apud Tunbridge p*re*dic*tam* in Com*itatu* p*re*dic*to* in quadam domo ib*idem* vocat*a* a playhouse et p*re*di*c*ti Edwardus Calvely Edwardus Oxly Sidneus ffrancis Ioh*ann*es homden et will*elm*us Beech adtunc et ib*idem* fecerunt affraiam inter se Et p*re*dic*t*us Edwardus Oxly adtunc et ib*idem* vi et armis &c in et sup*er* p*re*dic*t*um Edwardum Calvely insult*um* fecit et cu*m* quodam gladio vocat*o* a dagger valoris xij d. quod idem Edwardus Oxly in manu sua dextra adtunc et ib*idem* h*a*buit et tenuit p*re*fat*um* Edwardum Calvely sup*er* frontem ipsius Edwardi Calvely felonice p*er*cussit dans eidem Edwardo Calvely adtunc et ib*idem* cu*m* gladio p*re*dic*to* vocat*o* a dagger sup*er* p*re*-

dictam frontem predicti Edwardi vnum vulnus mortale de profunditate quarterij unius pollicis et de latitudine quarterij . . .[8] pollicis de quo quidem vulnere mortali predictus Edwardus Calvely a predicto vicesimo sexto die Iunij annis supradictis . . .[9] ad septimum diem Augusti Annis Regni dicti domini nostri Iacobi nunc Regis Anglie ffrancie et hibernie octavo et Scotie quadrage . . .[10] quarto apud Tunbridge predictam in Comitatu predicto languebat quo quidem septimo die Augusti Annis Regni dicti domini nostri Iaco . . .[11] nunc Regis anglie ffrancie octavo et Scotie quadragesimo quarto supradictis predictus Edwardus Calvely apud Tunbridg pre . . .[12] in Comitatu predicto de vulnere mortali predicto obijt Et quod predicti Sidneus ffrancis Iohannes homden et willelmus Beeche predicto vicesimo sexto Iunij Annis Regni dicti domini nostri Iacobi nunc Regis Anglie ffrancie et hibernie octavo et Scotie quadragesimo tertio supradictis apud Tunbridge predictam in Comitatu predicto felonice fuerunt presentes cum prefato Edwardo Oxly ipsum Edwardum ad feloniam et homicidium predictos in forma predicta faciendum felonice abettando procurando manutenendo auxiliando et confortando contra pacem dicti domini regis nunc Coronam et dignitatem suas Et sic predicti Edwardus Oxly Sidneus ffrancis Iohannes homden et willelmus Beech prefatum Edwardum Calvely apud Tunbridge predictam in Comitatu predicto modo et forma predictis felonice interfecerunt contra pacem dicti domini regis nunc Coronam et dignitatem suas /

per me Georgium pattenden Coronatorem
ponit se   culpabilis   cattalla nulla   legit
Edwardus Oxly
ponit se   non culpabilis nec reus
Sidneus ffrancis
ponit se   non culpabilis nec reus
Iohannes homden
ponit se   non culpabilis nec reus
willelmus Beeche

Kent Sessions
An indented inquest was held at Tonbridge in the aforesaid county on 18 September in the eighth year of the reign of our lord James by the grace of God king of England, France, and Ireland, defender of the faith, etc. and in the forty-fourth [year of the reign of our lord James king] of Scotland before George Pattenden, gentleman, one of the coroners of the said lord king of the county aforesaid, upon the view of the body of a certain Edward Calvely late of Tonbridge aforesaid in the county aforesaid, yeoman, lying dead there, by the oath of Nicholas Farmer, gentleman, Garret Gatlyn, gentleman, William Harry the elder, John Dann, Thomas Underhill, Robert Bourman, Alexander Rottenbridge, Walter Saker, William Harrys the younger, Thomas Bowle, William Harte, Thomas Hasselden, Moses Hodge, Henry Burden and Peter

Harrys, good and lawful men of the county aforesaid. They say upon their oath that the aforesaid Edward Calvely and a certain Edward Oxley late of Tonbridge in the county aforesaid, yeoman, Sidney Francis late of Tonbridge aforesaid in the county aforesaid, butcher, John Hombden late of Tonbridge aforesaid in the county aforesaid, butcher, and William Beech late of Ton-bridge aforesaid in the county aforesaid, tailor, and various other persons unknown to the aforesaid jurymen assembled together on 26 June in the eighth year of the reign of our lord James by the grace of God king of En-gland, France, and Ireland, defender [of the faith] &c and in the forty-third [year of the reign of our lord James king] of Scotland at Tonbridge aforesaid in the county aforesaid in a certain house there called "a playhouse," and the aforesaid Edward Calvely, Edward Oxley, Sidney Francis, John Homden, and William Beech did then and there make an affray among themselves; and [that] the aforesaid Edward Oxley did then and there by force and arms etc. make an assault on and about the aforesaid Edward Calvely and with a sword called "a dagger" of the value of 12d., which the same Edward Oxley then and there had and held in his right hand, did feloniously strike the afore-mentioned Edward Calvely upon the forehead of that same Edward Calvely, giving to the same Edward Calvely then and there with the aforesaid sword called "a dagger" upon the same forehead of the aforesaid Edward a mortal wound of the depth of one-quarter of one inch and of the width of one-quarter of [one] inch; [and that] indeed the aforesaid Edward Calvely was lying ill from that mortal wound from the aforesaid 26 June in the [regnal] years abovesaid [until] 7 August in the eighth year of the reign of our said lord James now king of England France and Ireland and in the forty-fourth [year of the reign of our said lord James king] of Scotland at Tonbridge aforesaid in the county aforesaid; [and that] indeed on that 7 August in the aforesaid eighth year of the reign of our said lord James now king of England, France [and Ireland] and in the forty-fourth year [of the reign of our said lord James now king] of Scotland the aforesaid Edward Calvely died from the aforesaid mortal wound at Tonbridge aforesaid in the county aforesaid. And that the aforesaid Sidney Francis, John Homden, and William Beech on the aforesaid 26 June in the aforesaid eighth year of the reign of our said lord James now king of England, France, and Ireland and in the forty-third year [of the reign of our said lord James now king] of Scotland at Tonbridge aforesaid in the county aforesaid were feloniously present with the aforementioned Edward Oxley by feloniously abetting, procuring, supporting, aiding, and encourag-ing that same Edward to commit the felony and homicide aforesaid in the form aforesaid contrary to the peace of the said now lord king, his Crown, and dignity; and [that] the aforesaid Edward Oxley, Sidney Francis, John Homden, and William Beech did thus feloniously kill the aforementioned Ed-ward Calvely at Tonbridge aforesaid in the county aforesaid in the manner and form aforesaid contrary to the peace of the said now lord king, his Crown, and dignity.

by me George Pattenden, Coroner

He places himself [to be tried before God and country.] [He is] guilty. [He has] no chattels. He reads.[13]
Edward Oxley

He places himself [to be tried before God and country.] [He is] neither guilty nor liable.
Sidney Francis

He places himself [to be tried before God and country.] [He is] neither guilty nor liable.
John Homden

He places himself [to be tried before God and country.] [He is] neither guilty nor liable.
William Beech

Assize Court Trial Calendar[14] (TNA: PRO ASSI 35/53/5, mb. 27)

Nomina Iuratorum inter Dominum Regem Et

Edwardum Hunter non culpabilem nec reum

non culpabilem nec reum
Sidneum ffrancis homicidam

non culpabilem nec reum
Willelmum Beeche homicidam

prisonarios ad barram.

Edwardum Oxly homicidam culpabilem cattallam nullam legit

non culpabilem nec reum
Iohannem Homden homicidam

non culpabilem nec ream
Abigallam Harte

Thomas Allen
Willelmus Hartridge
Willelmus Hyckmott
Thomas Iden
Willelmus Alfye
Matheus Browne
Thomas Daye
Iohannes Maynerd
Walterus Parson
Thomas Hale
Ricardus Cole
Edmundus Langlye

   } Iuratores

Nicholaus Gilborne
Miles Vicecomes

Names of the jurors between the Lord King and

Edward Hunter, not guilty nor liable

Edward Oxly, murderer, guilty, no chattels, he reads

not guilty nor liable
Sidney Francis, murderer,

not guilty nor liable
John Homden, murderer,

not guilty nor liable
William Beech, murder,

not guilty nor liable
Abigail Harte,

prisoners at the bar.

Thomas Allen
William Hartridge
William Hyckmott
Thomas Iden
William Alfye
Matthew Browne
Thomas Daye   } *Jurymen*
John Maynerd
Walter Parson
Thomas Hale
Richard Cole
Edmund Langlye

Nicholas Gilborne
Knight Sheriff

Further details about the participants in this fatal fray have emerged from the Tonbridge parish records, probate records, and other court records. The Oxleys were a prominent family of Tonbridge clothiers, descending from Edward Oxley, whose will, dated December 17, 1567, divided his property among five surviving sons and one daughter.[15] One of his sons, the clothier George Oxley who died May 28, 1598, ranked sufficiently high in the town to have served from 1580 to 1583 as one of the wardens of the town lands, responsible for repairing the bridges and paving the high street.[16] The will of George Oxley, dated May 26, 1598, reveals that he had three daughters and a son named Edward who had not yet reached "his full age of five and Twenty yeares."[17] Since the Tonbridge parish register of baptisms, which begins in 1585, does not mention Edward Oxley, he must have been at least fourteen years old in 1598 and probably in his late twenties or thirties in June 1610, when he assaulted Edward Calverley in the Tonbridge playhouse.[18] Foreshadowing this fatal fray in 1610, Edward Oxley's uncle David Oxley, another son of Edward Oxley (d. 1567) and brother of George Oxley (d. 1598), was himself involved in a fatal fray with Edmund Brystowe in Gravesend in May 1576. Apprehended in Queenborough, he was questioned before Queenborough magistrates and bailiffs, imprisoned at Canterbury Castle, and tried at the Maidstone assizes on July 16, 1576.[19] Also suggestive of things to come, on June 5, 1606, Edward Oxley of Tonbridge, clothier, stood surety in a recognizance for Thomas Woody of Tonbridge, tailor, to keep the peace toward John Collyns and to appear before the next court of quarter sessions.[20] In a conveyance dated July 2, 1612, following his conviction for murder and subsequent release from the bishop's custody, Edward Oxley, clothier, son and heir of George Oxley, clothier, sold to Thomas Busse of Pembury, clothier, the messuage or tenement on the west side of the Tonbridge high street between two of the bridges, Busse having first signed a bond dated July 1, 1612, to pay from the income of the property certain bequests to George Oxley's widow. After signing a release to Thomas Busse on May 19, 1615, following the death of his mother, Edward Oxley disappears from the Tonbridge records.[21]

The apparent ringleader in the assault on Edward Calverley was the Tonbridge butcher John Holmden (Hombden/Homden/Homeden), probably in his fifties at the time of the assault. The Tonbridge parish register shows that John Holmden and Fayth Copyng were married on January 10, 1579/80, and had three children: Sara, daughter of John Holmden, buried on August 8, 1585; John, son of John Holmden, christened on May 18, 1598; and Elizabeth, daughter of John Holmden, christened on August 17, 1600. He may also be the "old John Holmden" whose second marriage to Alice Somers took place on November 23, 1641, and the "old John Holmden" who was buried on April 14, 1653.[22] In his later life he served a three-year term as one of the wardens of the town lands from Michaelmas 1622 to Michaelmas 1625,[23] but during his younger years he was a known brawler, connected to Edward Oxley through their joint association with the Tonbridge tailor Thomas Woody (Wooddy/Wooddin/Wooden/Woodyer), and no stranger to the quarter sessions and assize courts. On August 15, 1597, John Holmden was bound by magistrates to keep the peace toward John Coles of Great St. Bartholomew's, London, informer, to appear in the quarter sessions court, and to answer for his part in the affray; and he stood surety for Thomas Wooddin of Tonbridge, tailor, also charged in the same incident.[24] A year later in a second affray he again stood surety for Thomas Woddye, tailor, on September 12, 1598.[25] On February 25, 1600, both John Holmden and Thomas Woody appeared before the assize court at Rochester, the former delivered from jail by proclamation and the latter released on bail;[26] and on April 1, 1600, they both appeared before the quarter sessions court at Maidstone.[27] Two years later, in trouble yet again, John Holmden was bound on April 3, 1602 "to be of good behaviour" and to appear at the quarter sesions, a recognizance that was eventually discharged on September 28, 1602.[28]

The third defendant, William Beach (Beech/Beche/Bech), also appears in both the Tonbridge parish register and the Kent court records, although at least two people by this name may have been living in Tonbridge in 1610.[29] The parish register shows that John Beach married Mary Plane on January

21, 1583/84, and produced at least two children—Humphrey, son of John, christened February 5, 1586/87, and William, son of John, christened June 1, 1589—before Mary Beach died on May 28, 1593. This William Beach, son of John Beach, would have been twenty-one years old at the time of the assault on Edward Calverley in June 1610. However, the parish register also mentions a William Beach, "brother of John," who was buried on April 4, 1636, suggesting that the John Beach whose son William was born in 1589 may also have had a brother named William who died in 1636. This suggestion of uncle and nephew both named William and both in trouble with the law is supported by the quarter sessions recognizances dated July 29, 1611, binding William Beach of Tonbridge, butcher, and John Beach of Tonbridge, laborer, to keep the peace toward Walter Thompson of Pembury, yeoman, to appear at the next quarter sessions court, and to answer charges concerning that fray. Confusion of the William Beach, butcher, in this case with his nephew, the William Beach, tailor, in the assault on Edward Calverley in June 1610 is further suggested by the confusion of William Beach's occupation in the first assize indictment (mb. 11), where "butcher" has been corrected to "taylor," followed by the correct designation of "taylor" in the redrawn indictment (mb. 26). In addition to William Beach, butcher, and William Beach, tailor, a possible third William Beach of Tonbridge, laborer, was also brought before the Maidstone assizes on July 4, 1627, for desertion, having enlisted as a soldier and received money to serve overseas in April 1627, but in June 1627 having deserted and returned to Tonbridge.[30]

The other two participants in the playhouse fray make only brief appearances in the Tonbridge parish register. The fourth defendant, Sidney Francis, butcher, appears only twice in the register, when "Sidney, son of Sydney ffraunces" was christened on January 12, 1611/12, and buried ten days later on January 22, 1611/12.[31] If Sidney Francis, the father in these records, were the same Sidney Francis involved in the assault on Edward Calverley, he may have been in his twenties or thirties at the time. Several generations of the Calverley (Calvely/Calverley/Calverlie/Caverly/Caverle/Caverlaye) family appear in the parish register, but only James Calverley (d. 1574) left a will, and not enough information survives to assign the victim Edward Calverley definitely to a particular branch of the family. Since his name does not appear in the register of christenings, however, he must have been born before the opening of the register in April 1585, thus making him at least in his late twenties at the time of his death. The register of burials does record the burial of Edward Calverlie on July 23, 1610, and adds the significant information that he was "Sir Anthony Dentons man."[32]

The reason for the fray between Edward Oxley, John Holmden, William Beach, Sidney Francis, and Edward Calverley in the Tonbridge playhouse remains a mystery, but the even greater mystery is why there was a playhouse in Tonbridge in the first place. Only four other playhouses are known to have existed outside of London before the Restoration: at Bristol Nicholas Wolfe's Wine Street playhouse between 1604 and 1625 and Sarah Barker's playhouse sometime before 1637, the York playhouse in 1609, and the Prescot playhouse in Lancashire sometime between 1592 and 1609.[33] In the early seventeenth century, Tonbridge was certainly not a logical location. Many incorporated Kentish towns were much larger than Tonbridge: Faversham had a population of 1,500, Dover and Maidstone each about 3,000, and Sandwich about 4,000. The city of Canterbury boasted a population of around 6,000. In contrast, the unincorporated market town of Tonbridge had a population of around only 600 in the early seventeenth century.[34] Even though Tonbridge had a Norman castle guarding the important River Medway crossing on the main road from London to Hastings, Rye, and Winchelsea,[35] the city of Canterbury with a population ten times as great as that of Tonbridge would surely have been a more logical location for a playhouse in Kent. So the mystery remains. Why did a small, unincorporated market town in the sparsely populated Weald of Kent have a playhouse in the early seventeenth century?

The answer to that question remains conjectural, but several strands of circumstantial evidence all point toward two powerful barons and sympathetic supporters of Elizabethan players and playhouses: Henry Carey, 1st Lord Hunsdon (1526–96) and George Carey, 2nd Lord Hunsdon (1547–1603). In the first year of her reign on January 13, 1558/59, Elizabeth I had created her cousin Henry Carey the first baron of Hunsdon, and on March 20, 1558/59, for the maintenance of his rank of baron she settled on him the reversions and rents arising from numerous estates in York, Northamptonshire, Berkshire, Hertfordshire, and Kent, including "the manors of Tunbridge and Hadlowe, the castle of Tunbridge, parks called Le Cage Parke and Le Posterne Parke in Tunbridge and a park called Le Northe Frithe, co. Kent."[36] Not many manorial records survive for the manor of Tonbridge; however, "A Rentall of so muche of the Manors of Tunbridge and Hadlow as is in the handes of S*i*r George Carey knight, knight marshall of her ma*ie*sties houshold & Captayne of the Ile of wight made By Richard Sutton gentleman Stewarde theire the ffirst daye of Ianuarye 1586 and in the xxixth yere of the Raigne of owr most gracyous Sou*e*raigne ladie Elizabethe by the grace of god Quene of England ffraunce & Ireland defender of the faithe &c." does list all the rents and quit-rents from properties, tenements, and inns in the town under the control of the Careys as lords of the manor.[37] After the death of George Carey, 2nd Lord Hunsdon in 1603, possession of the manor of Tonbridge passed to his daughter Elizabeth Carey and her husband, Sir Thomas Berkeley, who early in the reign of James I sold the manor to Sir Peter Vanlore, the Dutch merchant banker and jeweler to the courts of Elizabeth I and James I.[38]

In addition to the influence of Henry Carey, Lord Hunsdon, and his successors as lords of the manor of Tonbridge, Henry Carey also obtained from Elizabeth I on May 14, 1571, the grant of a weekly market on Fridays in the borough of Tonbridge and three annual fairs to be held on the eve, day, and morrow of the Nativity of St. John the Baptist (June 23–25), the eve, day, and morrow of feast of St. Luke (October 17–19), and Ash Wednesday, the morrow, and the day afterward (three successive days between February 4 and March 12 depending on the date of Easter).[39] Not only did these markets and fairs allow Lord Hunsdon's bailiffs to collect the fines and stallage fees, providing a further source of revenue and a visible demonstration of the authority of the lord of the manor, but they apparently also provided an opportunity for his lordship's players to perform before a large guaranteed audience drawn from the surrounding villages and parishes. The fray at the Tonbridge playhouse, it should be noted, happened either on June 25, or June 26, dates that coincide with the Midsummer fair and suggest that players may have come to Tonbridge specifically for the occasion.[40]

Whether such performances at the Tonbridge playhouse were a regular feature at fair time and when such a custom might have begun are open to speculation. The interest of the lords Hunsdon in players and playhouses, however, is well-documented fact.[41] From July 4, 1585, until his death on July 23, 1596, Henry Carey, 1st Lord Hunsdon held the post of Lord Chamberlain in the court of Elizabeth I. After a brief hiatus between August 8, 1596, and March 6, 1597, when William Brooke, 10th Lord Cobham held the position, George Carey, 2nd Lord Hunsdon became Lord Chamberlain until his death on September 8, 1603. For almost a decade between May 1594 and September 1603 father and son sponsored the most famous theater company of their time—the Lord Chamberlain's Men—until the company gained a royal sponsor in 1603 and became the King's Men.[42] Henry Carey's interest in theater, however, had begun long before May 1594. Throughout his life an enthusiastic and sympathetic supporter of players and musicians, he sponsored over the years two additional acting companies. Between 1564 and 1567 Lord Hunsdon's players performed as far afield as Beverley, Bridgwater, Bristol, Dartmouth, Plymouth, Gloucester, Leicester, Newcastle upon Tyne, and Norwich, as well as closer to Tonbridge at Canterbury, Dover, and Lydd in Kent.[43] This early acting company seems to have disbanded, since no other payments to Lord Hunsdon's players, apart from a single payment in 1575–76 to a lone player in Norwich, appear in the records until the payment to "my Lord of hunsdons servauntes beinge players of interludes" at York in September 1581.[44] Between 1581 and 1585, however, his players were once again on the road, performing in Bath, Bristol, Doncaster, Dover, Exeter, Gloucester, Ludlow, Maidstone, Norwich, and Nottingham,[45] and on December 27, 1582, Lord Hunsdon's men played at court during the Christmas festivities.[46] After the Privy Council's establishment of the Queen's Men in February 1583, and his own appointment as Lord Chamberlain in July 1585, Henry Carey's personal players took a lower profile, since in his official capacity of providing the annual Christmas entertainment for the court he consistently favored the Queen's Men. Only once between his appointment as Lord Chamberlain in 1585 and the reorganization of the acting companies in 1594 did his own acting company appear at court—a joint performance with the Lord Admiral's Men on January 6, 1586.[47] Nevertheless, his players did continue to play in the country during the late 1580s, payments having been recorded in Coventry, King's Lynn, Leicester, and Saffron Walden between 1585 and 1588.[48] During the late 1590s the Kent records also include payments to George Carey's players: Lord Hunsdon's players performed in Faversham "about Lamas" 1596 during Lord Cobham's short tenure as the Lord Chamberlain, and the Lord Chamberlain's players under Carey's patronage performed between Michaelmas 1596 and Michaelmas 1597 in both Dover and Faversham.[49] After the Lord Chamberlain's Men became the King's Men in 1603, they continued to tour the Kent circuit, payments to the King's Men having survived at Canterbury, Dover, Faversham, Folkestone, Fordwich, Hythe, Lydd, Maidstone, and New Romney between 1604 and 1625.[50] Of course, if Lord Hunsdon's players were playing at the Tonbridge fairs during the 1580s, or even if the Lord Chamberlain's Men were performing there after 1594 or the King's Men after 1603, no official record would have survived, since Tonbridge was an unincorporated town without mayor, aldermen, or chamberlain. As a result, when players came to town, there would have been no official mayor's play nor any town accounts in which official payments could have been entered. Only the judicial evidence of the fray in the Tonbridge playhouse during the Midsummer fair in 1610 survives to hint at the possibility of regular dramatic performance in the town at fair time.

In addition to their lordship of the manor and their establishment of the annual fairs, a third strand of evidence further strengthens the link between the lords Hunsdon and Tonbridge: the role of Sir Anthony Denton (1561–1615) whose servant Edward Calverley was fatally wounded in the playhouse fray. Sir Anthony Denton descended from William Denton, gentleman, of Southwark, Surrey, and Stedham, Sussex.[51] Shortly before his death in 1565, William Denton had acquired from Alexander Colepeper the rectory of Tonbridge including "all lands, tithes and the like in Tunbridge Warde *alias* Le Townewarde and Southborowe Warde, parcels of the said Rectory in Tunbridge."[52] With this purchase he joined Henry Carey, Lord Hunsdon as a leading landowner in the town. On May 26, 1567, William Denton's widow, Margery, was granted wardship of their son and heir, Anthony Denton, with an annuity from the estate, until Anthony Denton received license to enter into his inheritance on April 29, 1583.[53] Meanwhile, Anthony Denton had matriculated at Brasenose College, Oxford, on December 8, 1578, and entered the Middle Temple of the Inns of Court in 1581.[54] Styled armigero by 1601, Sir Anthony Denton was knighted on July 23, 1603, in the royal garden at Whitehall before the coronation of James I.[55] On May 25, 1601, Anthony Denton married Elizabeth Isham, daughter of Thomas Isham of Lamport, and established a country residence at Tonbridge in addition to his two London houses.[56] On August 26, 1615, he unexpectedly died at the age of 54.[57]

On the south wall of the parish church of SS Peter and Paul, Tonbridge, where Sir Anthony Denton lies buried beneath a recumbent effigy of a knight in armor, an inscription states that Sir Anthony was "one of the Honorable band of Pensioners (both to our late, renouned Lady Q. Elizabeth, & also to our now soverain Lord K. James)."[58] The Honourable Band of Gentlemen Pensioners, established during the reign of Henry VIII, consisted of an elite group of fifty knights who in rotation provided a royal bodyguard, standing guard with their gilt battle axes in the presence chamber and accompanying the monarch to the chapel royal or the House of Lords.[59] On ceremonial occasions all fifty gentlemen pensioners, dressed in identical livery, each attended by his servant, created a striking display of pageantry. Many of their quarterly account rolls are missing, but surviving gentlemen pensioners' rolls reveal that Sir Anthony Denton was serving as a gentlemen pensioner by at least September 1602 and continued in that post until his death in August 1615.[60] During the latter half of the reign of Elizabeth I the captain of the Honourable Band of Gentlemen Pensioners was none other than Henry Carey, 1st Lord Hunsdon (1583–96), succeeded in the post by George Carey, 2nd Lord Hunsdon (1596–1603). Since patronage of gentlemen pensioner places belonged to the captain, subject to the assent of the monarch, it was George Carey who recruited fellow Tonbridge landowner Anthony Denton to join the Honourable Band of Gentlemen Pensioners.[61] Once again, the fray in the Tonbridge playhouse, where Edward Calverley, "Sir Anthony Dentons man," was fatally wounded on June 26, 1610, ends with a link to the lords Hunsdon.

Given these three strands of circumstantial evidence that connect the lords Hunsdon to Tonbridge, suggesting a conjectural answer to the question of why a small, unincorporated market town in the sparsely populated Weald of Kent had a playhouse in the early seventeenth century, it may be time to revisit the well-known evidence, and to reconsider the implications, of another playhouse fray in June 1584 outside the Theatre and the Curtain in Shoreditch.[62] The details of this fracas need not detain us here; suffice it to take note that William Fleetwood's report to the Privy Council about the fray states that James Burbage had described himself as "my Lo. of Hunsdons man." A leading member of Leceister's players and also a member of the Joiners livery company, James Burbage and his brother Robert Burbage, a member of the Carpenters livery company, had erected in 1576 the first purpose-built theater in London, named appropriately, if unimaginatively, the Theatre.[63] When other players of Leicester's company were incorporated into the Queen's Men in 1583, however, James Burbage had not followed suit, nor was he part of the group of actors that accompanied Leicester to the Low Countries in 1585 and 1586. Instead, from at least June 1584 until his probable association with Pembroke's Men in 1591 and perhaps later, he was wearing Henry Carey's livery.[64] In the absence of any other evidence, it has been generally assumed that Burbage passed these years in London as landlord of the Theatre, managing the premises for any acting company who wished to hire it for their London performances. However, given the connection of James Burbage with lord Hunsdon during the 1580s and given the connection of the Lords Hunsdon with Tonbridge and the heretofore unnoticed existence of a playhouse in Tonbridge in 1610, is it not time to start asking what else this leading theatrical entrepreneur might have been doing during the 1580s in Tonbridge when he was "my Lo. of Hunsdons man"?

Notes

1. London: The National Archives (TNA): Public Record Office (PRO) ASSI 35/53/5, mbs. 11, 26, 27. See also J. S. Cockburn, ed., *Calendar of Assize Records: Kent Indictments, James I* (London: Her Majesty's Stationery Office, 1980), 94. I owe thanks to Dr. Christopher Chalklin for drawing this reference to my attention and to Abigail Ann Young for checking the Latin transcriptions and translations.

2. The August 7 date in the inquest for Edward Calverley's death disagrees with the July 23 date in the parish register for his burial, but the latter is more likely to be reliable, having probably been entered on the day rather than recalled almost two months later. The earliest surviving register of the ancient parish chuch of SS Peter and Paul, Tonbridge (Maidstone: Centre for Kentish Studies (CKS): P371/1/15), contains baptisms (1585–1687), marriages (1563–1687), and burials (1559–1685). The register's folios are not numbered, but each section is arranged chronologically.

3. William Beach appears on the list of prisoners delivered to the court (TNA: PRO ASSI 35/53/5, mbs. 40–41), but the membranes are damaged and many of the other names are illegible.

4. A contemporary account of legal procedure in criminal cases may be found in chapter 23 of Sir Thomas Smith's *De Republica Anglorum*, ed. Mary Dewar (Cambridge: Cambridge University Press, 1982), 110–16. Benefit of clergy, or the privilege of being tried in the ecclesiastical courts, which did not award the death penalty, was granted during the early modern period to anyone who could read a verse in Latin from the Psalter. In cases of homicide benefit of clergy was offered only on the first offense. If a visible brand on the hand demonstrated that a convicted murderer had already "received his clergy" for a prior offense, then he was sentenced to be hanged. Unfortunately, the act books for the diocese of Rochester consistory court and archdeacon's court have not survived for this period, making it impossible to follow Edward Oxley's case to its conclusion after he was handed over to the bishop's representative.

5. Words enclosed in < > have been inserted above the line in the manuscript.

6. Diue*rsi* alij *for* diue*rse* alie

7. De has been corrected over p*ro* resulting in *de funditate* for *de profunditate*.

8. 18mm tear in the manuscript for *unius* (?)

9. 18mm tear in the manuscript for &c vsq*ue* (?)

10. 14mm tear in the manuscript for *quadragesimo*

11. 14mm tear in the manuscript for *Iacobi*

12. 10mm tear in the manuscript for p*redictam*

13. As Sir Thomas Smith explains, the clerk of the court entered these abbreviated phrases above the names of each prisoner, indicating the result of the proceedings. When first arraigned, the prisoner had three choices: he could plead guilty, whereupon the judge proceeded directly to the sentence; he could remain mute and be pressed to death, but his estate would not be forfeited to the Crown; or he could ask for a trial, and a jury would be called. The second phrase indicates the verdict of the jury. If the jury declared the prisoner guilty, then the judge inquired whether he had any goods or chattels that could be confiscated by the court. If the guilty prisoner requested benefit of clergy, the bishop's representative confirmed whether or not the prisoner could read the verse from the Vulgate.

14. Prisoners were divided into groups, and all the cases in the group were heard before the jury retired to consider its verdict, thus accounting for Edward Hunter and Abigail Harte, both indicted in separate counts of grand larceny, being included in this trial calendar with the four men indicted for murder. See J. S. Cockburn, ed., *Calendar of Assize Records: Kent Indictments James I*; (London: Her Majesty's Stationery Office, 1980), 94.

15. CKS: Drb/Pwr13, ff. 341v–42v.

16. CKS: U422/Q7, 2.

17. CKS: Drb/Pwr19A, ff. 24–26v.

18. CKS: P371/1/15. It is possible that there were two Edward Oxleys in Tonbridge in 1610. John Oxley, another son of Edward Oxley (d. 1567) and brother of George Oxley (d. 1598), in his will dated November 16, 1575 (CKS: Drb/Pwr14, ff. 262v–63) divided his estate between his sons Richard and Edward, neither of whom had reached the age of twenty-one in 1575. Although the marriage of Richard Oxley to Anne Latter is recorded in the parish register on August 1, 1591, there is no further mention in the register of his brother Edward, who would have been a cousin of the Edward Oxley, son of George Oxley.

19. For the articles of examination and writ to the sheriff in this case, see CKS: Qb/ZB15–17. The record of the July 16, 1576 assize court is missing.

20. CKS: QM/SRc/1606/132.

21. This conveyance, bond, and release are among a bundle of title deeds in the Tonbridge Library Archives, TU1/T2.

22. CKS: P371/1/15.

23. CKS:U422/Q7, 23.

24. CKS: QM/SRc/1597/100 and QM/SRc/1597/102.

25. CKS: QM/SRc/1598/93.

26. TNA: PRO ASSI 35/42/5, mb. 41v. See also J. S. Cockburn, ed., *Calendar of Assize Records: Kent Indictments; Elizabeth I* (London: Her Majesty's Stationery Office, 1979), 454. To be delivered or "quitte by proclamation" means that, though the prisoner had been indicted, no one appeared to give evidence at his arraignment before the assize court, and thus the judge proclaimed him to be at liberty. See Sir Thomas Smith, *De Republica Anglorum*, ed., Mary Dewar (Cambridge: Cambridge University Press, 1982), 110.

27. CKS: Q/SR1, mb. 7.

28. CKS: QM/SRc/1602/61 and Q/SR3, mb. 11d.

29. CKS: P371/1/15; QM/SRc/1611/35; and QM/SRc/1611/36.

30. TNA: PRO ASSI 35/69/8, mb. 41; see also J. S. Cockburn, ed., *Calendar of Assize Records: Kent Indictments; Charles I* (London: Her Majesty's Stationery Office, 1995), 53. Earlier records of the Rochester assizes on March 26, 1599 (ASSI 35/41/2, mb. 69v): also include a William Beach (residence and occupation unknown) among the list of suspects delivered from jail by proclamation. See J. S. Cockburn, ed., *Calendar of Assize Records: Kent Indictments; Elizabeth I* (London: Her Majesty's Stationery Office, 1979), 441. If this William Beach came from Tonbridge, the date would be too early for William Beach, tailor, but could fit the criminal record of William Beach, butcher.

31. CKS: P371/1/15.

32. Ibid.

33. Mark C. Pilkinton, ed., *Bristol,* Records of Early English Drama (Toronto: Toronto University Press, 1997), xxxvii–xl and passim; Alexandra F. Johnston and Margaret Rogerson, eds., *York,* Records of Early English Drama (Toronto: Toronto University Press, 1979), 530–31; David George, ed., *Lancashire,* Records of Early English Drama (Toronto: Toronto University Press, 1991), xliv–xlv, 80–82, 240–41.

34. Christopher W. Chalklin, "A Seventeenth-Century Market Town: Tonbrirdge," *Archaeologia Cantiana* 76 (1962): 152–62. For a more in-depth study of the town, see Christopher W. Chalklin, "A Kentish Wealden Parish (Tonbridge), 1550–1750." Unpublished BLitt thesis (Oxford, 1960).

35. On Philip Symonson's 1596 map, "A New Description of Kent," Watling Street divides just west of Deptford, the main branch continuing eastward toward Rochester, Canterbury, and Dover, and the other branch dropping southeastward through the Weald to Bromley, Sevenoaks, Tonbridge, and Rye. See Henry Hannen, "An Account of a Map of Kent Dated 1596," *Archaeologia Cantiana* 30 (1914): 85–92, with facsimile of the map facing p. 85.

36. *Calendar of the Patent Rolls: Elizabeth,* vol. 1, 1558–1560 (London: Her Majesty's Stationery Office, 1939), 60–61, 115–18. See also J. F. Wadmore, "Tonbridge Castle and its Lords," *Archaeologia Cantiana* 6 (1886): 12–57, esp. 52.

37. CKS: U38/M1. Unfortunately, the rental does not contain sufficient detail to establish the location and use of most of the properties.

38. CKS: U55/T422 (title deeds for Tonbridge castle and manor); see also Edward Hasted, *The History and Topographical Survey of the County of Kent,* 12 vols. (Canterbury: W. Bristow, 1797–1801), 5:216–17.

39. *Calendar of the Patent Rolls: Elizabeth I,* vol. 5, 1569–1572 (London: Her Majesty's Stationery Office, 1966), 240.

40. On the first indictment (mb. 11) the fray is first said to have taken place on "xxv^{to} die Iunij" and then in a later reference on "eodem xxvj^{to} die Iunij." The second redrawn indictment (mb. 26) has June 26 in both places.

41. A convenient summary of the acting companies supported by Henry Carey, 1st Lord Hunsdon and George Carey, 2nd Lord Hunsdon may be found in Andrew Gurr, *The Shakespearian Playing Companies* (Oxford: Clarendon Press, 1996), 278–305. Performance dates, however, should be double-checked against those in the REED volumes.

42. Between August 8, 1596, and March 6, 1597, when Lord Cobham was the Lord Chamberlain, the acting company was known as Lord Hunsdon's Men.

43. David Galloway, ed., *Norwich, 1540–1642*, Records of Early English Drama (Toronto: Toronto University Press, 1984), 52; Audrey Douglas and Peter Greenfield, eds., *Cumberland Westmorland Gloucestershire*, Records of Early English Drama (Toronto: Toronto University Press, 1986), 300; J. J. Anderson, ed., *Newcastle upon Tyne*, Records of Early English Drama (Toronto: Toronto University Press, 1982), 45; John M. Wasson, ed., *Devon*, Records of Early English Drama (Toronto: Toronto University Press, 1986), 65, 237; James Stokes and Robert J. Alexander, ed., *Somerset*, Records of Early English Drama (Toronto: Toronto University Press, 1996), 49; Mark C. Pilkinton, ed., *Bristol*, Records of Early English Drama (Toronto: Toronto University Press, 1997), 52; and James M. Gibson, ed., *Kent: Diocese of Canterbury*, Records of Early English Drama (Toronto: Toronto University Press, 2002), 194, 465, 698. See also Andrew Gurr, *The Shakespearian Playing Companies* (Oxford: Clarendon Press, 1996), 302.

44. Galloway, ed., *Norwich, 1540–1642*, 58, and Johnston and Rogerson, eds., *York*, 397.

45. Stokes and Alexander, ed., *Somerset*, 13; Pilkinton, ed., *Bristol*, 124; Gibson, ed., *Kent: Diocese of Canterbury*, 477, 716; Wasson, ed., *Devon*, 159; Douglas and Greenfield, eds., *Cumberland Westmorland Gloucestershire*, 308; J. Alan B. Somerset, *Shropshire*, Records of Early English Drama (Toronto: Toronto University Press, 1994), 87; and Galloway, ed., *Norwich, 1540–1642*, 64–65. See also Andrew Gurr, *The Shakespearian Playing Companies* (Oxford: Clarendon Press, 1996), 302

46. E. K. Chambers, *The Elizabethan Stage*, 4 vols. (Oxford: Clarendon Press, 1923), 4:159.

47. Chambers, *The Elizabethan Stage*, 4:161.

48. Andrew Gurr, *The Shakespearian Playing Companies* (Oxford: Clarendon Press, 1996), 302; Malone Society, *Collections XI*, 64. Musicians and bearwards of Lord Hunsdon also performed throughout the 1580s in Coventry, as well as several times between 1574 and 1578. See R. W. Ingram, ed., *Coventry*, Records of Early English Drama (Toronto: Toronto University Press, 1981), 269, 270, 286, 300, 302, 310, 313, 317, 323.

49. Gibson, ed., *Kent: Diocese of Canterbury*, 484, 562.

50. Ibid., 271, 273, 495, 499, 513, 515, 566, 570, 586, 602–3, 633, 638–40, 710, 723–24, 806–8, 811–12.

51. William Berry, *County Genealogies: Pedigrees of the Families of the County of Kent*, 2 vols. (London: Sherwood, Gilbert and Piper, 1830), 451; TNA: PRO PROB 11/48, ff. 195v–97v.

52. TNA: PRO C.66/1016, mb. 33. See *Calendar of the Patent Rolls: Elizabeth I, vol. 3, 1563–1566* (London: Her Majesty's Stationery Office, 1960), 305.

53. TNA: PRO C.66/1039, mb. 25, and C.66/1236, mbs. 8–9. See *Calendar of the Patent Rolls: Elizabeth I,* vol. 4, 1566–1569 (London: Her Majesty's Stationery Office, 1964), 127. Various other title deeds relating to Anthony Denton's estate include a license to alienate, September 25, 1587 (TNA: PRO C.66/1316, mb. 8); a pardon for alienation of the rectory of Tonbridge, May 8, 1588 (TNA: PRO 66/1309, mb. 16); and a grant of the rectory of Tonbridge to Margery Martyn, widow; Anthony Denton, armigero; and William Denton, March 2, 1601 (TNA: PRO C.66/1548, mb. 9).

54. Joseph Foster, *Alumni Oxoniensis: The Members of the University of Oxford, 1500–1714,* 4 vols. (London: Parker, 1891), 1:395.

55. William Shaw, *The Knights of England,* 2 vols. (London: Heraldry Today, 1971), 2:120. Shaw mistakenly gives Sir Anthony's residence as Buckinghamshire, having confused the Dentons of Tonbridge with the Dentons of Hillsden.

56. Northamptonshire Record Office: I.C.3652B, Anthony Denton letter to Thomas Isham, November 19, "we are intended to continewe att Tunbridge vntill wee can make an end of our buildinge, and recover in some sort our expenses . . . I ame carefull concerninge my Sister Susan, but hither to I have mett with no encounter to my mynde, yf she hath not taken a surfett of Tunbridge, my wife and I would be gladd of hir company there"; I.C.3654, Anthony Denton letter to John Isham, March 15, "my house and furniture here in Kent hath coste me above six hundred poundes"; and I.C.4849, Elizabeth Denton letter to John Isham, n.d., "I was in good hope to have seene you heere this last terme, vntill my cosen Iohn Gilpin tould mee otherwise who was with mee at Tunbridge after his return from you." See also Mary E. Finch, *The Wealth of Five Northamptonshire Families, 1540–1640,* Publications of the Northamptonshire Record Society, 18, vol. 19 (Lampert, 1956), 26–27.

57. On September 18, 1615, Lady Elizabeth Denton was granted a letter of administration of his estate (TNA: PRO PROB 6/9, f. 32), and on November 2, 1615, an inquisition postmortem at Dartford found that by a prenuptial agreement with Thomas Isham, dated May 1, 1601, Sir Anthony Denton had settled on his wife the rectory of Tonbridge and other lands in Kent (TNA: PRO WARD 7/53/274). On April 20, 1625, sometime after her remarriage, Paul Dewes of Stowlaugh in Sussex and Dame Elizabeth his wife (widow of Sir Anthony Denton), granted to William Denton the elder of Tonbridge (brother of Sir Anthony), Ann his wife, and William Denton and Anthony Denton, their sons, all their interest in the rectory of Tonbridge with appurtenances (CKS: U55/T423).

58. A photograph of the monument appears in the anonymous booklet *The Story of the Parish Church of St. Peter & St. Paul Tonbridge,* [n.d.], 14.

59. For general background on the gentlemen pensioners, see W. J. Tighe, *The Gentlemen Pensioners in Elizabethan Politics and Government,* (Cambridge University Ph.D., 1983); also "An Account of the King's Honourable Band of Gentlemen Pensioners from its Establishment to the present Time," being part 2 of Samuel Pegge, *Curialia, or An Historical Account of Some Branches of the Royal Household* (London: B. White, 1791).

60. Each roll lists the names of the gentlemen pensioners, the number of days served, and the quarterly payments for wages (£46 13s. 4d. per annum) and board (2s. 6d. per diem). The following rolls contain payments to Sir Anthony Denton: TNA: PRO E 407/1/35, September 29– December 31 1602; E 407/1/36, September 29–December 31, 1603; E 407/1/37, March 25–June 24, 1605; E 407/1/38, March 25–1 January 1607; E 407/1/39, June 24–September 29, 1609; E 407/1/40, January 1–March 25, 1611; and E 407/1/41, March 25–June 24, 1613. See also Tighe, *The Gentlemen Pensioners,* 357.

61. TNA: PRO E 407/1/15-E 407/1/35; Tighe, *The Gentlemen Pensioners,* 41.

62. Letter of William Fleetwood to Lord Burghley, 18 June 1584, as quoted in E.K. Chambers, *The Elizabethan Stage* 4 vols. (Oxford, 1923), 4:297–8.

63. For a summary of James Burbage's life and theatrical career, see Chambers, *The Elizabethan Stage,* 2:305–6; William Ingram, *The Business of Playing* (Cornell, 1992), 182–218; William Ingram, "The Early Career of James Burbage," *Elizabethan Theatre* 10 (1988): 18–36; and Mary Edmond, "Yeomen, Citizens, Gentlemen, and Players: The Burbages and Their Connections," in *Elizabethan Theater: Essays in Honor of S. Schoenbaum.* ed. by R. B. Parker and S. P. Zitner, (Newark: University of Delaware Press, 1996).

64. Andrew Gurr, *The Shakespeare Company, 1594–1642* (Cambridge: Cambridge University Press, 2004), 1 and 8, asserts that in 1594 James Burbage had been wearing Henry Carey's livery for at least twelve years and implies that he continued to do so even after the reorganization of the theater companies in 1594.

Review Essays

This Strange, Eventful History . . .

Shakespeare's Serial History Plays, by Nicholas Grene. Cambridge: Cambridge University Press, 2002. Pp. xvii + 278. Cloth $80.00.

The Cambridge Companion to Shakespeare's History Plays, edited by Michael Hattaway. Cambridge: Cambridge University Press, 2002. Pp. xvii + 283. Cloth $70.00.

Reviewer: Andrew James Hartley

It is unsurprising that books on the histories should be so shot through with anxiety about what history actually is, how it is constructed, staged, and analyzed. But there is something more here, something shifting and opalescent concerning their own historical (or historicist) perspective, their own place in history and their sense of what might be better termed historiography, which seems almost deliberately indeterminate. In both books history becomes a catchall, though a catchall of different kinds, which facilitates the projects at hand and lends authority to their various claims and arguments without ever coming out into the light where the reader can see what it is.

Grene's book, as many readers will know, is the more controversial of the two, and seems to posit a claim for the sequential organization, composition, and staging for Shakespeare's first tetralogy, while making something like the reverse argument for the second, claiming that the plays were generated one at a time, the author keeping an eye on the box office for signs of when to stop. But I say "seems" advisedly, for the historical grounding of the thesis is oddly cursory, taking only the first 23 pages of this 278 page study. The core argument concerning the first tetralogy unfolds roughly like this.

1. The plays were written in sequence beginning with *1 Henry VI*—contrary to the opinion of the Oxford editors and others—as they appear in the First Folio. This claim rests less on new evidence than it does on new readings of old evidence ("ne" in Henslowe's diary could mean "newly licensed" rather than simply "new"), and much of it comes from a commonsensical reading of internal evidence within the plays. If we are to believe that *2 Henry VI* (published as *The First Part of the Contention*) was in fact written before *1 Henry VI*, we have to believe that Shakespeare chose to begin his history in 1444, an obscure period in the middle of a muddled reign, and that he chose to pass over all reference to

Talbot, the obvious hero of the French wars. This is, Grene suggests, beyond counterintuitive. The plays show evidence of careful "seeding" of characters who will be drawn upon later, and of a patterning of curse and prophecy that clearly knows where the sequence is going. Shakespeare the upstart crow, furthermore, was not beautified by the feathers of other writers from whom he had plagiarized. He began at the beginning of Henry VI's reign. He did not write of Talbot and the French wars in *2 Henry VI* because he had already covered them. He was the Johannes factotum who had dared to do what no other writer of the period had, and drawn up an epic historical series of four plays.

2. The plays were staged in sequence in the 1590s. This ingenious argument is grounded on evidence that, following the two parts of *Tamburlaine,* Henslowe regularly bought or commissioned sequels which, after their initial novelty value had worn off, were staged on the day following the original piece. Though all the hard evidence is for two-part plays (and there are numerous examples), Grene speculates that Shakespeare's first tetralogy did the same.

Grene is, of course, not the first to buck the Oxford editors' arguments about the sequencing of the first tetralogy (Michael Hattaway, editor of the *Cambridge Companion to the Histories,* has made similar arguments), though he is the first to utilize such a claim (and that about original performance conditions) to make a case for treating the first tetralogy as a unit— albeit an admittedly disparate one. It is premised on the assumption that the textual history is incomplete, that the shreds and patches on which the nonsequential argument is based indicates not proof but absence. The Folio was right all along, says Grene, and our overanalysis of incomplete records has led us to the wrong conclusions. There is something quite appealing about this, and many readers will concede that the evidence for the contrary position is indeed partial and open to reinterpretation, but it must also be said that a new perspective does not change the evidence at hand, and one is left feeling that Grene can offer only a leap of faith. The proof of this particular pudding (pending the discovery of new evidence) is less in the archives and more in what such a view of the tetralogy as a unit can generate for reading and performance.

The problem, of course, is that as he insists that the external historical evidence can be reread, others will say the same of his internal evidence. Yes, the first tetralogy features prophecy and curse in ways the more retrospective second tetralogy does not, but is this evidence of a different mode of composition or merely of their different positions within the larger narrative? After all "larger narrative" need not mean the histories as a series (or even *two* series), but might stand for history itself, the great swath of time that constructed crucial elements of Shakespeare and his audience's present. Grene seeks to affirm a continuity between the plays of the first tetralogy, though one, he says, is not "the Tudor Myth" of Tillyard, though it isn't clear what finally *is* unified about the series beyond their rootedness in a common his-

tory and a certain linkedness that would be expected in a single author's use
of repeated characters. Indeed, the different phases of the story, each embodied in a different play (patriotic war with France [*1 Henry VI*], internal jars
of faction and class [*2 Henry VI*], revenge and the brutal chaos of war [*3
Henry VI*], memory, moral collapse and renewal [*Richard III*]), might as
much affirm the separateness of each project as they do the discreet phases
of a single series.

By contrast, the second tetralogy, according to Grene, though written in
sequence was not mapped out as the first was. By the end of the 1590s, the
serial history play was a less sure thing in terms of marketability, and each
of the plays was thus given its own complete form and unity (even if, as in *1*
and *2 Henry IV*) it's the same unity, the author always being ready to pull the
plug on the sequence. Thus, the version of *Henry V* that is anticipated by the
epilogue to *2 Henry IV* bears little resemblance to the play that actually got
written. The evidence for this claim is even scanter than that offered for his
previous argument and, again, hinges mainly on internal evidence within the
plays. The second tetralogy, for example, is less shaped by prophecy and
curse than the first, working more by the retrospective rehearsal of what has
gone before, and there is less seeding of characters. But isn't this the inevita-
ble consequence of having already done the future in the first tetralogy? If
each play resonates with the past (as, say the *Henry IV* plays dwell on the
events of *Richard II*) doesn't that simply emphasize the significance and clear
causal links to the action that follows Bullingbrook's usurpation of the
crown? It seems that Grene falls prey to his own argument here. If he can
contend that Shakespeare would not have passed up a chance to write about
Talbot unless he had already done so and that it would make no sense to begin
the story with *2 Henry VI* because of the obscure events that that play initially
dramatizes, then how are we to imagine a Shakespeare who would only tack
on a play about *Henry V* because market conditions allowed him to, that he
didn't see a sequential logic building toward the reign of that particular king?
Internal aesthetic and structural evidence is a double-edged sword, and if one
lives by it in the first tetralogy, then surely one dies by it in the second. If it's
logical to begin the first tetralogy at Henry V's funeral, doesn't it make equal
sense that the second tetralogy was conceived to end immediately prior to
that event? My point is not that the second tetralogy *was* conceived and executed as a series, but that Grene's logic seems faulty and that his mode of
argumentation seems selective and depends on a sense of the artist and his
creative product, which is inevitably subjective.

While there is much interest in conceiving one tetralogy as a series and the
other as individual plays, there is finally little here to prove either case. That
is, perhaps, all to the good, for definitive proof, it seems to me, would close
off more than it opened, particularly in terms of how the plays might be explored onstage. Indeed, part of what is frustrating about the book is the way

that its (fairly halfhearted) argument about the historical composition of the tetralogies hijacks the many rich and suggestive readings of both the plays and their adaptation for various significantly different productions. One sometimes feels that the book would work better—be less distracting—if the whole was framed without the historical/textual claim at all, presenting itself as a study of the plays onstage in (and out of) sequence/series.

Grene's consideration of the plays in performance is a case in point. He begins with a narrative of the recent performance history of the plays as a series originating with the romantics (especially in Germany) as a national monument. Viewing the plays as series required tearing them from the unreverential hands of the eighteenth- and nineteenth-century actor managers. Grene argues convincingly that the (re)discovery of the history play series required the institutionalization of Shakespeare as a cultural monument and a concomitant development of noncommercial, subsidized theatres. Groundbreaking productions included "The Ten Chronicle Plays of William Shakespeare" at the Pasadena Playhouse in 1935 and the influential *1–3 Henry VI* series at the Birmingham Repertory Theatre. In the twentieth century, the tradition continued with such productions as *The Wars of the Roses* (Royal Shakespeare Company [RSC], 1963, Elizabethan Shakespeare Company [ESC] 1987–88), *The Plantagenets* (RSC, 1988), and *This England: The Histories* (RSC, 2000–2001).

The embedding of textual analysis with commentary on performances sometimes creates fissures of its own. When the petitioner who had faked blindness in *2 Henry VI,* for example, is ordered off to be beaten in modern productions, Grene says that sympathy tends to fall on his wife's "Alas, sir, we did it for pure need." "In an Elizabethan context" says Grene, "this may have been otherwise" (76). Well, yes, it *may,* but for which members of the audience? In every production? There is sometimes an oddly untheatrical sense of performance history here, one that seems to treat modern productions as adaptive and Elizabethan productions as somehow less so. While Grene concedes that there can be no such thing as a "straight" performance (then or now), his readings of the plays occasionally lean toward a univocality, which he comes close to equating with how the plays would have originally been staged and, apparently, received. He's too smart to say this outright, of course, but the idea seems to ghost the curious slippage from close textual analysis to performance history and review. Part of this stems also from a sort of neoconservatism in matters of authorship, Shakespeare the artist visible (as the original performances are visible) in the plays' textual traces, revealed almost cinematically by Grene as Shakespeare studying the pages of his sources (or at least, some of them: some get little coverage) as he carves out his masterpiece.

Where the analysis becomes grounded in description (what happens when you treat the plays as a series onstage?) rather than polemic (this is why they should/should not be considered a series), the reading experience becomes more enjoyable and more productive. Eschewing Renaissance history, for example, allows him to make a compelling case for why the twentieth century has found series productions fruitful because of the audience's familiarity with modernist long fiction and television series or soap operas, in which characters evolve over long periods. Grene argues that while the first tetralogy does not lend itself to a conventional (or a Bloomian) notion of character, the characters being largely driven by overarching historical narrative and depicted in stylized ways bound to rhetoric, they supply onstage (and he's careful not to say either consciously or textually) a series of independent scenes—stills—which, when dealt with as a series, create (the illusion of?) character development over time.

Grene goes on to detail certain performance approaches directors have taken in tackling apparent shifts in character in which directors invested in a larger view of character development create a sense of dynamism and fluidity in the execution of certain roles. Is York, for instance, a shrewd politician concealing his motives from everyone but the audience (Barton/Hall's *Wars of the Roses*), or a callow youth who gradually toughens, motivated in part by a genuine thirst for revenge (Jane Howell's BBC *1 Henry VI*)? His claim finally is cautious. On York, he says: "this need not have a sharp specificity of individual 'character,' the specificity that we associate with later Shakespearean characterization. Yet it makes for a complex, weighted sense of York's life as it comes to its end in the final confrontation with Margaret, whether that scene is played as grandly heroic in suffering or stoically enduring" (108). The key word here is "played," and it strains much of what Grene is trying to do, working against the idea he seems to want to hold on to that there is a direct continuity between text and performance, something some of his more adaptive directors clearly don't assume.

Similarly: "Even if we accept G. K. Hunter's proposition of the discontinuity of the character of the Queen—'Each Margaret (*Henry VI* I, II, III and *Richard III*) is in fact a different Margaret'—the effect of one actor playing those Margarets is likely to supply an illusion of continuity, of change and development" (117). This is an important point, one Grene prepares well in his discussion of twentieth-century notions of character, but his confessional use of the word "illusion" throws the value of the larger observation into question, at least for those critics who see such arguments as ultimately being about the plays as historical and textual entities.

The resultant problem is a familiar one in books about theater that build most of their arguments around what is said in play texts, and it raises doubts about what Grene is trying to do. Is this an argument about the plays as texts, the plays in the original performances, or in subsequent productions? As he tries to do all three, there is a palpable sense of the project fragmenting, of each section's interesting elements not quite making the bridge into the next section. Ambitious—even laudable—though it is to try and do textual analysis, history, and performance studies simultaneously, there seems to be inadequate explanation for how these disparate elements are supposed to relate to each other, or what larger argument their discrete parts are supposed to construct. It is ironic that a study of the plays as series should finally feel so episodic.

It might also be said that some of his better observations seem quite divorced from his larger thesis, and the more he tries to fit them into the "series" argument, the more the logic and eloquence seem to strain. "The chickens coming home to roost in *Richard III* have long been flying through the night skies of the *Henry VI* plays" (128), he says. This is certainly true in terms of the way that that last play builds on events already dramatized in the others, but to make this an argument about the coherence of the series *as series* in matters of character, narrative structure, the actual sequence of the writing and so forth requires a leap of imaginative faith like that which allows chickens to fly.

The book is perhaps strongest where it utilizes recent performance examples to explore issues such as the character "through-line" and leaves the question of whether or not that through-line is generated by performance conditions or textual traces. Grene argues that the genre is defined partly by its hybridity, and though the nature of that hybridity shifts from play to play it does not render the plays separate. Indeed, as he states in his conclusion, his primary claim (more than any argument about composition) is that "tetralogy thinking" (to use Barbara Hodgdon's phrase) does not necessarily suggest a Tillyardian, nationalist, historical epic or even plays of ideological or aesthetic uniformity. More problematic is his suggestion that the unfashionable nature of such "tetralogy thinking" and its often politically conservative manifestations is responsible for the "disintegration" theories of textual scholarship (246).

Companions to literature are curious beasts. Part of the problem lies in their polyvocality and the fact that those different voices are yoked together not in pursuit of a single issue but as part of a gesture toward the encyclopedic. They can be subtle, argumentative, even polemic, but they ultimately have to serve students as much as—or more than—academics. In this respect, the *Cambridge Companion to Shakespeare's History Plays* is more curious than most. While several of the essays are intelligent, insightful, and lucid, some seem out of place, poorly constructed, or polemic, which, in the context of a *Companion,* is peculiar, and muddies the book's purposes.

The book is divided into three parts titled "Contexts," "The Plays," and "Reference Material." The first two sections contain five and nine chapters respectively, the third being comprised of a list of principal characters and their histories along with various genealogical tables, and a further reading section. The longest section (157 pages) is devoted to readings of the plays, but it includes a chapter on "Theatrical afterlives" (Stuart Hampton-Reeves), one on the Roman plays (Robert S. Miola), and one on Shakespeare's "other" historical plays (R. A. Foakes), which deals with *Troilus and Cressida, King Lear, Macbeth, Cymbeline,* and *Henry VIII (All is True).* While these additional chapters are worthy of attention, they necessarily squeeze the space permitted for those plays that students are most likely to consider "histories."

The problem, of course, is what one means by history, and the Foakes and Miola chapters are both at pains to demonstrate that the plays they discuss show many of the same features as those of the tetralogies and *King John.* Miola offers a compelling reading of Rome as both strange and familiar to Shakespeare's audience, an object of fascinating Otherness and disarming proximity, while Foakes offers a model of history as being in dialogue with myth as it interrogates historiography. The problem with such definitions of the history play, of course, is that they are applicable to much (even most) of Shakespeare. All Shakespeare's plays manifest his present in dialogue with versions of the past, or explore ideas about government by analogy with other places. Many settings are both strange and familiar (Vienna in *Measure for Measure,* for example, or Venice in *The Merchant of Venice*), and while such plays insist less on their "pastness" than do *Macbeth* or *Troilus and Cressida,* they fulfill most of the other criteria. What about *Timon of Athens,* or *Pericles,* which get no such coverage in this collection? My point is not that they should, but that to call *Titus Andronicus* a history play when they aren't seems at best worthy of clarification, at worst inconsistent. This is a bifold issue because on the one hand it raises the philosophical question about what constitutes a history play, but on the other it raises the simpler, more pragmatic concern about what gets coverage (and I will return to that loaded term) in a collection such as this.

Such issues, like the plays, cannot exist out of context, and in this case we must surely take into account what students know about history. This is not the place to rehearse a familiar and arguable diatribe about what students no longer know, but it is a reasonable forum for asking what we expect them to need from a book like this and whether they are going to get it. I should begin by saying that some of the material in this book is extremely good, including the pieces by Foakes, Miola, and Hampton-Reeves. James C. Bulman's essay on the two parts of *Henry IV* is exemplary as a study of crucial political and thematic elements in the plays that is intelligently contextualized by matters such as the attraction and danger of the chivalric code to the court of Elizabeth and members like Essex in particular. Bulman is especially good on the link between acting and kingship and on the way that the second part of the play depicts the "other" England with its tavern and brothels and farms in contention with the ultimately faceless tools of political authority.

Similarly engaging and instructive is Robyn Bolam's "*Richard II:* Shakespeare and the Language of the Stage." As in Bulman, the chapter weaves a compelling blend of textual analysis and history, placing Elizabeth's alleged self-identification with Richard II in the context of their involvement in the deaths of powerful relatives (Mary Queen of Scots and Thomas of Woodstock), and using the details of the Essex rebellion to consider instabilities of text, meaning, and genre, which are essential to *Richard II* and how it was understood onstage. Bolam's consideration of verse form and other matters of language is rewarding, as is his use of four (all English) productions.

Similarly, A. J. Piesse offers a subtle consideration of *King John* and its shifting status within the canon, arguing that the play's apparent inconsistencies are emblematic of the play's notion of historiography: that the play's unstable characterization and structure reflects a similar view of history. In the context of Bale's *King Johan* and *The Troublesome Reign*, Shakespeare's play doesn't search for stability so much as examine complexity and discontinuity. While the bastard has drawn the most attention, the similarly unstable women characters seem to focus on the nature of writing and playing history. Indeed, they question what history means for women like Constance who can be politicians but are ultimately set against the male authority of the Church and who reveal their private worlds as wives and mothers, which matter "more than any kind of dispassionate chronicling" (134). King John himself is incomplete, a shifting, vascillating figure with no core self, dodging responsibility at every turn. In Arthur there is a potentially salvific "harmony between personal history and the broader notion of seeming and proper integrity" (137). But Arthur dies glimpsing the extent to which the King is England ("my uncle's spirit is in these stone"), demonstrating that England isn't nurturing, it is death dealing. "By constructing an eccentric central figure [the Bastard], and by making the obvious central figure centreless, Shakespeare continually and consistently draws attention to point of view in a way that a simple chorus figure cannot" (137). The bastard, Piesse contends, is unstable as a commentator, because history is unstable. "Prompted by the alternate views of history provided by Eleanor, Constance and Arthur, the various voices of the Bastard interrogate the legitimacy of the historical medium in which he has been drawn" (139).

Probably the strongest essay in the "contexts" section is Phyllis Rackin's lucid essay on the roles of women in the histories. She sketches a picture of the first tetralogy where women are either scary, even demonic destabilizers of the social order or sympathetically drawn passive victims. In the second tetralogy they recede, and where they are present without being scary, the mood shifts toward burlesque. This picture shifts however as we move to the margins of the canon, and Rackin argues that there is an inverse correlation between the prominence of women's roles in a history and its prominence in the canon, a relationship she suggests is causal. The dismissal of the *Henry VI* plays, *King John, Henry VIII,* and *Edward III* to the realm of immature hackwork is at odds with the plays' effectiveness onstage, particularly in the early modern period, something that may derive in part from the page's inability to convey the charisma of the women onstage, an argument she supports with reference to the size of the female audience at the first performances.

The women's roles in these plays invert the familiar truisms about women in the Renaissance in ways potentially aligned to the play's representation of history. In a play such as *Edward III,* for example (the authorship of which she is cagey about), the Countess of Salisbury resists military and sexual assault in ways proving her virtue and her defense of her husband's "property." This counters that canonical position "echoed by recent scholars who repeat it as an endlessly circulated 'truth' about Elizabethan culture" (79): the good woman is passive, the active woman must be a whore. Women can be virtuous or powerful, but not both. The author of *Edward III* deviates from his sources to make Queen Phillipa pregnant at the battle of Newcastle, conflating her military prowess with her impending childbirth and motherhood. There is plenty of evidence of women warriors in the medieval period, so Rackin suggests that it's unhistorical to assume this didn't happen even if such Amazonian behavior would have been burdened with negative assumptions in the Renaissance. "By the end of the sixteenth century," she says, "virtuous women no longer led armies: the constriction of women's roles which was to become one of the salient features of modernity was already well under way" (84).

Not all the chapters bear such fruit, however, and some are hard to justify in a collection of this kind. One such example is A. J. Hoenselaars's "Shakespeare and the Early Modern History Play," which attempts to place Shakespeare's histories in the context of contemporary histories, particularly with those written on the Continent. The latter, he says, have been woefully neglected, with Shakespeare and the English history player hogging the spotlight, though it is clear from what follows that the history play on the Continent is largely a seventeenth-century phenomenon. Such plays are interesting, particularly insofar as they are bound to matters of contemporary politics, and insofar as they shape the history play as a European, early modern phenomenon rather than an English Elizabethan one, but they don't so much contextualize Shakespeare's work as (at least in part) grow out of it. Hoenselaars calls for a decentering of Shakespeare (and, indeed, of England) from discussion of the history play so that we might better understand the plays as generated by a European traffic of ideas as manifested by non-English writers like Machiavelli, but his examples seem to foreground what most critics would assume: that while some elements of the plays and their ideological content derive from foreign nations, their main force is homegrown, their preoccupations ultimately domestic.

In terms of non-Shakespearean English histories, the argument for shaping context is, of course, easier to make and more immediately productive, showing as it does what Shakespeare does that is different from those romance-heavy "histories" by writers such as Munday, Greene, Rowley, and Dekker. Hoenselaars also sketches hagiographic histories such as Heywood's *If You Know Not Me, You Know Nobody*, and those biographical histories modeled on Foxe's Acts and Monuments (*Sir Thomas More, Thomas Lord Cromwell, Sir Thomas Wyatt*, and *Duchess of Suffolk*), forms of the genre in which Shakespeare seems to have had no interest. Following Helgerson, Hoenselaars sees Shakespeare as modeling a notion of nation that is abstract, a realm of centralized power and empire that is juxtaposed against that of many of his contemporaries (especially those writing for Henslowe) who saw nation as dealing with civic identity, a community of merchants, artisans, women, and children. The Lord Chamberlain's Men thus attempted to divest themselves of "such labels as 'popular', 'marginal', 'subversive', and 'folk' and the alienation of such qualities from their plays served this purpose" (30–31). This is, of course, in keeping with Hoenselaars's decentering of Shakespeare, and reinforces that Helgersonian vision of the playwright aiding the consolidation of central power in a deft act of self-promotion and upward social mobility, something the Bard's less iconic fellows were, apparently, guiltless of. So Shakespeare's plays frequently involve the Continent without being exactly Continental in the way that, say, Marlowe's *Massacre at Paris* or Chapman's *Bussy D'Ambois* are, plays that drew on foreign concerns that were still topical. Such a picture makes Shakespeare's histories seem remote, conservative, and providential in comparison with more classically inflected writers whose version of history is centered on the "antagonism between erratic fortune and human virtue" (32). But is such a picture fair? Does it not seem a tad reductive, stemming less from the political complexity of the plays themselves than from that (understandable) iconoclastic impulse to nudge Shakespeare out of the spotlight? By the end of the chapter, Hoenselaars is left wrestling with the paradox of wanting to see the history play outside Shakespeare's shadow while confessing that our sense of cultural nationalism has been directly shaped by Shakespeare and his nineteenth-century legacy in ways we can't escape. To want to see the play of history without seeing that play in Shakespearean terms is thus to want to divest ourselves of our own cultural dimension, something we can only imagine in the abstract.

If such an argument is odd in a companion to Shakespeare, it represents a pattern in the book, one further exemplified by David Bergeron's chapter on "Pageants, Masques and History." Forging a link through the appearance of Rumor in *2 Henry IV*, Bergeron explores court entertainments, triumphal entries, masques, and civic pageants, which, he says, like the history plays, enact history even as they make it. This perfectly valid and interesting idea nevertheless seems slim justification for the piece's place in the collection, and though he is careful to make some connections to the content of the plays, (royal entries into London seem recalled in the description of Bulling-brook in *Richard II*, pageantry seems to underscore moments like the garden scene in that same play) most of the connections feel thin. The issue, of course, is not whether such connections are there but that a collection of lim-ited scope should so privilege them. By contrast, Janis Lull's chapter "Planta-genets, Lancastrians, Yorkists and Tudors" is made to cover all three *Henry VI* plays, *Richard III*, and *Edward III* in seventeen pages. While *Richard III* shows up in other parts of the collection, this seems peculiar, and while Lull is shrewd and informative in her analysis, she just doesn't have the space to supply anything like coverage. But "coverage" even (especially?) for stu-dents has become something of a dirty word, and as the previous discussion of "decentering" Shakespeare suggests, this is not so much an oversight on the part of the collection as an agenda.

But it is one thing to decenter Shakespeare and another to decenter stu-dents. I am not sure what most of them would get from Dominique Goy-Blanquet's study of "Elizabethan Historiography and Shakespeare's Sources," not because the chapter is without value but because its style is so allusive and evasive, and its subject matter too large for so short a piece, covering as it does the entire process of history-writing as it came down to Shakespeare not just in the domestic chronicles but in studies of ancient Rome, and their respective intersections with censorship, moral edification, propaganda, theology, and so forth. This is a massive weight for any one chapter to bear. The chapter is also punctuated by curious interjections of faith that seem to invite contradiction: Bacon and some Shakespeare notwith-standing "there is no theory of Elizabethan progress" (60). (What about the Protestant revolution and English nationalism? Weren't they considered a step forward?) The Elizabethan period was characterized by a sense of new customs and an alienation from the past, something Shakespeare was aware of "alone of his generation" (60). In such a case the collection veers away from the grasp of most students and toward professional research without quite getting there, leaving it in a sort of no-man's-land where its final pur-pose is obscure.

More baffling still is Marie-Hélène Besnault and Michel Bitot's "Histori-cal Legacy and Fiction: The Poetical Reinvention of King Richard III," which sounds like it might be about Shakespeare's creation, after More, of the monstrous Duke of Gloucester in despite of historicity but, in fact, isn't. While much of what the chapter covers concerning the way Richard incorpo-rates various stage conventions is perfectly valid, the only sources discussed already contain those elements of monstrosity that characterize the protago-nist. Nor is there any interrogation of why Shakespeare ran with this particular version of Richard except for its innate theatricality, which would be fine if the chapter didn't constantly invoke problematic notions of history that are sometimes at odds with Shakespeare's creation, and sometimes, more confusingly still, somehow in accord with it. Thus: Richard "escapes from historical boundaries . . . to become a stylised, larger than life demonic figure" (108) (this despite presenting no evidence of a historical Richard who wasn't the demon of Tudor myth). "History has yielded to theatricality. But the latter is intrinsically linked with irony" (116), yet "as the dramatic action proceeds, [Richard] gradually dissolves into other stage archetypes such as the cunning Machiavel, the frantic Herod . . . or the ruthless Senecan Tyrant and finally into a more naturalistic, hence more potentially tragic, historical character" (116). The authors seem to be using "historical" in different ways here, ways I for one cannot track.

This shifting, amorphous sense of what history is ghosts the entire collection as it does Grene's book. Hattaway's introductory chapter tries to meet it head on, raising a couple of important arguments in the process. He contends that true "historicism may be impossible in the theatre" (11) because of the way theater functions dramatically. There can be no realism in terms of time or place there, no literal accuracy, the stage being better suited to Bakhtin's chronotopic representation of social spaces than to imitations of particular places (12). This sense of the stage as able to manifest only a kind of history, one that is subjective, polemic, even one-sided rather than somehow documentary is clearly alive in Stuart Hampton-Reeves's chapter on "Theatrical Afterlives," one of the book's most effective sections. Reeves details several productions in and out of series, in ways providing an excellent counterpoint to Grene, partly because it has less to prove and is able to find clearer ideas and a larger perspective, even where much of the ground is similar. Cycle plays (his term for series), requiring as they do ensemble casts and powerful directors, put history center stage, though the nature of that history is not consistent. Staging the histories with what Tillyard called "England" as the unseen central character presupposes a subordination of individual character to a larger collective consciousness, whether the shaping ideology of the show is about patriotism, the need for order, or the subversive exposure of the dynamics of power. Reeves perhaps puts too little emphasis on what audiences and critics thought they were seeing rather than what directors and program notes said they were (Grene's work suffers from the same problem), but he gives valuable space to productions Grene doesn't cover at all, particularly to productions of the two parts of *Henry IV,* which Grene (somewhat arbitrarily) thinks too insubstantial to be a series. The list includes Welles's *Chimes at Midnight* film, John Burrel's 1945 production with Laurence Olivier as Hotspur and Ralph Richardson as Hal, and Joan Littlewood's 1964 influential (on Bogdanov's ESC) conflation of *Henry IV 1 and 2,* none of which get discussed in Grene.

In his sense of what theater is Reeves is rather more savvy than Pamela Mason, whose chapter on *Henry V* bemoans productions' tendency to do the work for the audience, giving them a univocal perspective rather than giving them the play in all its complexity and letting it work on their imaginary forces. This is fair enough, of course, but it suggests a present-day audience's ability to decipher Mason's pointedly late twentieth-century, politically skeptical, and ironic reading (and I use that word advisedly) from the play's dense structural and verbal patterning. This is a common problem with armchair critics who privilege the text (and their sense of it) over the generation of something new and different in the air of performance, and it derives in part from a problematic (again) sense of stage history and the construction of an ideal audience member. Mason's reading is subtle and compelling, if not especially original, but to use it as a stick to beat productions that generated different meanings (even where they are limited or problematic) seems to misrecognize what theater is. Despite her sense of theater's reciprocal "labor," her complaints about modern productions/films pay little attention to those contingencies of the modern theater—the accumulation of history and the difficulties of Shakespeare's language—which make it increasingly difficult for audiences to decipher readings for themselves without directorial inflection, or how a production is supposed to generate such an *uninflected* production beyond using an uncut text.

Part of what Mason's chapter suggests—problematically, to my mind—is that the close reading of a text gives us access not only to an expressly theatrical product but also to a historical moment. Whether she is right or not, the collection as a whole seems undecided. There is surprisingly little of what might be called New Historicist method here, and not much more of that older, more monolithic history dealing with statecraft and large-scale national politics. Perhaps it is not the task of a companion volume such as this to supply such materials (beyond the useful list of characters that appears as an appendix), but I think it is part of its function to engage what history is since I don't think that can be taken as read, particularly for the target audience of a collection such as this. It is unfortunate that Dominique Goy-Blanquet's chapter on historiography is not longer and clearer because it could have provided a vital lynchpin for the book as a whole. Hattaway's own discussion of history (like the collection's handling of other controversies concerning the authorship of *Edward III* or the sequencing of the first tetralogy, which is so central to Grene's book) is noncommittal, even evasive. This is perhaps the nature of the beast, history in all its forms being a slippery category, but to say that the plays covered by the collection are best thought of as "political rather than 'historical' plays" (14) as Hattaway does, fudges the issue in ways that create as many questions as answers. If nothing else, such a position leaves the door open for much of the canon to be called "histories" in ways leaving little space for substantive exploration in a companion. Hattaway calls Shakespeare's histories (after Hutcheon) "historio-graphical metafictions" (19) and, countering Tillyard (20), says that if Shakespeare was writing to "edify" his audience he did so not in terms of moral exhortation, lessons in providential history, or repetitions of Tudor propaganda, but by offering a political edification. That sounds clear enough, but the nature of that edification or the edifice that is constructed by it, is left pointedly undescribed or argued for. "Handy-dandy, what is substantial, what is mere 'shadow'?" says Hattaway, "This is the question that Shake-speare in his great historiographical metafiction wickedly but wisely refused to answer" (22). It is the prerogative of greatness to withhold answers. Those that follow after should do otherwise, if only for fear that we will eventually run out of people who care to ask the questions.

Drugs, Medicine, and the Early Modern Stage

Drugs and Theater in Early Modern England, by Tanya Pollard. Oxford: Oxford University Press, 2005. Pp. × + 211. Cloth $74.00.

Beyond the Body: The Boundaries of Medicine and English Renaissance Drama, by William Kerwin. Amherst and Boston: University of Massachusetts Press, 2005. Pp. × + 290. Cloth $34.95.

Reviewer: STANTON B. GARNER JR.

IN 1996 Keir Elam remarked on "the *corporeal* turn" in Renaissance studies.[1] Ten years later we can appreciate how often this turn has been directed toward the relationship between theater and medical discourse and practice. The last two years alone have seen the publication of seven books in this area offering new perspectives on mercantilism and disease, pharmaceutical culture, diagnosis and cure, mental illness, and early modern anatomy.[2] That theater serves as the medium for these studies is no surprise. From the medical underpinnings of Aristotle's theory of *katharsis* through the anatomy theaters of Andreas Vesalius and the influence of humoral medicine on Elizabethan and Jacobean characterization, the two disciplines demonstrated a shared preoccupation with questions of embodiment, observation, and somatic representation. If theater is etymologically a "seeing place," then the modes of attention and diagnosis it engages are inescapably entwined with medicine's "theaters" of the body.

Tanya Pollard's *Drugs and Theater in Early Modern England* and William Kerwin's *Beyond the Body: The Boundaries of Medicine and English Renaissance Drama* examine the impact on English Renaissance drama of a changing medical profession and its often contending regimes of treatment. Pollard's book explores the representations of drugs in Elizabethan and Jacobean drama by foregrounding the medical and cultural debates within and surrounding early modern pharmacology. Kerwin's book covers some of the same ground, but in its treatment of medical practitioners and treatments, it raises broader historical and methodological questions of how one studies the medical in history and culture. In the end, both authors carry their concern with medical developments and controversies into the nature of theater itself.

Pollard approaches the theater in terms of a series of radical shifts in the pharmaceutical field of early modern medicine. The number and uses of medical remedies expanded in the late sixteenth century as New World explorers introduced Europe to medicinal herbs, including *Guiacum sanctum,* a tropical plant used to treat syphilis (which they also brought with them). In direct challenge to the humoral therapeutics of Galenism, Paracelsus and his followers introduced new, often toxic, chemicals into medical use. This crisis of professional authority contributed to a deepening ambivalence about drugs and other preparations. Remedial medicines could turn out to be poisonous, poisons could also have curative effects, and the same substance could work both ways depending on its prescription and use.

As Pollard suggests, the ambiguous, often dangerous, effects of drugs engaged a range of issues for playwrights, including the integrity of borders, bodily and otherwise; the relationship between the somatic and the mental; the unreliability of appearances; and the points of convergence between "the imagination and the body, the literary and the scientific, the magical and the rational" (22). In addition, the controversies surrounding drugs and their effects provided a discursive context for sixteenth- and early seventeenth-century debates about the operations of theater on its spectators. "A chorus of voices—from both attackers and defenders of the theater, as well as from playwrights themselves—saw the theater not only as a vehicle for representing drugs and poisons, but as a kind of drug or poison itself" (9). Pollard's book explores this pharmacological conception of the audience-stage relationship by discussing a range of drugs, remedies, and applications in relation to specific dramatic texts.

Chapter 1 considers drugs, poisons, and duplicitous doctors in John Webster's *The White Devil* and Ben Jonson's *Sejanus* and *Volpone.* Because these subjects have been treated by earlier scholars, the readings in the chapter have a familiar ring to them: Vittoria Corombona is presented as "a powerful but volatile medicine, intimately invasive, with dangerous side-effects" (37); the medical parody in Volpone's mountebank performance "identifies the dangers of medical charlatanism with the pleasures and perils of the theater itself" (45); while the notion of corrosive medicine serves as a figure for Jonson's moral and satiric aims. Chapter 2 offers a more unexpected and nuanced reading of sleeping potions in Shakespeare's *Romeo and Juliet* and *Antony and Cleopatra.* The fact that such potions operate in both remedial and harmful ways suggests that plays, for Shakespeare, are "misleadingly soothing potions that lull spectators into dream-like escapes, with uncertain consequences" (55). The proximity between sleep and death in *Romeo and Juliet* suggests the uncertain boundaries between the two states, and this reflects the phenomenological indistinguishability of the two in audience perception (it is hard to tell a "sleeping" character from a "dead" one). Through a provocative extension, Pollard links this indeterminacy with the ambiguous generic status of Shakespeare's love tragedies, which mix elements of comedy into their overall tragic structure.

Chapter 3 offers a fascinating discussion of cosmetics, which were closely allied to medical remedies in early modern thought. Because cosmetics were often linked with poisons (most cosmetics were made of mercury sublimate and ceruse, or white lead) and their operations were usually invisible, they created "a crisis of permeability, penetration and contagion" (83). Inevitably, face-painting was linked by moralists to other forms of contamination, concealment, and problematic interpretation: "concealing true faces behind false, they undermined the trustworthiness of bodily signs, leading to a broader crisis of semiotic reliability" (88). The extension to theater was a natural one, and cosmetics came to embody for antitheatricalists and playwrights together the dangerous seduction of dramatic performance. Chapter 4 explores the operations of this seduction in several plays that feature poisonous female corpses: Massinger's *The Second Maiden's Tragedy* and *The Duke of Milan,* as well as *The Revenger's Tragedy.* In all three plays the theatricality inherent in adornment is associated with the theater's own idolatrous appeal, as spectators are given a vision of the consequence of spectatorship.

Chapter 5 concludes Pollard's investigation of the body's vulnerable boundaries with an analysis of poison, language, and the ear in *Hamlet.* Pollard's reading of the ear in Shakespeare's play, in conjunction with Renaissance writings on the ear, links "early modern concerns about the integrity of bodily boundaries" (129) with the period's often physical conception of language's power over subjects and bodies. Here, too, the link with theater is crucial, and if Pollard is not the first to note the connection between poison's invasive operations and the effect of Hamlet's "Mousetrap" on Claudius—or the implications of this for the operation of Shakespeare's own dramatic creation—her analysis achieves its own originality through the pharmaceutical contexts she foregrounds.

It is not uncommon for books that turn a play's thematic preoccupations into reflections on the medium itself to overstate such connections, and Pollard's book does not avoid this temptation. The claims about theater feel strained at times, especially in chapter 4 ("If the Duke [in *The Revenger's Tragedy*] represents the audience, are we, the play's external spectators, tortured like him with the fatal spectacle of Gloriana?" [119]). But this is a minor reservation about an otherwise useful and informative book. Pollard's exploration of the "newly emerging world of ambivalent pharmacy" (147) directs our attention to an aspect of English Renaissance drama that otherwise exists on the periphery. Like the best examples of somatic criticism in recent Renaissance studies, *Drugs and Theater in Early Modern England* asks us to attend to the intense corporeality of Renaissance dramatic writing. As Pollard notes of the plays she discusses, "The worlds they present, steeped in medicines, ointments, drugs, paints, and poisons, insist that words, plays, and selves are all material, tangible, embodied presences" (148).

The theatrical, social, and discursive landscapes of *Beyond the Body* are embodied, as well, though William Kerwin's interests in this embodiment are different than Pollard's. As his title suggests, Kerwin explores the limits of a purely medical approach to the body as a historical entity. Unlike traditional studies of Renaissance medicine, *Beyond the Body* adopts the more socially directed approach of more recent medical historiography. This kind of history, Kerwin notes, "is often called 'externalist' to signify the importance of nonmedical history in shaping medical activities in contrast to 'internalist' history, which studies medicine or science as discrete bodies of knowledge" (5). Rather than analyzing the plays of Shakespeare and his contemporaries in terms of medical theory alone, Kerwin examines the ways in which non-medical controversies, economic factors, and historical trends determine the meanings of medical culture, medical practice, and their representations in Renaissance drama. As Kerwin writes in his opening chapter, "Medical stories are always also social stories, and in this book I present five case studies of how medicine's formation was a social contest in which different forces in society created multiple forms of the medical" (1). While *Beyond the Body* is detailed in its examination of medical debates and practices, its critical gaze is ultimately directed toward "group encounters that precede but shape embodiment" (vii).

A closer look at two of Kerwin's "case studies" suggests the methodological benefits of this approach. Chapter 2 addresses the influence on Renaissance dramatic texts of the pharmaceutical culture examined by Pollard. But whereas Pollard focuses on the operations of individual drugs and remedies and their metatheatrical appropriation, Kerwin explores the changing professions of apothecaries and alchemists in the context of "new markets, new class relations, and a new sense of the liquidity of wealth" (18). In the sixteenth and seventeenth centuries, apothecaries developed from a medieval guild to a medical profession able to take advantage of an expanding market economy and a rapidly developing urban world. The Friar and the unnamed Mantuan apothecary in *Romeo and Juliet* represent two historical moments in this transformation, and their juxtaposition underscores Shakespeare's skeptical attitude toward both drug cultures. Alchemists underwent similar transformation during the early modern period. Paracelsian alchemy paved the way for the emergence of modern chemistry and, in so doing, encouraged new market practices. Not only were chemical ideas "nurtured by modernizing economic forces" (46), but the new alchemy was also framed in terms of Puritan Reformation ideas (Paracelsus was referred to as the "Luther of Medicine"). These extramedical contexts allow powerful readings of Jonson's *Mercury Vindicated from the Alchemists at Court* and *The Alchemist,* which Kerwin sees as an investigation into alchemy's association with economic and religious innovation. As Kerwin argues, alchemy in Jonson's plays is not merely a metaphoric or thematic device; rather, it is part of a cultural formation that includes a broader sphere of economic and religious meanings.

Chapter 3 considers the social and theatrical presence of women healers in early modern England. As revisionist historians have demonstrated, women practitioners were central to health during this period, even going so far as to practice surgery. Predictably, these women were denounced as unlearned and dangerous by medical authorities, including the College of Physicians, which sought—usually unsuccessfully—to curtail their practice. (The efforts of the College to consolidate its medical authority in the face of emerging practitioners during the sixteenth and seventeenth centuries is one of the central narratives of *Beyond the Body,* and Kerwin works insightfully with the College's annals and other writings.) Given the prevalence of women healers in London and rural England, it is striking how seldom they appear on the English Renaissance stage. When they do, their portrayal differs from their denigration in official accounts. In Lyly's *Mother Bombie,* Shakespeare's *All's Well That Ends Well,* and Heywood's *The Wise Woman of Hogsdon,* women healers are given "a strikingly social authority" (64). In keeping with the range of contemporary social narratives in which these figures were described, playwrights "give voice to this ambiguous social position, drawing on the struggles of the historical woman healer to create a symbol of women struggling to work" (96).

The book's remaining chapters explore the intersection of medical and social discourses in other areas of early modern medical culture. Chapter 4 examines the importance of surgery for early modern notions of inwardness, surface, and the individual. As the cultural function of surgery expanded in the sixteenth century, surgeons assumed a central role in cultural negotiations about the line between private and public domains. In an engaging parallel to Pollard's analysis, chapter 5 considers the relationship of theatricality to professional medical identity. Whereas Elizabethan and Jacobean physicians used the language of antitheatricality to stigmatize their competitors for being "mere actors" (133), dramatists used the figure of the histrionic charlatan to describe members of the medical profession themselves. By the Caroline period attitudes toward acting had changed, and a new model emerged: that of the doctor-scientist, or *virtuoso,* who signaled his increasing social prestige through the performance of cures and social experiments. Chapter 6 turns to patients themselves and the ways in which early modern subjects defined their identities in medical terms. In *Twelfth Night,* Shakespeare satirizes the anchoring of identity through humoral categories and the discourses of spiritual healing. In keeping with the argument of the book as a whole, Kerwin's *Twelfth Night* debunks medicalized diagnosis that neglects the role of social determinations of lived experience.

Beyond the Body is an impressive contribution to the fields of Renaissance medical culture and theater. The link between these fields is stronger in some discussions than it is in others, and the analyses of medical developments and controversies are sometimes more illuminating than the play analyses they support. Moreover, Kerwin's insistence on the innovation of his externalist approach is not always fair to earlier scholarship on Renaissance medicine, much of which is aware of broader disciplinary, economic, and social developments even if it does not choose to foreground these. But the book's rhetorical strategies do not detract from its accomplishment. By taking advantage of the most recent trends in medical historiography, Kerwin offers a powerful account of the early modern body, its emergent technologies, and its complicated representation on social and institutional stages. Like Pollard's book, it reminds us how different medical practices could be in early modern Europe and how often these practices mixed the scientific with the magical; Shakespeare's age is never stranger than when it theorizes and treats the body. At the same time, its account of the crisis of medical authority that characterized the English Renaissance and the changes that medicine underwent as a result of the age's economic transformation establishes antecedents and surprising correlations to our own age of medical specialization, technological development, and alternative therapies. Four hundred years after Jonson's alchemists took the stage, the questions and possibilities raised by a medicalized culture are as urgent as ever.

Notes

1. Keir Elam, "'In What Chapter of His Bosom?': Reading Shakespeare's Bodies," in Terence Hawkes, ed., *Alternative Shakespeares,* vol. 2 (New York: Routledge, 1996), 143.

2. In addition to the books reviewed here, see Jonathan Gil Harris, *Sick Economies: Drama, Mercantilism, and Disease in Shakespeare's England* (Philadelphia: University of Pennsylvania Press, 2004); Stephanie Moss and Kaara L. Peterson, eds., *Disease, Diagnosis, and Cure on the Early Modern Stage* (Aldershot: Ashgate, 2004); Ken Jackson, *Separate Theaters: Bethlem ("Bedlam") Hospital and the Shakespearean Stage* (Newark: University of Delaware Press, 2005); Hillary M. Nunn, *Staging Anatomies: Dissection and Spectacle in Early Stuart Tragedy* (Aldershot: Ashgate, 2005); Maurizio Calbi, *Approximate Bodies: Gender and Power in Early Modern Drama and Anatomy* (New York: Routledge, 2005).

Reviews

Racism, Misogyny, and the "Othello" Myth: Inter-racial Couples from Shake-speare to Spike Lee, by Celia R. Daileader. Cambridge: Cambridge University Press, 2005. Pp. ix + 253. Cloth $70.00; Paper $25.99.

Reviewer: CHRISTY DESMET

In this book, Celia Daileader has set herself a large task. Spanning four centuries, her study of what she calls "Othellophilia" or the "Othello Myth" also moves back and forth across the Atlantic. Rather than detail lovingly the historical variations on her theme, Daileader pursues with a clear singleness of purpose the process by which Othello's story not only retains its currency, but also edges out other ideological variations on interracial sexual relations. *Racism, Misogyny, and the "Othello" Myth* "proceeds from the simple observation that in Anglo-American culture from the Renaissance onward, the most widely read, canonical narratives of inter-racial sex have involved black men and white women" (7). While a "desire to exorcise 'collective psychological demons'" might well be at work in the texts Daileader studies, she posits that Anglo-American culture's obsession with sex between black men and white women (a formula that inverts the sad realities of imperialism and slave culture) has less to do with race per se than with an imaginative appropriation of black men to control women, both black and white: "Othellophilia as a cultural construct is first and foremost *about women*—white women explicitly, as the 'subjects' of representation; black women implicitly, as the abjected and/or marginalized subjects of the suppressed counter-narrative" (10). While she argues strongly against the absorption of "sex" as a critical category into "race" in a monolithic story of marginalization, Daileader is not just making a plea for taking women seriously in tales of interracial relations. From her perspective, the Othello figure who spies on and murders his unfaithful wife is a raced stand-in for the reader or spectator in masculinist-racist discourse. The Othello myth lets the (male) (racist) reader have it both ways. Thus, Desdemona gets what she deserves because pitch always defiles, so that Othello's blackness must rub off on her. At the same time, by virtue of his race, within the narrative of miscegenation Othello himself can be disposed of as a cultural afterthought or abjected as just another manifestation of dark femininity.

On the surface, Daileader's project might seem unwieldy, at once too grand and a bit tenuous. Some of the texts she studies make little or no direct reference to *Othello* or its principal characters, and building a broad cultural argument on paradigmatic works is always a tricky business. On the one hand lies the Scylla of synecdochic fallacy (these select texts prove a global thesis); on the other, the Charybdis of the critical hobbyhorse (Othello and Othellophilia are everywhere, especially where one expects them least). I am happy to say that *Racism, Misogyny, and the "Othello" Myth* steers a clear path between these critical dangers and that Daileader's argument is, in the end, both provocative and persuasive. One reason for the book's success is the author's careful selection of texts. The chapters pair familiar with lesser-known texts, a strategy in keeping with the book's concern with canonicity and the question of why the Othello myth is so entrenched in Anglo-American culture. Within each chapter, the chosen texts speak energetically to one another. In some cases, the connection is historical; Harriet Jacobs, for instance, offered her story to Harriet Beecher Stowe before she gave it to Lydia Maria Child, establishing a factual connection among three of the authors discussed in chapter 4. Thomas Southerne's stage version of *Oroonoko,* discussed in chapter 2, is a clear revision of Aphra Behn's novel. More broadly, genre holds together the discussion of three Gothic tales in chapter 3. Daileader's talent for close reading solidifies the case for a persistent constellation of images and attitudes in the works covered by *Racism, Misogyny, and the "Othello" Myth.*

Grounding her argument in earlier work about race in early modern literature that has been produced by Kim Hall, Arthur Little, Joyce Green McDonald, Patricia Parker and Margo Hendricks, and Ania Loomba, among others, Daileader begins her study of interracial relations with a close reading of *Titus Andronicus, Othello* itself, Thomas Dekker's *Lust's Dominion,* John Webster's *The White Devil,* and William Rowley's largely unknown *All's Lost by Lust.*[1] Chapter 2 continues the story with Aphra Behn's *Abdelazar* and *Oroonoko,* followed by Thomas Southerne's stage adaptation of *Oroonoko,* Susanna Rowson's *Slaves in Algiers,* and Washington Irving's *Salmagundi.* Chapter 3 attends to Othellophilia in the Gothic, treating *Frankenstein* and *Dracula* in tandem with Edgar Allan Poe's *The Narrative of Arthur Gordon Pym.* Chapter 4 moves to the United States, pairing Lydia Maria Child's *Hobomok* with Harriet Jacobs's *Incidents in the Life of a Slave Girl* and Harriet Beecher Stowe's *Uncle Tom's Cabin* with William Wells Brown's novel *Clotel.* Chapter 5 studies the "handsome devils" of *Wuthering Heights, Gone with the Wind,* and Alice Randall's parody of Margaret Mitchell's novel, *The Wind Done Gone.* Chapter 6 brings together William Faulkner's *Light in August,* Richard Wright's *Native Son,* and Ralph Ellison's *Invisible Man.* The book concludes with a glance at some film appropriations of *Othello,* including Spike Lee's *Jungle Fever* and Tim Blake's *O.*

Racism, Misogyny, and the "Othello" Myth makes an important contribution to the study of Shakespearean appropriation and of *Othello*'s afterlives. It also engages vigorously with questions of canonicity by scrutinizing the ideological foundations of aesthetic endurance and attrition, the reasons why some texts seem eternal and others recede into oblivion. To some extent, Daileader's book is also an exercise in literary recovery. But her final, and most abiding, interest is in theory and models of critical practice.

The subterranean dialogue that *Racism, Misogyny, and the "Othello" Myth* carries on with critical discourses on race and sexuality is a crucial aspect of

Daileader's project. In part, she wants to break free from the national and chronological boundaries that seem to have entrenched themselves in the wake of New Historicism. Not that *Racism, Misogyny, and the "Othello" Myth* disdains the theoretical frameworks that have brought us to the place in which literary study finds itself today. Post-structuralism, psychoanalysis, and most of all, feminist theory are always in play. At the same time, Daileader seeks a new kind of rapprochement between feminist and what she terms "black" theoretical stances. The shorthand "black/feminist" that she uses to describe her work indicates the theoretical position that she wants to achieve. Daileader builds the bridges she desires by careful and respectful reference to work on race being done in other time periods of English and American literature. She also courts a rapprochement between feminism and race studies with a frankly polemical appeal to a theoretical "sisterhood." In this search, Harriet Jacobs's *Incidents in the Life of a Slave Girl* poses in its clearest form the problem that Daileader wants to solve by revealing how white women (as mistresses in the slave household) are pitted against black women (as slaves) through the institution of marriage: "In its searchingly honest discussions of female inter-racial rivalry, the book lays bare marriage—at least in the slave-holding class—as a racist-masculinist institution that pits white women against black" (130). The search for "Othello's sister" and the critic's own "sisters" is ongoing throughout the exploration of her chosen theme.

Racism, Misogyny, and the "Othello" Myth could have been a depressing book. After all, as Daileader concludes, "Racism will turn to misogyny on a dime; misogyny often obscures racism" (218). But with a clear sense of how critical practice (and teaching) are by definition explorations of ethics when so much is at stake, Daileader not only faults characters and authors when they slip into the old attitudes of Othellophilia, but she also points out those promising moments when texts slip the yoke and begin to change the story. She is concerned not only to unmask the strategies of racism and misogyny, but also to celebrate small textual triumphs, such as a heroine's *"refusal to commit suicide* at the ideologically appropriate moment" (118, italics in original). With its strong voice, polemical stance, and rich content, *Racism, Misogyny, and the "Othello" Myth: Inter-racial Couples from Shakespeare to Spike Lee* would be an excellent text for classroom use as well as private pleasure.

Note

1. Kim F. Hall, *Things of Darkness: Economies of Race and Gender in Early Modern England* (New York: Cornell University Press, 1995); Arthur J. Little Jr., *Shakespeare Jungle Fever: National-Imperial Re-Visions of Race, Rape, and Sacrifice*

(Stanford, CA: Stanford University Press, 2000); Joyce Green McDonald, *Women and Race in Early Modern Texts* (Cambridge: Cambridge University Press, 2001); *Women, "Race," and Writing in the Early Modern Peri*od, ed. Margo Hendricks and Patricia Parker (London: Routledge, 1992); and Ania Loomba, *Shakespeare, Race, and Colonialism* (Oxford: Oxford University Press, 2001).

Humoring the Body: Emotions and the Shakespearean Stage, by Gail Kern Paster. Chicago: University of Chicago Press, 2004. Pp. xiii + 274. Cloth: $35.00.

Reviewer: ERIC JOHNSON-DEBAUFRE

The emotions—those seemingly most transhistorical of objects—undergo a thoroughgoing defamiliarization in Gail Kern Paster's recent work. In contrast to the contemporary tendency to read early modern literary representations of the emotions through a post-Cartesian lens of dematerialized affectivity, Paster argues for their rematerialization by recognizing that "what is now emotional figuration for us was bodily reality for the early moderns" (26). According to Paster, the tendency to read the emotions represented in early modern literature through a residual post-Enlightenment framework of mind-body dualism bedevils our efforts to read them "with historical care" (26). She thus embarks on an ambitious project to reconstruct a "historical phenomenology of the early modern emotions" (10), carefully treating a range of early modern texts on the emotions and demonstrating how this project might extend our understanding of early modern dramatic literature. Particularly notable are her readings of less familiar texts such as Thomas Wright's *The Passions of the Minde in Generall* (1604) and Edward Reynolds's *A Treatise of the Passions and Faculties of the Soule of Man* (1640), as well as familiar plays like Shakespeare's *Hamlet* and *Othello,* and Jonson's *Every Man in His Humour.*

Chapter 1 uses Paster's argument for the ontological coextensiveness of the early modern subject's emotions with the "particular social and physical environments in which those emotions arise" (27) as an opportunity for rereading several important moments in *Hamlet* and *Othello.* The goal in each case is to reveal the physicality and materiality of the early modern understanding of the emotions as well as to demonstrate the subject's participation in and penetration by a social and physical environment conceived of as pregnant with its own latent affective impulses. The effect, in the case of *Hamlet,* is an enriched understanding of the meaning of both Hamlet's response to the Pyrrhus speech and his objectives in the Mousetrap scene, as well as a more nuanced understanding of the complexity of the early modern English conception of human subjectivity. Thus in *Hamlet,* the attention paid to the time, place, and circumstances of Pyrrhus's slaying of Priam reveals the way that "agency is vividly produced and just as vividly decentered, emanating from Pyrrhus's body and its extensions of sword and armor without being specific or exclusive to them, being redistributed outward to a universe of desiring elements and sympathetic affordances" (42). Likewise, Paster's reading of Desdemona's concern for whatever "[h]ath puddled [Othello's] clear spirit" makes visible "the work of physiology rather than metaphor elsewhere in the play" (64) as well as how the porousness of the early modern body makes it susceptible to penetration and contamination by "the fetid materials of the outside world" (76).

Chapter 2 takes up the issue of women's affective change within a humoral economy that generally regarded them as invariant and their bodies as naturally colder and moister than men's. Given what Paster calls the "Galenic commonplace that 'the Minds inclinations follows the Bodies Temperature'" (77), such an understanding had significant, negative consequences for early modern understandings of female subjectivity and were frequently used to explain "the sex's limited capacity for productive agency, individuality, and higher reasoning" (79). Here Paster puts to good use the insights gained in chapter 1 about the influence that the larger, affectively charged social and physical environment has on the individual subject. Paster's focus here is on the "nature and causation of behavioral and expressive changes in Desdemona, Rosalind, and Katherine Minola" (86), which she situates in relation to the early modern "rediscovery" of green sickness.

Broadening further Paster's argument for the affectively full nature of the physical world, chapter 3 examines early modern attributions of affective states to animals and the implications this has for an understanding of human subjectivity. In an argument that ranges from a discussion of Falstaff's citation of the melancholy of cats in *1 Henry IV* to Cleopatra's species-barrier crossing identifications in *Antony and Cleopatra,* Paster demonstrates both the affinities early moderns observed between human and animal affectivity and the sometimes surprising transactions that occurred between the species.

From movements across the animal-human species barrier in chapter 3, Paster moves to a discussion of the "mobility and fluidity of social relations" (232) in Jonsonian city comedy and of the humoral thinking that underlies the self-conceptions of Shakespeare's Shylock, Corporal Nym, and Malvolio. Paster's goal here is to "rescue the humors from their critical relegation as an annoying and psychologically archaic feature of early modern city comedy and argue for their importance, instead, as a key heuristic in the troubled representations of male individuation" (200). Her readings, particularly of the affective privilege claimed by characters in Jonson's *Everyman in His Humour* and of the humoral quarreling that takes place in *Bartholomew Fair*'s game of the vapors, are among the most convincing in the entire book and form a satisfying conclusion to her impressive study.

A strength of Paster's work—namely its persuasive argument that early modern affective states are rooted in the dynamic interaction of the material body with the larger physical and social world—is also a source of its potential limitations. Given the sheer variety and complexity of that world and its multiple vectors of affective pull, how did early moderns—and by extension, how do we—delimit the factors believed to exert a determinative influence on a character's behavior from those that do not? Moreover, if at times the early modern humoral body seems remarkably porous and open to the sympathetic influences of the affectively charged outer world, as in the case of Hamlet or Othello, at others it remains stubbornly resistant to such influence. Thus Hamlet's proclamation, "Now could I drink hot blood," results in part from the environmental influence exerted on his body by midnight and by the "noxious exhalations" of churchyards (56). Here Hamlet's characteristic melancholy gives way to a momentary desire to enact Pyrrhus-like vengeance, in part as a result of "his natural embeddedness in the world and his openness to the cues of time and season" (57). Recognizing the humoral body's susceptibility to environmental factors of time, place, and circumstance here renders more intelligible Hamlet's abrupt, if transitory, release from his dispositional melancholy into a fleeting choleric absorption. But a consequence of this recognition is only to make the workings of the passions the more mysterious as when, in the case of Shylock, we are faced with characters whose bodies appear resistant to affective influence by the larger affect-laden environment.

Thus Paster's immensely valuable study points to the need for further understanding of the mechanisms by which the early modern humoral body was believed to negotiate its transactions with the affect-laden world, to discriminate between competing and contradictory affective pulls, and to regulate their influences. *Humoring the Body* is an enormous achievement that greatly enriches our understanding of the epistemic gulf separating the early modern and post-Enlightenment understandings of the emotions and has the potential to alter substantially how we conceive of early modern subjectivity. For this as well as for the fine readings it offers of many key early modern dramatic texts, *Humoring the Body* will be required reading for anyone working in early modern studies.

Shakespeare's Violated Bodies: Stage and Screen Performance, by Pascale Aebischer. Cambridge: Cambridge University Press, 2004. Pp. xiii + 221. Cloth $75.00.

Reviewer: DENEEN SENASI

Shakespeare's Violated Bodies: Stage and Screen Performance begins with a tantalizing scenario of regendering and recuperation, a "story of loss"

(1) based on a passing reference to an unexpected casting choice and a performance that might have been. In handwritten rehearsal notes in the archives of the Shakespeare Centre for the 1989 Royal Shakespeare Company's production of *Hamlet,* the author discovers a reference to the Second Gravedigger as "the gravediggers daughter" (1). While she finds no additional references to this figure, Aebischer nevertheless imagines the implications of the gravedigger's daughter as a "modern woman" who, at the grave of Ophelia, "could meet her Shakespearean tragic equivalent" (3). She envisions a "healthy young gravedigger's daughter, the smutty, intelligent working-class girl who is sensitive to social injustice, nailing the trap lid over the over-refined body of her 'privileged' ancestor" (2–3). While this is certainly an intriguing scenario, there are difficulties as well, since such an encounter between the "healthy" modern woman and her "over-refined" opposite could be accurately described as such only if the production's presentation of Ophelia was somehow truly a "privileged ancestor" rather than an equally "modern" performance.

Aebischer moves from the elusive gravedigger's daughter to other, less fleeting instances of "loss" in the Shakespearean canon through which she describes the expulsion of female bodies from theatrical space as an enabling act in the phallogocentric tradition of tragedy. Citing Peter Brook's description of the "act of theatre" as "an empty space filled by a man walking across it" (4), she envisions her analysis as an intervention that reconfigures the constituencies of that space in Shakespearean tragedy. As Aebischer writes, "The project of this book is to find the moments at which the empty space of theatre is created in Shakespearean tragedies and prevent Brook's generic man from walking across it. Instead, I will seek to fill out those spaces with narratives about how those gaps come to be, about the mechanisms that lead to the expulsion of some bodies from both playtexts and their critical reception" (5). Such instances of expulsion emerge as the primary "violation" with which Aebischer is concerned. This is an intriguing, imaginative strategy, but it is also not without some implicit difficulties. For example, the focus on female bodies violated and expelled by male subjects emphasizes the material body at the expense of the dramatic subjectivity of characters like Cordelia, Ophelia, and Lavinia, whose rape and mutilation serve as a recurrent touchstone throughout the text.

In addition, while there is a brief reference to the boy actor in the introduction, the analysis does not address how the presence of the boy's body, at the time of the characters' inception, complicates the history of these bodies and their marginalization. Like the "unruly corpses" (64) described in the text's chapter on *Hamlet,* the boy's body persists as a spectral presence, a residual trace of one of the primary "mechanisms that lead to the expulsion of some bodies" (5) from early modern texts and theatrical spaces. Aebischer's assertion that "it is in relationship to present concerns that Shakespeare's violated bodies can be made to mean in performance, and it is within the context of present-day spectators' culture that they demand to be read" (5) seems designed to situate the plays and her analysis of them exclusively in the present, but this contradicts the idealized encounter between the "modern" gravedigger's daughter and Ophelia, as her "privileged ancestor," with which the text begins.

Aebischer argues that these bodies "may come centerstage in performance and performance studies" where, she suggests, their "absence" in the text may be "compensated for by their physical presence" (5). This compensatory gesture effectively collapses the female dramatic subject into a utopia of the recuperated, recentered body. While she envisions the "white *male subject* of tragedy" (emphasis added) being forced to "give way for his gendered and racial Others" (5), Aebishcer imagines filling that evacuated space not with a *female subject* but with a *body.* Such a substitution ironically reenacts the cultural bias that assumes that a woman is first and foremost a body. While the book's project is described in terms of the recuperation of those bodies "under threat of erasure" in the text, Aebischer asserts that because of that threat, they are "like Desdemona, 'fair paper,' blank pages/empty spaces onto which the interests, beliefs and anxieties of production teams and spectators can be projected" (5). Such logic treats these characters as already erased or readily eraseable, thereby reenacting the "threat of erasure" described as a feature of the texts. This approach also seems to suggest that those characters not under "threat of erasure" are somehow not subject to "projections."

Aebischer's study characterized by these kinds of imaginative, sometimes problematic, scenarios combined with an unapologetically proactive sense of critical agency. This results in an approach less interested in analyzing Shakespeare's tragedies as they have come down to us, in all their mediated complexity, than in reconstructing them as they might be reimagined through the transformative dynamics of performance. Individual chapters include a reading of the spectacular in *Titus Andronicus* juxtaposed to the "textual gap left by Lavinia's erasure" (25), an intriguing analysis of *Hamlet*'s meaningful corpses, a broadening of the discussion to include racialized bodies in *Titus* and *Othello,* and a final chapter on *Lear* focusing on how female bodies have been literally and figuratively pushed "out of the frame of the play" (151) in performance as well as in the text. This is an intensely personal piece of criticism throughout; the author repeatedly emphasizes her own moments of choice or resistance as a reader of the plays and their critical reception. The motive force here seems to be loss, as she explicitly replaces the suffering of the white male subject of tragedy not only with the bodies of his "Others" but also with her own "outrage" (189). Like Titus, Aebischer seeks to "wrest an alphabet" (3.2.44) out of silence and loss, and this is simultaneously the greatest allure of her text and its most disconcerting parallel.

The Early Modern Corpse and Shakespeare's Theatre, by Susan Zimmerman. Edinburgh: Edinburgh University Press, 2005. Pp. viii + 216. Cloth $80.00.

Reviewer: HEATHER HIRSCHFELD

Susan Zimmerman's *Early Modern Corpse* is a wonderful paradox: steeped in the contemplation of death, decomposition, and putrefaction, its language, critical argumentation, and theoretical and historical insight are continuously vibrant, vital, and intellectually *alive.* Zimmerman's overarching achievement lies in bringing together, in historically responsible ways, Reformation religious debate with contemporary theory, thereby generating a series of sharp insights not only into the structure of individual early modern tragedies but also into the shapes and commitments of competing Reformation doctrines. Ultimately the book demonstrates the tremendous rewards of bringing postmodern theories of tragedy and the gendered subject to bear on early modern concerns about theological and scientific meanings of the body.

Zimmerman's project, as articulated in the introductory chapter, is to assess the staging of corpses—that is, the staging of live bodies as though lifeless—in relation to the early modern theater's participation in "ongoing controversies concerning the dead" (10). Although those controversies have been the object of considerable critical scrutiny, including recent monographs by Michael Neill and Robert Watson, Zimmerman locates them specifically at the root of Reformation doctrinal conflict, and she offers a focused account of the terms of Catholic-Protestant hermeneutical debate by concentrating on the status of idols, relics, and saints as a particular illustration of the logics of confessional differences in understanding the material and spiritual body. Looking at the Homily against Idolatry and John Foxe's *Actes and Monuments,* Zimmerman carefully lays out the structure of iconoclastic controversy, identifying the Reformers' "virtually intractable dilemma" of "reformulat[ing] the prevailing concept of the body/soul relation so as to counteract the materiality of Catholicism, but without repudiating the paradoxes at the heart of Christian doctrine" (25). This dilemma reaches its apogee in the figure of the corpse—"the ultimate relic," as Zimmerman says, since it "foregrounds most dramatically the complexity of the relation between redeemed and debased bodies in the Christian system" (27). Relying on a substantial survey of historical scholarship to trace the movement from Catholic to Reform notions of corporeality, Zimmerman explores Foxe and the Homily as two works that "reconceptualise the materiality of the body and of the corpse in self-conscious opposition to Catholic beliefs and practices" by "envisage[ing] its materiality, like that of the idol, as dead" (46). It is in her reading of these kinds of texts as "exercises in demystification" that Zimmerman proves the dexterity and sharpness of her critical and theoretical methods, as she traces in both works a shared horror of bodily

process and a shared effort to represent the corpse not as something potentially transcendent and redemptive but as something fundamentally dead and
empty (65).

The following chapters, which pair the tragedies of *The Second Maiden's
Tragedy* and *The Duchess of Milan, The Revenger's Tragedy* and *The Duchess of Malfi,* and *Macbeth* and *Hamlet,* translate the theological resonances
of the corpse to the realm of the theater, a realm already preoccupied with
the dilemma of representing soul and body. Influenced by Walter Benjamin's
theories of *Tragodie* and *Trauerspiel,* Zimmerman offers a compelling account of these plays' melodramatic excesses—particularly their characters'
necrophilic obsessions—in relation to idolatrous tyranny; even more important, she explains the plays' seeming ideological inconsistency (their simultaneous iconoclasm and spiritual investment in the corpses of dead women)
as the performative effect of early modern theatrical display, particularly
but not restricted to the cross-dressing of boy actors. The next chapter connects *Revenger's* and *Duchess* based on the plays' mutual trafficking in
popular notions of the corpse—particularly notions of its mysterious, semi-
animate status—in ways informed not only by theological discourses but
also by scientific and anatomical ones. Here Zimmerman weaves together a
series of contextualizing materials—from transi sculptures and the *danse
macabre* to psychoanalytic theories of the blurring of sex and death—to
explain the uncanny power of the corpse in the period and thus to highlight
the efforts by Protestant reformers as well as anatomists to de-fetishize or
demystify it. As in the chapter on *Maiden's* and *Milan,* Zimmerman is especially effective in noting the gendered status of the corpse, the way that the
Duchess and the skull of the dead Gloriana provide "dual emblems of material dissolution and of transcendent wholeness" associated with woman as
mother, virgin, whore—all figures of generation as well as dissolution
(135). If Zimmerman's argument about Vindice as a morally ambiguous
avenger is not new, it nevertheless identifies in fresh terms the ways in
which his specific use of the skull of Gloriana becomes the source of his
own undoing: when Vindice dresses up what remains of his fiancée, he initiates "the collapse of gender-based defences against putrefaction itself"
(141). Contrasting Vindice's glee to the nightmarish quality of *Duchess,*
Zimmerman offers a particularly powerful interpretation of Bosola and Ferdinand's melancholia in relation to the material and spiritual body of the
female protagonist. The psychoanalytic tenor of this part of the chapter is
especially noticeable, as Zimmerman puts herself in dialogue with critics
such as Lynn Enterline to suggest the ways that the Duchess serves as a
screen for the men's revulsion from physical processes and the ways that,
even after her death, she continues to exert an influence over the men's
imaginations: "Ferdinand and Bosola find an inescapable oppression, an

even worse torment, in the after-life of her corpse" (144). Such a reading allows her to offer a striking explanation of Ferdinand's lycanthropy as an approximation of the experience of the corpse, which "dooms *him* to 'non-being' of a peculiar sort and simultaneously allows him to violate the grave-yard that she will soon inhabit" (155).

Zimmerman saves Shakespeare for last, violating chronology (as she does within the chapter itself, since she looks first to *Macbeth* before turning to *Hamlet*), in order to highlight the role of the corpses of Duncan and Hamlet Sr. on the unsettled, haunted atmosphere of these plays. It is here that her sustained analysis of the theological and psychic significance of the corpse comes to fruition in provocative, original readings of plays burdened by long critical traditions. Working from well-established interpretations of the fact that in *Macbeth* "nothing is totally obliterated, nothing is final," Zimmerman explains the power of Duncan's corpse, figured by Macbeth as both mascu-line and feminine, to control the protagonist's demise. Equating Duncan's corpse with his blood, Zimmerman sees that "by the end of the play, Mac-beth's cosmos has been horrifically enlarged by the encompassing sea of Duncan's blood—a sea in which materiality provides no anchor, and sexual-ity itself is inextricably bound up with death" (180). Her approach to *Hamlet* brings new critical energy to the time-honored questions asked of the Ghost, as she reads for the corpse *inside* the "figure like your father, / Armed at all points" and for the ways in which this indeterminate revenant defines the world of the play and justifies Hamlet's uncommon mourning: "At the center of Hamlet's struggle to cope with his terrible grief and rage is an apparition that is uniquely his: the invincible fantasy father corroded from within by the mindlessness of mortality" (184).

For all its excellencies—its eloquent insight, its dexterous handling of the plays' structure and language—there are some flaws here. The most discon-certing of them is Zimmerman's comparison between early modern theologi-cal and anatomical treatments of the material body. She makes a compelling and important case for their similarity—indeed, the book's blurbs praise pre-cisely this aspect of the book—but the role of scientific anatomy remains peripheral to her larger arguments about Reformation hermeneutics and to her more specific analyses of plays. The ideological interests of Renaissance anatomy feels more like an appendage, as it were, to her claims; the space devoted to this issue might have been better used in elaborating more fully the dynamics of cross-dressing than Zimmerman does at present. But these are small reservations; overall this is an erudite and significant contribution to contemporary scholarship about the English stage and the Reformation which proves the value of bringing theory and history together in the literary analysis of religious culture.

Performing Blackness on English Stages, 1500–1800, by Virginia Mason Vaughan. Cambridge: Cambridge University Press, 2005. Pp. xiv + 190. Cloth $75.00.

Reviewer: **Francesca T. Royster**

When I teach about blackface conventions in my undergraduate Shakespeare classes, I often ask students to cull from their own experiences of blackface performance. Most are from an American context: many of them have seen Spike Lee's *Bamboozled,* or caught a clip of Al Jolson (or Bugs Bunny imitating Al Jolson) singing "Mammy." A few have been lucky enough to have seen Marlon Rigg's groundbreaking documentary of blackface and its American roots, *Ethnic Notions.* In the United States, blackface performance has been forged in the ovens of slavery and postslavery race relations. In the sexual stereotypes of U.S. blackface images, we find lurking fantasies spawned from the systematic breeding and trade of black bodies; in the mixture of violence and humor of blackface, we might see a spectacular transmogrification of the post-Reconstruction Black Laws, ever-present threat of lynchings, and the rise of Jim Crow. And in the careers of blackface performers, white and black, we see reflected the tenuous act of becoming white and protecting whiteness borne from the history of U.S. immigration. The late twentieth and early twenty-first century brings a whole new trajectory of blackface appropriations shaped by U.S. experiences, including the critical use of blackface in the art and performances of Fred Wilson, Chris Rock, Whoopie Goldberg, and Michael Ray Charles, whose modern racial kitsch figures appear in Spike Lee's film, *Bamboozled.* But while our most familiar associations of blackface tradition might most likely be informed by the American historical context, Americans did not invent blackface. As Virginia Mason Vaughan discusses in her powerful study, *Performing Blackness on English Stages, 1500–1800,* the early modern period in England has yielded several examples of white actors performing in blackface for the popular stage, and we can reach even further back to blackfaced devils in medieval mystery plays, or further still to black slave characters in classical Roman productions. Vaughan's *Performing Blackness* is valuable for its history and analysis of English blackface traditions in their specificity; at the same time, the work provides an important conceptual framework that might help bridge blackface traditions across time, nation, and audience.

Vaughan's study focuses on the relationship between text and performance in the flesh: "appearance, linguistic tropes, speech patterns, plot situations, the use of asides and soliloquies, and other forms of dramatic signification" (2–3), that shaped the ways that blackness was "performed," read, and understood by white audiences. Here, she applies Toni Morrison's concept of "Africanisms," first conceived to explain the production of fictionalized blackness to forge white American identity, to consider patterns of fantastical blackness as they are performed to forge white identity on the British stage. Blackface in the imaginative work of the stage is, after all, not about black people, but really about fantastic notions of blackness that tell us more about the (white) author and audiences. As Vaughan writes, "When all is said and done, the black characters that populated early modern theatres tell us little about actual black Africans; they are the projections of imaginations that capitalize on the assumptions, fantasies, fears, and anxieties of England's pale complexioned audiences" (4–5).

The challenge of any study of live performance is the difficulty of reconstructing audience response. This is particularly true for the early modern period, where few commentaries by audiences, actors, and playwrights about stagecraft and methods or the impact of those techniques survive. Vaughan nevertheless successfully brings this past to life by integrating historical context, illustrations, actor's handbooks, property books, reviews, and diary entries, as well as clues within the plays themselves, to reconstruct the material aspects of blackface as a stage tradition. Vaughan presents glimpses into the material practice of blackface as it shifts and adapts. For example, we learn that as blackface performances shifted from silent to speaking parts, there evolved new techniques and technologies that allow for greater visibility of the actor and of the performance of emotion. We see actors move from the use of coal or charcoal, and/or black lawn veils or other, more obscuring techniques of blackface, to experiments with different pigments. The increasing frequency of contact between the English and black and brown Moors, whether captured Africans who were brought to England as servants or visiting merchants and dignitaries like Abd-el-Ouahed ben Messaoud ben Mohammed Anoun, a Moroccan ambassador to Elizabeth I, also influenced variations in blackface technique and style, including a range of skin colors, from black to tawny, as well as clothing and speech. Throughout the text, Vaughan effectively outlines the technologies and stagecraft of blackface performance, and the ways that blackface conventions grew to be a site for professional development—a way of showing one's performance chops and also one's viability for other forms of performance.

Blackface performances in the early modern period shift from medieval uses of blackness as a relatively simple analogy of moral and religious meanings, where blackness equals damnation, to "polyphonic" meanings and functions. These shifts in performance mark the development of a "racially defined discourse of human identity and personhood" essential to our notion of English modernity (2). In medieval visual art and mystery cycles, Lucifer bore the mark of blackness, signifying his shame-worthiness and exclusion from the Christian Kingdom of God. Medieval mystery plays also include more positive imagery, such as the blackfaced king in the image of the Three Magi. In this case, the king's black alterity ultimately demonstrates the universal reach of Christianity. As blackface characters move from silent displays to speaking parts—the "talking devils" and "avenging villains" of the Elizabethan public theater—characters become more dynamic and more memorable. Drawing from early modern travel literature and England's emerging participation in the transatlantic slave trade, these new configurations combine older associations of blackness with devils, with newer ideas of the blackface figure as warrior and sexual trickster. Trickster figures like Aaron in Shakespeare's *Titus Andronicus* and Eleazor in Thomas Dekker's *Lust's Dominion* raise stereotypical fears of miscegenation and black rape (47–54). Yet the characters sometimes also embodied complex psychologies. For example, George Peele's Muly Hamet, from *The Battle of Alcazar,* the first public English play with a black speaking character, is both bloodthirsty warrior and loyal leader, sentimental lover and verbal threat to his enemies—and audience (42).

Vaughan continually asks us to think about the ways that blackface necessarily intertwines race with nation, gender, and class. These interconnections came most alive for me in her fifth chapter, "Bedtricksters." The bedtrick is a dramatic device of switching one bedmate for another, resulting in confusion, the questioning of identity, humiliation or crisis, leading to sometimes comic, sometimes more serious resolution. Vaughan argues that the figure of the Moor as a substitute bedmate in these early modern plays brings up anxiety about sexuality, the stability of gender markers, and changing ideas about marriage and property, all informed by race. These anxieties are also linked to deeper issues of "self" linked to the sexual act, what critic Wendy Doniger calls "'the tension between the urge to diverge and the urge to merge'" (74).

Why are these bedtricks so often linked to black bodies—or more accurately, to the performance of blackness? Blackface figures, usually servants, as they become involved in these sexual intrigues, often highlight (by contrast) the white women's chastity, at the same time allowing for the sometimes vicarious expression of sexual desire. Black female servants act as forbidden doubles, sites of fantasy and projection. Black male servants are also objects of desire or tools for revenge. Vaughan foregrounds these roles in the cultural context of growing populations of black servants and, later, slaves in England, and therefore increasingly more intimate interactions between blacks and whites in domestic spaces. These shifts accelerate the already circulating fantasies of sexual desire and pollution from travel literature and other earlier, more distanced images (76).

Bedtrick episodes sometimes highlight tensions in class identity, where sleeping (mistakenly) with a black servant becomes punishment for attempting to climb the social ladder. In John Fletcher's play *Monsieur Thomas,* written between 1614–17, Thomas, a fortune seeker, dresses up as a woman in order to win the financially well-placed Mary. Thomas is "punished" by finding himself in bed with a black female servant, Kate, rather than his desired love. These "tricks" often present sexually loaded and sometimes ambivalent expressions of desire for the other. When Thomas discovers his black bedmate, he cries,

> Holy saints defend me!
> The devil, devil, devil! O the devil! . . .
> I am abused most damnedly, most beastly;
> Yet if it be a she-devil—

(5.2.30–35)

In Vaughan's reading, "At first, Thomas is horrified and reads Kate as the blackfaced devil of the homiletic tradition. His fourth line, 'Yet . . . ,' suggests that after the initial shock dissipates, Thomas has second thoughts; perhaps if the devil is female, she is beddable after all. But then he beats Kate, crying, 'Plague o' your Spanish-leather hide!' (5.2.39) and runs away" (81).

Black servants, particularly male servants, were also used in these bedtrick devices to complete acts of revenge and to perform implied or explicit sexual violence, as in John Marston's *The Wonder of Women, or The Tragedy of Sophonisba,* (1606). The villain Syphax threatens the white virgin Sophonisba that if she does not yield to his advances, he'll use his two black male servants to hold her down. The rape is averted by Sophonisba's substitution of Syphax's sleeping black male servant, Vangue, in her bed. When Syphax discovers that he has leaped into bed with a black man, he is so humiliated that he kills Vangue. As Arthur Little, Jr. has noted in his *Shakespeare Jungle Fever,* sacrificed black bodies help regulate the economy of desire in a society often fearful of its own "jungle" impulses.[1]

But as Vaughan shows, there is also pleasure to be had in becoming that dangerous black body, and this was exploited theatrically by having European characters black up onstage. In her seventh chapter, "Europeans Disguised as Black Moors," Vaughan argues that blackening up gives another kind of social mobility, providing the opportunity to trick, humiliate, avenge, rape, or otherwise punish by becoming the other. In late Jacobean and early Caroline plays like John Webster's *The White Devil* and Samuel Harding's unperformed *Sicily and Naples,* black disguise adds a new life to the increasingly conventional aspects of revenge drama. Thus, Harding's play *Sicily and Naples* takes the image of the Machiavellian villain and "supersizes" him, by having him blacken up onstage. This play so pushed the envelope of propriety via the graphic acts of its blacked-up villain, including incest, murder, and rape, that it was never able to be produced. This play continues the association between blackness and devils that has now become a "naturalized" association onstage. Perhaps we might think about the ways that white characters continue to appropriate black style, music, and identity in films, music, and other forms of performance, as a means of expressing socially dangerous ideas and freshening up putrid writing and stock characters or forms. Take, for example, Mike Judge's recent film *Office Space,* and its sometimes self-mocking use of a gangsta rap sound track to express primarily white, middle-class corporate workers' frustration and anger at (white) corporate norms.

Useful chapters focusing on Shakespeare's *Othello* and Aphra Behn's *Oroonoko* shed new light on these more familiar plays and show their influence on theatrical conventions and genres. Shakespeare's *Othello* becomes an important and special case throughout Vaughan's analysis, in part because of its influence on other blackface plays in the period—a phenomenon that Celia Daileader has described as "Othellophilia"[2]—and because of the play history's influence on current attitudes toward blackface in contemporary theatrical productions.

In her chapter on *Othello,* as well as in her "Afterthoughts," Vaughan asks us to think harder about the social uses of blackface now. Going against the grain of much contemporary theatrical practice, Vaughan argues for the continued usefulness of blackface productions of early modern theater, if presented sensitively and within their own social context. This, she argues, is not only because "Othello was a white man"—performed by and to some extent always remembered to be white and male by his original audience, as Dympna Callaghan points out in her book *Shakespeare Without Women*[3]— but also because the artiface of blackface can tell us much about the fears and anxieties of white audiences in the past (and, I'd argue, now). Vaughan uses the illustration of the reconstructed Globe Theatre on Bankside, which she says, through its recent all-male productions of *Antony and Cleopatra* and *Twelfth Night,* has shown the erotic charge of cross-gender casting as it might have been experienced by earlier audiences. She asks, "Could we not have an experimental *Lust's Dominion* or *Oroonoko* that demonstrates black performance at work? Would the resulting impersonations be seen simply as derogatory racial slurs? Or would some other qualities—dignity and courage, perhaps—capture the audience's attention?" (174). I agree with Vaughan that this might be a risk worth taking in contemporary theater, one that we saw in slightly different form taken in Spike Lee's film *Bamboozled,* but which might have even more immediate impact in live production. Perhaps, though, Vaughan sets up an unnecessary dichotomy by imagining such experimental blackface productions as only being cast with white male actors, and only telling us about white fantasies of blackness. Blackface can also be performed by black bodies, and can tell us something about the ways that we have all been shaped by white supremacy. In many ways, we might think of performances of Othello by Paul Robeson, Ira Aldridge, and more recently, Laurence Fishburne, as forms of blackface. These actors, while of African descent, were still performing within a history of fantasized "patterns of blackness" expressed by character, speech, and gesture. The "fact" of their black bodies does not erase the artificiality of the conception of black identity as it is manifest in Shakespeare's play. At the same time, such performances enabled these actors to gain a limited form of social power that might arguably be conceived as "white." Perhaps, then, a more expansive conception of a historically informed experimental production highlighting blackface dynamics might be one that acknowledges the *ongoing* ways that blackface performances have been constitutive of our identities, white and nonwhite. As we continue to think about the formative impact of performance on the identity of audiences, we have to revise our histories and our view of the present to include audiences that are not only white and male, and whose politics of looking might not only be to replicate a white and male social position. Vaughan's study will be an important tool for readers to think about the formations of fantasized blackness that we have all inherited.

Notes

1. Arthur Little, Jr., *Shakespeare Jungle Fever: National-Imperial Re-Visions of Race, Rape and Sacrifice* (Stanford, CA: Stanford University Press, 2000), 14–15.

2. Celia Daileader, "Casting Black Actors: Beyond Othellophilia," in *Shakespeare and Race,* ed. Catherine M. S. Alexander and Stanley Wells, 177–203 (Cambridge: Cambridge University Press, 2000).

3. Dympna Callaghan, " 'Othello Was a White Man': Properties of Race on Shakespeare's Stage," in *Shakespeare Without Women: Representing Gender and Race on the Renaissance Stage* (London: Routledge, 2000), 75–96.

Masculinity, Anti-Semitism and Early Modern English Literature: From the Satanic to the Effeminate Jew, by Matthew Biberman. Aldershot: Ashgate, 2004. Pp. xii + 260. Hardcover $89.95.

Reviewer: PETER BEREK

Matthew Biberman's book on masculinity and anti-Semitism reflects wide reading, imaginative ingenuity, and great ambition. But the book is better at identifying provocative issues than at convincing this reader that its argument hangs together point by point.

Early modern English literature is only a starting point for Biberman's argument. For him, representations of Jews both reveal and enable a series of turning points in Western culture. The first turn, from a classical conception of masculinity apparently synonymous with Christian knighthood to modern capitalist bourgeois subjectivity, seems to occur in the brief moment between *The Jew of Malta* and *The Merchant of Venice.* Modernity then gives way to postmodernity at Hitler's holocaust, an event that, according to Biberman, empties anti-Semitism of content and makes it a purely aesthetic phenomenon.

Biberman asserts that classical masculinity is in conflict with Christianity because of premodern culture's embrace of a gender ideal that excludes women. The "hypermasculine" figure of the Jew-devil offers Christian culture a way of stigmatizing excesses of masculinity by projecting them onto the Jew. As capitalism's more feminized version of manhood emerges at the start of the seventeenth century, a new, more "sensitive" man sees the feminized "Jew-sissy" as the floor beneath which he cannot sink, just as the Jew-devil was a ceiling above which hypermasculinity could not rise (the structural metaphor is Biberman's). Yet the spectral presence of the Jew-devil haunts the Jew-sissy, and nineteenth-century Gothic makes both available to Nazism.

This narrative of Western history is not on its face compelling; one wants evidence and details, which Biberman tries to supply. He does so in chapters that attend to specific, and largely literary, topics. Chapter 1 analyzes medieval and early modern representations of Jews in works such as Chaucer's "Prioress's Tale," the Croxton *Play of the Sacrament, The Jew of Malta,* and *The Merchant of Venice.* Chapter 2 talks about Jewish women: Marlowe's Abigail, Shakespeare's Jessica, and (astonishingly) Jonson's Dol Common in *The Alchemist.* Chapter 3 contrasts Donne and Milton. Donne's masculine poetry evinces "ecstatic discourse offered by a male to a male deity" (5); the more modern Milton heteronormatively acknowledges that a male poet needs a female (and therefore non-Christian, says Biberman) object of devotion. Modern heterosexuality, Biberman says, impedes men's intense identification with Christ and also mutes the demonization of the Jew. Discussing both Milton and Elizabeth Cary, chapter 4 argues that divorce was more available than usually thought in Renaissance England (Biberman cites no new legal or historical evidence). One version of divorce—Mariam's—renounces sexuality. But Milton and Cary's Salome see divorce as a way of changing sex partners, and in this sense links divorce, feminine carnality, and Jewish sinfulness. Thus divorce "secures the Jew-sissy's ascendancy in the cultural imagination" (5). Chapter 5 shifts to the twentieth-century "Milton controversy" and argues that T. S. Eliot's anti-Semitism created Eliot's antipathy to a Milton whose grand style was in fact a polyglot, cosmopolitan Jewish babble rather than the plain speech of laudably Anglican Donne or Herbert. Chapter 6 reads Mary Shelley's *Frankenstein* and Bram Stoker's *Dracula* as rewritings of *The Merchant of Venice* that attempt to materialize the Jew-devil to replace the Jew-sissy. The book ends with a brief discussion of Otto Weininger's 1903 *Sex and Character,* which Biberman says calls for an elimination of both women and Jews in order to facilitate a reunion of God and God's creation. Biberman sees Weininger's ideas as enacted in Nazi policies about Jewish-Christian intermarriage.

Postmodern theory shapes hypotheses about cultural change and cultural meaning, as no doubt it should. Unfortunately, one can then hear creaks and squeals as evidence from older texts gets bent, sometimes painfully, to fit the shape theory predicts. Sometimes the issues are local. Needing to accommodate Gerontus, a universally admired Jewish character in Robert Wilson's 1583 hybrid morality play, *The Three Ladies of London,* to the paradigm of "Jew-devil," Biberman implausibly calls the play a parody of the morality genre in which every asserted value is to be read as its opposite. (Curiously, he resists the frequently made argument that *Merchant of Venice* should be read ironically with Shylock as its oppressed hero.) Shylock, Biberman acknowledges, begins his play as "Jew-devil," but when Gratiano taunts him for having lost his stones, daughter, and ducats, he becomes an emasculated sissy. Is Shylock still a sissy as he whets the phallic knife with which he wants to penetrate Antonio? Wisely wanting to make gender a central issue in his analyses, Biberman talks about Jessica, Abigail, and their conversions. But then he adds Dol Common to his list of "Jewish" women because she feigns madness by babbling Hebrew terms drawn from Broughton, and one of her gulls, Sir Epicure Mammon, calls her "Madame Rabbi." Dol, says Biberman, helps decouple Jewishness and hypermasculine deviltry and moves culture on to the more modern "Jew-sissy." But why is Biberman then silent about Rabbi Zeal-of-the-land Busy in *Bartholomew Fair?* Is he devil or sissy or just another goy? The list could go on, chapter by chapter, of ways in which particularities are bent to fit an overall scheme.

More serious than these local concerns are basic issues of definition within Biberman's argument. What does "masculinity" mean? Biberman announces a "classical" conception broad enough to include ancient Greece, Rome, medieval knighthood, Antonio in *Merchant,* and the speaker of Donne's "Spit in my face, you Jews"—all somehow at odds with Christianity. Modern masculinity includes Portia (as Balthasar), Milton on divorce, and Count Dracula as revitalized Jew-devil. Same-sex and opposite-sex sexuality can be either masculine or feminine, depending on where they appear in the book's argument. Rightly, Biberman leaves Jewishness undefined; he persuasively argues that the concept he analyzes is a screen or projection for the fantasies and anxieties of non-Jews. But the same cannot be said for Christianity. Arguing wittily if implausibly for a "Jewish" Milton, Biberman effaces distinctions between Catholic and Protestant, Anglican and Puritan. Except where convenient for his overarching thesis, Biberman pays little attention to actual conflicts or affiliations within the cultures he studies. If contemporary theory leads one to hypothesize a conflict at some moment in the past, Biberman finds that conflict precisely in the theory's own terms. He largely ignores the vocabularies of the authors he studies. Though we construct the history we study, the past is not mute, and its voices should be in dialogue with our own.

Still, to echo Doctor Johnson on metaphysical poetry, to write this way it is at least necessary to read, and to think. Biberman's book is sometimes irritating, but never dull. He is never self-important, and sometimes endearing in his efforts to cram all his exciting ideas into a single project. *Masculinity, Anti-Semitism and Early Modern English Literature* is worth reading.

Index

A Knack to Know a Knave, 195, 196, 197, 198, 199, 200
A Knack to Know an Honest Man, 195, 196, 197, 200
Acting, 17–45, 187–203, 225–35, 265
Actors, prejudice against, 29–30
Aebischer, Pascale, 286–88
Africans, 47, 55, 60, 61, 63, 65
Africanus, Leo, 63, 90
Alciati, Andrea, 98
Alleyn, Edward, 20, 34, 197, 200
Andrewes, Lancelot, 114, 115
Anti-Semitism, 297–99
Apes, 65–67, 95–6
Aristotle, 64, 273
Armin, Robert, 225, 226, 227, 231, 233
Astington, John H., 225–36
Aubrey, John, 22, 69
Augustine of Hippo, 51, 53

Bachinger, Katharina, 93
Bacon, Francis, 269
Baker, Robert, 62
Barbot, John, 54, 63
Barclay, Alexander, 70
Barnes, Barnabe, 161
Barthelemy, Anthony, 47
Baskervill, C. R., 69
Bassano, Leandro, 66
Battle of Alcazar, 20, 29, 154
Bear-baiting, 143
Beaumont, Francis, 91, 125
Behn, Aphra, 296
Bell (inn and playhouse), 227
Benjamin, Walter, 17
Bentley, G. E., 187
Berek, Peter, 297–99
Bergeron, David, 268
Bernard, John, 70
Besnault, Marie-Hélène, 269
Best, George, 23, 61, 69

Bevington, David, 160, 196
Biberman, Matthew, 297–99
Birde (alias Bourne), William, 29
Blackface makeup, 46–84, 87
Blackfriars playhouse (first and second), 157, 160, 163, 168, 169, 170, 171, 173, 176, 177
Blake, Tim, 282
Boemus, John, 63
Bogdanov, Michael, 270
Bolam, Robyn, 266
Borch, Gerard ter, 177
Boskin, Joseph, 65, 70, 71
Bourne (Birde alias Bourne), William, 29
Bowes, Sir Martin, 226
Brant, Sebastian, 69
Braudel, Fernand, 86
Bridges, Gyles (Third Lord Chandos), 230–31
Brome, Richard, 30, 170
Brook, Peter, 144, 287
Brooke, Nicholas, 176
Brown, John Russell, 169, 163
Bruster, Douglas, 86, 97, 99
Bull (inn and playhouse), 227
Bulman, James C., 265
Bulwer, John, 96
Burbage, James, 33, 227
Byrd (alias Bourne), William, 29

Callaghan, Dympna, 20, 21, 22, 28, 29, 30, 32, 47
Calverley, Edward, 236–50
Calvin, John, 54
Cane, Andrew, 225, 227, 232, 233
Carleton, Dudley, 29
Carpenter, Sarah, 50
Cartwright, William, 29
Castle of Perseverance, 52
Catholicism, 24, 111–135
Cecil, William (First Baron Burghley), 24, 46

Cecilia, Princess of Sweden, 46
Chambers, E. K., 87, 162, 177, 230
Chandos portrait, 33
Chapman, Alison A., 111–35
Chapman, George, 58, 72, 169, 176, 197, 268
Charles I, 66
Chaucer, Geoffrey, 66, 92, 298
Chester cycle, 48, 142
Chettle, Henry, 19, 197
Cobb, Thomas R. R., 70
Cockpit (Drury Lane), 156
Cockrell, Dale, 49
Colonialism, 26, 29
Cox, John D., 50
Cromwell, Oliver, 59
Cross Keys (inn and playhouse), 227
Curtains (on stage), 151–86

Daborne, Robert, 22
Daileader, Cecilia R., 281–84
Dance, 85–107
Davenant, William, 170, 176
Davis, David Brion, 65
Davis, Natalie Zemon, 69
Day, John, 155, 166, 169
Dekker, Thomas, 51, 70, 155, 159, 165, 166, 168, 174, 176, 197, 213, 214, 215–16, 268, 294
DeWitt, Johannes, 151, 156, 157, 177
Desmet, Christy, 281–84
Dessen, Alan, 155, 156, 171, 176
Devils, 48–49, 50, 51, 52, 53
Dixon, George Washington, 49
Dolan, Frances, 130
Doniger, Wendy, 294
Donne, John, 126
Drayton, Michael, 70
Drew-Bear, Annette, 87
Dudley, Robert (Earl of Leicester), 228, 229, 230

Eden, Richard, 20
Edward IV, 60
Edward VI, 129
Edwards, Philip, 165
Edwards, Richard, 58, 72
Elam, Keir, 273
Elizabeth I, 17, 61, 62, 230
Elizabeth (Princess), 91
Ellison, Ralph, 57

Evans, G. B., 172
Eyre, Simon, 174, 226

Fabyan, Robert, 23, 60
Faulkner, William, 282
Field, Nathan, 30, 155, 176
Fisher, F. J., 86
Fitzpatrick, Tom, 157
Fleck, Andrew, 204–24
Fletcher, John, 85–107, 172, 294
Floyd-Wilson, Mary, 94
Fo, Dario, 59
Foakes, R. A., 152, 174, 265
Fools, 46–84, 225–35
Foreign languages on stage, 204–24
Fortune Playhouse (first and second), 21, 165, 175, 210
Foster, Donald, 17, 18
Fowler, William, 61
Foxe, John, 289
Frederickson, George M., 65
Freeman, Arthur, 111
Frith, Mary, 21, 27

Galen, 274
Gaming, 142–43
Garner, Stanton B., 273–79
Gates, Henry Louis, 68
Gayton, Edmund, 21
Geneva Bible, 54, 140
Gibson, Gail McMurray, 114
Gibson, James M., 236–55
Globe Playhouse (first and second), 33, 151, 158, 160, 161, 163, 171, 173, 176, 177, 189, 207
Golding, Arthur, 95
Gosson, Stephen, 30
Goy-Blanquet, Dominique, 269, 271
Gray's Inn (Gentlemen of), 164
Greenblatt, Stephen, 26, 111, 117
Greene, Robert, 19, 51, 72, 156, 164, 268
Greg, W. W., 162
Grene, Nicholas, 259–72
Grotius, Hugo, 136–50
Groves, Beatrice, 136–50
Gurr, Andrew, 20, 22, 155, 157, 187, 230

Habib, Imtiaz, 17–45
Hagiography, 111–35
Hakluyt, Richard, 20, 22, 62
Hales, Sir James, 128, 129

Hall, Kim, 66, 88, 90, 94, 282
Hampton-Reeves, Stuart, 265, 270, 271
Happé, Peter, 50, 51
Hartley, Andrew James, 259–72
Hattaway, Michael, 170, 259–72
Haughton, William, 51, 72, 155, 197,
    209, 210
Hawkes, Terence, 26
Hawkins, John, 60, 61, 62
Hawkins, William, 60
Hedrick, Donald K., 100
Hegel, Georg W. F., 68
Heminges, William, 166, 169, 174, 177
Hendricks, Margo, 282
Henrietta Maria, 66
Henry VIII, 66
Henslowe, Philip, 19, 169, 197
Heylyn, Peter, 63
Heyward, Richard, 233
Heywood, John, 58, 72
Heywood, Thomas, 72, 153, 154, 168,
    268, 277
Hirschfeld, Heather A., 111, 289–91
History plays, 259–72
Hobbes, Thomas, 28
Hodgdon, Barbara, 264
Hodges, G. Walter, 168
Hoenselaars, A. J., 267, 268
Holbein, Hans (the younger), 67
Honigmann, Ernst, 19, 154
Hooker, Richard, 114, 115
Hornback, Robert, 46–84
Hosley, Richard, 152, 156, 157, 161,
    171, 174
Howell, Jane, 263
Hume, David, 68
Hunter, G. K., 263

Ichikawa, Mariko, 157
Impersonation, 17–45
Interludes, 55–58
Irving, Washington, 70

Jacobs, Harriet, 283
James VI and I, 91
Jameson, Frederic, 26
Janson, H. W., 66
Jeffes, Anthony, 29
Jenkins, Harold, 111
Johnson, Richard, 88
Johnson, Samuel, 288

Johnson-DeBaufre, Eric, 284–86
Jones, Eldred, 20, 23
Jones, Inigo, 156
Jonson, Ben:
—Plays: *The Alchemist*, 276, 298; *Bar-
    tholomew Fair*, 285; *Cynthia's Revels*,
    168, 172; *The Devil is an Ass*, 51;
    Every Man In His Humour, 18, 284,
    285; *Every Man Out of His Humour*,
    200; *The Masque of Blackness*, 29, 30,
    87, 95; *Sejanus*, 274; *Volpone*, 151,
    158, 161–62, 163, 174, 193, 274
Jordan, Winthrop, 65,

Kaiser, Walter, 70
Kant, Immanuel, 68
Kelley, Donald, 116
Kemp, Will, 86, 87, 226, 228, 231
Kennedy, John Pendleton, 70
Kent (county), 236–55
Kernan, Alvin, 158
Kerwin, William, 273–78
Kettlewood, John, 226, 229, 231
Kiefer, Frederick, 151–86
Killigrew, Henry, 170
King's Men, 151, 159, 160, 161, 171
Kirkham, Francis, 59
Knutson, Roslyn L., 187
Kyd, Thomas, 165, 204, 206, 207, 209

Lady Elizabeth's Men, 152, 175
Lawrence, William J., 177
Lee, Spike, 282, 292, 296
Leggatt, Alexander, 21
Lennam, Trevor, 58
Ligon, Richard, 65
Little, Arthur, 94, 282
Littlewood, Joan, 270
Lok, John, 60, 61
London, 23, 24, 228
Lonyson, John, 228, 229
Loomba, Ania, 22, 29, 32, 282
Lopez, Jeremy, 187–203
Lord Admiral's Men, 33, 156, 161, 164,
    169, 174, 195
Lord Chamberlain's Men, 33, 172, 268
Lord Strange's Men, 20,154, 195
Lowin, John, 22
Lydgate, John, 53
Lyly, John, 277

MacDonald, Joyce Green, 94
McClintock, Anne, 65
McMullan, Gordon, 159
Machiavelli, Niccolo, 267
MacLean, Sally Beth, 187, 229
Madness, 111–135
Mankind (play), 51
Marlowe, Christopher:
Plays: *Doctor Faustus,* 166; *The Jew of Malta,* 20, 297, 298; *The Massacre at Paris,* 154
Marriage, 117, 118
Marrow, James, 140
Marston, John, 155, 172, 177, 211–13, 214
Mary I, Queen of England, 61
Mason, John, 87
Mason, Pamela, 271
Massey, Charles, 29
Massinger, Philip, 171, 173, 176, 275
Matar, Nabil, 22
Mazzio, Carla, 204
Meckenem, Israel van, 67
Mehl, Dieter, 165
Merbury, Francis, 57, 72
Middleton, Thomas, 87, 152, 160, 175, 210
Miller, Jonathon, 143
Millyard, Wendy, 157
Milton, John, 299
Miola, Robert, 265
Mitchell, Margaret, 282
Moorishness, 85–107, 293, 294, 295
More, Sir Thomas (play), 58
More, Sir Thomas, 269
Morris dance, 85
Mortlack, Elizabeth, 124
Mullany, Steven, 204
Mulryne, J. R., 165
Munday, Anthony, 30, 58, 87, 164, 268
Mystery plays, 136–50, 293, 292
Mytens, Daniel, 66

N-Town plays, 140
Neely, Carol Thomas, 124
Neill, Michael, 124
Nelson, Alan H., 162
Northbrooke, John, 30
Norwich (city), 53
Nunes, Hector, 23

Olivier, Sir Laurence, 270
Ostovich, Helen, 158, 208
Ovid, 137, 145
Oxley, Edward, 236–50

Paracelsus, 274
Parker, Patricia, 89, 282
Parker, R. B., 151, 158
Paster, Gail Kern, 284–86
Patrides, C. A., 22
Paul's Boys, 159, 169
Peele, George, 20, 34, 175, 294
Percy, William, 157
Petrarch, Francesco, 100
Philo, 64
Phoenix Playhouse, 168, 171, 175, 176
Piesse, A. J., 266
Plato, 63, 64
Plautus, 137
Plutarch, 137
Poe, Edgar Allen, 282
Poel, William, 163
Pollard, Tonya, 273–78
Pollard, Thomas, 233
Pory, John, 90
Potter, Lois, 94
Prager, Carolyn, 54
Prince Henry's Men, 165
Prynne, William, 141
Purchas, Samuel, 22

Queen Anne's Men, 152, 153, 154, 159
Queen Henrietta's Men, 166, 171
Queen's Men, 164, 225, 227, 229
Queen's Revels Children, 155, 157, 169, 176

Rackin, Phyllis, 266, 267
Rastell, John, 58, 72
Reay, Barry, 69
Red Bull Playhouse, 152, 153, 154, 158, 159
Red Lion Playhouse, 33
Reynolds, Edward, 284
Reynolds, George, 152
Rhenanus, Johannes, 22
Richardson, Sir Ralph, 270
Rice, T. D., 49
Roberts, Sasha, 152
Ronayne, John, 168
Rose, Jacqueline, 26

Rose playhouse, 23, 29, 32, 154, 156, 163, 164, 174, 175, 197, 206, 207
Rowan, D. F., 165
Rowley, Samuel, 29
Rowley, William, 175, 268, 282
Rowson, Susanna, 282
Royster, Francesca, 292–97
Russell, Jeffrey Burton, 51
Rust, Jennifer, 111

St. George play, 87, 90
Said, Edward, 85
Salgado, Gamini, 87
Salisbury Court Playhouse, 166, 168, 175
Sampson, William, 152
Sandys, George, 145
Scarry, Elaine, 146
Schwarz, Kathryn, 101
Senasi, Deneen, 286–88
Seneca, 137, 145
Seng, Peter, 125
Seven Deadly Sins, 52
Shakespeare, William:
—Plays: All's Well that Ends Well, 126, 189, 277; Antony and Cleopatra, 32, 157, 193, 274, 285, 296; As You Like It, 18; The Comedy of Errors, 191; Coriolanus, 189; Cymbeline, 166, 189, 190, 265; Edward III, 267, 269, 271; Hamlet, 18, 111–35, 167, 168, 187, 188, 194, 275, 284, 287, 288, 290; Henry IV, Pt. 1, 98, 167, 192, 193, 195, 285; Henry IV, Pt. 2, 154, 168, 192, 193; Henry V, 154, 193, 207, 208, 209, 214; Henry VI, Pt. 1, 195; Henry VI, Pt. 2, 88, 154, 195; Henry VI, Pt. 3, 195; Henry VIII, 159, 172, 175, 194 ; Julius Caesar, 194; King John, 193; Love's Labors Lost, 192; King Lear, 129, 136–50, 265; Macbeth, 138, 265, 290, 291; Measure for Measure, 102, 112, 189, 200, 265; The Merchant of Venice, 17–18, 30, 95, 158, 204, 265, 297, 298, 299; The Merry Wives of Windsor, 167; A Midsummer Night's Dream, 86, 88, 91, 98, 99, 101, 102, 112, 122; Much Ado About Nothing, 112, 167; Othello, 18, 30, 32, 52, 72, 87, 154, 194, 281–84, 288, 296; Pericles, 94, 189, 265; Richard II, 153, 195; Richard III, 21, 195; Romeo and Juliet, 98, 153, 274, 276; The Taming of the Shrew, 89, 188; The Tempest, 156, 200; Timon of Athens, 193, 265; Titus Andronicus, 17–45, 195, 265, 288, 294; Troilus and Cressida, 200, 265; Twelfth Night, 159, 192, 277, 296; Two Gentlemen of Verona, 191
Shannon, Laurie, 102
SHAXICON, 17, 18, 19, 22, 25, 31, 32
Shelley, Mary, 298, 299
Shirley, James, 171, 176
Shuger, Debora, 114, 115, 117
Sidney, Sir Philip, 136, 204, 205
Slavery, 49, 50, 59, 61–62
Smallwood, Robert, 174
Smith, Irwin, 170
Somer, Will, 66
Sophocles, 137
Southern, Richard, 162
Southern, Thomas, 282
Spenser, Edmund, 119–21
Stage setting, 151–86
Stern, Tiffany, 155, 187
Stoker, Bram, 298
Stowe, Harriet Beecher, 282,
Strachey, William, 69
Stubbs, Philip, 30, 87
Stuttgart Psalter, 33
Sutcliffe, Chris, 229
Swan Playhouse, 151, 152, 156

Targoff, Ramie, 111
Tarlton, Richard, 225, 226, 227, 228, 230, 231, 233
Taussig, Michael, 17
Taylor, Joseph, 22
Theater/Theatre (playhouse), 33
Thomson, Leslie, 155, 156, 171, 176, 177
Tillyard, E. M. W., 272
Tintam, John, 60
Topsell, Edward, 65, 67, 95
Towneley cycle, 138, 139, 140, 142, 143, 144
Towrson, William, 60
Turks, 22
Twycross, Meg, 50

Vaughan, Virginia Mason, 47, 49, 67, 292–97

Vesalius, Andreas, 273

Wager, Lewis, 145
Wager, William, 52, 53, 55, 56, 58, 72
Wakefield cycle, 47, 48, 51
Walsingham (place), 127–28
Walsingham, Francis, 24
Watson, Robert N., 151, 289
Watson, Thomas, 100
Webster, John:
—Plays: *Northward Ho,* 168; *Satiromas-*
tix, 176; *The Duchess of Malfi,* 163,
167, 290; *The Revenger's Tragedy,*
290; *The White Devil,* 159, 163, 274,
295
Weimann, Robert, 21
Wells, Stanley, 174

Welsford, Enid, 70
Whistler, Henry, 65
Whitefriars Playhouse, 155, 176
Wickham, Glynne, 138, 151
Wilson, Arthur, 170
Wilson, Robert, 299
Windham, Thomas, 60
Woodbridge, Linda, 69
Woolf, Rosemary, 141
Wright, Richard, 282

Yachnin, Paul, 188
York cycle, 48, 56, 136, 138, 142, 144

Zimmerman, Susan, 289–91
Zitner, Sheldon, 207